George Frideric Handel (originally Haendal) was born in Saxony in 1685 of impeccably German parentage, but after the composition of some operas and oratorios he settled permanently in England in 1712. His opera *Rinaldo* had already been successful at the Queen's Theatre, London, in 1711.

From 1718 to 1720 he was organist to the Duke of Chandos, during which period he composed *Esther*, his first English oratorio, and *Acis and Galatea*. From 1720 to 1728 he directed an operatic venture known as the Royal Academy of Music, but really came into his own when he was appointed court composer in 1727. His most famous oratorio, the *Messiah*, was first produced in Dublin in 1741. Handel's fame justifiably rests upon his oratorios: his instrumental compositions are good but certainly no better than that of his contemporaries, but his choral music set a high-water mark that has not yet been exceeded. Handel died in 1759 and was buried in Westminster Abbey.

Newman Flower

George Frideric Handel

his personality and his times

Panther

Granada Publishing Limited
Published in 1972 by Panther Books Limited
3 Upper James Street, London W1R 4BP

First published in Great Britain by Cassell &
Co. Limited 1923. Reprinted five times. This
revised edition published 1959
Made and printed in Great Britain by
Richard Clay (The Chaucer Press) Ltd.,
Bungay, Suffolk
Set in Monotype Times

to Desmond

NOTES ON SIR NEWMAN FLOWER'S HANDEL COLLECTION

SIR NEWMAN FLOWER's Handel collection is unique in several respects. It contains, in about seven hundred manuscripts bound into approximately three hundred volumes, the bulk of the great Aylesford Collection originally written out for Charles Jennens, Handel's friend and librettist of his *L'Allegro*, *Belshazzar*, *Saul* and *Messiah*. The manuscripts, later bequeathed to the Aylesford family, are in the spotless condition in which they left the hands of John Christopher Smith, Handel's secretary, and his immediate circle of copyists. In addition to fifty-five full scores of Handel operas and oratorios there are fifty-two cembalo or organ scores, together with a nearly complete set of instrumental and voice parts for all the operas and oratorios. Such parts are of the greatest rarity and value to the editors of critical Handel editions.

The score of *Jupiter in Argos* and a full score and set of instrumental parts for the complete *Water Music* call for special mention amongst a plethora of still unknown treasures which could bring surprise and delight to Handelian editors for many years to come.

Amongst a wide range of first and early printed editions of Handel works, Sir Newman's collection is specially rich in rare libretti, particularly of contemporary performances of Handel operas in Germany. Of the greatest rarity is a superb copy of the libretto of *La Resurezzione*, engraved in Rome in 1708 for the Marchese Ruspoli. Another unique libretto is the 1741 Italian-English version of *L'Allegro ed Il Penseroso*. This alone has enabled the present editors of its critical edition to solve problems which have baffled Chrysander and his successors for over a hundred years.

WALMER
JAMES S. HALL
March, 1958

AUTHOR'S NOTE
TO THE NEW AND REVISED EDITION, 1959

Two hundred years have passed since Handel was buried in Westminster Abbey, and I feel this is the occasion to issue a new and revised edition of my life of him, first published in 1923.

During these years I have pursued my research into his life and works, and have discovered fresh things which throw light on his activities, and enable me also to correct certain facts and dates.

The popularity of Handel in Britain has increased greatly during recent years due to the performances in this country of many of his works which had seldom or never been performed before. The B.B.C. has done much to make these unknown Handel works known to the people of this land. It has been realized at long last that some of the richest musical treasures of Handel have lain for ages buried as jewels in the deepest seas.

I feel that this book, as now presented, embodies all that is known at this period about Handel, the man and his activities.

I wish to express my warmest thanks to those two great Handelians, Mr William C. Smith and Dr James Hall, for the assistance they have given me in my attempt to make this edition as accurate and complete as possible.

N. F.

PREFACE
TO THE FIRST EDITION

No attempt has been made in this volume to survey the works of Handel in any technical sense, nor to deal with his music in any technical form. This has already been done exhaustively by Dr Chrysander, Mr Rockstro, Mr Streatfeild, Mr P. Robinson, and other able pens.

I have endeavoured, rather, to outline Handel the Man—the striking personality who never admitted defeat, but rose superior to whatever powers a surfeit of enemies could and did exert. In order to convey, however poorly, this Handel, I have attempted to sketch a background of the times in which he lived, and the people with whom he had to deal.

In the course of some years of Handelian study, induced by a sincere admiration of the man's genius, I have discovered certain facts which are not included in the Handel biographies. I felt they would not be without interest to other ardent lovers of the Master, and in this belief I attempted this book. The accepted story of the *Water Music*, for instance, which began with Mainwaring, and has gone on ever since, is quite incorrect, as recent investigation in Germany proves. Delvings into the archives of Prince di Ruspoli at Rome have revealed some interesting details concerning Handel's Italian journey. I am also indebted to the authorities of Halle University for much new matter bearing on Handel's birthplace. From my own collection, which includes the Aylesford transcripts—the copies of Handel's works made by his amanuensis Christopher Smith, and given to the Earl of Aylesford by Jennens after the death of the Composer—I have derived certain points of interest, especially concerning *Jupiter in Argos*, that mystery work of Handel's which was never performed, and of which I have the copy of the songs Smith made for him. There are many other details concerning his life and death which I believe are new to the Handel records, and these are my excuse for attempting a new life of Handel.

Handel's music is really a reflex of an extraordinary

character, acting and reacting upon a beauteous and rich imagination. His actions, even in times of great adversity— actions often abrupt and motiveless superficially—reveal, on investigation, the thinking man behind them. They represent the thoughts of one who could survey Humanity and translate into music the impressions formed. It is questionable whether any music, composed in this country or imported into it, has reached the heart of the people so truly as his. He caught the moods of the world and set them to song.

To admire the music of Handel above all other is often considered to be the taste of a heretic. There are some, too, who have striven, not very nobly, to show that Handel stole all his better music. Lacking such knowledge, it would be difficult for me not to appear self-conscious in the company of these comedians, so I am grateful to be numbered among the heretics.

I would like to take this opportunity of acknowledging my gratitude to those who have so kindly assisted me in the research which has resulted in this volume. I am particularly indebted to Mr William C. Smith, Assistant Keeper of Printed Books in the British Museum, to Mr E. van der Straeten for research in Germany and elsewhere, and to Mr L. A. Shepherd of the British Museum for research in Italy. To the Earl and Countess of Aylesford, to Earl Howe, to the Prince di Ruspoli for permitting the search in their archives, or the reproduction of pictures. To Mr Arthur F. Hill for permission to reproduce the portrait of Farinelli of which he is the possessor, and for continuous help in other directions. To Herr Foss of Berlin, the direct descendant of Dorothea Michaelsen, Handel's sister, who has allowed me to include their family portrait of Handel, which has not hitherto been reproduced. This is believed to be one of the last portraits painted during the Composer's lifetime. I am also indebted to Professor Michael, of Freiburg, for the *Water Music* information, to Professor Arnold Schering and Dr Weissenborn, of Halle University, to Dr Kinsky of the Hayer Museum, Cologne, Professor Dr Wahl, Professor Dr Reinke of Hamburg, and Professor Werner of Bitterfeld. All these friends have made this work possible.

As regards authority for the statements made in the volume, I would refer my readers, not only to the footnotes, but to the bibliography at the end, made by Mr William C.

Smith above mentioned, which I think can be claimed justifiably as the most complete Handelian Bibliography yet compiled.

I cannot hope by this book to bring more admirers to Handel than his own music has already found for him, but if the book helps any student or lover of Handel's work to a better understanding of this Master, then the years of research this volume has entailed have not been given in vain.

N. F.

CONTENTS

BOOK I *MORNING*

BOOK II *NOON*

BOOK III *EVENING*

BOOK I

MORNING

CHAPTER I

OF SOME RELATIONS

GENIUS is seldom admitted as such save when it can achieve over Circumstance, and the Circumstance that governs the ways of Mankind is so contrived to hinder rather than help the weakling idea. Existence, as humanly conceived, would mock at and poke into seclusion those tendrils of thought which, if developed, would produce a voice to which the world might listen.

This same Circumstance did its utmost to prevent the genius of George Frideric Handel from fruition.[1] It pegged him about from his early years with absurd obstacles. It fought him with all the strength of precedent in its favour. Nor did it yield him even the favour of happy chance. It tried to stifle a voice that ultimately turned a world to melody.

The child who was born at the little Saxon town of Halle on 23 February 1685 was never followed by what is known as good luck. In a gamble with chance he was certain to lose every time. But he made his way to his ultimate destiny by genius and personality.

Nothing was expected of George Frideric Handel when he was born except a commonplace yet circumspect life. His father had reared many children, and George Frideric— following after by the grace of a second wife—was just one of a herd, as ordinary as his name. No great ability was anticipated of him. The suspicion of any musical genius in him would have shocked his father, the barber-surgeon, into disowning him. All that his parents demanded was that he should become a good citizen and pay his way in some respectable craft; be God-fearing, if not God-chosen; ultimately marry and rear children, and, in the fullness of time, pass to

---

[1] For the purpose of this book, and to avoid confusion, the name of Handel, both as applied to the composer and his relatives, is spelled in English fashion. There are documents in existence in which the composer spelled his name in several ways, notably Hendel. This form of spelling was usually adopted by his relatives, and his descendant had a bookshop in Halle with the name OTTO HENDEL over the door. In England, however, the composer always kept to the English form of Handel.

an honoured corner in the Halle churchyard, to be remembered with respect.

The Handels had always done things that way. They had never been original, but ever respectable. From the time that they first settled in Breslau in medieval ages, till and after grandfather Handel—Valentine by name—came and established the Handel respectability at Halle, they had been the same. He opened a small coppersmith's shop to which he attended very vigilantly. He was unimaginative, and unsuspecting that any grandchild of his would one day demand the silence of kings.

In 1685, when the birth of the future musician occurred in the Am Schlamm at Halle, Middle Europe was in a curious state of unoriginality. It had its own scheme of things; its slow progress was a change as slowly conceived. It was rather hidebound with Lutheranism, relieved with patches—very eruptive patches—of Judaism, and occasional upheavals of Catholicism and free thought. Its business was as respectable as its religion. It did not wish to do anything in a new way. It made things and sold them. This Middle Europe of 1685 wanted to go on making things and selling them in the same fashion for ever. There was no political disturbance that tore at the roots of industry nor thrust them rudely up into the glare of progress. One was born and educated and trained to narrow issues, and taught above all things to be supremely careful. But to strike out and be a pioneer—that was one of those acts which the better circles abhorred because such peculiar conduct was not understood. It was a form of heresy usually purged from the higher families by disowning the offender. A pioneer in a Saxon family in 1685 was not talked about. The drawing-rooms, which were dovecotes of righteousness, insincerity and trivial scandal, did not mention these pioneers, these few. Its people were too well bred of their time. The few pioneers usually drifted into the cities, became debauchees, and died very namelessly, as those families that had once owned them hoped they would do. There was a singular connivance between Fate and the smug conscience in those days.

Moreover, 1685 was a rather mean age. It was an age of snobbery in saving money. It was ungenerous. It was interested in the suffering, in the charities of the time, only by an occasional mild mood of religious revivalism, and extreme

Church ceremony. There was little secret charity. To trample on the weak was the act of a man who really had achieved some object in getting born. The weak were there to be trampled upon, and a man was the better listened to at the dinner-table according to the heaviness of his step.

The Handels were a rather peculiar family. They succeeded in Middle Europe at this age because they were so clearly typical of their age. They were extremely efficient, quiet people. They had no family scandals, no skeletons hidden in the family cupboard. They made no noise; they rose to no honours. They did not attempt to govern. They married just the kind of people they were themselves, for they adventured neither in business nor in marriage. They made their profits in their occupations, and paid their debts, and were buried, as they would have wished to be buried, with the little pompous funerals of seventeenth-century Germany. They lived very gamely and straightly round the narrow arc which their mentality perceived, and came to the same very revered end. Just dust to the earth that had yielded it. Dust and few memories.

Suddenly this very circumspect family developed an eruptive mood. Early in the seventeenth century Valentine Handel packed himself up, bag and baggage, at Breslau and went south to Halle. He followed the usual custom of the time for an apprentice who had become 'Gesell' to take to the road. The Saxon town had no special call for him. So he responded to a mood. Like some irresponsible bird of passage, he did what no Handel had ever done hitherto—he went out to discover. To fight.

It is possible that *en route* he stopped at the neighbouring town of Eisleben and worked in the copper-mines for some time. Scarcely a year before his arrival at Halle, he married an Eisleben girl, Anne, the daughter of the master coppersmith, Samuel Beichling, who was to be the grandmother of the musician. At all events it is on record that on Tuesday after 'Reminiscere', (14 March) 1609, he took the oath as a Halle citizen, and paid the citizen-right's fee of six guilders. He was then twenty-six years of age.

He arrived at Halle with his few sticks of belongings, and the knowledge of his craft as a coppersmith—the only stable things to which he had pegged his adventure. Often he must have meditated on the complete lack of object which had drawn him to Halle. It was a call from some vague destiny, just as the sea in these days will drag a man from an office stool, or a sudden mood will send a driven city slave to the wildest ends of the earth in pursuit of a shadow.

Valentine Handel settled down in a little narrow street off the Market-platz known as 'Unter den Kleinschmieden' (street of the small smith). There were other coppersmiths there before him, but the records show that he was a brilliant craftsman in the more delicate forms of the work. He became known as such and prospered. Rapidly he climbed the ladder till the citizens of Halle held such respect for him that they put him into the Council with the important position of bread-weigher.[1]

In a short time his shop was one of the foremost of the period. We can picture this man approaching old age, busying himself in his shop, a rather mournful but efficient figure with a small, close-fitting cap on his head. A man more than a little mean, but a man whose word was his bond.

Valentine Handel made money, and he saved money. As proof of it, let it be said that he bought two of the principal houses in the adjoining main street. No tradesman in those days could afford to buy houses unless he were making money in a considerable manner.

The Handel stock was particularly strong in this man. He had no ideas outside his business. He did not know one note of music from another. He was conscious of no appeal from any Art. He lived a rather closeted, furtive life, taking no chances unless he had previously measured every step that led to them. But he was alert, and very conscious that in his epoch commercial Germany was about to be sold to the Jews. So he prospered; he prospered because he had been manufactured so closely to the pattern of his age. Also he lived in a manner that became his lineage, a clean-trading, rather ignorant person, with ideals and beliefs in the hereafter for those who kept themselves unsullied from the Jewish vices which were breaking out in gross and disturbing fashion in the larger cities. A person rather dour and sanctimonious.

He died in the same unostentatious fashion in which he had lived, just as the Handel precedents ordained. His financial affairs very simple and arranged, and with a clear conscience that those for whom he had worked should never be troubled

[1] Julius Otto Opel: *Periodical for General History*, 1885.

with any irritating annoyances about their heritage. He had thought all these things out beforehand, and so planned his death that it should be as simple and understood as had been his life. He had been always a very safe person, rather difficult to live with at times, one may gather, but worthy of the elegant inscription they put upon his tomb. And when he died at the coppersmith's shop that had borne his name for so long and honourably over its portral, he left his two elder sons, Valentine and Christoph—already trained to his own pattern as coppersmiths—to succeed him. Two other sons he had lost, but the fifth, George by name, never appears to have interested him. George had no inclinations towards the craft of the smith. He was ambitious, dreamy. He lived a solitary life, out of joint with the family and its affairs. Yet Destiny was to choose him as the father of one of the world's greatest musicians.

This youth had just turned fourteen years when he followed his father's bier to its last resting-place. He was of no more importance in that procession through the Halle streets than the family cat might have been. A small, insignificant creature in a great concourse of people. A solitary child.

Valentine and Christoph, in the strenuous life which followed immediately upon taking over the business, were not interested in him. His mother left the shop to the sons and supported herself chiefly by distillery. He could wander from the family roof-tree as soon as he liked. And he did.

Possibly it was this solitude which built the strength of character in George Handel. Certainly it did not hinder him, for six years later he was the most respected burgher in Halle as a barber-surgeon. At the end of his life he was in his turn to pass on that strength of character to his last son George Frideric. This gift was the only thing that George did for that son of his late years.

Nevertheless it was this gift which brought the son in the fullness of time to Westminster Abbey.

When they had buried the old coppersmith of Halle in 1636, George, the boy of fourteen, was left more than ever to the seclusion of his own ways, to his own thoughts. Whatever destiny there might be for him had given no sign. He had no one to turn towards for guidance, and, says one historian, he walked the streets and the wooded paths beside the banks of Halle's wonderful river, the Saale, 'trapped by a great sense of ambition'.

Then the destiny of George Handel began to shape itself. He became an apprentice to Christoph Oettinger, a barber-surgeon, one of the successful young men of Halle. He went into the Oettinger household and began to pick up the rudiments of surgery. Oettinger was thrifty and prospering. He had no dream in the world beyond money, and he hammered this boy into being what he meant him to be—just a pawn in his game of building up success for himself and a handsome substance to leave behind him. Not that there was a great deal to learn in surgery in those days. The average medical student of modern times could master in a week the whole gamut of surgery as it was then known, and be glad enough to forget it afterwards. But the life was hard, the trivial round remorseless and unending. This was not so with the usual youth of Halle at this period. They roistered and loafed. They spent half their days and more than half their nights in the billiard-rooms, where the *billardeurs*, or room-keepers, did a thriving trade plying them with tea, coffee, and chocolate, and then retired, comforably off, to senile ease.

Eventually and with startling suddenness, Christoph Oettinger died, and his young wife, Anna, was left with her thirty-one years and no children, but a considerable business hanging on her hands. In the ordinary way she should have disposed of it, and, with the aid of the comfortable fortune which Christoph had left, set about to find some eligible mate for her middle age.

But if Christoph had been thrifty, Anna was more so. She had helped him to build up this business, and she was giving nothing away. She resolved to go on. One can imagine her seeking and striving to pick up the threads where Christoph had laid them down, without the world, which was Halle, discovering those deficiencies that were hers. Wrestling with this problem and that, finding something new which Christoph had never told her about, wondering, then, beaten, going to that tall, slim youth, George Handel, who alone could help her out.

Thus she ran her business, relying on young Handel. More and more relying upon him. This quiet youth who said so little, yet always seemed to know. Odd thoughts must have passed through the minds of these two; Anna just thirty-one, and George Handel not yet twenty-one. To both there may have been apparent the certain fact that union alone would make their success. Success was the one almighty god that stirred in these twain.

Christoph Oettinger had not long become dust before George Handel married his widow. It was the one certain thing that had to happen. It proved to be a marriage exceptional in the fact that it was successful where the average marriage based on a business foundation is not. George Handel was at once a burgher of the town. Also Frau Handel held an equal importance with her husband in the conduct of a business which, under the full force of their youth and his cleverness, rose to be the principal establishment of its kind in the place. They made money rapidly. Valentine and Christoph in the coppersmith business discovered at last that the despised little brother had become a power in the town. They knew of him in Weissenfels; Leipzig had spoken of him. Then doubtless they realized that there might be some pride in the relationship.

This union, blessed as it had been by the object for which it was connived—on the part of George Handel an outlet for his brain without the terrible battle for a career, and, on that of Anna, the salvation of a business which she had helped to make—was a failure in other respects. Anna bore her husband six children, but only two of them—a boy and a girl—grew to maturity. Though George Handel, the barber-surgeon, studied, with the passage of years, even more deeply that duty to his home, the sense of which he had gained from his forebears, he became with those years more morose, often bitter, intensely severe, silent, and unpopular in the main. The will of Anna Handel, who had once owned the business, and who, in some sudden flight of lover-like fancy, had taken his youth to her bosom, must have wilted and died slowly, like some power reaching its extremity and then quietly subsiding.

Whereas she had owned the business in the Neumarkt which was to make George Handel, she now dropped out of it, and became the subdued *Hausfrau*. The disappointment of their children had hit them hard. Instead of bringing the twain closer, it hung as a heavy weight and forbade union and understanding.

As Handel grew older he became more a person to himself. He worked indefatigably. Night and day the tall, sinister figure, with the face that never smiled, was seen walking the streets, knowing no one, dreaming, just as perchance the boy had dreamed at the coppersmith's funeral. For at times the wings of a death epidemic swept over Halle and would wipe out the inhabitants of half a street, just as a gust of autumn gale can clear the leaves from one side of a tree. Halle was ill-drained, its streets too narrow. The wisp of disease would percolate from this point to that like some vile searching thing that was brought to a halt, not by the people's prayers in the Moritzburg, but by some peculiar dispensation of God at His own particular time.

For long after her marriage Frau Handel was kept continually busy with her cradles. They were, perhaps, mainly responsible for that gradual falling away of interest in what had now become her husband's business. But when they had been married nine years Handel was so definitely established as the finest barber-surgeon of the district that he was appointed (in 1652) the surgeon of Giebichenstein, a suburb of the town. What he achieved in Giebichenstein is not recorded. It is significant that shortly afterwards he was appointed Surgeon-in-Ordinary and Valet-de-Chambre to Prince Augustus of Saxony, a dissolute gentleman, a past-master in the art of Love, whose mistresses were scattered high and low over the immediate district and beyond it.

Meanwhile, with the coming of affluence, George Handel bought himself a house in the Schlamm in 1666. This particular locality is in the centre of the town, and only a couple of minutes' walk from the street in which his father had started his career in Halle as a coppersmith.

The house was known as 'Zum Gelben Hirsch' (The Yellow Stag) and the barber-surgeon determined to leave no stone unturned to make money. For nearly forty years the house had been licensed as a wine-house, and, when he bought it, the wine-pole—which distinguished the house as a wine-inn—was attached. Then he soon found himself in difficulties with the Governors of Halle, who refused to renew the licence. The barber-surgeon went over their heads and appealed to the Elector, who ultimately (in 1668) confirmed the privilege the house had always enjoyed.

The battle between the barber-surgeon and the town of Halle over this house went on for years. In spite of the Elector's ruling, the burghers prohibited Handel's wine from coming into the town. Many lawyers from the Leipzig University were called in to settle the dispute, but they made no headway. The Elector became annoyed. He threatened the town of Halle with penalties if they did not let the barber-surgeon pursue his wine-selling in peace. But things moved slowly in those days. Halle took no notice of any Elector. It appealed to forgotten Councils, who assembled in great state and put their hands together, ate sumptuous banquets, and did nothing.

The barber-surgeon was goaded into a fighting mood. That thin underlip had become thinner yet, and straight and firm. There was a smouldering fire in his eyes. Documents were prepared—pages of documents. They all cost money. The barber-surgeon, who hated parting with a pfennig, decided that his last pfennig should go to beat the town, since he was fighting for a right which he had bought with the house. The Elector wobbled between the clamours from right and left. He decided once more against the town, but gave it the right to appeal. The barber-surgeon fought on.

Then some bold fellow marched up to Handel's house with a document summoning him to appear before the Town Council, and the knave threw the summons through George's window. The blood of Handel was fired anew. The insult! If the rapscallion had only delivered the document into his hands and waited while he made suitable comments thereon! But he had hurled in his paper and run from the lion he had prodded.

Again the barber-surgeon went to the Elector. Again the Elector was bored to tears. This silly squabble was becoming a nuisance. He wrote finally to the town of Halle and said that unless they desisted in annoying the barber-surgeon he would fine the town 500 gold florins and, if need be, put in troops.[1]

That ended the business. The barber-surgeon had won. Disgruntled burghers sneered at him in the streets. But the keen eye of the man never swerved nor was afraid. He went on selling wine at The Yellow Stag for years, then, feeling that he could rest on his victory, he handed the licence over to the town—a victor who now performed a gracious act.[2]

It had been a bitter battle and a hard-earned victory. But its record is necessary because the whole affair is so typical of

[1] Report of the case in the State Archives at Magdeburg.
[2] G. F. Hertzberg: *Geschichte de Stadt Halle*, Vol. II.

the barber-surgeon. Could a man with that mouth, that violent pugnacity, sit down calmly while they stole a single right from him which his money had bought? He would have fought Europe single-handed for a case which had the vestige of right hidden somewhere in it. He was a strong man. A strong man of vast principles. Bigoted over principles. Narrow. Intensely disagreeable. If he won a victory he would, in common parlance, 'rub it in'. A man with a rather withered heart that blossomed weakly at times like some late October rose, unfragrant, a little stale with the day to which it had been born. This Handel never warmed to the sun of human understanding. He was a creature aloof whom most citizens feared.

Judging from the area on which it stood, the house which the barber-surgeon took to himself after his marriage must have been of considerable size, large enough, in fact, to house three families.

The biographers of George Frideric Handel, the son of this barber-surgeon, have, since the middle of the nineteenth century, for some unknown reason, followed each other in making a mistake about the Handel-house in Halle until lately. They have declared that the house in which the barber-surgeon lived, and in which his son George Frideric was destined to be born, was the house adjoining. They have depicted it with photograph and sketch. As a matter of fact the house that has been gilded with a frame it never earned is even now decorated with bays, with the names of George Frideric's oratorios on its plaster front, and with a bust of George Frideric over its doorway. It has been stared at, photographed—decrepit, deceiving thing. But the child who was later to decoy this world with his music never stumbled down its dark passages. That child's first cry on waking to a world of hurt and distress was never heard by its walls, its low dank ceilings. True, the boy must have played often in the courtyard that lies within its gate. The narrow cobbled street knew the patter of his feet, the roof, ageing then, and so much older now, stooped over him as if in benison, but that venerable house, with all its fabled romance, was never the Handel-house.

The mistake continued until it became almost old enough to be veracious. But, some years ago, a Professor of Halle University and a great Handel student[1] discovered undeniable evidence that Handel was never born in the house

[1] Dr Bernhard Weissenborn.

that claims him, but in the adjoining building, a corner house built at right angles with fronts on two streets—or, rather, in the building that stood on the site. The present house, Nicolaistrasse 5, which stands on the site of the musician's birthplace, was built in 1800.[1]

Eleven years after the barber-surgeon had bought his palatial house in the Schlamm, disaster overtook the district. On 2 May 1676, a house in this quarter suddenly burst into flames.[2] House after house was involved as a strong wind, rushing up the narrow lanes, hurled the sparks and flaming debris in all directions. The parsimonious builders of those days had bunched the houses together in huge clusters, separated only by the narrowest alleys. In a very short time the Schlamm was a blazing cauldron. It was night—the original fire was only discovered at ten o'clock—and most of the respectable citizens of the Schlamm were in bed. In a short time the adjoining streets, the Great Ulrichstrasse, the Dachritz, the Barfüsser (Bare-foot monks' street) made a palisade of fire about the Handel mansion, and before very long thirty-eight houses lay in heaps of charred and smoking

[1] In an advertisement which appeared in the *Wöchentliche Hallische Anzeiger* in December 1783, the house which stands on the site of Handel's birthplace is described as the former house of Handel, afterwards of Flörke, who was the husband of George Frideric Handel's niece. This house then bore the number 976; the old number was 528, afterwards 528A. The next following building, 975 (old number 529), which was rebuilt about 1720, was put up for sale in 1801 in the *Hallisches Patriotisches Wochenblatt*, and described in detail. The large courtyard, extensive garden, side wing and 'a front of twelve windows' can only be applied to the building which today appears decorated as the 'Handel-house'. Through my discovery of these two advertisements it is proved that the house in which Handel was born therefore stood on the spot where the corner house stands today—Nicolaistrasse 5—Dr Weissenborn.

Further evidence that the house at the corner of Nicolaistrasse and Kleine Ulrichstrasse is the house in which Handel was born is to be found in this letter which was published in the *Wiener Theaterzeitung*, 22 October 1806, over the signature of a man named Pokels. 'The widow of the late Ratmeister, Mrs Reichhelm, has told me that her great-uncle, the famous Handel, was born in the corner house of the "Kleine Ulrichstrasse", and that her late husband had for that reason caused the house to be rebuilt to dedicate it to the lasting memory of this famous man, and that he had intended to erect therein a special monument in honour of Handel, if sudden death had not overtaken him.' This Mrs Reichhelm was a granddaughter of Mrs Michaelsen, Handel's elder sister.

[2] Dreyhaupt: *Chronik des Saal Kreises*, Vol. II.

wood. Those houses which escaped actual destruction had their backs burned away. Eleven barns followed the houses to the ash-heap, and women and children were killed and injured, or disappeared in the flames.

How far the Handel mansion—and it undoubtedly was a mansion for the period—suffered in the conflagration there is no record, but the barber-surgeon saved himself and his family. Thereafter, the disaster was closely followed by others, which brought increasing anxiety into the lives of the Handels.

Four years later Prince Augustus of Saxony died, and the town of Halle passed from Saxony to Brandenburg. All the honours which George Handel had striven for and attained in royal circles thus fell away at a stroke, and the removal of royal patronage, even by death, was a catastrophe of the utmost magnitude in those days.

The silent surgeon of the Schlamm was not content to drop back from the proud position he had fought for. One imagines the varying emotions of depression and hopelessness that passed in succession across his mind. One can picture him daily growing more morose as he had been ever morose, more difficult in the family as he always had been difficult in the family since those days when the burden of his affairs first occupied his every thought. And Anna, dropping a little more into that subservience, that easy slide downhill from the independence she had known as Christoph Oettinger's widow.

Handel was disgruntled, his pride was smashed. Then the Halle Council, consisting as it did of many of his enemies, brought a charge against him of intriguing against the late Prince by supplying information about his condition to the Elector of Brandenburg, who had become the successor. They tried to harass Handel in Halle. Perhaps they hoped to drive out so gloomy a person from their midst. But with the tough courage, which he eventually passed on to his son, the barber-surgeon refused to budge an inch.

A little later his health began to fail. Possibly it was only a mental miasma that had caught him, a melancholia provoked by the agitation at the loss of his honours. He took a bold step. He wrote to the famous Privy Councillor von Dancklemann. 'I wish,' he said, 'to thank you herewith most humbly and obediently to pray, to be so gracious, as I am an old most humble servant, and according to the will of God have only to live one or two years, that on the occasion of the present visit of His Electoral Highness (to Halle) I may receive the document,' i.e. the renewal of the appointment to the various offices he held.[1]

It may have been the humility of his letter—had the pompous old fellow ever grovelled so completely before?—or it may have been out of pity for an old servant of the Court, but the Elector gave back to the barber-surgeon all the honours he had lost. Once again George Handel became surgeon to the Court, at first without salary.

Hardly had he been reappointed than he was suddenly taken ill. He grew worse. Would that life remaining to him, which he had said had but one year, two years to run, pass out so soon? They prayed for him in the churches. The Superintendent Olearius, his confessor and a distant relative, came and administered the last Sacrament. It was obvious that the old barber-surgeon was dying.

Then came an amazing change. He rallied. This man, whom they believed to be gasping out his last breath, was suddenly found walking about in his room. Death! Who had spoken of death? There was so much he had to do, so much for him to think about, and Death could not interrupt these things. His recovery was a sheer achievement of will-power—the will-power that hustled Death away even as it peeped in at the bedroom door. He flung aside the leech, he dispensed with Superintendent Olearius, and a surprised town saw him suddenly appear, a white, slow-moving ghost, towards his seat in the Liebfrauenkirche and drop painfully to his knees, till only the shower of silver hair was visible above the pew. For long he knelt thus, thanking his Maker for his new lease of life.

Honour was restored. A new sense of ease and achievement crept into the Handel establishment, and probably no one felt the relief more than Anna. Only for a space did Fate allow the barber-surgeon any respite. Scarcely a year after the new distinction had been given, Anna Handel died suddenly. If the barber-surgeon was stupefied by the blow he did not show it. His life went on imperturbably as before. He buried her without a coffin, without any ceremonial whatever, just as if he were hiding in the ground some finished thing that had once been a piece of his home. In his later years he had not

[1] Opel.

shown the adoration for Anna which he professed whilst she was Oettinger's widow. Now that she had gone he picked up the threads of his life, no more solitary for her loss. But a corner-stone had been knocked out of the domestic edifice which had grown about him, and as the months passed his life accommodated itself anew to his work, altering its shape, adapting itself to every call which the daily round demanded.

The upheaval did not change him. He went steadily on without varying the lines of his life by a fraction. Possibly he spoke a little less than he did before to those about him, but otherwise there was no perceptible change in this man. He never showed at any time of his life, by any expression or by any act, anything that he felt. He took his misfortune as he took his success, with a calm, even strength.

He was still floundering in the rut of misfortune, when further disaster overtook him. Plague broke out in Halle, the last epidemic of plague Halle was to know. During the disaster, nineteen of the principal citizens of the town formed a union for purposes of mutual help during the plague. The union came into being on 8 May 1682, and each member paid five thalers into its fund, but how the money was applied there is nothing to show. Indeed it is odd that one of the rules of the union was that the money was to be returned to the subscribers after the plague *plus interest*! How the plague could have been turned into a money-making concern is a problem. The members were required to invoke daily prayer hours in their establishments, and pray regularly in places of worship; to follow with their families a moderate mode of life, consume good diet, and keep their houses stocked with good provisions. And, finally, if a member were to fail in his provisions or medicines and became infected, the others were to come to his aid from their own stores. The nineteen members were made up of doctors (including George Handel), pastors, town inspectors and grocers. Excellent fellows of high standing in the town, whose names and vocations have been preserved.[1]

But in spite of these precautions, these prayers, the plague swept away Gottfried, one of the barber-surgeon's two surviving children. The surgeon, with years gathering as a mighty weight upon him, was left practically alone in the great house in the Schlamm, a strong, unbroken but piteous figure.

[1] *Hallische Tageblatt*, No. 303.

Even this blow did not bring him to his knees. He waited a little while considering how he could best remedy the havoc that had been made in his life. Six months elapsed. Not for any trivial move did he wait.

All through the years since he had been made surgeon to the suburb of Giebichenstein—and exactly thirty anniversaries of the event had passed over his head—he had been a regular visitor there. In spite of his strange reticence for finding friendships he had so far thawed as to make a friend and confidant of the pastor of the district, George Taust. The Taust household for long had been a kind of sanctuary, which he visited when Giebichenstein claimed his service, possibly he dined there frequently. In any case, he was a close intimate of the family.

He was now sixty years of age. The tall figure had bent, the face had thinned, the mouth become more stubborn, more firm. As he aged, his long hair whitened in curls about his shoulders. He dressed always in black, with a black skullcap, a coat of black satin and a collar of white lace. Early in 1683—only a very few months after the unromantic Anna had passed to her account—George Handel announced to the few cronies who frequented his house in the Schlamm, and had his confidence, that he was engaged to be married to Dorothea Taust, a woman of thirty-two, quiet, subdued. At his age, and with his experience, George would never have tolerated any woman who was not subdued. His new era of love-making was as violent as the first had been subtle. He attempted in his strong, selfish fashion to thrust an urgent marriage upon her. But the plague, which now had been stamped out of Halle, was still lingering in the suburbs, and some of the Taust family were stricken with it.

In vain did George Handel press the matter of an immediate marriage. Subservient as she was, Dorothea had a greater instinct in her—that of humanity. She refused to leave her relatives till they were convalescent. Plead as he might he could make no impression. Not until April burst in loveliness over the Saale plain did George Handel make his second marriage. Certainly he had not wasted much time, for Anna had now been dead only six months, but he would have wasted less had it not been for the confounded plague which had worried and overworked him for nearly a year.

So did Dorothea Taust come to the mansion in the Schlamm.

A nervous woman, very fearful of the rather celebrated personage whom she had married, the old man with lingerings of youth in him still, his certain faithfulness, his extraordinary set sense of duty in everything.

As soon as he had married, George Handel shut himself up again to his secret life as he had done before. Possibly it meant very little to him whether Dorothea Taust faced him across the dinner-table or Anna Oettinger. He was in his fashion extremely sexless to *difference* in women. He had never philandered, nor had he ever understood women. He had never wished to understand them. They had not intrigued him. He would have lived and died a celibate but for ulterior reasons that made him respond in lukewarm fashion to their charms. Either of the two women who married him could and did always count on extreme fidelity–this fidelity, this cold fidelity, he gave.

A year after their marriage Dorothea brought into the world a son, a weak child, who died at birth. The Fates still juggled with old Handel. If it were not for the excuse that he ultimately reared one of the greatest children in the world's history, it might be said that he was never meant to bring children to maturity because he did not understand them nor did he want them. When his wife ultimately bore a child of genius he thought the child a fool.

So when, on 23 February 1685, passers down the Nicolaistrasse or Schlamm heard the small cry of a newly born child come from the big building at the corner, they interpreted nothing in it at all, except that they hoped, no doubt, that the doctor would have better luck this time.

Not that it could signify at all on that February morning that George Frideric Handel had been born into the world.

CHAPTER II

THE HALLE DAYS

ON the day following the birth of the child in the Schlamm a few people gathered about the font in the Liebfrauenkirche, situated only five minutes' walk from the residence of the barber-surgeon. There was the barber-surgeon himself, standing white-haired beside the font and looking at the small scrap of humanity carried in the arms of his sister-in-law, Anna Taust. Anna Taust, the curious spinster lady with the warm heart, who, in the process of time, was to drift into the Handel circle and exercise a wonderful influence over this child, because she understood children as neither of the Handels ever understood them.

Whatever her joy in this child may have been, however envious she may have been of her sister Dorothea, who had brought him into the world, it is doubtful if Anna Taust knew but a small part of the elation which the coming of the child had created in the heart of the barber-surgeon. This child was the child of his old age. It marked the beginning of a new family circle which was his. After all, the family that had come to him by Anna Oettinger had ceased to count in his life. Few had survived; those few who reached maturity had crept away and left him in his solitude. Possibly his taciturnity had hastened their departure. Only one of those children had counted in his heart, and that was his son Gottfried, whom the plague had killed three years before. Gottfried, who had done everything he had been told to do, who had become a surgeon as he meant him to be a surgeon, and who had achieved some little fame and much respectability in Halle as all the Handels had before him. He had married well, this Gottfried; he had raised unto himself a sound practice and had earned a good income. The old barber-surgeon must have seen in this son something of an ideal as it had framed itself in his mind.

But when Gottfried fell before the plague-storm that swept the streets of Halle he left no issue, only a young widow. Had there been a child the old barber-surgeon might never have married a second time. He wanted some youth about him. All the taciturnity and sacrifice of self to the altar of success had left him a man desolate of heart. It was this searching for youth which made him marry Dorothea Taust of Giebichenstein. It was the same yearning that made him bring into the world George Frideric, whom they were baptizing this day in the Liebfrauenkirche.

'Unto us a child is born.' Those words must have been very present in the mind of this man as he waited beside the font while his father-in-law, old George Taust, christened this child George Frideric, thereby performing an office which was to be one of the last of his official life, for within a few weeks of his leaving the church, filled as he doubtless was with the great pride of owning a first grandchild, death claimed him. 'Unto us a child is born.' And this very child upon whose forehead they set the cross of water now was to put those words to the wonderful music in little over a half a century's time.

He would have been a brave fellow who had suggested to the barber-surgeon that day that his child would in the ensuing years make his living by music. It would have horrified the barber-surgeon; it would have been a suggestion of scandal upon the whole Handel family. Music in those days had failed to find respectability. It was a sort of pedlar's calling, cheap huckstering when all else failed. The family blacklegs turned to music; people sang in the streets, wrote and sang ephemeral melodies in the taverns, and counted themselves well paid when the equivalent of a few pence rewarded them. A few escaped to higher spheres, and were included in the select and exclusive choirs that earned for them some shadow of respectability.

The barber-surgeon, who had lost Gottfried and found salvation in George Frideric, had higher ambitions for this son. But George Frideric was to disappoint him; he was to frivol with musical instruments ere his parent passed to the Handel tomb. Though his mother Dorothea from the Giebichenstein parsonage was to live to see this child go out and find fame in the doubtful ways of music, she never understood what it meant. This son was to grow up and depart from her, and would, in the fullness of time, send short messages of affection to her from his sanctuary in England. But, having no knowledge of music, she never realized his worth. He ultimately became to her a being she had created and sent forth into some strange vortex of public life. She always cared for him, though he departed from her for ever when just emerging from his teens, and when she died Death dealt the greatest blow to this son his life ever knew.

From the time that the christening party left the Liebfrauenkirche, life for the Handel child was to drop into the common rut of the better-bred Halle children. Ere the year had ended Pastor Taust of Giebichenstein, left weak and ill as he had been by the plague, passed quietly away, and Fräulein Anna came to live with her sister Frau Dorothea Handel at the Schlamm. Her coming banished all question of the child's education in the tender years. Frau Dorothea was occupied with other cradles. She raised two girls, one of whom was in later years to have the proud knowledge of her brother's achievements. Upon Anna Taust depended the main upbringing of this boy, and his mother, left with the nurture of two tender children, watched the influence of Tante Anna work itself upon this first child she had been able to rear.

Of some things concerning that boy she remained unaware, even though Anna Taust clearly understood them. She did not know of his interest in church music, she did not see him fascinated by the first dawning understanding of the notes of the organ. He went to the Liebfrauenkirche regularly. To Frau Handel his object in doing so was to serve his Maker as he had been taught to do. That the organ music in the Liebfrauenkirche stood in the place of his Maker to the boy who groped his way to understanding never occurred to her. And, if it had, she was doubtless so shaped in her mental outlook by the creed of her husband that probably she would have sent young George Frideric to one of the lesser places of worship of simple faith which existed in Halle at the time, and at which music was unknown.

It is not easy to understand immediately this dislike of the Handels towards any form of music, without inquiring a little into the life of Halle at the time when George Frideric was in his childhood. Halle was then a small town confined within the radius of its medieval walls, a town of houses constructed of wood and plaster covered with thatched roofs. As a house fell into disrepair it was pulled down and a new building created out of the remains of the old, with the addition of more modern material.[1] Thus the town kept in its own little circle, with only the suburbs of Glauchau and Neu-

[1] G. F. Hertzberg: *Geschichte der Stadt Halle.*

THE BAPTISMAL ENTRY IN THE BOOK OF THE LIEBFRAUENKIRCHE AT HALLE

Showing the record of Handel, and proving the year of his birth—1685 markt apart. It was in the latter that the barber-surgeon had his practice.

Moreover, the people of Halle were severely solitary in their existence. They were situated in the centre of a group of warring tribes, which had fought and triumphed over each other since very early times. Halle was a sort of buffer state ringed about by the denizens of the salt-marshes, a strange people of ancient Wend and Frankish blood, who from the beginning of time had worked the salt wells, and been a law unto themselves—a people so powerful that they were able to support an army of six hundred men.[1] But music had always been an art, ardently pursued and much better practised at Halle than in all Saxony. The glories of the old courts, the moods of successive rulers with the pomps and ceremonies at the old Moritzburg[2] in the town, whence archbishops and princes ruled with rods of iron, had kept song alive throughout Halle. And the glorious memory of Halle's court music, which lasted until shortly before the birth of the child George Frideric, was undoubtedly still with the people at the time of his infancy.[3] Many choirs existed in the town at the time when his infant intelligence first began to understand. The town choir, and choirs from the schools—choirs that sang in the streets in front of citizens' houses, and thrived on chance charity cast from the windows to put an end to what was too frequently an irritating noise. Someone was always singing somewhere in public in Halle in those days. Occasionally the singers were given pieces of cloth and a spasmodic education by some ancient charity according to the regularity of their singing. To become musical, therefore, was to ally oneself with a species of street vagrants, to descend in public esteem, and to be the certain occupier of a charitable cubicle at the end of it all.

Such a prospect for their son jarred badly on the Handels. It was not entirely his fault that the barber-surgeon strove to exterminate, as he might some rank weed, the first interest in music which showed in his son. The Handel pride was considered a God-given gift above music. It had found its birth in a great record of honourable men, and it was not going to slip into the common huckstering of sounds and noises if the

---

[1] Brockhaus: Lexikon *Halloren.*
[2] Built in 1478 when the Archbishop conquered the town.
[3] Dr Weissenborn.

old barber-surgeon could help it. Aunt Anna, when she cast aside neutrality and threw all the weight of her sympathies to the child in whom the first knowledge of melody was dawning, who took him to the Liebfrauenkirche that he might listen to a wonderful organ on Sundays, and brought him back again, was risking a great deal in what she did. Had her lack of neutrality been revealed, it is certain that she would not have been tolerated for very long in the Handel household. In aiding this child to understand the meaning of music, in cultivating that new-born creed in him, she was hiding a secret sin. It is certain that the barber-surgeon did not know, and equally certain that his wife, Dorothea, was equally unaware that the saintly Anna was leading a double life. If she did smuggle in the clavichord for the child, which some biographers will insist upon, although there is no evidence of her having done so, then she was a woman of still greater daring than history has ever credited her with possessing. The barber-surgeon was weary of hearing the various choirs sing daily sacred airs in chorus manner and in parts under the conductorship of a Praefectus at stated hours in front of the citizens' houses.[1] They were a sort of public nuisance in the Schlamm, the melancholy nuisance familar in our Christmas waits. Daily repetition may well have urged a certain decision in his mind when thinking about his son: 'If that boy ever shows the first inclination towards music, or noises disguised as such, I will kill it.' And all the while that delightful old maid in his house, Aunt Anna, was deceiving him, tolerating little George Frideric, if she did not actually encourage him, in this awful vice. Tremendously proud of his rebellion in her secret soul no doubt. Trammelled about as they were by the fussation and importance of the barber-surgeon in the Schlamm house, it is so easy to see how it all happened. Probably if there had been no Aunt Anna there might have been no Westminster Abbey for George Frideric, though it is hard to believe that a soul so crowded with melody would have failed to find its destined and appointed place.

The greatest characteristic about the barber-surgeon throughout his life had been selfishness. He had been selfish from his youth, and his selfishness had been aided by great strength of personality. Everything he did—as far as history

[1] G. F. Hertzberg: *Geschichte der Stadt Halle*.

reveals—had been guided by self-motives. His marriage with Anna Oettinger, a diplomatic move for self; his great honours the result of cleverness, but as cleverly planned. His second marriage, a sop to self. A supremely selfish, clever man, he had ever been with two weak women, one after the other, vainly striving to play a very inferior second fiddle, a half-dumb instrument in the family orchestra which was all 'George Handel, barber-surgeon of some renown'.

When the child of his late years was seven years old a new problem occurred to the barber-surgeon. He had to educate him. Halle at that date was full of schools, both good and bad. There were poor schools and orphan schools in the Glauchau, and in the Vineyards. There was a school of Catholics, a school of French commune, a great number of private schools. There was also a Jewish school in the town conducted by a Rabbi, and free to pupils. The Rabbis usually came from Poland and were married men whose wives and children remained in Poland. By their laws these Rabbis were compelled to return to their wives after two years in Halle, and live with them for at least one year. If, at the end of that time, they came to the end of their earnings they were considered free to go back to Halle for another term and so continue on the jog-trot of life, now here, now there.[1] There was also the Lutheran Gymnasium or Halle Grammar School, not renowned for the breeding of its scholars, for if a boy did not enter it by legitimate means he could enter it by charity.[2] If he were the son of the poorest tradesman he could arrive there by this means or that. It was denied to no one. As often as not the Alms-treasury paid the fees for the boy. The school had a good philosophical and theological library if no standing as a seminary of teaching. It had ten classes, divided irrespective of the children's social standing.

Into this mixed quarter the barber-surgeon sent his son, for no apparent reason revealed by record except to save money. There were good private schools in Halle in plenty,

[1] Dreyhaupt.
[2] Some of Handel's biographers have maintained that Handel was first a pupil at the Latin School at Halle, but this was not opened till 1698. The register of the Stadtkinder (town-children school) does not contain his name, consequently there is only the Lutheran Gymnasium to which he could have gone. Unfortunately the school register of this seminary was not kept by the Rector Praetorius during the years of Handel's childhood, and was only recontinued in 1705.

but he avoided them all. And, though he meant his son to be a lawyer, which in those days entailed the best education possible, he decided to save fees by sending him to the Grammar School, a carefully thought-out move which proved a boomerang. The head of the Grammar School when young George Frideric entered was a music-loving Rector Praetorius. A puritanical spirit of pietism was spreading in Halle at that date, and the head of this school had been caught up in it, and believed in the power of music to develop religious thought. It was into the hands of this man that the barber-surgeon unknowingly pushed his son, believing that all the nonsense of music would be worried out of him by the demands of school-work, as the Grammar School work was notoriously excessive and unproductive and diffuse. It led nowhere, but the pupil met and rubbed shoulders with the children of common tradesmen or nobody at all, and picked up a smattering of miscellaneous knowledge, which had no beginning and no end, because it had no object. The alms-child had as good a chance as the child of the notorious barber-surgeon.

The uncouth urchins, who were his companions, and the cramped means of education, must have given the child cause for a diversion of thoughts. They taught him at this seminary Latin and the sense of his God. The latter he had already discovered under the protection of Aunt Anna in the mysterious dusk of the Liebfrauenkirche. He had never revealed it even to her. But religious music had an intense fascination for him. The range of the organ—poor in comparison with the range of that same organ today—on which his fingers first learned to play, was the discovery of a new soul seeking its destiny. When he was not at the Grammar School, he seems to have been left to playing with street companions. He was, as the old barber-surgeon had been in his youth, intensely lonely. There is no record of the boy George Frideric having found a single friend in his early days. They were just companions of youth's irresponsible pathway, who pass as unknown as they come.

He had the courtyard at the back of the Schlamm and its wide garden as a playground. Beyond it some odd barns and fields. On the town side he had an old courtyard, which still stands with its surrounding buildings as he knew it—the ancient palace of Cardinal Albrecht, a medieval ruffian, who playcd havoc with the Church and the hearts of women.

The child, of course, knew nothing of Cardinal Albrecht or his works and his love passages. But Albrecht had been a sixteenth-century demigod of Halle, who had left out of his riches a rather desolate courtyard between a cramped run of buildings, in which the child George Frideric Handel was to play. The story of that courtyard is worth recording, since it must have been one of the principal haunts of the boy. It stands opposite the place where he was born, dull and shabby and with all the overburdening sense of lost romance. The daintily clad mistresses of the Cardinal who built it havc gonc down in the dust. The glories of the Moritzburg, which the Cardinal inhabited, are as a tale that is told. All the memories of high rank, of riches, of life that sailed above that which Halle knew in this age have passed just as worldly things pass in their appointed time, leaving an old courtyard, melancholy, seldom stirred by the sound of feet.

The courtyard is still as he knew it; from his bedroom window he must have viewed its solemn entrance. Originally the main building in it had been a chapel, but in the early sixteenth century the Cardinal Albrecht found a Court favourite in one Hans von Schönitz. This fellow Schönitz amassed enormous wealth by transactions which did not admit of strict investigation. He built himself a palace in this courtyard, which had a single entrance from the Schlamm, and which in its day consisted of a row of stately buildings, including the Kühlebrunnen (cool-born spring or well). This Kühlebrunnen, the possession of the town, received the only wine and spirit licence apart from the Rath-cellar. To construct this palace Schönitz had used a great deal of material from the Church of St Ulrich. He accumulated building material from anywhere without paying for it. Most of it was purloined from churches which he thought needed pulling down. Thus he slowly built his palace, an ugly, medieval building still. On the first floor there is a large room, where the Town Council used to hold their meetings, and underneath was their spacious cellar. In a room by the side of it there was, in the days of the child Handel, a very old wooden bedstead—it existed until 1755. And it was in this room that the Cardinal used to visit his mistress; the room had a secret staircase going in from a small door in the courtyard.[1]

[1] G. F. Hertzberg: *Geschichte de Stadt Halle*, Vol. I.

The man Schönitz had built this palace by illicit gains, and by equally illicit means he came to his fall. The Cardinal had no objection to the barefaced robbery of his purse, since he could make good the deficiencies by heavier taxation on the people of Halle. But when von Schönitz in this building, every brick of which, apart from those purloined, the Cardinal had paid for, stole away one of the Cardinal's favourite mistresses, the matter came to a climax. The Cardinal dragged his favourite out of his lair, and beheaded him in 1535. It was the only thing to do. Still the palace yard, no better than an East End London alley, went on undisturbed and became the haunt of a lonely child, who probably knew nothing of its story. The building that was a palace and its yard still stand; all the romance gone from the desolate windows and doorways, uncurtained and grim, changing itself not at all, but standing sure and defiant against the ravages of time, long after the scuffle of those young feet over its stones had ceased.

Some miles distant from the town of Halle is Weissenfels, which at this period was celebrated chiefly because the Duke kept his Court there. Much of the pomp, which in earlier times had annoyed the citizens of Halle with endless restrictions and ceremonies, had since passed to Weissenfels. Halle now was a town making money, with its coal and salt industries, its lace and ribbon factories, its silk and wool. It had to a great extent broken free from the serfdom which had found its ruling from the Moritzburg. Weissenfels had taken the place of Halle since the established Court there had drawn thither many of the rich drones of public life and their accruing vice.

Meanwhile, the fame of the barber-surgeon had continued to grow. They had heard of him as far away as Leipzig. The richest people of the outlying towns came to him. Then at this period (1692) he performed an operation under peculiar circumstances, which made his repute a matter for common talk everywhere. A boy of sixteen named Andreas Rudloff, the son of a peasant of Maschvritz, near Halle, held in his mouth a fair-sized knife with a stag-horn handle. He had the misfortune to fall and the knife was pushed down his throat. Those present, finding they could not get the knife up, decided to wash it down with cold and hot beer and olive oil! This they did and followed the beer with medicines to corrode the blade of the knife. For nearly a year the boy lived with this knife inside him, suffering greatly, and the subject of medical experiment all the time. But medicines and masters proved of no avail—the knife remained wedged at the base of the stomach. Finally a boil appeared under the heart, and on opening it the barber-surgeon Handel discovered the point of the knife. He fastened a silk thread to it, and daily attempts were made to pull the knife a little farther out. This had to be done with great care, because it caused intense pain to the patient, followed by rapid fits of fainting and vomiting. It was on 18 June that the barber-surgeon found the point of the knife, and he did not succeed in removing the weapon till 2 August. The boy who had walked about with the knife in him for one year, thirty weeks, and three days, then recovered completely, was nicknamed the 'Halle Sword-Swallower', and in the fullness of time became a military surgeon.[1] What he had endured doubtless enthused him towards barber-surgery.

As surgeon at the Weissenfels Court, the father of the child Handel travelled there at regular intervals by coach. And it was one of these journeys which decided the question of music for this child for all time. That Weissenfels journey was a divine accident or a premeditated act of equal inspiration. George Frideric Handel was now between seven and nine years old,[2] but how it came about that he went with his father to Weissenfels there is nothing to show. Historians declare that he ran after the coach in which his father was travelling and overtook it![3] One can scarcely imagine a boy, even of nine years of age, being able to overtake a coach, slothful as the coach must have been on the bad roads. Others declare that the coach broke down, and the boy, following on foot, came upon the benighted barber-surgeon unawares, and cried so piteously to be taken that his father had perforce to bundle him into the vehicle. This story, like the other, is probably more fragrant with romance than veracity, for no child would follow a coach blindly in the hope that it would break down. The probability is that the barber-surgeon left the house at

[1] Dreyhaupt.

[2] Mainwaring, Handel's first biographer, says that the child was seven years of age; Chrysander declares that he was somewhat older, but there is no record as to his actual age.

[3] Mainwaring, Chrysander, Schölcher, Rockstro, and Streatfeild, all maintain this story, though it probably originated in the imagination of the first-named, for there is no record to support it.

the Schlamm with the child in the coach beside him. There were times in his life when he took a spasmodic interest in the members of his family. In a heart that had known little tenderness and much severity there were moments of human understanding, which came at intervals like the glow of a short burst of sunshine over ice. He may have promised the boy the treat of a journey to Weissenfels; or it is even possible that out of his own vanity—which was superb—he decided to take this child of his late years to the Court for show purposes, since his cleverness in his craft had made him a *persona grata* there. It is difficult to believe that he would have taken his child to Court without some definite permission, for ceremony reigned supreme, and a presumption of this kind might have produced a crisis which the barber-surgeon could ill afford to risk. In any case the child was taken and lodged with Georg Christian Handel, the son of Georg Friedrich's half brother Karl, who was engaged as valet de chambre at the palace.

At Weissenfels the child immediately took possession of the affections of many, for he was intelligent beyond his years. Georg Christian, interested no doubt in his small relative, took him into the chapel. After that the child would go to the chapel for rehearsals, until the organist began to recognize the quaint little wondering figure. One day the organist seated the child at the instrument, and was astounded to find that he had some instinctive knowledge of music.

It was a Sunday service which was the means of drawing the Duke's attention to the child Handel. On this occasion the boy was allowed to attempt a voluntary at the end of the service. To a child something under nine, a modern organ would have been unmanageable, but the instrument in question was small, and the little fingers found melody and played.

In the chapel the Duke listened. The notion of this child seated at what was in comparison a mighty instrument, amused him. He had more than average discernment where music was concerned, and he sent for the boy and his father. When the barber-surgeon took George Frideric to Weissenfels he had no suspicion of what was going to happen. The Duke in his remarks was brief and to the point. This child, he declared, had abnormal gifts; he had never known a child play in such a cultured manner before. He must be trained.

In vain the barber-surgeon expostulated as energetically as he dared. He intended the child for the law, and no minor talents must defeat what the doctor believed to be the boy's destiny. But to ignore gifts like these in a child was to fly in the face of God, the Duke answered. He produced some money and filled George Frideric's small pocket with it. Whatever passions rose in the surgeon's breast, he lost by this incident the battle for his son's future. There was nothing left for him to say. The Duke insisted that the child should be taught music, and to decline or break the command would have meant risking his post at the Court. He was a prudent man, ready, when someone greater than himself so demanded, to sacrifice even his own inclinations. He took George Frideric back to Halle and put him into the hands of Zachow, the organist at the Liebfrauenkirche, for his musical education.

Zachow was a curious character. A thinker, an extremely able man, with qualities far in excess of those required by his post at the Liebfrauenkirche. He was thirty years of age when the barber-surgeon came to him about this wayward son who had begun to disappoint him with his musical proclivities. Zachow came from Leipzig, where his father was Stadtmusikus, and he had an extremely wide knowledge of all forms of music, and instruments. He could, in fact, play all the instruments then in general use. He was a zealot of the highest order, deeply impressed by the sense of those great ones who had preceded him at the Liebfrauenkirche organ—Wolff Heintz, Samuel Scheidt, and others. He composed regularly and well, church cantatas and fugues, and, if his music never rose to great heights, it was at least graceful and lacking only in imagination. He adopted the boy Handel as the object for the outpourings of his whole musical enthusiasm. The boy had genius and Zachow was only second to the Duke in recognizing the fact. He gave to that genius all the service he knew, sparing himself nothing.

The result was that Handel derived far more than a musical teaching from Zachow; he was imbued with a certain amount of his style. There are, in several of Handel's compositions, distinct leanings towards Zachow, although Zachow's organ music, when played today, seems like the innocuous trifling of an inferior musician compared with the imagination of Handel. The latter had genius, whilst the former merely possessed talent and a great ardour. The world's debt to Zachow lies, not in his musical remains, but in the sound and strictly accurate tuition which he gave to the boy Handel. He worked him ruthlessly at all instruments, and in Italian and German forms of composition, so much so that, had not the hours with Zachow been a joy rather than a burden to the boy, the heaviness of the instruction would have broken his heart. No doubt it would also have achieved what the barber-surgeon most desired—the satiation of his son with music for ever.[1] Young Handel composed, so it is said, a Church Service every week, and when in his later years Lord Polwarth discovered one of these volumes of his boyhood somewhere on the Continent, and Weidemann the flute-player showed it to Handel, he laughingly admitted the work as his own. 'I used to write like the devil in those days,' he said, by way of self-excuse.[2]

He had three years under Zachow—three years during which he probably achieved a greater understanding of music than Zachow himself. Zachow had taught him the rudiments of counterpoint and harmony; he admitted now that he could teach his pupil no more. This precocious boy had a mind that thought in the same tones of music as that of his master. He desired means for expansion and it was decided that he should go to Berlin.

Most of Handel's biographers have declared that he was sent to Berlin to meet Ariosti and Bononcini, whose fame was then common talk throughout Germany. Some write of the boy Handel sitting on Ariosti's knee and being trained to the difficult ways of music, but at that period the Dominican monk was still in Italy.[3] When Handel, now eleven years of age, went to Berlin in 1696, neither of the two musicians had been there. Ariosti was the first to arrive, a year later; not until five years afterwards did Bononcini, like some flashing

[1] Some proof of this was to be found in the volume of choruses, fugues, and airs, transcribed by Handel at this period from the works of Zachow, Alberti, Krieger, Ebner, and others, which, according to Coxe, was dated 1698. It passed into the possession of Lady Rivers, who was remarkably careless with her Handel possessions, and then disappeared.

[2] Burney.

[3] Grove's *Dictionary of Music* is wrong in stating that Ariosti became Maestro di Cappella to the Electress of Brandenburg in 1690.

firework, lighten the musical circles of the Electress and disappear again.[1] There was therefore no apparent reason for Handel to have gone to Berlin. But it would suggest a certain relinquishing of the spirit of antagonism to music in the mood of his father. For a boy of eleven to set out on such a mysterious journey—the barber-surgeon was then too ill to accompany him—was romantic even for a romantic age. He must have gone with someone. Whom? Did Zachow take him there to show the boy a world in which music was supreme? Certainly the barber-surgeon must have financed the mission.

At that time Berlin was taking definite shape in European affairs as a centre of music. It was entirely the work of one woman, the Electress Sophia Charlotte, wife of the man who was to become Frederick I of Prussia. For years she had made of her Court a 'mad riot of music', to quote an historian of the period. She set all Berlin by the ears on account of her eccentric behaviour. She held concerts at all times—often in the dead of night—and in all places. Her husband she regarded as a puppet. He was content to remain so, and own to a pride in the wonderful musical fervour which was making the Berlin Court talked about in London, Paris, and elsewhere. Moreover, the Electress was certainly stirring the musical dovecotes of Florence, whence some of the best Italian musicians were migrating northward to the welter of colour and exclusiveness, which Berlin, under Sophia, offered to the Europe of her day. Sophia, clever and with a certain sense of music, had composed a few very uninspired but dignified pieces, and she had at one time been trained by Steffani, who had been *Kapellmeister* to her father the Elector of Hanover. She was a woman who had no belief in rank; a creature from the gutter might play the violin well and be her friend. He could sit at her table and eat the rich foods for which the Berlin Court was famous, or if the singing of his violin were better than that of other violins he would be treated as the guest of the evening. Those who still clung to the Court, aware that the Court had now been turned topsy-

---

[1] There is a letter in existence from the Cavaliere Fra Alessandro Bichi, written from Berlin in 1695, in which he gives all the names of the painters and musicians in the city at the time, but neither Bononcini nor Ariosti are mentioned. This would suggest that neither of them was in Berlin at that period.

turvy by this woman, had to bow to the figure of musical ability who came to the table in rags if the Electress demanded, or stay away and drift towards the quiet backwaters into which those of political thought, with not a note of music in them, slowly and certainly eddied.

All political progress at a Court consecrated to Art alone was out of the question. Sophia's husband was sequestering himself with a wealth of mistresses, while his Consort rubbed shoulders with all kinds of weird figures who carried instruments through the palace gates. Unknown people found some mysterious entrée to the palace, and came away famous; were called upon by Sophia in disreputable by-streets given over to humble lodgements. It was a kaleidoscopic Court of peoples and manners, of big drawing-rooms, where the lights blazed till the first shafts of daylight were very certain intruders, where half the visitors could not utter a word of German, but spoke to the Consort of Germany's ruler in the notes of an instrument, and had no other means of communication with her.

That a boy of eleven should come up from what was practically an unknown town, and drop directly into this vortex of cosmopolitan life is at first a little mysterious. But his coming to Berlin had, it would seem, nothing to do with the Court. That he reached that Court and was exploited was entirely due to the acumen of the Electress, searching as she always was for some feverish sensation to create a new mood in music among the members of her circle. She had compelled her husband to run an opera-theatre, or rather a theatre at which the Italian operas and Italian musicians were prominent. Probably the good man never knew the manner in which his money was being expended, but was only conscious that he was running the Italian opera by the fact that unknown figures who gabbled in a southern tongue of which he had no learning, appeared and reappeared at the palace with ever more alarming frequency.

Everything points to the fact that Handel's first performances in Berlin were of the humblest nature. He certainly did not come in with a storm of precocity under the aegis of Ariosti or Bononcini. But his remarkable skill on the clavichord and the organ, considering age, began to astonish the little thatched town of twenty thousand inhabitants which Berlin then was, and he created an immediate sensation.[1] The

[1] E. David: *G. F. Händel et Sa Vie.*

neurotic Electress, tired and distinctly nervy with a surfeit of high life, heard of him, and when she heard of a musical curiosity she sent for it. She commanded the attendance of the boy Handel, and for a wondrous hour he was the most talked-of personage in Berlin.

Consider for a moment the circle into which this boy had been drawn. All the musical genius of Europe had assembled at this Court as if it had been some vast concert room. Italy, the heart from which the music of Europe throbbed at the end of the seventeenth century, had had its best blood drawn from it by the attractions of this extraordinary Court. The boy Handel was caught up and whirled off his feet by the panegyrics of a people who must have appeared to him strange if not a little mad. The Electress herself directed the orchestra, the Prince and princesses played and sang, and musicians, accustomed to lead at other and inferior Courts, humbly took their places in the orchestra.[1] That young Handel created a stupendous impression there is no doubt. Only a few months after his arrival in Berlin we find the Elector—inspired, no doubt, by the whims of his weird and wonderful wife—appealing to the aged barber-surgeon at Halle, now laid to the bed on which he was so soon to die, to permit him to take the boy into his service. He offered at the same time to send him to Italy to have him trained—which really showed his ignorance of musical affairs, for there was very little about music at this stage which the young Handel did not know.

It is hardly possible that the barber-surgeon weighed the letter in his mind for very long. He knew the ways of Courts; he had breathed the exotic atmosphere of such places. He knew possibly that there was something strange about his son George Frideric which he had never deeply fathomed, because he had never understood the moods of the boy. He had talents doubtless above those of the School Choir and Town Choir, whose singers came bothering him with their dim religious music in the Schlamm at all times and in all moods and weathers. These effete tuneless nuisances, as they must have appeared to his tuneless soul! The boy had thriven with his Latin and general knowledge at the Grammar School. And quite probably Zachow, with that ardour which he always felt

[1] W. S. Rockstro: *Life of G. F. Handel*, p. 15.

for his extraordinary pupil, had met the father in the street at times and expounded his revolutionary theories of what the boy ought to do in the world of music. Of one thing the barber-surgeon must have been quite certain: this boy of his had got him out of his depth. So he did what all the race of Handels would have expected him to do: he refused the Elector's offer, and ordered his son to return to Halle forthwith.

This took place at the end of 1696. George Frideric, receiving the call from Halle, answered it.

It was a dreary journey by coach covering ten days, for there was no main road between Berlin and Halle at that period. When Handel reached Halle the venerable barber-surgeon breathed his last in the house at the Schlamm on 17 February. The dour old gentleman with the white locks, whose bent figure had crept rather painfully through the streets in his later years, who was still more proud of a reputation which had extended for many leagues than ever he was to be of a son who alone was the cause of his name being remembered, had dropped asleep for ever. For years he had been a waning figure, a man living in the memory of dead yesterdays, growing more and more to himself as the stress of age pressed in upon him. Silent, feared, remote.

A sense of infinite responsibility must have come to the child of twelve as he stood in the death-chamber. This aged father, whom he had never understood, had been the axis around which the Handel family revolved. He had caused the ordering of everything without explanation. Now the boy had stepped into his shoes, and, looking to him as the head of the house, was a widowed mother, forty-five years of age, Aunt Anna, and two small sisters.

His first act was to write a poem to the memory of his father. It appeared in a pamphlet issued on 18 February 1697, three days after the barber-surgeon's death, and it was the first occasion on which the name of George Frideric Handel appeared in print.[1]

But there were more material things to be considered. There was the Handel practice to be disposed of. It would never be of any use to George Frideric, and the family was in need of ready money. The barber-surgeon had left no secret store, indeed it is doubtful if in his later years he had made much

[1] Opel.

money. Rearing two families, economically as he had planned the task, had reduced his savings. The big Schlamm house had cost him a great deal to maintain, and there is even a suspicion that the restaurant of 'The Yellow Stag' had been none too profitable.

Frau Handel, therefore, was left with no alternative but to sell the practice at once, and she sold it to Christopher E. Möller. Where Möller came from, or how far he was competent to carry on a practice hitherto held by a man who knew his work backwards, there is nothing to show. Nevertheless the enterprising Möller soon found himself in trouble. No sooner had he bought the practice than he was sued by the Barbers' Company of Halle, the nearest approach to a trade union which the seventeenth century could produce. The three parishes of Halle, Neumarkt, and Glauchau at that time were separate, and it was against the jurisdiction of the Halle Barbers' Company that one barber-surgeon should practise in all three.[1] Why Handel was allowed to do so, there is nothing to show, but the Barbers' Company was not willing to admit the same privilege to his successor. Handel, having rushed blithely through all trouble with the Barbers' Company, was certainly an instance of 'casus singularis', which in future was not to be permitted to recur.

When Möller acquired the Handel business in Neumarkt, there was at that time no vacancy for a barber-surgeon in the place, but the Company were prepared to offer him a vacancy at Glauchau. This Möller would not accept. Handel had always practised at Neumarkt, and he intended to do the same. The case went to the Elector, much as Handel's fight over his wine-selling had done, and he decided in Möller's favour. A decree was issued, but the Barbers' Company appealed and had the decree rescinded.

It was an urgent little war at which the Handel family had to sit down and look on. Frau Dorothea, doubtless very bored with the stupid, sordid nature of it all, was perhaps in great anxiety lest she should have to refund some of the money she had received for the practice her husband had left her. But Möller ultimately won his case, was satisfied with his bargain and pursued the steps of the barber-surgeon

[1] All documents relating to this case were, before the Second World War, at the Geheimen Staats Archiv, Berlin, and the Staats Archiv, Magdeburg, and details have not been hitherto published.

Handel before him. What Möller paid for the practice no one ever knew except Frau Dorothea and perhaps Aunt Anna.

Change then began to creep into the household as the influence which had ruled inviolate over it for so many years departed and left nothing of its power. Frau Dorothea cut the Schlamm house into two halves; she lived in one half with Aunt Anna and her children, and let the other. Such a thing as letting half the family domain would have shocked the pride of the dead barber-surgeon. Now that he had gone, his widow began to gain something of that sense of independence which she had never known since the days when, as Dorothea Taust, she made the barber-surgeon wait till her own chosen time for their wedding. Thirteen years of married life in the Schlamm house had not entirely crushed out that sturdiness of character which had formerly been hers in the Giebichenstein parsonage, when she arranged the affairs of the Taust household. The Schlamm house had been large and rather solitary in its extent, with its low corridors and square ugly rooms. It was imposing as the barber-surgeon had always been imposing, needing space, carrying importance.

The Möller case settled, the Schlamm house divided up and made more comfortable and compact, Frau Dorothea devoted her life and energies to the training of her children, whom she educated to a belief in God and the best instincts of the home. Probably due to this strong Lutheran faith of hers, which she so carefully passed on to her son, the great influence of religion began to stir in the boy, which later found its true expression in his church music and *Messiah*. His first visits to the Liebfrauenkirche with Aunt Anna, later his work there with Zachow, had made his mind ready to receive the seeds of religious thought which came from his mother, and was an influence directly traced to that period which followed the barber-surgeon's passing.

One unwritten commandment made by the barber-surgeon remained. The boy was to train himself for the Law, and, when the venerable figure had gone, George Frideric pursued his studies with greater zeal than ever. All his leisure from his legitimate studies he devoted to music: so much his father had agreed. Zachow was still helping him, and Zachow was doubtless responsible for the boy securing certain audiences for his playing which in the ordinary way he could not have obtained. Certainly Handel acquired a local reputation. People came from a distance to hear him perform. Georg Philipp Telemann, who was later to achieve a great vogue in Germany by his church music, heard the young Handel play and wrote about him in the autobiography which, at a later date, he contributed to Mattheson's *Ehren-Pforte*. Telemann was four years older than Handel. His rise was meteoric; his Passion music a forerunner of the greater qualities of Handel. But his reputation fell away after his death with the same ease as it had arisen, because, in the main his music was artificial, and had only a certain ripeness, insufficient to carry the work to posterity.[1] He was a person of peculiar conceit, who yet had the fairness of mind to admit the genius of Handel. There is evidence that at a later stage a warm friendship sprang up between them, which remained unspoiled by any sense of rivalry. Indeed Handel had a keen admiration for Telemann, who he said could, 'write a motet for eight voices more quickly than one could write a letter'.[2]

Five years almost to a day (10 February 1702) after the death of the barber-surgeon, George Frideric Handel carried out what would have been his father's most ardent wish—he entered Halle University as a student. But he did this purely for the sake of his social position, and not with the intention of embracing any particular study. His biographer, Chrysander, declares that he went to the University to study Law, but Handel did not enter himself among the law students, which is proof that obedience to the old barber-surgeon's dictum had ceased to count. He had already chosen his career. The University at this period was comparatively new and was the outcome of the old academy for the nobility (Ritter Akademie), which the Elector of Brandenburg had founded in 1691. When Handel signed his name on the students' record it was under the direction of Pro-rector Buddeus.

Student life at Halle in 1702 was far removed from drudgery

---

[1] Rockstro says that Telemann heard Handel play in 1701 whilst on his way to Leipzig. But he must have been in error, for Telemann went to Leipzig in 1700. If he heard Handel play at a later date it would have been during a subsequent visit to Halle. The fact that he came from Magdeburg and would therefore pass through Halle on his way to Leipzig would suggest that 1700 was the year in which he met the Handel prodigy, then fifteen years of age.

[2] Hawkins: *A General History of the Science and Practice of Music*, 1776.

or abnormal toil. Roistering was frequent, duelling openly indulged in, and sport and copious drinking of wine and beer part and parcel of the students' day and night. The University itself possessed a privilege for a wine and beer house, which it let yearly to a magistrate or a private individual, and so found a source of income to supplement its none too plentiful funds. It also ran a coffee shop. Duelling had assumed such aggravated proportion among the students here and elsewhere that, six weeks after Handel joined the University, a royal decree was issued that it should be excluded from all royal universities, but the high spirits of the students soon broke out in other directions. They made periodical attacks on the town hall and other public places, and, after ringing the 'storm-bell', armed citizens had to come to the aid of the town guards to quell the disturbance.[1]

Not that Handel had much heart for these jousts, for the extraordinary energy which characterized his life began in these years. Barely a month after he had joined the University a scandal occurred at the Cathedral, or Dom-Kirche, attached to the Moritzburg, where one Leporin, a Leipzig musician, had presided at the organ for the past four years. Leporin was a dissolute character, but a master of the instrument. He drank, he roistered. Often when the congregation foregathered to worship, the organ was lacking a player, for Leporin was either in a drunken stupor or away on one of his regular carousals. Some of the earliest biographers of Handel threw much of the blame for Leporin's behaviour on Zachow of the Liebfrauenkirche, with no reason at all. A more flagrant injustice cannot be imagined. Zachow at all times had been of temperate, even puritanical habits, and often absurdly mean in the matter of luxury. The man was too keen on his work to be otherwise, and when he died in 1712 it was in peculiarly humble circumstances.

The Leporin scandal at the Dom outraged Halle. The Lutherans at the Liebfrauenkirche blamed the Calvinists, to whom the Dom belonged, for permitting such impious behaviour to endure. In March 1702 the Calvinists took action. They threw out Leporin, and they put in the student Handel as a temporary measure. A certain section of the Calvinists of the town took exception to the decision, because Handel was a Lutheran. The step had been under consideration for some

[1] Dreyhaupt.

HANDEL AS A STUDENT

His signature—at foot of page—as he wrote it in the register of Halle University on the day he entered as a student.

time, for negotiations were in progress when he first joined the University, but his religion, his extreme youth, were points for doubt. Strictly speaking, he had no right at the Dom whatever, but as the appointment was for a year's probation at an annual salary of fifty thalers, the controversy quickly subsided, and the Calvinists continued their worship in peace. In addition, Handel was given lodging at the Moritzburg 'below by the gate', but he failed to live there; instead, he let the apartment for sixteen thalers a year.[1]

For over a year he presided at the organ of the Dom. But all the while big resolves were forming in his mind. He had no desire to serve his life as an organist, much as he loved the instrument. His ambition was goading him beyond the narrow confines of Halle, with its petty feuds and commercial smugness. Some searching instinct suggested to him that on the far horizon attainment might be found. He was intrigued by the stories of Italian music which had stormed Europe, of the melodious glories of Hamburg. A new school of music was seeking birth in the German city.

He was eighteen years of age—a year of decision, and against the desire for independence and travel, the home ties could offer but a poor defence.

In 1703 he resigned his post as organist at the Dom, and was succeeded by Johann Kohlhart,[2] oddly enough another Lutheran. Handel wasted little time. Leaving the University he packed up his few belongings at the Schlamm, bade farewell to his mother and sisters and Aunt Anna, and set out in the early summer for Hamburg.

Happily for himself, the old barber-surgeon slept on in his grave, unknowing that all he had striven for had broken down. The son of his late years had failed him.

[1] Chrysander credits Handel with considerable activity in connection with the town music during his appointment at the Dom, but is sadly in error. He had read in Dreyhaupt (Vol. I, p. 991) that the church music performances were divided amongst the various churches. But the Dom is not enumerated amongst these churches. As a matter of fact, the town choir was entrusted with these performances, and this choir belonged to the Gymnasium. Teachers of the Lutheran Gymnasium, were, according to the custom of the time, also Cantors of the town churches, and they employed their choir in the church music performances. The *reformed* organist could have no part in these; in consequence Handel's activity was restricted to the Dom church. Chrysander is therefore far from the mark when he says (p. 63): 'In this manner it was an easy matter for Handel to possess himself of the entire musical government. Whatever he composed was performed without delay.'

[2] Johann Kohlhart was born at Wettin, 11 January 1661; was Cantor at Glauchau 1682, and Octavus at the Lutheran Gymnasium 1701. Besides his duties at the Dom church he had to take over the Cantorship of St Ulrich Church in 1712. He died 9 April 1732—*Hallische Schul-Historica*, III, p. 12.

CHAPTER III

THE HAMBURG ADVENTURE—1703–1705

HAMBURG was the city of adventure. In 1703 it was an evil spot for a youth of eighteen without a friend, and certainly with very little money. Moreover, there was in prospect for Handel no definite means of earning his living. He had left Halle aimlessly to find fortune, and Hamburg was the beginning of the great search.

For thirty years, Italian music had swept in a tide across musical Germany. The theatres resounded to the singing of Italian words. Italian *maestri* found a welcome; too often to the detriment of more talented musicians of native birth. But in 1703 the musical glories of Berlin were fading, and Hamburg, a city free from any subjection of its arts to Electoral control, was the centre of new and uprising thought in music. Keiser, that strange figure who produced operas—some hundred and twenty in all—as easily as he could pour water from a bottle, was on the crest of the wave. He was a force in German music. In addition to his operatic achievements he was then running concerts, where the very best music was heard, and the best food and wines could be consumed. He was making money and spending money in sensuality, yet working like a Trojan. An idol of the people who, after forty years of adulation in Hamburg, was to disappear in the slough of vice that enthralled him. Musicians, artists, writers mingled in a life of gaiety and poverty, with occasional affluences, which were dissipated in debauchery of every kind. Yet Hamburg was full of clever men at the period, debauchees many of them, who spent their money as they earned it, but clever men for all that.

In 1690 Rathmann G. Schott had founded and owned the first opera house there, and four years later he let it to a Jew, Jacob Kremberg, on a five years' lease with the machinery, scenery, costumes, etc., and with the additional loan of all the operas previously performed there at Schott's expense.[1] Schott was very opposed to the inroad of Italian music. He had built that opera house to exploit German work, and soon after Kremberg took over the place trouble occurred.

[1] State Archives. Hamburg.

Kremberg began to run Italian comedies, many of them lewd and lacking in cleverness. But so long as he paid his annual rental of six hundred reichstalers, Schott was more or less powerless to interfere. In vain Schott protested; Kremberg was drawing good houses and went on. Then Schott appealed to the Syndic Lucas van Bostel to prohibit these performances. How long the squabble might have continued there is no knowing, but Kremberg struck a bad season, ran heavily into debt and compromised with Schott. The matter, however, did not end there. In 1702—just a year before Handel reached Hamburg—Schott died. Hardly had they buried him than Kremberg broke out afresh with an orgy of foreign, and, in most instances, indifferent pieces. Stung to anger, Schott's widow sought an injunction against him. But it was never obeyed, and just as Handel came to the city she complained to the courts that their order had been set aside.

Handel, therefore, found the opera in a strange state of disorder. What his thoughts may have been when he discovered that the new heart of Germany's music was kept pulsing by dissolutes, that Art was prostituted by lewdness and debauchery of the worst type, one can imagine. He had lived a sheltered life at the Schlamm. He had never come face to face with that gaiety of the epoch which found expression in the larger cities. Halle, with its strong Lutheran and Calvinistic traits, can have known little of it. Apart from a students' 'rough house' none of the boisterousness of real youth had been known to Handel.

It was probably fortunate for him that he fell in with Johann Mattheson almost upon his arrival at Hamburg. For Handel it was indeed a happy meeting, since he possessed the wilful self-assurance that comes to youth at eighteen— assurance which had to suffer many blows in the hard school of experience in the city. Fortunate, too, for Mattheson was this meeting, since his assocation with Handel has kept alive his name which otherwise never would have passed beyond the frontiers of Germany.

Mattheson was a creature of conflicting personality. He had sprung from nothing with the aid of a good education and his own cleverness. He was four years older than Handel, and his father was a collector in the Hamburg customs. At nine he had been proficient at the organ and harpsichord and possessed of a wonderful treble voice. At sixteen he was singing in opera at the Hamburg Opera House, at eighteen his first opera *Die Pleiaden* was produced there, with himself in one of the principal parts, and conductor of the orchestra when he was not on the stage. His was a brilliance which carried him high, only suddenly to lose its strength. He was vain with a consuming vanity; more than a little mean, pedantic in dress. He composed well, sang and acted well, wrote well—always a swift moving spirit that never rested or was still. If he had been gifted with genius instead of mere cleverness he would have been one of the most uplifting figures in the musical history of his age.

There was nothing Mattheson loved better than his art—except himself. Throughout his life he had a supremely good nature, which he exercised generously, because he felt that the world could produce no serious rival. Towards Handel he adopted the attitude of the experienced and worldly-wise teacher. Later, when he wrote about Handel in his *Ehren-Pforte*, he appears rather like a nursemaid taking the little boy out. 'Handel came to Hamburg rich in ability and good intentions,' he says. 'I was almost his first acquaintance and, through me, he was taken round to all the organs, choirs, operas, and concerts.' And later: 'He composed long, long arias and absolutely endless cantatas, but he had not yet got the knack of the right taste.' And later still, a gibe at Handel's poverty, sugared by an admission of help: 'He mostly came for free meals to my late father's, and in return revealed to me certain special tricks of counterpoint. I for my part helped him considerably in dramatic style.'

Time has proved the irony of this statement. Mattheson's vocal music has been forgotten because it was too declamatory, and Handel's 'long, long arias', are even still, too often, beyond the powers of singers who attempt them.

Very soon after Handel reached Hamburg he secured a post as second violin at the opera house. How he was able to drop so readily into a salaried position, without previous experience at a theatre, no record remains to prove. Mattheson may have been in some way responsible. It is perhaps only natural that Handel should have gone at once to the opera house in search of employment, for the Hamburg Opera House was most probably the Mecca he had in his mind when he shook the dust of Halle off his shoes. Musicians who wandered towards Hamburg from all parts of the country

—they were many, and poverty-stricken most of them—went directly to the opera house as if it were the objective of a pilgrimage. Therefore, Handel may have gone in there, as those many others had done before him, his violin under his arm, and asked for a hearing in the ordinary way. If he had a hearing his skill would have secured him the post, especially if it were Keiser himself who first listened to his playing, for Keiser was a past-master in his knowledge of the instrument. If Mattheson and Handel first met beside the organ of Maria Magdalena Church[1] in Hamburg, then it is possible that Handel's curiosity to see the organ had led him there, and a chance conversation drew from Mattheson that help which was rather typical of his treatment of Handel in the early days.

Whatever the cause that brought them together, their friendship ripened at once. For all Mattheson's patronizing behaviour and later jealousy, it was one of the greatest friendships in the lives of either. By ambition their minds were tuned to the same key. They were plunged together into the great conflict of jealousy and intrigue which the changing moods of music of their day provoked about them. All youth and dreams. Possessing only sufficient money to provide the needs of the hour, but very certain of themselves. Burning the midnight oil, journeying together, comparing their work, helping, criticizing. Ardent, and secure above all the bitterness that surged beneath. Zealots who meant to sweep the stars.

In the days that followed their meeting they were inseparables. Mattheson describes a period that must have been full of the joy of youth. In his *Ehren-Pforte* he hints at little happenings, of no particular import, but which meant everything to the friend who shared them. Probably after jealousies and intrigue had driven a wedge between these two, Handel, with that great human nature which was always his, smiled at the remembrance, and was glad that the memories had not faded from the mind of his early friend. Mattheson recalls the pastry-cook's son who blew the bellows for them when they played at the Maria Magdalena Church at Hamburg—and this may have been, and possibly was, on the occasion of their first meeting. He writes of a water-party in those first days, and adds: 'Hundreds of similar incidents come back to me as I write.'

Whatever may have been Mattheson's shortcomings, and
_____
[1] Chrysander, Vol. I, p. 84.

they were many, he always wrote of Handel in a way which suggests that he was intensely fond of him. In his later works, notably his *Critica Musica*, it needs little discernment to perceive that he had a great love for this friend of his youth who rose to the heights, a love too strong to be hidden in secret.

Only a few weeks after the organ in the Maria Magdalena Church had brought them together, they went off on a great adventure. On 17 August they set out for Lübeck, because the head of the Lübeck Council, a worthy named Magnus von Wedderkopp, had asked Mattheson to compete for the post of organist to the Marienkirche in that city, in succession to the organist of the day, Dietrich Buxtehude. Mattheson writes:[1] 'I am certain that if he (Handel) reads this he will laugh inwardly, for he rarely laughs out loud. Especially if he remembers the pigeon-dealer who travelled with us by post to Lübeck.'

Mattheson took Handel with him for the need of a companion. It is suggestive of the friendship which existed between them at this period that, although Mattheson alone had been invited to compete for the post of organist, he arranged with Handel during the journey that Handel alone should perform upon the organ, and that he should play the clavicymbal.

Had either of them been impressionable at this age the Lübeck journey might have produced an unlooked-for result. Herr Wedderkopp was a discerning person, and seems to have been attracted by the playing of both. But what he had as closely at heart as the necessity of good music at the Marienkirche, was the equal necessity of benefiting the city taxpayer in any way he could. The custom at Lübeck at the time was that whoever succeeded to the post of organist should marry the daughter or widow of his predecessor. There was reason and economy in this from the city's point of view, for the city maintained the female relatives of a dead organist. It therefore welcomed a release from the cost when some enterprising musician came along and married one of the daughters as the penalty—or prize—attached to succession to the post of organist.[2] Thus, before Buxtehude had been given the

[1] *Ehren-Pforte*, p. 93.
[2] Frederick Stahl: *Franz Tunder und Dietrich Buxtehude*.

post at the Marienkirche he had married the daughter of his predecessor Franz Tunder.

Wedderkopp, with a shrewdness that characterized him, put the proposition fairly and squarely to Mattheson and Handel. Whichever would marry Buxtehude's daughter should have the post of organist. Buxtehude was getting old, he was becoming a martyr to rheumatics, and it could not be expected that he would hold the post much longer. As it chanced, the daughter was a buxom wench twelve years older than Mattheson. Apparently both Mattheson and Handel were too scared by the notion of marriage to wait to set eyes on this lady, for they scuttled out of Lübeck with all possible speed, more than a little pleased that their celibacy was secured from violation.

Incidentally, this did not deter Buxtehude. He meant to have his daughter's future provided for ere the organ passed to another's keeping, so three years later he asked the Church Council to favour the girl at his demise by compelling his successor to marry her. He knew or guessed that his sands had nearly run out, and he was living in the *Werkhaus* close to the church with a little garden in which to stretch his ageing limbs. He was terribly conscious that he had not a thaler with which to endow those dependent upon him, and that this was the best arrangement he could make. When he died a year later, a musician named Schieferdecker—one of the roués from the Keiser gang at Hamburg—took the plunge, married Buxtehude's daughter, and presided at the keyboard in his father-in-law's place at the Marienkirche.[1] Had Handel yielded to this marriage as the price for a post which must have appealed to him all the more because of his impecunious condition, the whole course of his life, doubtless, would have been changed. To the end of his days he shunned matrimony as he would the plague, and Mattheson, who was not a much greater success as a gallant, remained single until, at the wane of his career, he married the daughter of an English clergyman.

The months that immediately followed the return from Lübeck were vital in Handel's life. They definitely shaped his career. It was a gay season, given up in the main to

[1] The same post with the same condition attached, is said to have been offered to J. S. Bach in 1705, but because of the marriage clause he refused the contract.—Spitta, I, p. 313.

Keiser's *Claudius*, a brilliant work which brought its composer good money. Keiser, reckless and well in funds, swept along in wild abandon and luxury. There was no form of high living which he did not explore. Following after him like a flock of sheep, were the people from the opera house, eating the rich dinners for which he paid, drinking his wines. Keiser knew—and no man better—the art of mixing luxurious idling with supreme hard work. He wrote his operas—and at this period they were original and striking, tender, and melodious—with amazing speed. He would return from a bout of debauchery in the first hours of daylight, work feverishly as the sun rose, rehearse, organize, sleep but little, and so hustle one day into another. He had no hours—no sense of hours. His women hung about him everywhere, except in the opera house. Though his mistresses were many among those who, for professional reasons, frequented the theatre, he kept aloof from associating with them in the precincts of the building. At the opera house he ruled. He was an uncrowned king, flattered, and aware that most of the flattery had been earned. Keiser in his greatest moods was not very far removed from genius, and he had all the madness and vice which often accompanies genius. To him, then, Handel was just a clever youth, very useful in his theatre. Mattheson was his star. And only a madman would have told him in 1703 that either of the twain would ever hurt his fame, or even arouse in him the first moods of jealousy. Ere long, jealousy of Handel was to inspire most of his acts.

Licentiousness therefore, under Keiser's example, ruled at the opera house. Hamburg nights blazed with windows from which the lights never drooped till morning came. Mattheson kept fairly free from the great stampede to vice, saved by his economical turn of mind, which would not permit him to spend money except to propitiate some little turn of vanity. He hung on to the Keiser set of debauchees because it contained so many who were necessary to him in his work, but he was not of it.

Handel went quietly on with his fiddling. As the opera season always ran from the end of August till the Easter following, he was to some extent continuously employed. His engagement kept him in lodgment and food and little else. It was Mattheson who turned the tide for him. He introduced him to the household of the British representative at Hamburg, John Wich, an estimable fellow of good birth and culture, who carried out consular duties in the city. Wich was a diplomat. He was plausible, and possessed a wonderful library. It is doubtful if England had a more scholarly consul in her foreign offices at the time. He was enamoured by Handel's playing, and promptly engaged him to teach his small son the harpsichord. To Handel, anxious to augment the slender funds he received at the opera house, the engagement was fortunate. It brought him into touch with influential people in the city, so that soon he had a string of pupils.

The dreary round of the opera, with its ceaseless rehearsals, and the still more dreary work of teaching, would have sapped the ambition of many. To Handel this work was merely the background against which he was going to set his career. His playing began to make him talked about, and his organ work especially attracted the attention of the aged poet Christian Postel, who had written the libretti of more operas than he could count. Many of these Keiser had set and produced with marked success and profit. Postel soon discovered that Handel was a youth out of the ordinary. This quiet fiddler in the orchestra sheltered the lamp of genius which might, if given the opportunity, shine with penetrating power. It was Postel who gave Handel his chance; he wrote a libretto for him.

Meanwhile, the opera season was waning, and the end of the winter 1703–4 approached. Mattheson had departed to Holland, not upon any definite task, but he had some vague idea that he would get through to London. English music was in a state of curious disorder and required a leader. He would be that leader. At any rate for a while he aspired to be that leader, and probably he would have achieved considerable success had he gained his object. His wandering, restless spirit needed new fields to conquer; he wanted to be alone in the limelight.

He found in Holland the success which he believed awaited him in London. He ran a series of concerts at Amsterdam which whirled him into notoriety. Dutch music, which had been but a poor echo of German melody, assumed a certain form, and acquired an interest with the cultured classes of Amsterdam. Then Haarlem came forward and offered Mattheson £150 a year as organist at the city church. But Mattheson did not possess the organist's soul; he wanted the honours, the applause of audiences.

All through the latter part of the season, Handel had been working on the Postel libretto, the *Passion of St John*. Postel, who had written tragedies and dramas, had become a convert to religious thought. Handel, whose consciousness to religious influence had been awakened in the Liebfrauen-kirche at Halle, was ripe for Postel's words. He had finished the music in March, rehearsals were in progress for the first performance at Easter. The precocity of the youth whom he had employed as a second violin ripieno amazed Keiser, then angered him. He saw in Handel's effort a challenge to his own popularity. This Postel had set up the standard to which the youth should march—Postel who had shared Keiser's own successes in the past, but who now had become a sick religious aesthete, and withdrawn into his shell. Postel was beginning to prepare himself for his entrance into another world. An example which Keiser, little more than thirty years of age, and in the heyday of youth, considered it quite unnecessary to follow at the moment.

Keiser was going to seed, and the whole organization of the opera house looked like breaking down. Had any such suggestion been made to him he would have stormed. But it was the truth. Accordingly, just as he had completed his Passion music, Handel wrote to Mattheson at Amsterdam. He wanted his friend back to share with him the joy of his first performance. He wanted him back to save the opera before the Keiser orgies destroyed all chances of success for the next season. Mattheson records that on 21 March he received at Amsterdam a letter from Handel in which he said:[1]

'I very much wish to have the pleasure of your conver-sation, and this loss will very soon be made good, for the time is approaching when they will be able to do nothing without you. I therefore beg you to notify me of your de-parture so that I may have the opportunity of fulfilling my duty, and come and meet you with Mlle Stübens.'

In spite of the appeal, Mattheson did not return in time to be present at the performance of Handel's first work in Holy Week, and was therefore then unfamiliar with the music which,

[1] *Ehren-Pforte*, p. 94.

nearly a quarter of a century later, he attacked so viciously in his *Critica Musica*. Nevertheless, the entrance of Handel into the sacred circle of the composers stirred Keiser, although it is probable that he was more annoyed by Postel having provided Handel with his libretto than he was by any possible rivalry Handel might offer. That he regarded Handel's own assault upon his position seriously is proved by the fact that he sat down and wrote a Passion also,[1] based upon a libretto by Menantes, a poet of some quality. Neither Keiser's nor Handel's *Passion* achieved much success. The former was forgotten as soon as Holy Week had passed, and the latter, which possessed dignity and sweetness, bore small promise of the achievements to come.

It was a beginning, however, and it brought Handel a little local notoriety. People began to wonder whether this youth would prove a rival to Keiser. His pupils increased. Mattheson returned to find that, in his absence, Handel had achieved at least something. His curious, inordinate vanity was hurt. If Keiser had to fall—and it certainly must have been obvious both to Mattheson and Handel that he would fall—Mattheson knew no two opinions as to who should be his successor. As soon as he reached Hamburg again he set a miserable diatribe by Frederick Feustking[2] called *Cleopatra*. On 20 October he produced it at the opera house. Mattheson himself played the principal part of Antonius, and when he had accomplished his death-scene on the stage, usually returned in costume to accompany the rest of the opera for half an hour before the fall of the final curtain.

It was this action on the part of Mattheson which eventually provoked the famous duel between himself and Handel, and ended in the latter nearly losing his life.

To realize the state of tension that had sprung up between the two since Mattheson's return, it is necessary to consider some salient points. Mattheson was unquestionably irritated by Handel's Passion music, even if it had met with little success, and he retaliated. He had considerable influence with John Wich, whose son was Handel's principal pupil, and, in October 1704, Mattheson was made tutor to the boy, without any consideration for Handel's position. Handel was at once

---

[1] *The Bleeding and Dying Jesus.*
[2] Feustking was a local student who showed very indifferent ability in his search for the poet's crown.

deposed. His chief pupil had been taken from him by his best friend—an act which can create an aching wound at the age of twenty. Yet when Mattheson produced his *Cleopatra* during the same month, Handel supported him at the harpsichord, and left the instrument when Mattheson, his part on the stage finished, resolved to take the musical honours as well as those of the singer.

It is obvious that *Cleopatra* was a success. It gave promise of filling the opera house for the season. Keiser, meanwhile, was out of the bill, and Mattheson's star was fast rising in the firmament. His vitriolic vanity was soothed by great achievement. He had scored a palpable hit. Handel seems to have repeatedly given up his place at the harpsichord to Mattheson when he came off the stage,[1] but on 5 December he rebelled. What provoked rebellion has no record. Handel throughout his life was discreetly silent about the affair, and when once he referred to it in London he kept the name of his opponent secret. On the occasion in question, when Mattheson left the stage and sought the harpsichord, he found a raging Handel who refused to vacate the instrument. An altercation, violent and bitter, immediately sprang up. One can imagine a crowded house hugely enjoying this unrehearsed effect, for in 1704 no opera, no play carried any dignity. An encounter and fisticuffs were common events; a foul epithet hurled by a leading lady to a rival across the stage merely a diversion. Too frequently the audience joined in what was usually only a private quarrel, finding more entertainment thereby than from the play itself.

The quarrel on that December night must have produced no little excitement in the theatre, for it is said to have lasted half an hour.[2] The end was a sordid affair in the Goosemarket outside the theatre. A crowd—no doubt the audience, which had been regaled by the commotion—followed the angry pair to that point in the square where they faced about and set upon each other with swords. It is odd to see Handel engaged in an affair of this sort, for his temperament was not given to violence; but Mattheson's wounded vanity would have carried him to any adventure. Fortunately the combat quickly

---

[1] Romain Rolland in his life of Handel declares that he gave up the harpsichord only on two previous occasions.

[2] Chrysander, Vol. I, p. 104. Chrysander also says that Mattheson struck Handel.

came to an end. Mattheson's sword struck the button on Handel's coat and splintered in his hand.[1]

They spent the Christmas season in a state of enmity. But on 30 December a Town Councillor and the lessee of the opera house reconciled them. They celebrated their fresh understanding in a royal manner. Youth, so quick to fire, alone knows the full joyousness of reconciliation. They dined together at Mattheson's house. After the meal, they went on to the rehearsal of *Almira*, an opera which Handel had written to a queer libretto by Feustking, on the recommendation of Postel, built up—partly in Italian and partly in German— from his translation of an Italian olla podrida. From that day forward Mattheson and Handel were better friends than ever.[2]

They threw themselves heart and soul into the rehearsals of *Almira*. They were joint adventurers, searching with the brazen effrontery of youth for recognition. Little more than a week later the piece was produced, with Mattheson playing the role of the principal tenor. Although they were close friends again, the applause which greeted Handel, when, on 8 January 1705 he stood, flushed with success, at the fall of the curtain, did not enhance that friendship. *Almira*, from its initial performance, was a success, and Mattheson had no soul for a big dramatic success by Handel. His own *Cleopatra* had been followed by a work from his friend, which promised to become an equal achievement. There was a freshness in the music of *Almira* which was warmly welcomed by Hamburg. This youth of twenty had given the burghers something to talk about. It was evident that Keiser, and even Mattheson, might have to look to their laurels.

Handel was fired with zeal by the reception of *Almira*, and set about composing a new work to succeed it. He meant to strike while the iron was hot. It was the first expression of a characteristic in him, which became evident throughout his entire later life—to strike, and strike hard, at opportunity. He lived in the simplest manner, avoided any kind of pleasure removed from the pursuit of his art, saved money, worked

---

[1] Mattheson in his *Ehren-Pforte*, p. 95, describes the episode thus: 'Urged on by others when we left the Opera we came to blows in the public market before a large audience. The duel might have ended very badly for us both, if by God's mercy my sword had not broken in coming into contact with a hard metal button of my opponent's. So no great damage was done.'

[2] Mattheson: *Ehren-Pforte*, p. 95.

all day and the greater part of the night. His energy was unceasing and tireless.

Although Feustking had been a weak collaborator when he supplied the *Almira* libretto, Handel went to him for the book of his next work *Nero*. It turned out to be the poorest book Handel ever set in his life, so poor that he complained that it was painful to have to try to set music to such stuff. But it must be said in excuse for Feustking, that probably he was rushed off his feet in his haste to produce the words for the impetuous composer. Postel, though aged, would have provided Handel with a libretto of some quality, but Postel with his new tendency towards religious mania would not have been capable of so profane a work as *Nero* proved to be. With *Almira, Queen of Castille*, filling the theatre on account of its big dramatic effects, any departure from drama in its successor would have been imprudent. Of this Handel must have been well aware.

Almira ran continuously until 25 February, and on that day Handel's second drama, *Love Obtained Through Blood and Murder; or Nero*, was put on. It had been better if *Almira* had run longer, but it was taken off to make way for *Nero*, because the latter was believed to be a better work. He was probably wrong, although there is no means of comparing the two achievements, for the music of *Nero* is lost, but Feustking's miserable libretto exists.[1] Mattheson sang the part of Nero, but he could not save the piece. It ran for three performances, then stopped.

The two operas, whether they were financially successful or otherwise—and as they had both been staged in an elaborate fashion there cannot have been a great deal of profit in either—provoked a storm of discussion. Handel had the flair. He was an oasis in a desert of staleness. Or he was like a crystal stream after the later turgidity of Keiser. He had shown himself able to get dramatic effect with his music. His achievement drove Keiser to distraction. Piqued and angry, he reset *Nero* with a view to showing Hamburg that, after all, he and not Handel was the master, but when his version was produced in the autumn it also failed miserably. Nothing daunted, he reset *Almira* under another title and produced it the following spring. Again came failure.

[1] I have a copy of the 'book of words' sold in the theatre at the time, one of the only two existing—Author.

The outpourings of jealousy and bitterness by Keiser and the gang of kindred roués, who still clung about him, stung Handel. The treatment began to wear him down. Mattheson, too, was drawing away from his friend. Friendship that had been so strong had snapped under the attacks of jealousy. Handel was left in his lonely furrow, and he pursued it in his own fashion. For a while he ceased to write for the theatre. Instead, he applied himself more closely to his teaching, and his compositions were confined to sonatas and miscellaneous pieces for the use of his pupils.[1] That he had no lack of pupils at this period is borne out by the evidence of Mattheson, and the fee he received for his instruction was probably in the region of that of his friend, who drew the equivalent of eighteen shillings a month, or thereabouts, from every pupil.

The blast of bitterness and intrigue which now descended upon Handel would have broken the spirit of many. Keiser had always borne the honours, and, being a popular man, who, in a magnetic career, had shown amazing ability, his position would have appeared difficult to assault had Handel been pledged to attack. But no such campaign was in Handel's mind. He had revelled in the success of both Keiser and Mattheson. He envied them in a big heart that knew only the excitement of life. That they should turn upon him now, because some of his first fledglings had not failed, hurt him, but did not spoil his courage. They had yet to learn that nothing ever would spoil his courage.

The tactics of these people did, however, cause Handel to change his plans. The opera was sinking so rapidly under the Keiser régime that Handel saw himself being involved in the wreckage of disorder, and the antagonism towards himself brought decision. He had met in Hamburg during the winter of 1703–4 a wandering Italian princeling, Gaston de' Medici, who at the time was engaged in a hopeless squabble with his wife, Princess Anna Maria of Saxony-Luxemburg. No greater rascal strolled through Europe at that age than Gaston de' Medici, but, like many rogues, he had one redeeming quality, and that was his love of music. It was this redeeming feature which intrigued Handel when they met. The Prince had a sound knowledge of Italian music of the day. He had once played wonderfully upon the flute, and he had

[1] Burney states that he procured some of these at Hamburg in 1773.

the true instinct of the Italian for good music. He singled out Handel at once as a youth who would go far, described to him the glories of Italian music at Florence and Rome, and convinced him that he was wasting his time in Hamburg. His rightful place was that Mecca of Genius—Florence.

It was this rogue who ultimately proved to be responsible for one of the most decisive developments in Handel's life. Whatever Gaston's past may have been was of little count to Handel, in whose eyes he was redeemed by his musical knowledge. Prince Gaston was then very well known throughout Europe by the blatancy and ostentation of his vice. He gambled heavily, he had mistresses in every city, and he wandered from one to the other in careless abandon. His wife alternately tried to reform him and then cast him out, only to take him back again. Not that Gaston ever stayed long. The call of the paths of unrighteousness was too strong. He disappeared with his mood in search of a pretty face here, or some gamester there, for whom he had no other respect than that he had money and could drink him under the table. And such champions with the cup were few and far between.

It is the common story that Gaston de' Medici offered to pay Handel's expenses to Italy. But, if he ever made such an offer, de' Medici could not have intended it seriously, for he never had money to give away. To him money was only the passport to a fresh haunt of vice, so he had little to spare for the costly journey of a chance friend. Nor was he that peculiar vagabond who would spend on a friend money which he could dissipate in a fresh burst of vice. There is in existence a letter from the Prince to his sister, the wife of the Elector Palatine, which proved that he was in dire penury when he left Hamburg for Prague and Vienna in March 1705.[1]

But his words took root in Handel's mind. To the young musician, amidst all the riot and upheaval which had come to the opera house, Italy became a lure. He was saving money, stinting himself, his life had become a self-denial on the altar of ambition. He no longer received remittances from his mother at Halle; on the contrary, he was now sending her small sums at Christmas and at other times. Keiser, hampered with debts, which had not been moderated by the absconding of his partner, Drüsicke, was broken on the wheel, and the

[1] Ademollo: *G. F. Haendel in Italia.*

theatre passed into the hands of a Jew, Johann Saurbrey, who made it his first business to approach Handel to write him an opera. Verily the compliments must have pleased the youth after the efforts that had been made to bear him down. He wanted money—money to take him to Italy.

It was Saurbrey, a gentleman who, if he ever possessed an artistic soul, had long since pawned it to commerce, who started Handel composing again. For Saurbrey, Handel wrote a long opera—so long that to perform it occupied two evenings. The enthusiasm which Keiser had striven to kill in him had broken out anew in such violent ecstasy that he could not curtail the length of his songs. He wrote on and on. It had only required the slightest encouragement to make his sensitive spirit rise like some bird afresh on the wings of the morning.

Thus did Saurbrey become possessed of a work which must have frightened him not a little by its length. To produce it would require an all-night sitting of the audience, and even Hamburg, proud of its understanding of musical quality, was not prepared for that. There was only one thing for Handel to do—cut it in two: thus *Florindo* and *Daphne* came into being. Handel received his money down and, without a regret in his soul, left Hamburg. He did not even stay to bid farewell to Mattheson, whom he never saw again. Probably Mattheson's later lament of the fact was only simulated. The tide of jealousy had been too strong.

Not until long after Handel had passed out of Hamburg as unostentatiously as he had entered it did his twin operas find production. He was then far beyond acclamation or criticism. In his absence these operas provided Hamburg's musical event of 1708. The city then had been denuded of all talent, and in the year following, Keiser, like some wandering ghost, reappeared again. Hamburg did not know he had arrived till he had captured the opera house by a manoeuvre. It was a great return. His sins were forgotten; his services to music remembered. Where had he been? No one inquired; no one wanted to know. It was sufficient that he had returned. He had rushed back to his old place. The haunts where he had ruled and patronized found new life, the former bacchanalians crept from their secret haunts and gathered about him with their 'Hail, master!' During the year of his return Keiser composed and produced eight operas, and in some of them was the tender spirit of his old fire. He made money once more, and spent it as readily. He rushed into matrimony with the daughter of one of the principal patricians of the city. But his vices, the Hamburg that was his, wore him down. The flames that came from the stirred fire dropped away into embers, and Keiser passed out, leaving a Hamburg from which the glories of its art had departed. He drifted away. He died.

A contemporary paragraph which appeared after his death best describes the wreckage:[1]

'Mad.Neuberinn (Neuber) will this summer, as it is thought, produce comedies again at the opera house. Stage, costumes, and scenery are quite used up. Monza was obliged to leave Hamburg utterly destitute and covered with debts. Mme Keiser, as well as Monza, have again tried to get the opera, but up till now without success. The former is quite unable to do so, partly because she has no money, partly also, because she has lost all her esteem. Moreover, she has no singers. Monza, however, is amply provided with those, and might sooner attain his object, but the old debts will not permit him to return. The theatre is ruined, there are no costumes, and the building itself is very dilapidated. Some old amateurs still allow the 'Kaiserinn' (Mme Keiser) to enjoy their former munificence, and these as well as something more (the daughters' *savoir-faire*) keep her.'

A trail of ruin; threadbare costumes and broken scenery and a widow trying to make a living. All that was left of what had once been Reinhold Keiser! What an artist he had been! How he had loved life. How he had worked. How he had played. He had stormed his way with the courage of a gladiator, and dropped out, a forgotten husk of a man.

But the youth whom he had first known as ripieno violin had now passed along the solitary way that led to the more certain memories of the great.

[1] *Matthesoniana Politica* (Hamburg State and University Library).

CHAPTER IV

THE ITALIAN JOURNEY

HANDEL arrived in Italy as mysteriously as he had left Hamburg. By what route he travelled, or how long the journey occupied him there is no knowing. He was doubtless alone, for there was not a single soul in Hamburg in whom he had sufficient interest to solicit his companionship for the exploit. It is more probable that he embarked on the journey with the same impulse he had shown when he left Halle for Hamburg. He had no engagement in view; no means of earning his living except by his talents, and, as this was not an age when musical talent always came by its own reward, the adventure was beset with some risks and considerable difficulty. Of material things it seemed to offer nothing. But it must be remembered that Handel was a dreamer; throughout his life he remained a dreamer who expected or hoped to meet the realization of his dreams at the turn of the road.

Handel's position when he reached Italy was little better than that of the strolling musician, so far as his prospects were concerned. Doubtless he had written to his erstwhile friend Prince Gaston de' Medici announcing his coming, for as soon as he reached Florence he went to the palace of Pratolino in the hills beyond the city, where Ferdinand, Prince of Tuscany, brother of Prince Gaston, kept a palace of extreme extravagance and indolence, but brightened by the most wonderful music in Italy. Doubtless, too, Handel acquainted his mother at Halle with his decision to seek fresh fortune in Italy, for he was in regular correspondence with her. One can imagine the consternation in the Schlamm house which such news would occasion. They must have known, Dorothea and the simple-minded Tante, that the boy had little money. Probably he had told them all about the two hundred ducats he had saved. To throw off the land of his birth, to seek a nation of whose language he could not speak a single word, to abandon all his Hamburg engagements and travel far with no money and only a single friend at the end of the journey, must have filled them with anxiety, if not alarm.[1] One may conceive that many prayers went from the Schlamm house to high heaven on behalf of the youthful traveller. Oft-times Frau Handel must have desired that the imperious barber-surgeon had been alive again to restrain this wild strain of adventure in their child.

Once in the atmosphere of real music again, Handel became a slave to work. He produced a score of cantatas, he rewrote part of *Almira*—the only work of his which had in any way justified his belief in himself as yet. The flame of ambition began to blaze up stronger than ever. But he did not remain long enough in Florence to create any impression. He went on to Rome.

There was probably sound common sense in this decision. The music at the Pratolino Court, though beautiful—the fact that Alessandro Scarlatti had been in charge of it till shortly before Handel's arrival, is sufficient proof of its quality—cannot have been of the nature likely to bring Handel any means of livelihood. The musicians there were drawn from the best talent in Italy, so that this youth, who had yet to prove his brilliance to the Italians, cannot have been very seriously regarded as a composer, however efficient he showed himself to be as a performer. The two hundred ducats were running low, and there was need for something more substantial than the associations of an extravagant Court. The Prince can have had little need for him at this period or he would not have let him go. Rome, on the other hand, was the home of religious music, and its musical circle was extraordinarily gifted. The wealthy Roman families gave all the time and energy to good music which such families in many other Italian cities devoted to gambling, drinking, and loose living generally. In many ways the Florentine music which Handel knew differed from that of Rome. It must have been obvious to Handel, then, that if Italy was to offer him a career, knowledge of Rome and her form of art was vital.

Hitherto there has been a great deal of uncertainty as to exactly when he arrived in Rome. Because he put the month of April in the autograph of his *Dixit Dominus*, which was performed there at Easter, it is generally concluded that he arrived at the capital about that period. The dates in dispute

[1] Chrysander says that Handel spent the Christmas of 1706 with his mother at Halle on his way to Italy. But this is an entirely erroneous conclusion, for he was in Rome on 14 January 1707.

—4 and 11 April—are now accepted. But there is an entry in the Valesio Diary in the Archivio Storico Capitolino at Rome, and dated 14 January 1707, which sets the matter at rest. The paragraph in question reads as follows:

> 'There has arrived in this city a Saxon, an excellent player on the cembalo and a composer of music, who has today displayed his ability in playing the organ in the Church of St John (Lateran) to the amazement of everyone.'[1]

Handel thus established himself as a musician from the time of his arrival in the capital. Moreover, the letters of introduction he carried enabled him to get into the Roman salons.[2] At this period opera, as such, was forbidden in Rome under the Papal Edict, but religious music in its various forms was at its height. To this form of composition Handel at once devoted himself. He set several of the Psalms, and produced a stream of fragmentary pieces for the voice, or for this instrument, or for that, which showed that his versatility was breaking out in a rapidly maturing form. Nevertheless, all that Rome gave him at this time was experience—experience in religious expression, which was to shape itself with the years.

There was little he could do in Rome that would prove profitable. Whilst studying the Roman music he had been secretly composing his first Italian opera *Rodrigo*.[3] Who provided him with the libretto there is no record to show, and the quality of that libretto offers no claim for the preservation of the author's name. It was a wretched affair. Even the book of *Nero*, which had worried Handel so extremely at Hamburg, could not have been much worse. But in July, Handel, with *Rodrigo* complete, left Rome and returned to Florence to produce the work under the auspices of Ferdinand at a theatre in the city.

[1] This information, which was found by Mr L. A. Shepherd of the British Museum, searching in Italy on my behalf, of a certainty refers to Handel, who was usually called 'Il Sassone' by the Italians. The point is important, because if Handel arrived in Rome on or before 14 January it makes impossible Streatfeild's suggestion that his Opera *Rodrigo* was produced at Florence during the carnival season of this year. The fact that Handel played the organ of St John Lateran was also hitherto unknown.—Author.

[2] Romain Rolland: *Handel*, p. 40.

[3] Puliti declares that Handel composed *Rodrigo* in Florence. He may have begun it there, but he cannot have completed it, else he would hardly have left Florence before its production.

The Prince welcomed the wanderer. He was considerably startled by *Rodrigo*. There was a freshness in its airs which interested him, and the opera was different from that form of music which had ruled so long at the Pratolino. It was so unlike what he had termed the melancholy of Scarlatti, for which he had dismissed the *maestro*, at all events temporarily. The Florentine experts did not think so much of *Rodrigo* as did Ferdinand, who gave Handel the equivalent of £50 and a porcelain dinner service for the work. They were sullen in their reception of the Saxon's achievement. Maybe, like Keiser, they saw the possibility of this youth's uprising. He had captured the Prince's approval. This at least was dangerous to them, and might bring about any dramatic event at the hands of an employer so fickle as Ferdinand. Therefore they quietly argued that *Rodrigo* might be good music, but they thought not. Even Handel was a little uncertain of the fact himself, for at a later date, when speaking of *Rodrigo*, he frankly confessed that he had failed thoroughly to understand the Italian style.[1] As he had been in Italy less than a year this is conceivable.

Had Handel at this period confined himself to one form of musical composition he might then have achieved more success than he did, in spite of his barely twenty-two years. But he was experimenting, breaking out irresponsibly like a bird soaring and swinging now here, now there, on varying winds. From his Passion music he had passed to the romance of *Almira*, to the pomposity of *Nero*, hurrying aside into cantatas and exquisite fragments of song, all youth, all joy. Then the influence of Rome, the dignified, sombre music of his Psalms; now, caught by a new mood, throwing all his thought into utilizing the violin as a means of expression in *Rodrigo*—*Rodrigo* with its breezy airs, its best pieces from *Almira* retrieved and improved. But he knew that he had hardly begun to draw upon that tremendous treasure-house of melody which was stored within him. His productions so far had been a brilliant effort for a man of twenty-two. He had passed through Hamburg, then the most critical city in its musical affairs of all the cities of his homeland, had already become feared by the *maestri* of Florence, and had flashed through the Roman salons—to which he was so soon to return—with the swift brilliance of a comet.

[1] Mainwaring.

It was a period of glorious uncertainty for Handel. Indeed many have been the attempts made to crowd it with more romance than those Florentine weeks actually produced for him. Some of his biographers have charged him with a love-affair that never happened, but which, by all the laws of romance, should have happened.[1] They say that the great Italian contralto Vittoria Tesi fell in love with the handsome young Saxon, played in *Rodrigo*, and then, bent on following him everywhere, went from Florence to Venice in his footsteps, and played in his later work *Agrippina*, laying siege to his heart the while. Nothing of the kind ever happened. Vittoria Tesi was only seven years old at the time[2] and some nine years had yet to pass before she began to appear as the woman of splendour who captivated the hearts of most of the richer-born males in Italy. From then onward she was a disturbing influence in all the Italian cities. She swept through her country, a queen of song without morals or pity, to die as such women so often die—forgotten in her later years by the crowds that had thronged the stage door to touch the hem of her cloak. The Vittoria who did figure in *Rodrigo* was Vittoria Tarquini, better known as Bombace, who had for a long time been attached as soprano to the Florentine Court. She was a woman well advanced in middle age, with nothing more than an average voice, who would probably have been the last person to make any physical impression on Handel.

At this period—one of the most illuminating in his career —Handel had no interest in women. Later, when he mellowed to that tenderness towards mankind which brought out some of the best of his melodies, he had a liking for feminine society. He became the genteel gallant—never the courtier. But whilst in Florence, at any rate, he can be quite safely exonerated from intrigue with an actress or any other woman. His art was his life. No woman could have taken its place, or even shared that place. It drew from him everything he had to give.

In spite of the moderate stir which *Rodrigo* had aroused, Handel remained in Florence but a few weeks longer. He

---

[1] Mainwaring began the story, and Chrysander amplified it. Even Rockstro was caught by the notion of this Court actress hunting down the young composer, and gave credence to the fabrication.

[2] Signor Ademollo claimed to have her birth certificate.

had established himself with Ferdinand, who for years afterwards was his firm friend. Ferdinand was guided in most of his motives by economy, and had apparently no desire to support another rising musician. Florence therefore had little to offer Handel, save the gathering jealousies of those whose successful talents or disguised mediocrity had been threatened by his coming. He had no wish for a second bout of the intrigues of Hamburg.

Venice was calling him in no uncertain voice—Venice the home of dramatic music, with its many theatres and opera houses, its regular concerts, its wealthy patronage of the musical art. At the close of the year he departed for Venice with apparently no object at all. He wrote nothing whilst there. He did not attempt to introduce his talents into the operas which were then in full swing. How he made his living—for he can have possessed little money—no one knows. But he made a friend who came to occupy much the same place in his life as Mattheson had done, and with a greater sense of fidelity, Domenico Scarlatti, the wonderful son of a wonderful father.[1]

Scarlatti was Handel's senior by a couple of years. He had the same ambition that yearned for nothing save achievement in music, and the friendship, thus begun, continued for years. When later, in 1720, Handel met Scarlatti again in London they were the same friends still. It was always a great friendship. Handel went on to his honours in London; Scarlatti to be *maestro di capella* of St Peter's in Rome. But in those first days in Venice they were inseparables. The salons received them as twin youths of exquisite quality who would go far. True, Scarlatti's harpsichord brilliance was eclipsed by Handel's equal talent on Italy's accepted instrument, the organ. But in musical endeavour Venice was not inclined to be pedantic, even if the other Italian cities suffered from a surfeit of conservative opinion and fetish.

It is not surprising that Handel wrote nothing in Venice. The wonder is that his head was not turned by the favours heaped upon him and his companion. Prince Ernest of Hanover, a personage accompanied by two very dissolute counts

[1] The story goes that they met at a masked ball when Handel was in disguise, and that Scarlatti exclaimed: 'This is either the wonderful Saxon or the devil!' It seems rather improbable, since Scarlatti had no cause to suspect the presence of Handel in Venice.

during his Venetian stay, sought the acquaintance of Handel and urged a visit to Hanover when the Saxon turned again from Italy. It has been said that this helped towards the foundation of Handel's British citizenship, for Prince Ernest was the younger brother of the monarch who afterwards sat on the British throne as George I. In the same Venetian circle was the Duke of Manchester, who had just been appointed English Ambassador at Venice. He was a man of singular talent, and of whom they said that he sold his fortune to buy melody. Certainly he was a true patron of music and one of the first English noblemen to extend the hand of greeting to Handel when ultimately he came to England.

Venice was busy with its repertoire of accepted Italian composers, the opera houses swung to the mood of a vacillating taste. Their Venetian audiences wanted some new thought in music, but those who controlled their tastes were afraid of experiment. The fame of Handel had to ring through musical Italy before Venice staged his *Agrippina*. But the hour for that was not yet. Accompanied by Scarlatti he went off with his old impulsiveness to Rome at the beginning of 1708. Probably both of them had in the ardour of youth dreamed that they would sway the musical population of the capital. And in a manner, they did.

Rome, when Handel reached it again, was turbulent with a great movement of religious music. The Papal ban against the opera was in part responsible, but the influence of Cardinal Pietro Ottoboni had raised the religious music of the city to a higher level than it had ever attained before.

The Cardinal was the most striking and probably the most unostentatious personality Rome produced at this period. His riches were fabulous; he was one of the wealthiest men in Southern Europe of his day. But, however ardent he had been towards his Church, he was equally ardent in his exploitation of the arts with his open-handed generosity.

Since he was the close friend of Ferdinand, Handel claimed his interest on arrival. The Cardinal was no respecter of age. He hailed the young man of promise as he welcomed the *maestro* whose name was known throughout Europe. The Ottoboni *ménage* at this time was a striking affair. Corelli, the violinist and composer, was chief of the Cardinal's music, which rivalled in grace that of the Vatican. In the palace was a concert room where musicales were held every Monday evening. Strange gatherings of men appeared there, for the Cardinal had formed an academy of poets, painters, and musicians, a circle that had no god to serve save art. Every musician of promise, were he Italian or foreigner, found himself drawn into this circle by some subtle influence. Handel's financial embarrassments were swept away by the same magic hand. Before the world knew of his talents he was in the Ottoboni circle, which included Alessandro Scarlatti, father of Handel's friend, Pasquini, and others—the elect of musical Europe.

There were no half-measures about Ottoboni. If a man was clever, his music true to his Art, his standing, his affairs became of no count. He found himself in the circle, and, though he had been unable to buy himself a square meal for a month, he came in and rubbed shoulders with the rich, sat at a board where only the choicest dishes from the palace chef were served in monotonous succession, and found his glass ever brimmed with the richest wines of the south. Art and the knowledge of art was the only entrée to the Ottoboni circle.

All Europe talked about Pietro Ottoboni. His powers were infinite. The nephew of a Pope, he was raised to the Purple at the age of twenty-two—almost an unprecedented happening. When Handel and Domenico Scarlatti came into his orbit in 1708, he was a little over forty—thin, ascetic, seldom seen except by those members of his coterie to whom he was just a brother in Art. He ran his circle like a modern literary or musical club, only without the same bickerings and internal jealousies. No one knew his qualities, because he kept himself and his affairs supremely aloof. He worked in a most mysterious way among the poorer classes, whilst his guests ate and drank untold wealth from his hospitable board. He ran a free bakery for the poor; he kept three doctors at their beck and call. Money spilled through his fingers into the homes of the very poor by secret ways, whilst he walked about among them as the high prelate, his benevolence all unsuspected. They accused him of pomp and power, although, unknown to them, he fed their hunger. This secret charity was a form of eccentricity. The more mysterious it became, the more he loved it.

He had begun by accumulating the most wonderful collection of historical MSS. in Europe, a library of priceless treasures. But music was his passion. He had no interest in the middle classes. He loved the beggar of the streets, and he loved the genius, who in poverty warped in a hidden corner. In his secret hours he composed; an opera, some oratorios, a mass of disintegrated church music without distinction. In truth, Ottoboni was a rather ordinary man trying to touch the stars.

What he achieved was a triumph of personality and wealth. Social Rome at this period was in a rotten state. The rich hectored and bullied the poor. Amusement, dances, the theatre and the like, being suppressed by the Pope, the need for excitement broke out in wilder directions. Sensualism was rife; drinking carried to the utmost stretches of debauchery. Secret dancing of the lewdest order was prevalent, and the priests, masked, attended these orgies by permission of the Vicar-General. But Ottoboni and his circle were a rock in a muddy tide. It carried high the loftiest thinkers in religious music, just as the better always rises, sure and apart, in the days of reaction and decadence. Bribery had been brought to a fine art. If one called on a friend his servants waited at one's doorstep next day to compliment 'the noble stranger' on the honour he had to see his master or mistress, and to receive in consequence *la buona mancia*, i.e. the usual tips. It was even the case after an audience of the Pope. 'One owes them (the servants) about 30 lire of our money each time one is admitted to an audience of his holiness,' wrote l'Abbé Richard.[1]

Into this vast vortex of contrasts Handel was flung at a moment in his life when he was beginning to shape the power of expression that would respond to his moods. Venice, with its light operas, its bawdy comedies, was forgotten, and the religious motif that moved in the Ottoboni household captured him. Among the members of the Academy was Prince Ruspoli. Until shortly before Handel's arrival, the Prince had been the Marquis di Ruspoli, but an act of grace on the part of the Pope had just raised him to the principality. Prince Ruspoli was a person of artistic soul and extreme wealth. His magnificence, his patronage rivalled that of the Cardinal himself. By some means he lured young Handel to come and stay in his palace in March 1708—a remarkable palace of marble pillars and Grecian statuary. Handel stayed

[1] Abbé Jerome Richard: *Description Historique de l'Italie*.

there just a month, and during that time wrote and produced for the Easter festivities *La Resurrezione*. It was his first great religious effort. He was moved by the stress and storm of the Roman atmosphere at this hour, and he put all that was roving in his young thoughts into his notes. *La Resurrezione*, which was only just sufficiently removed from being an opera to enable it to escape the Papal wrath, has a great and haunting beauty, if immature. It is the product of youth waiting at the gate.

It has always been supposed that *La Resurrezione* was first given at the Ottoboni palace. Most of the biographers have assumed that Handel was still under the Ottoboni influence, but the archives of Prince Ruspoli clearly prove that it was not so. Apart from which, the manuscript is dated as having been written for *la Festa di Pasqua*, held at the Marchesa Ruspoli on 4 April 1708. The libretto, which was written by Carlo Sigismondo Capece, a poet of indifferent talent, states that the work was sung 'nella Sala dell'Accademia del Signor Marchese Ruspoli'.

As a matter of fact, Ruspoli seems to have been more impressed by Handel's quality than anyone else in Rome at the time. He had intended to amuse himself during the carnival that year by improvising comedies at his castle at Vignanello, but at the eleventh hour refrained from doing so because the Pope, being informed of what was afoot, made it understood that such productions would not meet with his approval.[1] As the Prince had so shortly before been raised from the Marquisate to a Princeling, he could not incur the Papal displeasure. Therefore he decided to remain in Rome and employ Handel. This probably accounts for Handel having written *La Resurrezione* in such a hurry. A religious work, even if it were shaped like an opera, would provide the Prince with all the diversion he required, and at the same time escape the wrath of the Pontiff. It was another instance of Handel's growing characteristic of grasping impulsively at opportunity.

The Prince produced Scarlatti's oratorio *Della Santissima Annunziata* in his palace on 25 March, after which he set about the preparations for Handel's work in earnest. He took Handel into his household. This was not the Palazzo Ruspoli in the Corso, but the palace in the Piazza SS. Apostoli,

[1] Diary of Valesio, Archivio Storico Capitolino, Rome.

which the Prince had taken from the Duca Bonelli for a term of years because his own palace was in process of being restored. Such rehearsals as the shortness of time permitted, were thus carried on in his presence. He even went to the expense of constructing a temporary theatre in the palace. The Ruspoli Archives still contain the accounts of Crespineo Pavone, the carpenter who had the work in hand and which say:

> 'Making a theatre with raised seats on the occasion of the sacred oratorio in music which His Excellency had performed in the hall of his palace in Piazza SS. Apostoli, with stage and seats for the players of various instruments, making other conveniences and works for the same occasion.'[1]

Handel, it would seem, arrived at Prince Ruspoli's palace as a guest, on or about 18 March, for there is an entry in the Archives under that date as follows: 'Paid for the carriage of the bed and other things for Monsù. Endel 10 bajocchi.' (Fivepence.) A little later is another entry: 'Paid to the Jew for hire of the said bed and counterpanes for one month, 70 bajocchi.' (2s. 11d.) Obviously the Jew was not extortionate!

A further entry gives us definite proof of the date of production, for we find the following: 'Sunday April 8, Easter Day. This evening in the Bonelli Palace at SS. Apostoli, the Marquis[2] Ruspoli had a very beautiful musical oratorio performed, having made a well-decorated theatre in the hall for the audience. There were present many of the nobility and some cardinals.'

Doubtless Ottoboni was there and all the Roman Arcadians, for the production was carried out on a more elaborate scale than any of the Arcadian productions for some time. The orchestra consisted of 20 violins, 4 violoncelli, 5 bassviols, 5 double bass, 2 trumpets, 1 trombone, and 4 oboes, the performers being paid from 2 scudi 50 (about 10 shillings)

---

[1] The present Prince Ruspoli permitted a thorough search to be made in his family archives for details of Handel's stay with his ancestors, and these details, and those that follow are the result. They are interesting as throwing new light upon Handel's movements at this time.

[2] It is odd that Prince Ruspoli is here entered in the Archives as Marquis, since he had held princely rank for some months.

to 4 scudi 50. Arcangelo Corelli's name does not occur on this list (in the archives all the names of the performers are given), but there is a separate account signed by the Prince which reads:

'Angelo Valeri, our Steward, you will pay to Sig. Arcangelo Corelli the above-mentioned 244 scudi 50 bajocchi, that he may pay the players named, each according to his mark, for their complete and final payment of all their services rendered, as shown in the present list, and receiving this from the said Signor Arcangelo, they will be properly paid. This day 11 April 1708.'

Corelli, be it said, received 20 scudi (£4 3s. 4d.) for his services on this occasion. The total cost of the production seems to have been 528 scudi 40 bajocchi (about £110), no mean sum for a private performance, taking into consideration the money value of those days. Nothing that could add to the comfort of the guests seems to have been overlooked, for among the items of expense is the cost of making fifty-six candlesticks for lighting the theatre with wax candles, while two men drew a scudo apiece for helping with the refreshments in the buttery at the oratorio. In fact, the Prince paid for everything, even the cost of printing and publishing the libretto, and for a copy of it, bound in Cordovan leather, which was presented to Cardinal Gualterio, to whom it was dedicated.

Yet, in spite of the great care, one incident occurred which must have troubled the Prince a little. Among the singers a woman had been employed, and on the day after the performance came the announcement: '9 April Monday. His Holiness has issued a reproof for having a female singer in the Oratorio yesterday evening.'[1] What the objection was to a female singer performing cannot be said, since women were regularly employed in performances at the time. Perhaps the Pope, irritated in the belief that Prince di Ruspoli had merely dodged his edict regarding Easter productions, found in this woman's playing an excuse for a reproof which eased his feelings.

The triumphant production of La Resurrezione was the talk of musical Rome. The young composer—only just past

[1] Diary of Valesio.

his twenty-third birthday—had, in spite of his simple Lutheran faith, blended with the Cardinals of Rome, and brought them to his feet in acclamation. This, his very first production in the capital, caused him to be accorded the honours which the capital only gave to a tried composer. Not that he waited long in the Ruspoli palace to enjoy them, for, under the date of 30 April 1708, the Ruspoli records have this entry: 'Paid for return of the Jew's bed hired for Monsù. Endel 20 bajocchi. Paid for food for Monsù. Endel and companion 38 scudi 25 bajocchi.' This would appear to be the cost of the food consumed by Handel during his visit, and for some reason, known only to the Prince, classified as a separate item in the household accounts. The entries make it clear, however, that Handel was only at the palace in the Piazza SS. Apostoli one month, and when he left at the end of April, came once more under the sway of his first patron Cardinal Ottoboni.

Instantly he set to work again. He had no longer to use his talents on indifferent libretti, such as the atrocities with which Feustking had provided him in Hamburg. His association with the Roman Arcadians made him sure of a good 'book'. Cardinal Panfili, who went by the name of 'Fenizio' among the Arcadians, gave Handel a libretto almost as soon as the applause for *La Resurrezione* had died away. Panfili was an aged prelate who had known a curiously diverse career. He climbed down from his Cardinal dignity and wrote words for any musician who had a tuneful note in him. He wrote dramas, comedies, poetical works for the stage, and in fact anything that would put his name on a programme. Not that he was deficient in talent. True, he 'pot-boiled', and that he was ever present when there was any chance of figuring in a production. But in the main his work was good. His libretto for Handel, *Il Trionfo del Tempo e del Disinganno*, was merely a flight of fancy. In it two characters, Beauty and Pleasure, vainly endeavour to seduce Time and Truth, and sing violently against their rivals throughout the attempt. It is rather surprising that Handel should rush into a work of this sort after the careful music of *La Resurrezione*, which, even if hastily completed, had moments of genuine harmony and thought. *Il Trionfo* had neither. It was produced under the Ottoboni régime, and probably, fully conscious of its deficiencies, Handel put it away in his mind, only to resurrect it later in different forms during his years in London. *Il*

Trionfo achieved nothing in Rome, and Handel, whose sensitive nature was easily piqued, may have suffered some burning of the spirit on account of its failure.[1] When the Arcadians failed to acclaim, he was possibly more conscious of failure than were his critics. Whatever the cause, he promptly hurried out of Rome. It is true that the quarrel between the Pope and the State was brewing up into a siege of Rome—the Pope had already closed many of the gates in preparation for it. Handel may have imagined he would be wise to get out of trouble, the nature of which he did not understand. So he went to Naples. The Scarlattis, father and son, are believed to have gone with him. Probably all were rather sure that a siege had no elements in it that tended towards the making of good music.

The Naples journey was merely a diversion. Handel had nothing to gain by going there, and had it not been for an accident he would not have composed a note during the sojourn. Certainly, he carried no partially completed work in Naples, and just as certain is it that he had no idea of having anything performed in the southern city. Yet he wrote his *Acis, Galatea e Polifemo*, and produced it in Naples.

For years this has puzzled his biographers. But quite recently the last leaf of the serenata was recovered under peculiar circumstances, and in addition to the signature, is given the date 'Napoli, li 16 di Giugno 1708', and the mysterious words: 'd'Alvito'. It is these words which give the key to Handel's object in composing a fragmentary work which can never be regarded as a serious effort, but which he put aside, as he had done *Il Trionfo*, for elaboration and serious production in his later years. As it happened, d'Alvito is the title of an important Neapolitan family of great antiquity which still exists, though now known by the higher title of Prince di Colobrano. The then Duca d'Alvito was married with great festivities on 19 July 1708, which must have been almost

---

[1] One reason for its failure may have been that much of the music was too difficult for the period. It would seem that after the success of *La Resurrezione*, Handel 'aspired'. Corelli falling foul of some of the intricate parts, Handel is said to have snatched the violin from his hands and played the notes, to which Corelli replied: 'But, dear Saxon, this music is in the French manner, which I do not understand!' The story may be a canard, but if it is not, then Corelli was a better-tempered genius than has been thought.

immediately after Handel arrived in Naples.

It is not too much to surmise, therefore, that he wrote the serenata for the occasion.[1] He had come with the finest credentials from Florence and Rome. Italy, linked up as it was in matters musical at this time more closely than in political things, knew little about him. He was a youth who had flourished in Germany in a very mysterious way. Probably the mystery surrounding him was a pique to curiosity. He had shown no wild uplifting by his success; on the other hand his modesty had rather hindered his notoriety. Moreover, the Duca d'Alvito was a patron of music, since on 11 September there was performed at his house a serenata by Sarro called *Amore, Eco e Narciso*, on the occasion of the acknowledgment by Sardinia of the Emperor Charles.

The marriage of the Duca d'Alvito was one of the most gorgeous functions seen in Naples for years. It is hardly possible that Handel, freshly arrived in a city which was beginning to assume all the decoration for an event of distinction, would wish to be out of it. Throughout his later life he was always equal to the making of music for a particular occasion, and this may have been his first attempt at topical composition.

The Naples he found was a city of flowers. The roistering in the streets went on throughout the week, for the great social marriages of Italy of that day had functions which encouraged roistering. Now, on the eventful day, the Archbishop Pignatelli went to the palace, and, in the presence of all the high society of Naples, married the Duca d'Alvito to the Donna Beatrice Sauseverino, daughter of the late Prince di Monte-Miletto. And the same evening the bride was accompanied by all her relatives to her husband's palace at Chiaja—a building which had been sumptuously decorated, where the rich tapestries, flowered velvets, embroideries, brocades, jewels, statues, pictures, and other objects were inestimable, and there they all revelled magnificently.[2]

What shall we surmise then, since Handel wrote 'd'Alvito' at the foot of his *Acis* of the Neapolitan days? He came to Naples, a youth in whom was all the romance of youth. Youth ever ready to suit its richness to the mood of the moment, to

---

[1] Mainwaring declares that he wrote it at the behest of a Portuguese or Spanish Princess, named Donna Laura.
[2] *Gazetta di Napoli.*

the solemnity of an Easter Passion, to the *festa* of a decorated city. Striving for opportunity. Youth so sure. And, in his case, Youth aided by the knowledge that it could yield as votive offering the gift of a few—music worthy of the hour of rejoicing.

He may have played his part at the ducal marriage, or he may have been just a bawler on the edge of the crowd—if his enthusiasm led him so far. But he certainly made no money in Naples. The opera, for the greater part, was passing through a wave of licentiousness. Cheap music, cheap humanity. It had a dramatis personae of mistresses rather richly kept. Its productions were too often hatched out in drawing-rooms, where the attractions of the women were incentives to the policy of those productions. There were jealousies to be avoided, the tenderness of certain people's whims to be studied. The result was that Naples of 1708 produced nothing to be remembered, though Italy was walked at that time by the feet of genius.

That Handel had little interest in Naples is fairly obvious. But at least, during the visit, he made one good friend who was to stand him in good stead. This was Cardinal Vincenzo Grimani, the celebrated Viceroy. The elegance of Handel's extemporizing attracted him at once. There were endless possibilities in Grimani, as Handel soon discovered. For one thing, his family owned the unsuccessful San Giovanni Grisostomo theatre at Venice. Also Grimani was a poet. Before very long the inevitable occurred—he wrote a libretto for Handel, the best libretto, be it said, with which Handel had so far been provided. Doubtless they talked the story over together long before Grimani wrote a word of it, and, full of enthusiasm, Handel set it to music in three weeks. Thus did *Agrippina* come into being.

When the work was finished, Handel did not hurry into immediate production with his wonted fervour. There were difficulties at the Venetian theatre, for a heavy run of operas at the two rival theatres had captured the city. He left Naples and repaired to Rome with *Agrippina* in his pocket. But Rome seemed to hold little for him now—all the promise of the future appeared to lie in Venice.

In Rome, where the greater musicians and the greater performers were to be found, opera, and all the ways to opera, were still under the ban. The musical gathered at pseudo-religious oratorios, because in Rome it was the thing to do. But no theatres ever contained audiences so poor in enthusiasm for the players on the stage. The rich bought boxes at high prices, wherein to hold extravagant orgies. They burned candles in these boxes, and had card tables there, whereat they played scudi, quite oblivious to what was passing on the stage. Their theatrical life was a lurid farce, and was really an excuse for licentiousness. The boxes were little used except for bawdy gatherings, which the Pope's edict had unconsciously legalized. All the rottenness of Roman life seemed to boil to a head at the instigation of opera and religious oratorio.

So Handel found Rome when he reached the capital again, and so he left it. Towards the end of 1709 he appeared suddenly at Venice, accompanied, it is said, by Cardinal Grimani. Immediate arrangements were made for staging *Agrippina*, which was to be the first production of the Carnival season—a season which opened each year on 26 December.

Agrippina was an enormous success from its first performance. The audience went mad, and at every pause broke into loud shouts of 'Viva il caro Sassone!' and other acclaimations of praise.[1] The fortune of the old San Giovanni Grisostomo theatre was restored. The attractions at the two rival houses, presided over by two of the greatest musicians and producers of their day, Gasparini and Lotti, failed to draw. *Agrippina* was performed for twenty-seven nights during the season, a remarkable achievement for a Venetian opera in those days. It made Handel in Italy, indeed, it carried his name through Europe. Its dramatic power and extraordinary melody appealed to the Venetians at once. They fêted him, he became the idol of the city. This youth, who had come to Italy goaded by a keen sense of adventure, became in a few nights the veritable musical ruler of the Venetian people. *Agrippina* was unquestionably the finest work he had produced in Italy or elsewhere, and it was the means of getting him back again to his native land.

Throughout the run of the opera Prince Ernest of Hanover —a musician to the soul—sat in a box. He never tired of the work, it possessed some extreme fascination for him. Handel had come in contact with him during his previous Venetian

[1] Mainwaring, p. 53.

visit. *Agrippina* confirmed the Prince in the surmise he had previously formed of Handel's possibilities when he invited him to go to Hanover. Now again he pressed the invitation.

There was nothing left for Handel in Italy. He had seen the various cities. The best musical circles of the country had accepted and been proud of him. He had achieved—how much more he had achieved than he had anticipated when he set out on that long journey from Hamburg! If he had made little money, he had attained recognition. Now, strong in him, was the desire to see his own land again, and to wander to other fields.

He made up his mind. He would go to Hanover.

But Hanover was only the resting-place of a bird of passage. Handel in his youth, as in his maturity, was all moods, and there is much to suggest that the Hanover journey was, as ever, the result of a mood. Witness the erratic dash from Florence to Rome, from Rome to Florence, the sudden motiveless descent on Naples. When the shouting had died down in the Venetian theatre for *Agrippina*, mood caught him and flung him north again. One can almost trace the workings of his mind. He had arrived, an unadorned Lutheran, into Catholic circles and been accepted. True, efforts had been made to convert him to the Catholic faith, but when these met with a blunt refusal, he was still accepted for his art. It is not a little remarkable, and certainly indicative of the musical enthusiasm of Rome at the period, that on no occasion was his religion a hindrance to him in the highest circles of the Roman Church. They had acclaimed him, these people, given him recognition, his first taste of the sweets of fame. And the Italy that ruled the music of Europe had fostered him. It is possible, then, that in deciding upon his journey, he was stirred by some wish to return to Germany with the same humble vestments of the prodigal son—but a prodigal who, if weary of feet, yet returned with laurels which he would not wish to hide.

Or it may have been Steffani who urged the journey. Handel is said to have met Steffani at the Ottoboni palace at Rome, although there is no authority for this, and still less for the statement that the twain were pitted against each other in musical competition there. Considering that he was fifty-four when Handel met him, and one of the truly accomplished figures in music, Steffani would scarcely be likely to hoist his dignity by an act of this sort with a rival less than half his own age. It is certain that he was in Venice during the run of *Agrippina*, however, and equally certain that he recognized Handel's brilliance, and gave him unstinted praise and encouragement.

Agostino Steffani was one of the most extraordinary Europeans of his day. He bobbed up everywhere like a cork on a sea of musical and political intrigue, religious fervour and courtly pomp. No one knew who his parents were, but he was born at Castelfranco just thirty years before Handel saw the light at Halle. Somebody picked the boy out of the ditch because of his beautiful voice, and made him a chorister at St Mark's, Venice. He drifted to Munich, and was educated by the Elector Ferdinand Maria; later he reappeared in Rome and turned up mysteriously at the Court as a musician. His voice in maturity proved to be even more beautiful than it had been in his youth. He composed, and his church music found a vogue throughout Europe, though practically none of it has remained. Still unsatisfied, he studied theology and philosophy and became a priest, then turned to writing operas! Ultimately he tired of the Munich Court and passed to that of the Elector of Hanover, who made him *Kapellmeister*.

Even this did not satisfy Steffani. He wanted diplomacy, so this extraordinary creature was made Ambassador to Brussels, by the Elector. There was very little he could not do, and anyone more unlike an Abbé—the rank he held—could not be imagined. He joyed in the luxurious life of the Court, dined at the royal table, and, in some subtle manner, managed to keep himself free from the intrigue which swept through the courts.

Steffani's fifty-four years had mellowed him to the ways of all peoples and all classes. One can imagine this person of experience, therefore, impressing Handel, and possibly pointing out to him the advantages of rich patronage, which he might expect at Hanover, in preference to the wandering happy-go-lucky existence the Saxon had been leading.

Unlike Mattheson, Steffani had no sense of jealousy. There was too much of the wanderer in him. At all events, when Handel arrived at Hanover he at once put his footsteps on the right road. 'When I first arrived in Hanover I was a young man,' Handel said in later years,[1] 'Steffani received me with great kindness and introduced me to the Princess Sophia, and the Elector's son, giving them to understand that I was a virtuoso in music.'

Steffani exercised a greater influence over Handel than any of those with whom the young musician became acquainted during his Italian years. Steffani was, indeed, a master. His word was accepted everywhere. He was amiable and kind, and possessed an exquisite courtesy.[2] But he had a quick temper, an easily wounded dignity. Soon after Handel arrived at Hanover, Steffani quarrelled with his singers. The affair seems to have been due to his punctiliousness on insisting that his singers kept precisely to the score as written. Whatever the cause, the master's dignity suffered rebuff, and without waiting for further argument he threw up his post and went off to Rome.

Such an incident might have proved a musical debacle at the Court. Certainly if it had taken place a couple of years earlier it would have done. Steffani, who had ruled so long, who had brought the music of the Court to a precision hitherto unknown there, left Hanover, never to return. And Handel stepped into his shoes, at a fee equivalent to £300 a year. He became *Kapellmeister*.

For a youth of twenty-five the honour was exceptional. And in more ways than one. Handel had not proved himself to the Elector at the time the appointment was made. He was largely taken on trust, to some extent on the recommendation of Steffani, whose last act before leaving the Court was to urge that Handel should succeed him. He therefore had everything to satisfy him, and yet his first request was for leave of absence to go to England. No call had come to him from England, no invitation from high quarters. It was the old demand of impulse. He obtained his permission just when summer was in full blaze at Hanover, and set off at once for Halle instead of going direct to London.

Much had happened at the Schlamm house since Handel left it. His youngest sister, Johanna Christiana, had died the year previous, and his elder sister, Dorothea Sophia, had effected a successful marriage with a well-to-do official, Dr Michael Michaelsen, who later became a prominent member

---

[1] To Sir John Hawkins.   [2] Chrysander, Vol. I.

of the Prussian Imperial Service, War Councillor, and Lord of the Manor of Eptingen. Handel found Frau Dorothea ageing fast,[1] cast about as she was by penurious habits for which there does not appear to have been any real necessity. Not that she was well off, but the sale of her husband's practice to Möller must have kept her from want. Solitude and lack of direct interest in things was doubtless responsible for her circumstances. As for Aunt Anna, she was Frau Dorothea's sole companion in the large house. Two ageing women alone, slaves to an overriding piety, so ignorant of the ways of the world that this dashing from one country to another on the part of George Frideric must have amazed them.

Into the house one day walked George Frideric with all the dust of travel upon him. No longer the stripling who had set out for Hamburg. No longer the youth seeking fortune on a high road strange to his feet. Nevertheless he remained only a very few days, and took the mail-coach towards Düsseldorf at the invitation of the Elector Johann Wilhelm. The Elector was an ardent patron of music, and his wife, Anna Maria, was the sister of Prince Gaston, who had lured Handel from Hamburg to Italy. None of the German Courts had music equal to that at Düsseldorf. The Elector ran operas on a magnificent scale, but if the motive that lay behind the invitation to Handel was to secure his services, he failed signally, for, with a gift of plate from the Elector to mark the visit, Handel left him and set out for Holland.

By that route he reached London. The autumn of 1710 was waning when he set foot on these shores, friendless, unable to speak a word of the language. Other German musicians had come before him and settled down in comparative affluence. There was Pepusch, there was Haym; both must have wondered what had drawn Handel to London. Pepusch openly mocked.

Handel did just what he had intended to do. He put up an opera in London, made an extraordinary hit with it, then went quietly back to the Hanoverian Court to answer his parole.

By which time, no doubt, Pepusch had ceased to laugh, and Haym had serious thoughts of writing a libretto for the

---

[1] Mainwaring declares that Handel found his mother blind, but she did not lose her sight till 1730.

Saxon who came here and did things in this stampede fashion.

Handel was a force to be reckoned with. Haym knew it, even if Pepusch's more solemn intelligence had failed to absorb the fact.

CHAPTER V

THE FIRST VISIT TO LONDON

WHEN Handel arrived in London, Purcell had been dead fifteen years.

Purcell had carried English music to the heights, and the years that followed his passing found it at its lowest point of mediocrity. Only just before his death, Purcell had said:

> 'Music is yet in its nonage, a forward child which gives hope of what he may be hereafter in England when the masters of it shall find more encouragement. It is now leaving Italian, which is its best master, and studying a little of the French air, to give it somewhat more of gaiety and fashion.'[1]

Prophetic words. After the death of Purcell, English music collapsed. The woeful efforts of men who knew nothing of the first rudiments of harmony and counterpoint appeared on the London stage, failed miserably, and cost their patrons small fortunes. Itinerant Italian musicians had begun to flock to London, drawn by the knowledge that London looked to Italy to retrieve its opera from the 'slough of the devil'. Operas of indifferent worth were staged with Italian and English words, so that the audiences only understood half that was sung and were bored to death.

So important was this Italian influence that Addison of *Spectator* fame had made a special journey to Italy to study it. When he returned he put on *Rosamund* to Thomas Clayton's music, a perpetration of noise which irritated audiences for three nights only, and then dropped into permanent oblivion. The failure fired Addison's blood. He hectored and advised through the *Spectator* on the absurdities of Italian operas. He esteemed them as no higher than the devil's artless strumming, so that when Handel arrived with his Italian reputation behind him, Addison—a slave to his liver through over-dining, and with a pen ever ready to tilt at the first excuse—settled himself into his chair and waited for him.

London in 1710 was in a curious state of discord. Operas

[1] *Court and Society from Elizabeth to Anne*, Vol. II, p. 339.

failed one after the other. Their attractions were so few that the inhabitants of the town thought again before venturing into the night for a theatre with the risk of being waylaid and robbed on the way home. A wave of crime had swept over the metropolis. Robberies were enacted in Piccadilly; houses in Bond Street openly pilfered in broad daylight. Night watchmen were trussed like fowls in the principal thoroughfares while my lady's coach on its way to the theatre passed within a few yards. The streets were ill-lit and stank of stale garbage, and the courtyards that led from them were thieves' kitchens and murder shops. One was arrested on the word of an informer for nothing at all when passing down a main London street at night. The Haymarket Theatre played continuously to a losing box-office. Drury Lane—a forbidding thoroughfare, which only the boldest would traverse at night —turned out failure after failure. Small wonder, then that those who alone could keep a theatre open preferred to linger over their wine and gaming, rather than venture through a gauntlet of marauders, to hear indifferent music and piffling libretti.

When Handel arrived in London, every condition of the theatrical world was against him, and was heaped as a mighty load upon the burden he already had to bear in his ignorance of the language and his lack of influence. By some means he came in touch at once with Aaron Hill, who was running the Queen's Theatre in the Haymarket, and finding it impossible to make the box-office balance the expenses.

Hill was a figure of opportunity, and he was precisely Handel's age. He had knocked about the world, after being left unprovided for as an urchin of fourteen in the London streets. At fifteen, he went to Constantinople, where his relation, Lord Paget, was English Ambassador. Lord Paget was surprised to have this scion of his poor relations thrust upon him in a strange capital. He was considerably annoyed. Being rather a proud and pompous person he almost responded to his first inclination to send the boy home by the same way that he had come. But upon second thoughts he mellowed. He found the youthful Aaron a tutor. He educated him, sent him through Palestine, Egypt, and parts of the East, and brought him back to England in 1703. In 1709 young Hill astonished the London literary circles by writing *A History of the Ottoman Empire*, much of the material for which he secured whilst in Constantinople. Then he published a poem in favour of the Earl of Peterborough. So easy were things achieved in those days by the critical pen, that the Earl in return put him in charge of Drury Lane Theatre, from whence he migrated in due course to the Haymarket. His mind was curious; his adaptability unbounded. He stepped out of the theatrical orbit for a time to put on the market a patent for extracting oil from beechmast.[1] Then he finished his life by running a distillery at Pitlochry, where he died.[2]

When Handel found him, or he found Handel, he was at the height of his vigour. The Drury Lane company had passed from that ancient street to the Queen's Theatre in the Haymarket in 1708, and Aaron Hill with it. In vain he had struggled with adverse fate at the Haymarket. He knew better than anyone that there was something distinctly wrong with the musical fare that was being put before the London audiences. So, when Handel came, he hailed him as a man whose fame in Italy he had heard of from afar. The next thing he did was to call Handel into the theatre, where he gave him his own translation of a play by a wandering Italian, Giacomo Rossi, who had adapted the story from Tasso. Handel set Rossi's libretto as fast as the Italian, halting and hindered by the adaptation of Italian styles to the English stage, could produce it.

And so *Rinaldo* came into being. It was composed in a fortnight. Handel, ripe to the new adventure, and eager to figure in an English theatre, let the music pour from him. It was a great effort. The notes of *Rinaldo* carried in them all Handel's surging youth, all his mentality fresh and unspoiled. The work came at a time when his whole soul was in tune with his task. On the night of 24 February 1711 *Rinaldo* made the name of Handel famous throughout London.

He had been lucky with his singers. There was a good deal of brilliant talent in London at the time—people to whom the bad music of the epoch denied a chance. The *Rinaldo* singers may have been of Aaron Hill's choosing, but they were more probably Handel's. There was Giuseppe Boschi, the greatest *basso* of his day in Europe; a man whom his most violent enemies could not tear down on the score of the quality of his voice. He had just come to London from

[1] Rees: *Cyclopædia.*
[2] P. R. Drummond: *Perthshire in Bygone Days*, p. 403.

Naples with his wife, Francesca Vanini, a lady older than himself, who possessed a worn-out contralto voice. Boschi had never sung in London, but both he and his wife had sung in Handel's *Agrippina* before coming to England. Boschi was young, vigorous, his voice rich with all the powers of youth. He was waiting for a chance in the English capital. Handel engaged him for the part of Organte, and also gave a part to his wife, and so began a big partnership. He became Handel's greatest *basso*; his voice, with its melodious thunder, interpreted Handel's heavier recitatives as few other voices probably have done since. His voice stormed London.

These *Rinaldo* singers require reference, because the *Rinaldo* casting was really the foundation of much of Handel's later casting for his operas. His sweetest singer in this work was Nicolini, who had come from Italy rather less than three years before, and who first appeared in London in a work of the elder Scarlatti. Nicolini was a sensation. He had a remarkably fine soprano voice which dropped with his later years to a rich contralto. He was a faddist, a dilettante. He wrote poetry. He supped at the richest tables of Venice and Rome. He had all kinds of organizing schemes, among which was one to reorganize the London opera on the Venetian system, and he urged that the first thing to be done was to get a thousand guineas out of Queen Anne, which, be it said, he failed to do. He wrote precious letters—the sort of letters one hesitates to destroy on account of the beauty of their language.[1] He sang with the voice of a nightingale. It was Bononcini who first discovered Nicolini in Rome, Bononcini whose hatred of Handel ultimately led to one of the sensations of a musical epoch. But it was Handel who brought Nicolini out, for until *Rinaldo* was produced the Italian had not reached the heart of the English people.

Rinaldo was a masterpiece, and it reshaped the whole fabric of London music at the time. Addison, with the recollection of the three solitary performances of his *Rosamund*, drew into his corner, vicious and hostile, waiting his chance to strike. Eventually he came out with a torrent of abuse of *Rinaldo*, but the only criticism he was able to bring home to the society ladies who read him was that the wild birds let loose during the opera, and which got mixed up with the

[1] One of his original letters in possession of the author, is a study in adjectival courtesy.

candles and snuffed them out,[1] were likely to prove a nuisance to the heads of those in the audience. Sir Richard Steele, who had just acquired the concert rooms in York Buildings, which found good patronage because London offered little better music elsewhere, decided at once that Handel must be crushed. At York Buildings, Steele was offering his patrons stale fare as compared with *Rinaldo* at the Haymarket, and his audiences were thinning rapidly.

Handel had all pride in his singers, but less in his librettist. Rossi had served him badly. The *Rinaldo* 'book' was inane, stupid, but Handel rescued the work from the pit by the sheer beauty of his composing. He was all passion, seductiveness, tenderness—a soul aflame.

The opera caught on in a night. London came crowding to Handel's box-office in the Haymarket—Society in its carriages and chairs, the others from the dark lanes and byways. The narrow Haymarket began to hold crowds of unsurpassed magnitude. Drury Lane, with its dangers of poor entertainment, became obscured as might some ancient house from which the glories had fled. This must have angered Steele more than his diminishing concert audiences, for he held the patent of Old Drury. Addison let loose his first shafts of *Spectator* invective, and Steele was at his side goading him on. They worked like a couple of demons in harness. It was a battle of two brilliant Englishmen against a youth who, with the international gift of melody at his fingers, could speak little more than a dozen words of the English tongue in retort.

Rinaldo played fifteen times between February and June, and not once to a vacant seat. The effect on Society was peculiar. The denizens of Mayfair had scurried away to country houses owing to the boredom in entertainment which London provided. Now they came back in couples; in threes and groups they went to *Rinaldo*, and wrote long screeds to cousins and friends. They talked Handel into success, they wrote him into success. This Handel, this unknown who had dropped into their midst from nowhere! The *Rinaldo* tunes swept with swift insidiousness to all comers. To all drawing-rooms. To drinking dens. Years afterwards Pepusch used some of them for his *Beggar's Opera*. They paraphrased them. They danced to them.

These 'dull English' crowded about Handel and bore him

[1] Duke of Manchester: *Court and Society*. See also *The Spectator*.

high. He was invited to Society's tables. Musical circles sought his company with them as they might have done to an imported and unexplained freak. As for Handel, he went everywhere, saw everything, knew everybody, and laughed at Addison's violent assault upon him in the *Spectator*.

Mary Granville, afterwards the famous Mrs Delany, wrote of her first meeting with Handel in 1711 when she was quite a child:

'In the year '10 I first saw Mr Handel who was introduced to my uncle by Mr Heidegger, the famous manager of the opera, and the most ugly man that was ever formed. We had no better instrument in the house than a little spinet of mine, on which the great musician performed wonders. I was much struck with his playing, but struck as a child, not a judge, for the moment he was gone, I seated myself at my instrument and played the best lesson I had then learnt. My uncle archly asked me if I thought I should ever play as well as Mr Handel. "If I did not think I should," cried I, "I would burn my instrument!" Such was the innocent presumption of childish ignorance.'[1]

Thus did Handel, aided by Heidegger and Aaron Hill, work his way through drawing-rooms of the city. His brilliant *Rinaldo*, and the introduction of musical friends, obtained the entrées for him, but it was his performances on the harpsichord that made him popular. He had lifted London's music up from decay they said. He played at the harpsichord, he improvised. Soon that little circle which clustered about Piccadilly knew that a rather unobtrusive giant had indeed arrived, and somehow been accepted on his own guarantees.

Mary Granville's record is important, because it proves Handel's early association with Heidegger, although they were not to be partners in productions during Handel's first visit to England. Heidegger at the time was manager of the opera house: an enterprising person, astute, stupidly generous. He had come to England a beggar three years previously, under very peculiar circumstances. The Heideggers were an old Nuremberg family. The grandfather of this man of ugliness had departed from the German town and gone to Zürich on a business tour. He had only intended to stay in the town a few

[1] *Life and Correspondence of Mrs Delany*, pp. 5 and 6.

days before leaving for the Strassburg Fair, and during this period he ordered a suit of clothes from a tailor which was to be ready in time for his departure by the lake boat. The clothes did not arrive. Heidegger could not go without them, so the boat departed, leaving him rather melancholy on the landing-stage. But ere it had reached Fahr it was wrecked and everyone on board was drowned.[1]

Heidegger was evidently pleased with the tailor's sloth since he owed the preservation of his life to it. So he settled in Zürich. His grandson, grim and ugly, had a love-affair in the town, and, on being thrown over, travelled as a valet throughout Germany. In 1707 he turned up in England to confer with the English Government upon some unknown subject on behalf of the Swiss.[2] Probably he was an opportunist, glib of tongue, who failed. The English Government would have none of him, so he entered the Queen's Life Guards as a private.

People like Heidegger ultimately seldom fail. He got out of the Guards. He connived his way into the highest social circles by 'his elegant manners and amiable personality'. They called him the 'Swiss Count', simply because he looked like one. He gathered together some money from loiterers round Society's dinner-tables and began to produce operas. Out of one he cleared five hundred guineas. So he went on, a delightful opportunist, so revoltingly ugly that women feared to look upon him.

Heidegger had a hypnotic personality. His hideous appearance began to be out-balanced by his sheer cleverness. When Handel came to England he was undoubtedly the most brilliant adept at stagecraft in London. His sense of drama was astonishing. He made money, drank it, tossed it away. He stalked through the drawing-rooms as Poe's plague-figure did at a later age in the *Masque of the Red Death*. And then the very ugliness of him seemed to create a sense of fascination. He had a wonderful, mellow voice that made it difficult to break away when he was speaking. Women—Society women—from sheer revulsion, changed to interest in the man. The way he commanded, the way he talked, the way he drew a whole room towards him, wrapped him about with a subtle mystery. Then he began to receive offers of

---

[1] Theodor Vetter: *Johann Jakob Heidegger*.
[2] *Ibid*.

marriage, and was soon accepted as a hero who had been forgotten by God somehow—a man, handicapped by his hideous appearance, who fought and conquered adversity through open courage and direct personality.

This was the Heidegger who introduced Handel to that child Mary Granville. What his age was no one knew, for he seemed to pass year after year without changing. Later, beside Handel, he found the heights and the depths, to fade away in the end as secretly as he had come, mysterious and never understood. Some said that he rejoiced in the fact that his ugliness made him ever conspicuous. Be that as it may, no one understood John Jacob Heidegger save the person of that name. But few people understood Handel so well as he.

Meanwhile, Handel went the rounds. Any person who loved sound music was good enough for his friendship. He wandered about London, spluttering his few words of English, trying every organ worth consideration, regaling Society's drawing-rooms with his performances on the harpsichord, attending concerts held in concert rooms or in the back parlours of taverns, or anywhere else if the musical fare was good. One of his first friends in Society was the Earl of Burlington who had a wonderful mansion in Piccadilly. The Burlington House concerts were extravagant in the hospitality of the Earl to his guests. In fact, Burlington House was more or less open at all times to the best musicians.

The talk of musical London at this period were the coal-house concerts of Thomas Britton. There has never been anyone like Britton before or since. He started life carrying a basket of coal on his back round the poorer districts, and selling it in small portions. Then he bought a handcart, and in this fashion continued peddling. He saved money and spent his savings on old music, until he had amassed a collection of extraordinary interest and value. All this music he kept in a loft over a stable in a back street near Clerkenwell Green. Down in the stable he piled his coal. To reach the loft, which he had made into a concert room, one had to climb up a precipitous flight of steps fixed outside the building—steps which 'could scarce be ascended without crawling'.[1]

How Thomas Britton organized his extraordinary clientele is a mystery. Society and the artistic professions flocked to the loft over the coal cellar, and were seen clawing their way

[1] Hawkins.

crazily up the rough steps. They filled the room for the concerts Britton held there every Thursday night. Not that they can have been particular as to their comfort, for the room was so low that a tall man could not stand upright, and the atmosphere of beer and tobacco during the progress of the evening deterred them not at all. Pepusch was invariably there playing the harpsichord. It was probably here that Handel first met him, for throughout the spring of 1711 Handel was one of Thomas Britton's regular patrons. Woolaston, the painter, was an enthusiast, so also were Hughes, the poet and Obadiah Shuttleworth, who became organist at St Michael's, Cornhill. Banister and H. Needler were first violinists at the concerts. Sir Roger l'Estrange, the best amateur viol da gambist in town, came regularly with the Earl of Burlington and the Duchess of Queensbury To this assorted gathering Handel used to play on a little chamber organ, with five stops,[1] whilst Thomas Britton himself performed upon the viol da gamba. So popular indeed did Britton and his concerts become that a song was composed in his honour, the chorus of which ran:

> '*Altho' disguis'd with smutty Looks,*
> *I'm skilled in many Trades.*
> *Come hear me Fiddle, read my Books,*
> *Or buy my Small Coal, Maids.*'[2]

With the coming of June and the close of the opera season, Handel left London. To remain longer would be to incur displeasure at the Hanoverian Court. Indeed, there was some risk of this having taken place already. He stayed a few days *en route*, with the Elector Palatine at Düsseldorf, in order to advise him about some instruments, and the letter of excuse which the Elector gave him to take on to Hanover suggests that Handel was cognizant of possible trouble for his tardiness when he reached his destination. 'Your Ld's *capellmeister* Handel,' the Elector wrote from Düsseldorf to the Elector George Ludwig at Hanover,

'who will have the grace to hand you this, I have kept here with me for a few days, to show him some instruments

[1] Rockstro: *Life of Handel*, p. 74.
[2] Edward Ward: *Clubs and Societies* (London, 1745).

and other things, and to obtain his opinion about them. Therefore I beg of your Ld. in cousinly friendship, most urgently, you will not put to account and express your disfavour at this delay which has occurred against his will, but to retain him in your grace and protection as hitherto so also in the future.'[1]

Still there was some doubt as to the nature of the reception Handel would receive at Hanover, for a few days later the Elector Palatine wrote a second letter setting out more copiously his excuses for the musician. Armed with these two letters Handel started for Hanover. If there was any remonstrance it must have been trivial, for it is unrecorded. It may be that they were fully aware of his London triumph, and knew that to call him to task might, and doubtless would, have caused him to leave Hanover for ever.

The incident passed. Handel settled down to an active period of chamber music at the Court. He wrote duets for the Princess Caroline, the stepdaughter of the Elector, who was destined to be the first Hanoverian consort on the English throne. He produced songs, sheaves of them, and most of them had a tenderness distinctly their own. To England he wrote regularly. Strange indeed were the desires and ambitions stirring within him. His country was ceasing to call to him. There was something solid in the London triumph; something that appealed to him in the English people. Addison and Steele were mere fussers on a flood of popular approval. Handel never remembered his enemies for long—his life was too full to bother with them. Had Mattheson been subjected to half the bitterness and concerted attack that Handel was to know, his heart would have broken. It was never so with Handel. His enemies did more than the applause of a nation to make him. He answered them back, not in words, but in music.

In November he was granted further leave to proceed to Halle. Here he was present at the baptism of his niece, Johanna Frederica Michaelsen, the daughter of his only surviving sister. The Michaelsens were flourishing, they were at the moment the only branch of the family making good money. This, their first child, was named Frederica after Handel, for

[1] Dr Alfred Einstein. Letter discovered by him in the Secret State Archives of Bavaria.

his growing fame was knowledge to them, even if they scarcely understood it. It is doubtful if they had even heard him play. There had been practically no opportunity, and it is tolerably certain that they had never listened to a note of his composing. In an age when reputations travelled slowly, the genius of the brother who had left the Schlamm when little more than a child must have been very vague and misunderstood. Maybe they appraised him chiefly for his royal associations. His income was not extraordinary—although *Rinaldo* had paid him well— so that they did not know him on that account. His brother-in-law Michaelsen was certainly making more. He was the rich relation.

Like his visit of the year before, this one was brief. Handel returned to Hanover to his chamber music, his royal pupils, his *Lieder*, growing restless the while, with a goading desire to break out again.

He did not wait long. In the following autumn (1712) he obtained permission to return to London. He wanted the opera, and there was no opera at Hanover. That he intended to go back to London had been obvious for a long time, for he had been studying English,[1] and corresponding regularly with Hughes and other of the friends he had met in England.

He had in truth become the complete cosmopolitan. Any country was his that held the best chance for his genius, and wisely he chose England, and chose it at the very time when the poverty of English music made a setting for his own genius. England was ripe for him, and he was ripe for England.

It was the chance that comes in every lifetime and he took it. At the beginning of November he stepped off the coach in London.

He had come back for all time.

[1] Letter, July 1712, to his friend Andreas Roner.

CHAPTER VI

THE LAST DAYS OF ANNE

IF English music had been lifeless when Handel first came to London, it was certainly barren of melody when he returned in November. No production after his *Rinaldo* had found success. Meanwhile, Aaron Hill had left the Queen's Theatre, and its management had been taken over by an adventurer named MacSwiney, who knew little about music, but was a producer of some skill.

Following his sudden decision to return to London, Handel had prepared the outline of a new opera on a poor libretto by Rossi entitled *Il Pastor Fido*. A foolish diversion on the part of Handel, for the work showed traces of haste, and was from the start a failure. Immediately on his arrival in London he went to stay at the town house of an English admirer, a Mr Andrews, but it is clear that he must have brought the greater portion of the opera with him, since it was ready to go into rehearsal on 4 November.

Il Pastor Fido was produced on 22 November and failed. It was given six performances. Nor did the success he had with his singers in *Rinaldo* follow him with the new work. Nicolini had returned to Italy, so the principal part was given to a singer newly arrived from that country, Cavaliere Valeriano Pellegrini, an artificial soprano of little execution. Valentini was the only outstanding singer of those who had been heard in *Rinaldo*. They were a poor lot. Not that they can be held responsible for the failure of Rossi's atrocious words, and Handel's hastily written music, with its rare moments of beauty.

Long before Christmas, Handel was aware that his first opera after his return was laughed at by the English as being scarcely better than the poor stuff to which lately they had been accustomed. The failure must have been a quick blow to him. The very patron who had admired him so much kept away from the new work. Early in the New Year (1713) *Il Pastor Fido* was played for the last time in that form. In later years Handel, after working over the music afresh, and adding some choruses, revived it.

The failure of the opera taught Handel the important lesson that London audiences, poverty-stricken in musical fare, were certainly not prepared to accept anything. Those two cronies, Addison and Sir Richard Steele, revelled in the failure. The German had come back full of conceit and found defeat! It did a lot to wash the taste of the *Rinaldo* success from their palates. Not that Handel wept over the ashes of his first English failure. He sat down and composed a new opera in twenty days, completing it on 19 December 1712, and it proved to be one of the usual triumphs that came out of his adversity.

Nicolo Haym had written the 'book'—and excellent it was —the Haym, who with Pepusch, had jeered when Handel arrived in England for the first time! A composer himself, he had recognized the latent strength in the invader, and his libretto of *Teseo* was an attempt to give to Handel the best that he knew.

Teseo was produced on 10 January 1713. It was a triumph of passionate strength. *Teseo* is a character fired with every emotion known to man. All the youth, the vigour, the yearning in the human conscience was caught by Handel's violins and carried high in his great waves of singing. He understood human frailty and desire more truly in *Teseo* than in any other of his early works.

The effect of the *Teseo* production was magical. But the opera had started badly. After the second performance MacSwiney disappeared with the proceeds of a ripe box-office, the singers unpaid, and most of the expenses of the production still unliquidated. It was one of those eternal tricks which fate was always playing upon Handel—lifting him to the top of the wave only to drop him rudely down on the other side. He probably made little out of the opera, for, in consequence of MacSwiney's delinquency, he received nothing till the last performance, which was given for his benefit. Things might have been desperate with him had not Heidegger come in and taken over the control of the theatre.

Heidegger verily saved Handel at this hour. The theatre kept open. The ugly man discharged the bills. *Teseo* went on; its patrons forgot the scandal of the absconding manager and filled the boxes. This was the beginning of the big friendship between Handel and Heidegger. The former did not forget that, but for the little 'Swiss Count', he would have been sent back to Hanover a pauper. As it was, *Teseo* proved to be the biggest success Handel had yet had in opera.

In spite of the fortune of *Teseo*, which certainly set the musical dovecotes chattering, this opera remained unpublished for many years until Dr Arnold brought out his edition. Not that Handel had kept aloof from music publishers. Walsh, the foremost music publisher of his time, had come to Handel when *Rinaldo* found its public, and secured the publishing rights on terms which no one but Handel and himself ever knew. They were probably small, for Walsh afterwards boasted that he only paid Handel twenty guineas for the publishing rights of an opera. Walsh kept an army of apprentices who worked almost with the rapidity of the modern press in turning out music sheets, and he asked Handel to permit him to include *Rinaldo* in his series of Italian operas. The fact that Walsh made a large sum out of the publishing rights of *Rinaldo* annoyed Handel, who told him that he should write the next opera and he (Handel) would publish it.[1] Yet we find him allowing Walsh to publish portions of *Il Pastor Fido*, after which he refused to publish again with Walsh till 1722.

Walsh had the mean streak highly developed, and his son, who succeeded him, surpassed him in this characteristic. Both of them made fortunes. Both of them kept their apprentices busy rolling riches into their coffers on sweated wages, and when they could not fix a contract with a composer they pirated him. The Walshes would have made a capital pair of convicts in these days, but, in Handel's epoch a music publisher was a prowler, with dishonourable intent most of the time, and if he did fix up a contract with a composer, it was an accident of conscience usually on the right side as regards himself. John Caulfield, whose father was apprenticed to Walsh, said that Walsh used to leave pieces of gold about on his desk to test the honesty of his clerks, and workpeople, and that he was very rich.[2] In short, Walsh was one of those difficult and irritating people sometimes met with in life, with no soul beyond self; so wrapped up in self that they seem to be characters out of an exaggerated novel. But he was unquestionably the greatest music publisher of his time.

[1] E. David: *G. F. Händel et Sa Vie*, p. 73.
[2] V. Schölcher: *Life of Handel*, p. 91.

Teseo brought Handel back to his former position. The lack of interest in *Il Pastor Fido* was forgotten: he might never have conceived such a work. Haym had dedicated the libretto to the Earl of Burlington. After all, Burlington had been and remained one of the few people in London who maintained his faith in Handel. Throughout his life he looked upon Handel as some magician whose creations would never die. Ephemeral personage as he was, and young at the time when he supported Handel—he was only seventeen —his sentiments remained that of the ages. He was a rich idler, yet unlike most rich idlers of his time he chose a branch of art and gave his riches to it, without expectation of reward. He had not been drawn into the throes of loose living. The ladies at the lesser theatres were common game, but not if he could help it in those productions with which he was associated. Drury Lane was a bawdy-house; the concert rooms were teeming with the mistresses of rich backers—ladies caught up for their pretty faces, and too often possessing voices which might have achieved something had they been capable of an honest pronunciation of the English tongue, or some semblance of melody. The clubs roared with merriment at the concert programmes which revealed the secret *amours* of those who should know better. But Burlington House was the home of the Arts, and it escaped the gibes.

Teseo well launched, Handel packed his baggage at Mr Andrew's and went at the Earl's request to live at Burlington House. The palace then stood in the middle of some fields, well back from the streets, as can be judged by its present position as the Royal Academy.[1] No more ideal spot for a composer could be found. There was no disturbance, no noise. He was given his own suite of rooms, where he remained, living a life apart from the titled circle. The Earl's object, no doubt, was to have the first call on Handel for all the musical functions at the Palace. At these functions Handel met Pope and Gay for the first time, the former very poor, very proud, but not too proud to accept the Burlington patronage in the shape of an allowance, when he took a little house at Chelsea. Gay, on the other hand, was the wastrel, the man with a perpetual liver, with a gift for cynicism and retort unequalled by anyone

[1] The Burlington House of Handel's time was burnt down in 1854, but part of the old building—the ground floor of the right wing—still remains.

in town—a man who lived entirely for pleasure, who turned and rent his best friends on the slightest provocation.

Handel's first composition to be performed was the Queen Anne *Birthday Ode* probably at Windsor. He had been presented to the Queen at the time of his first visit, and doubtless his object in composing this *Birthday Ode* was to ingratiate himself at Court, and with the English people. The success of *Teseo* had convinced him that his future lay in London.

The *Birthday Ode* was produced on 6 February 1714, whilst *Teseo* was running, and was the first occasion on which Handel had set English to music. He had not yet acquired the art of thinking in English. He always thought in Italian, and wrote his thoughts in Italian upon his music pages all through these early years in London.[1] As he grew older he thought in German, and even his last compositions bear these thoughts written in German on the margins, for he never really mastered the English tongue. In two years he had become proficient in Italian, yet the greater part of a lifetime spent in London never gave him the same knowledge of English. He spoke it badly, with a strong German twang. His music, up to the very end, shows repeatedly the limits of his understanding of English by his frequent bad accenting in composition. It is evident that the *Birthday Ode* was completed with considerable speed.

In January he had composed a Te Deum, known as the *Utrecht Te Deum*. This he put away till the festivities for the Peace of Utrecht took place, and it was performed for the first time on 7 July. Ostensibly, the Queen was as delighted with it as with the *Birthday Ode*, for she promptly settled upon Handel a yearly pension of £200. The real cause of her pleasure was not the music itself, seeing that she 'was too busy or too careless to listen to her own band, and had no thought of hearing and paying new players however great their genius or vast skill.'[2] By pensioning Handel she had—to use a popular phrase—got one back at the Germans, whom she hated with every fibre in her tightly corseted body. It rejoiced her to have lured from a German Court a genius, as people called him, though her knowledge of music was too meagre to confirm or refute the opinion. The crotchety old lady must have been really pleased by her achievement. The

[1] Schölcher.
[2] Duke of Manchester: *Court and Society*, Vol. II, p. 337.

fact that Handel with his music had not made himself so precious to her, in spite of the pension of £200, is suggested by the fact that, having pensioned him, she let him alone as if in no need of his services. He did not appear at Court; he was not required at Court. With her prayer meetings, her combat with the Duchess of Marlborough, and her German hatred, the Queen was too fully occupied. She fretted and fussed with the grievances, lived with them, and starved herself of pleasures which neither Handel nor any other musician or composer could provide.

Handel continued to live at Burlington House, and apparently did little except continue his tour of the town organs, and fraternize with the St Paul's choir at the Queen's Arms Tavern in St Paul's Churchyard, where he idled hours away with a harpsichord at the weekly evening meeting. Society still strove to pamper him, but he moved little in the Burlington circle outside Burlington House. The dinners and social functions of the town had small attraction for him, but a harpsichord and a beer-mug in the house of a musical friend, however lowly in birth, made him a happy man. He showed no desire to return to Hanover, which is odd, since his strictness to the letter in a business contract was a commercial acumen never departed from in his later life. Possibly Hanover held little to interest him. Chamber music to a handful of people, who in the main failed to understand it, can have been a poor lure by comparison with the real joy of operatic production in London.

The months rolled by, and all idea of returning to Hanover seems to have drifted out of his mind. It is obvious that the Elector would not have kept the post of *Kapellmeister* open if he had thought that Handel intended to settle permanently in London. There is certainly no evidence that the Elector at any time pressed for his return. But in August 1714 Queen Anne made rather a muddle of the situation. She died. On the same day the Elector of Hanover was proclaimed King of England. Little more than a month later he landed at Greenwich; in another month the English crown had been placed firmly upon his brow. He came with 'a compact body of Germans'; he had his faithful German chamberlains, his German secretaries; his negroes, captives of his bow and spear in Turkish wars; his two ugly elderly German favourites Mesdames Kielmansegge and Schulenburg, whom he created respectively Countess of Darlington and Duchess of Kendal.[1]

Handel was in a curious predicament, but it did not worry him. Queen Anne, with all her German hatreds, her petty quarrels, her strained attempts to show animosity to Germany and its princelings, was safely buried beneath the Abbey stones. But Handel, moving in London political circles as he did, must have known for some time that, on the death of the Queen, the Elector, to whom he was playing truant, might reign in her stead. Anne could not live for ever with her chronic indigestion and general internal troubles. The point is important, because Handel would not have neglected the situation as he did if coming events were likely to prove dangerous to him.

Doubtless he was ready with his excuses when the new monarch would summon him. He sat down and waited. But the King did not summon him. He ignored the existence of Mr Handel. He asked for no Te Deum for his accession, nor received one. Indeed, if there was no actual breach between the King and Handel, the attitude of the former towards the musician at this stage was that of a sovereign who was to follow him later upon the same throne, and who, after an unpleasant incident with a subject, exclaimed: 'We are not amused.'

[1] W. M. Thackeray: *The Four Georges*, p. 33.

CHAPTER VII

THE 'WATER MUSIC',
AND A JOURNEY ABROAD

HOWEVER surly George I may have felt on account of
Handel's failure to return to Hanover, his anger became
appeased. He soon discovered that the name of his runaway
Kapellmeister was everywhere. Society had enshrined him
as the only figure who counted in English music. It was
therefore particularly gratifying to the German monarch to
find that the musician he claimed to have cultivated was
idolized by his new people. Not that George had much liking
for the English; he hated their ways. He came here a German
—and died as German as he came. Only one thing about
the English ever allured or interested him, and that was their
music, which Handel carried to the skies. For the rest, the
English had little appeal to him. Even his mistresses were
mainly German importations.

According to Handel's biographers, King George was so
furiously angry with him that it required a trick on the part
of Baron Kielmansegge, who had become Master of the
King's Horse, to bring them together again. But a document
was discovered in the State Archives at Berlin a few years
ago, and given to me by Professor Michael of Freiburg, which
disproves that delightful romance about the reconciliation
of King George and Handel over the *Water Music*, which
has wandered down the years.

Kielmansegge was a licentious, roving individual who owed
his place at the Court to the King's affection for his wife.
She was past forty years of age when George came to the
throne, and she had the utmost difficulty in getting out of
Hanover to come with him, on account of her many creditors.
Ultimately she got away in disguise in a post-chaise to Holland,
whence she embarked with the King and arrived at his side in
London.[1]

Madame Kielmansegge in her youth had been a remarkably
beautiful woman, but she ultimately became a fat, heavy
individual who had 'two acres of cheeks spread with crimson,

[1] Lady Mary Montagu: *Letters*, Vol. I, p. 7.

an ocean of neck that overflowed and was not distinguished from the lower part of her body.'[1] She remained almost to the time of her death in 1724—except for certain tiffs—the King's chief mistress. The Prince of Wales called her 'Aunt'. When Society required the presence of the monarch at a supper-party, the bait used to draw him was Madame Kielmansegge, albeit she was intensely unpopular in social circles on account of her coarseness and Germanic habits.[2] Kielmansegge, on the other hand, was a philanderer who fawned at the King's feet, who spent his riches like water in trying to please a monarch from whom he received few favours in return.

The romance of the *Water Music*, as history has recorded it, is as follows:[3] In 1715 the strained relations between the King and Handel had reached such a pitch that Kielmansegge decided to step into the breach and patch up the quarrel. As it happened, the King had organized a triumphal procession in barges down the river from Whitehall to Limehouse on 22 August, for which Kielmansegge was charged with the arrangements. This was the Baron's chance. He went to the Earl of Burlington and arranged for Handel to write certain music, which should be played under the musician's own direction, and from a barge which followed the King's so closely that the monarch, on the stillness of the river, would hear every note.

Everything chanced as the Baron decreed. The King, charmed by the music, sent for the Baron, and, congratulating him, asked for information concerning the composer. What more could the Baron do than drag Handel from his hiding-place on the second barge, and lead him to the King's feet? Then ensued excuses, apologies, the royal melting, and, ultimately, the royal clemency and congratulations.

[1] Horace Walpole.
[2] Streatfeild relates a delightful story of Madame Kielmansegge which deserves preservation. When she arrived in London she could speak but little English, and that badly. Once, when out driving, her carriage was surrounded by an anti-German mob, whereupon Madame Kielmansegge put her head out of the carriage window and cried: 'Good people, why do you abuse us? We come for your goods.' 'Aye, damn you!' exclaimed someone in the crowd, 'and for our chattels too!'
[3] This story was begun by Mainwaring and has been slavishly copied by the biographers ever since.

The story is so ridden with romance that it is precisely what ought to have happened. As a matter of fact, the *Water Music* was not produced until 1717, and then under very different circumstances. The document in the Berlin Archives, recently disclosed, is the report made by the Brandenburg envoy to the English Court, Frederic Bonnet, and is dated 19 July 1717. It gives the whole story of the *Water Music* shorn of its romance. It shows that the righteous anger of the King, which had been aroused by Handel's failure to return to the Hanoverian Court, did not exist. The King may have had his annoyance, but, at any rate, when the *Water Music* was produced they were the best of friends. The importance of this document is such that it is of interest to give it in detail.

'Some weeks ago the King expressed a wish to Baron von Kilmanseck to have a concert on the river, by subscription, like the masquerades this winter which the King attended assiduously on each occasion. The Baron addressed himself therefore to Heidegger, a Suisse by nationality, but the most intelligent agent the nobility could have for their pleasures. Heidegger answered that as much as he was eager to oblige his Majesty, he must reserve the subscription for the big enterprises, to wit, the Masquerades, each of which was worth from 300 to 400 guineas to him.

'Baron Kilmanseck, seeing that H.M. was vexed about these difficulties, resolved to give the concert on the river at his own expense, and so the concert took place the day before yesterday. The King entered his barge about eight o'clock with the Duchess of Bolton, the Countess of Godolphin, Mad. de Kilmanseck, Mad. Were, and the Earl of Orkney, gentleman of the King's Bedchamber who was on guard.

'By the side of the Royal barge was that of the musicians to the number of 50 who played all kinds of instruments, viz. trumpets, hunting horns, oboes, bassoons, German flutes, French flutes à bec, violins and basses, but without voices. This concert was *composed expressly for the occasion*[1] by the famous Handel, native of Halle, and first composer of the King's music. It was so strongly approved by H.M. that he commanded it to be repeated, once before and once after

[1] The italics are mine.—Author.

supper, although it took an hour for each performance.

'The evening party was all that could be desired for the occasion. There were numberless barges, and especially boats filled with people eager to take part in it. In order to make it more complete Mad. de Kilmanseck had made arrangements for a splendid supper at the pleasure house of the late Lord Ranelagh at Chelsea on the river, to where the King repaired an hour after midnight. He left there at three, and at half-past four in the morning H.M. was back at St James'. The concert has cost Baron Kilmanseck £150 for the musicians alone, but neither the Prince nor the Princess took any part in the festivities.'

Frederic Bonnet's report, made only two days after the performance in question, is undoubtedly reliable, and explodes all the myths which have endured so long about the *Water Music*. Far from giving any expression to the royal anger, if it existed, King George set about patronizing Handel ere he had scarcely settled down on the throne. Before he had been in England a couple of months he attended a performance of *Rinaldo*, which had been revived in connection with the festivities following the Coronation.[1] He joined at once in the national adulation of Handel. Even if he did not call him to the Court, he was sufficiently a musical enthusiast to realize that the work of this brilliant young German must be respected.

Handel, however, clove to his retirement at Burlington House. If he joined in the national rejoicings it was only as an interested spectator. Nothing came from his pen to celebrate the event. Instead, he wrote a very slight work called *Scilla*, which does not seem to have been performed outside Burlington House.

It was, however, only a prelude to greater things. All the winter he was working on his new opera *Amadigi*.[2] This was the work intended to greet the royal advent. Everything was in his favour. Heidegger had written him a good book, a

[1] Professor Wolfgang Michael: *Englische Geschichte im 18 Jahrhundert*; quotation from report of Frederic Bonnet, dated 24 December 1714.

[2] For a long time the manuscript of *Amadigi* was lost in private ownership, but in 1870 it came into a London auction room and was sold for £35 10s. The score consisted of seventy-three pages. This appears to be the same autograph that was sold in 1844 for £5 5s.

book which ranked with that of *Teseo* as the best he had ever had the joy of setting in these early years. Moreover, Nicolini was back in England, in expectancy of the musical Elector making a great boom in music in London, now that he had the power of the throne behind him.

Amadigi was a love story, tense with great dramatic moments which gave Handel all the chance he wanted, and it was superbly staged. Never before had such scenery been put on at a London opera. Not the least surprise that greeted the spectators, when the work was produced on 25 May, was a real fountain playing on the stage. Crowds rolled up to the doors on the first night, and still greater crowds were turned away. It was the greatest opera night that had been known in London for years.

The King was not present at the first performance of *Amadigi*, but he was a constant visitor afterwards. The opera, together with *Rinaldo*, was frequently given during the year, until the season ended in July. During that time the King was in the habit of going to a play of some kind, or a concert, most evenings. There was no form of musical entertainment in London which he did not patronize continually, for he appeared to be concerned more about music than he did about the best way of understanding his new subjects. He invariably went to the Handel operas incognito, in a hired sedan-chair, and bought a private box, which accounts for the fact that there are few, if any, references to his visits to these operas in the newspapers of the time.[1] On every occasion he was accompanied by one or other of his ladies; sometimes by a party of half a dozen. This blatant parading of his *amours* in front of London in such thin disguise, did little to add to his popularity. The more serious patrons of music became a little disgusted with it. The others found that it added piquancy to Handel's own good entertainment.

The performing honours in *Amadigi* fell to Nicolini. Never had he been heard in better voice; never had he been presented with a part that suited him so well. His love-making as 'Amadigi' carried the house. Brilliant as had been his performances in London before, he had now risen to the heights which were to hold him for so many years.

Associated with him in *Amadigi* was Mrs Anastasia Robinson (as Oriana), a brilliant singer, who had started as a sop-

[1] Frederic Bonnet, report dated 17 July 1717.

rano, but after a fit of sickness her voice sank to a contralto.[1] Mrs Robinson was one of the romantic figures of the eighteenth-century stage, and almost alone in the fact that her morals from first to last were above reproach. She was the daughter of a portrait painter who had a house in Golden Square, a much-travelled personage, who spoke a number of languages. Eventually he went blind, and Anastasia, little more than a girl, was called upon to keep him. He had educated her well. Finding that she had a voice out of the common, he started a series of weekly concerts at his house, to which people of all grades of society came to hear the girl sing. Mrs Delany, who knew Mrs Robinson well, is the better person to describe her. 'She was of middling stature, not handsome, but of a pleasing modest countenance, with large blue eyes; her deportment easy, unaffected, and graceful; her manner and address very engaging, and her behaviour on all occasions that of a gentlewoman.'[2]

From the Golden Square conversaziones Anastasia Robinson passed on to opera, and, in spite of the comparatively short seasons, she was able to make as much as a thousand pounds a year, while her presents and emoluments amounted to as much again. Admirers flocked about her in plenty. Among the many was the elderly Lord Peterborough, a peer chiefly notable for his violent fits of temper, who, after the death of Mr Robinson, settled Anastasia and her mother in a house which he took at Fulham. One day, towards the end of his life, the irascible gentleman called all his friends together, including Anastasia. After extolling the lady's virtues in a long preamble, he announced that he had been married to her for years! Consternation ran through the social dovecotes. How the secret had been kept was a puzzle to everybody. Anastasia, to whom so many of them had openly made love, aye, and in the presence of the husband himself on occasion! The affair became the talk of the town. Then, having made the announcement, Lord Peterborough took his wife off to Lisbon and promptly died. A happy release for the lady whose 'principles and fortitude of mind, supported her through many severe trials in her conjugal state'.[3]

Yet she had a curious respect for him, just as he always

[1] Burney.
[2] Mrs Delany: *Life and Correspondence*, Vol. I, p. 72.
[3] Mrs Delany: *Life and Correspondence*, Vol. I, p. 73.

exercised a strange and unexplainable fascination for her. After his death she discovered that he had written his secret memoirs, in which he declared that he had been guilty of actions that reflected very much upon his character.[1] Whereupon, with that respect she might give to a god of stone, she burnt them. A great and wonderful fidelity. How opposite to the Georgian principle, which, instead of respecting the dead, explored their faults in order to decorate oneself with virtue for having endured them!

How now had the gaiety of London changed under the influence of this Hanoverian importation? The secret pleasure gangs—which did not dare to prate too loudly while the pious Anne held the throne, breathing alternately texts and venom against all Germans—now hid themselves no longer. The King was everywhere; pleasure haunts lured him. The Court was packed with bright-eyed women, who talked against each other in differing languages. The King knew no English and did not wish to know any. When his dulled intelligence did assimilate ultimately a few words, he pronounced them in such German fashion that both the English and German followers looked askance at each other as if to inquire whether the King was talking in a tongue unknown to either of them.

The old roistering monarch had become corpulent. He waddled painfully and sat a horse like a loose sack of hay. He was faithful to a few mistresses. Madame Schulenburg, Duchess of Kendal, was the favourite, which upset Madame Kielmansegge extremely, so that one day she went to the King and, in a storm of tears, asked why he had passed her by. The dull old courtier fell back on the usual lie. He considered her the greatest beauty of his Court; he had always done so. 'Then why do you spend all your time with Madame Schulenburg, and I hardly ever receive the honour of a visit from you?' persisted the outraged lady.[2] George took refuge in a silly laugh. The obese madame had won her battle.

In his declining years George abruptly changed his mind about women, and imported to St James's Palace a wondrous dark-eyed beauty, Anna Brett. The 'Maypole', as they had nicknamed the Duchess, on account of her height and leanness, was forgotten. Salons laughed and jeered. For once the King

[1] *Ibid.*, Vol. I, p. 74.
[2] Lady Mary Montagu: *Letters*, p. 9.

had chosen an English mistress. What honour! Then when the old rascal died miserably of a seizure in a coach in Holland, the lady was spirited out of St James's with the same suddenness as she came to it. One of those unnecessary chattels that pass so soon when death claims a King.

Ten years afterwards, Anna Brett emerged again. She flung a challenge to the social dovecotes by marrying Sir William Leman, a lover who had been in the background during the time when the fancies of the fatuous monarch from Hanover had held her in thrall. The marriage was performed by a Fleet parson. Lady Montagu wrote to the Countess of Pomfret about the affair. She was frank. Anna had no heroism in her eyes. 'I knew not whether to say Sir William Leman was very unlucky in not dying two years before he had committed such a folly which will make his memory ridiculous; or very fortunate in having time given him to indulge his inclination, and not time enough to see it in its proper light.'[1]

Poor George! Your secret love in a royal palace lost all its romance when you died in that Osnaburg coach. And your spirit which haunted another of your left-handed widows as a black raven, must have been sorrowful when the Fleet parson set agog all the tongues of Society! Anna Brett! Your sudden discovery, the lady with the Spanish black eyes!

When the opera season came to an end in June 1716, the King was all haste to be off. He had endured as much London as he could swallow in one portion. So, at the beginning of July he packed himself up bag and baggage, Madame Kielmansegge, Madame Schulenburg, and departed for Hanover, very vague as to whether he would ever come back. Handel, who was now so strongly in his graces that he had been appointed music-master to the little princesses, went with him.

Once back in Hanover, George set to work to enjoy himself. He was sick with over-abundant dinners of English food, which execrable fare, he declared, always upset his stomach. He wanted his heavy plain German meals. He wanted to wallow again in German beer, as he always made a point of doing, usually in the rooms of his ladies, after the principal meal of the day. His beer and tobacco! They were more necessary to him than the crazy crown of England that sat so awkwardly on his brow. He loved to lie hunched up in the biggest chair in the room, his ruffle and vest spattered and

[1] *Ibid.*, Vol. II, p. 107.

stained with snuff, his feet extended, a long pipe in his hand, and a copious draught at his elbow, while Schulenburg digressed upon anything, or spat venom at Madame Kielmansegge. To which George laughed and rolled with the discomfort of the over-fed animal. But even Schulenburg must soon have tired him with her moods, or her temper, which was violent. Suddenly he sent her off to drink the waters, and betook himself to Herrenhausen and its linden trees.[1]

Unlike his royal master, Handel had no inclination to idle. Success had come to him. Youth, strength, a mental activity that was never still, were his. What had Germany done for music in his absence? He would go and see. He left Hanover. Hamburg knew him again. He went to Halle. Here he found that old Zachow, who had first trained his youthful fingers to the mysteries of the organ in the Liebfrauenkirche, was dead. More than that, he had left an ageing widow in a state of penury. Infirm during the closing years of his life, the old man had slipped lower and lower, hiding his hurt under a veneer of pride. The hermit life had closed in about Zachow. The power to compose passed as sight passes from the eyes of the very aged. The only joy of those last slow years was occasional letters from his old pupil in England. Verily was Handel's visit to Halle that autumn a melancholy one. How often that big generous nature had declared that it owed all to Zachow. The only consolation now left to Handel was to help the widow Zachow had left behind.

From Halle, Handel went on to Anspach, where he met Johann Christoph Schmidt, an old friend of his university days. Schmidt had a large family and not a pfennig with which to keep them. His was precisely the sort of case that appealed to Handel. He could not leave Schmidt to his penury. Schmidt could be useful to him; he would make him useful. So he told Schmidt frankly that he could not afford to transport him and all his belongings to England, but if he had a taste for adventure he might leave the family behind in the care of friends, and return to London with him. Schmidt agreed. He found someone willing to assume responsibility for his family in Anspach—a thing easier done in those days than now—and set out for England with Handel. It was the beginning of a great friendship. Schmidt became

[1] Letter from J. Clavering, Esq., to Lady Cowper, 4 September 1716.

plain Mr Smith in London, and soon spoke the King's English quite elegantly. A year later he had saved enough to send to Anspach for his family, and soon the whole tribe of Schmidts were nestled under the wing of Handel; including little John Christopher Smith, then five years old.

The two Christopher Smiths, father and son, stand out as strong, strange figures in the subsequent life of Handel. See what happens. The father becomes a sort of general factotum to the composer. He writes his letters, and in association with other scribes, copies his music, and practically assumes the position of business manager.[1] Later on, little Christopher, who has shown distinct signs of musical ability, is taught his notes by Handel, then Dr Pepusch takes him over and completes the training. The years roll on. More and more the lives of these twain move into the life of Handel. He cannot do without them. In later life the younger Smith begins to compose. He produces some stray pieces, he produces an opera, then another, an oratorio, he sets Shakespeare. He is a satellite swirling round a constellation, never to be more than star-dust lost in the fires of the other. Handel's influence shaped him, made him. Throughout Handel's later years, when *gutta serena* blinded his eyes, it was to the elder Christopher Smith that he dictated his work. No man was ever better served than Handel by the elder Smith.

The association of these Smiths with Handel is the romance of a friendship, which started at a university. They shared his triumphs, they stood by him in his failures, and neither the crustiness of age nor the waywardness of circumstance ever broke that loyalty which the younger Smith yielded as votive offering to the genius.

But to return to Anspach. What trivial mission sent Handel there no record has revealed. Some have said that it was an errand on which he had been sent by the Princess. Certainly

---

[1] The Smiths, mainly the father, appear to have made three copies of all Handel's music. A portion of one set is divided between the British Museum and the Fitzwilliam Museum at Cambridge; a number of copies of the second set, containing Handel's pencilled corrections, are at the Hamburg Museum. The third set was given to the first Earl of Aylesford by Jennens, who was associated with Handel in *Messiah*, and has now passed into my possession. In addition to the copies made by the elder Smith, Handel employed other copyists—or else the Smiths did, for there are copies of parts in many hands.—Author.

he did not stay very long. He had, as a matter of fact, set to music—as Keiser and Telemann had done before him—the Passion of Senator Barth by Heinrich Brockes of Hamburg, a vain fellow with a certain cleverness and knowledge of poetry. Brockes had been a student at Halle University, and actually left the University in the year that Handel entered it. Mattheson declared that Handel sent his setting over from London, that it came in 'uncommon close-written score',[1] but Mattheson was unquestionably wrong. Handel, full of success with his operas, would scarcely have wandered off on such a side-track without some inbreaking influence being responsible. With one of his little conceits, he set the Brockes Passion so that the German people should judge between his setting and those of Keiser and Telemann. A couple of years later, Mattheson made a fourth setting in the hope of obscuring his three rivals.

All of which must have been distinctly diverting to Brockes. Vain to a degree, the commotion and rivalry between the principal composers of the day to set his words would be a joy to his heart. He was a short, fat person, a student of sorts, and his poetry was good. Where he came from no one knew. Who his parents had been was a matter of conjecture. But he emerged from the underworld in Rome in 1703, and was eventually closely associated with Corelli and the stars of Rome's musical firmament.

Brockes' own story of what made him write this Passion is worth recording. The self-appraise and snobbery is so typical of him. Says he:

'When, however, I became aware that poetry, in so far as it is not directed to a particular and that is a useful end, be but an empty play of words, not deserving of any great esteem, I endeavoured to choose such objects for my poetical art by which the people, apart from a permissible amusement, might derive edification. Thus I wrote firstly the *Passion-Oratorium*, afterwards translated into several languages. I had it performed very solemnly at my house, which, as something uncommon, brought me to not only the whole foreign nobility, all the Ministers and Residents with their ladies, but also the greater part of the most eminent Hamburg people, so that over 500 people were

[1] *Ehren-Pforte*.

present, which gave me no small pleasure, the more so, as everything, praise be to God! went off in the best order without all confusion, and to the enjoyment of the whole audience.'[1]

Brockes's adventuring was not confined to his own literary efforts. His love-affairs caused him to call even more frequently upon his Maker. About this time—shortly before the Handel version of his Passion came into being—he was on the look-out for a rich wife, and tried his fortune in various quarters, proceeding in a most business-like fashion. This vulgar little person is seen on his own showing darting about, making inquiries concerning dowries, no matter how plain or beauteous the maidens, and still more careless as to their sentiments towards himself. When a bargain did not come off he wrote: 'Whereas I perceived all the more God's wise direction, I recognize more than too well the great cause I have to give thanks to Him.'[2]

Ultimately, he did secure a bride, and then the paean of praise to his Deity rose in a falsetto of delight. He made the acquaintance of Fräulein Anna Ilsabe Lehmann, 'and as she was by the gifts of body, mind, and fortune—especially after the recent death of her father—one of the most considerable parties, I formed the resolution, in God's name, to sue for her hand, wherein, Praise be to God! I succeeded. And with the said A. I. L., my fiancée, I was married Ao. 1714 Febr, by Pastor Heinson. The great God from whom all good doth flow, be praised!'[3]

Unless they had met as students at Halle University, it is doubtful if Handel ever saw this wretched little man, whose eyes were on the money-bags and his glib tongue on his God. Handel's version of the Passion was performed in Hamburg after his return to England.

The King left Hanover for London at the beginning of January 1717, and Handel followed quickly in his train. *Rinaldo* and *Amadigi* were immediately revived and played to full houses. With the return of the King the old gaieties—

[1] *Zeitschrift des Vereines für hamburgische Geschichte*, Vol. II, p. 167, *et seq.*
[2] *Ibid.*
[3] *Ibid.*

the over-eating and drinking, the licentiousness—the concert rooms and the lesser theatres, took to themselves a new vitality. But opera collapsed. French comedies and lewd farces captured the mood of the town. Also, they pleased the King and his ladies.

So London reverted to its old habits. A London more decadent. A London from which all musical art had for the time being passed. Promoters would no longer put up the money for opera when lewdness paid better.

Meanwhile, the King had his oysters and beer and made merry.

CHAPTER VIII

CANNONS

WHATEVER plans Handel may have made for the future of opera when he returned to England, were quickly destined to yield him nothing but disappointment. London wanted no more opera. The changed mood of the people must have disgusted him. Musicians of quality were sent out of business; the foreigners returned to their native cities. The English performers migrated to the concert rooms and coffee-taverns, or picked up a precarious living by means of promiscuous engagements in Society. For nearly three years opera ceased to exist in London.

Things were desperate for Handel. He had his pension and his £200 a year for teaching music to the Royal Princesses. Beyond that his income had ceased, save for the lesser fees which a few aristocratic pupils brought him. It was useless for him to compose; no one would back him. His savings, if he had any, must have been meagre, for others had taken the greater portion of the money which his brains had brought to the Haymarket. 'Any musician worth the name must now turn a gentleman and be sure of a patron,' exclaimed Heidegger, who, never at a loss to improve the shining hour, was engaged in earning a living by running masquerades of very doubtful morality.

It was then that Handel discovered James Brydges, Earl of Carnarvon, or, more probably, the Earl discovered Handel. Carnarvon was a rich rogue. He had been Paymaster-General during the Marlborough Wars, and had made a very good thing out of it for himself. He became in some mysterious manner fabulously rich. People began to talk. A royal commission was set up to inquire into the Army's accounts, and the Earl's connection with them, but, after sitting for a considerable period and wasting everybody's time, it had to admit that, if the Earl had been a plunderer—as he unquestionably had—then he had hidden his guilt very well.

But the exoneration of the Earl did not allay the talk of the town. The ex-Paymaster played a careful game. He would give them something to talk about. As it chanced, he had inherited a considerable estate at Cannons, near Edgware, through his first wife. Therefore, in 1712, when the whole of England was calling him a thief and a robber, and Swift was aiming shafts at him to the effect that the man who plundered the nation was losing the money in stocks, the Earl set out to build such a palace at Cannons as the King himself might envy.

He did so. Two hundred and thirty thousand pounds that house cost him. It had marble columns, an amazing marble staircase, which afterwards went to Chesterfield House. A theatre with a Jordan organ. A dining-hall with a large music-room opening from it, where his band played during meals. He brought painters from Italy to paint the ceilings. He had eight old campaigners from Chelsea, who were dressed as Swiss Guards, and were given comfortable houses in the grounds to live in, with the duty of guarding the palace by night, and calling out the hours of the clock through the watches. There was no luxury, no notion of comfort belonging to that epoch, which he did not adopt. It was his answering challenge to the public which had suspected him.

The first portion of the house was ready for residence in 1713, and the Earl moved in with great state, and installed Dr Pepusch as *Kapellmeister* over a big gathering of Italian and English musicians. Then, as if to throw a sop to the people, he reconstructed the beautiful little church of Whitchurch hard by, put in its Grinling Gibbons carvings, and its paintings by the same Italian artists who were at work on the mansion. This done, he presented it with a set of Communion plate bearing an inscription to the effect that the church had been restored by that 'most honourable man, James Earl of Carnarvon'.

In short, the Earl had no enmity with his conscience. He spent money lavishly; he looked after the poor. Then in 1718 he got rid of Pepusch. The music of Pepusch was becoming dull. That of Handel was never brighter. The Earl, who knew —or thought he knew—good music as he understood good wine, changed his *Kapellmeisters*.

Whatever may have been the purpose for which the Earl threw over Pepusch to secure Handel, it could not have been for composition, for Handel composed little at Cannons. It may have been that the calls upon his time as *Kapellmeister* were heavy, or else there was lack of incentive. The Earl entertained heavily, the Prince of Wales, dukes and lords—all the aristocracy who could be induced to brave the dangers of the Edgware Road for a meal, rendered on rather sumptuous lines, were welcome, if they did not mind having their pockets picked on the way. At that time the Edgware Road was notorious for footpads. The Earl was held up. More than once he came to the rescue of other unfortunates, for he certainly had courage. A man who could deftly purloin vast thousands of the public's money without a tremor, and, at a time when discovery of the default meant death, had no lack of courage. Cannons was the show-house near London; it was a treasure-house of luxury. The Prince of Wales, eager to take up anything of which his father did not approve, smiled genially upon the gallant embezzler who ruled in regal state there.

As regards big work, Handel was merely marking time. He wrote his *Chandos Te Deum*, which was privately performed in the Chandos Theatre or the adjacent Whitchurch. The Earl now resided for the main part in Albemarle Street, and Handel, with his royal music lessons, could scarcely afford to be shut up in a deserted palace to which his patron came only when the mood took him. That he composed *Esther* on the organ at Whitchurch, as the plate on the instrument still declares, is pure fabrication. To begin with, Handel never composed on the organ. If he had occasion to use an instrument for this purpose it would most probably have been the harpsichord, or, if he had wanted an organ to achieve the work, the very beautiful instrument in the Earl's chapel adjoining the mansion, and which is now at Gosport, would have been sufficient for his requirements.

Rejoicing in the fact that he had the greatest *Kapellmeister* in England, the Earl threaded his way through those centres of Society which rejoiced in the cult of good music. He was an odd creature, sternly apart in culture from those in whom was the strain of real art. What art he possessed was bought. The gorgeous painted windows of his chapel were secured by the outpouring of gold to buy the best that money could tempt. His marble staircase was bought because it was marble. He secured Handel because Handel stood at the head of representative musical thought of the day. With his campaigners disguised as Swiss Guards, he attempted a pomp which might throw equality at the King of England. He was tolerably moral, and he allowed three wives to suffer him without unduly straining their fidelity.

The biographers have recorded that once when he was out riding he discovered the groom of a neighbouring nobleman unmercifully thrashing his wife. The Earl gave the man a good pommelling, then bought the woman from him. She was young and he educated her, and the drunken husband quickly went to the grave with the aid of the Chandos money, and the liquor it purchased. About this time the Duchess of Chandos died, and the Earl, more than a little perplexed at what to do with the bargain he had secured, married her.

Of course the story ought to be true. They tell it still about Whitchurch as a remnant of the majesty of Chandos that once graced the neighbouring fields till, within a century of its erection, the mansion and all its treasures were sold for £70,000. But, unhappily for the story, it was not the Earl, but his son Henry, who bought the woman. He may have married her or he may not, but one thing is certain, the Earl married three wives—all from the peerage—and two of them lie at his side in the tomb at Whitchurch.

The life at Cannons was certainly the quietest period in Handel's life. It was the lull before the storm. When he finished at Cannons he was to go into the whirlpool of management, to the pit of execration from his rivals. But that day was not yet. There is no record that he composed his *Suite de Pièces pour le Clavecin* at Cannons, and they had been more or less his lessons for his royal pupils. A musical publisher of the prowling variety had obtained the lessons and published them, so that Handel was compelled for his own sake to put out an authoritative edition, with a comment to the effect that 'I have added several new ones to make the work more useful, which if it meets with a favourable reception I will still proceed to publish more, reckoning it my duty with my small talent to serve a nation from which I have received so generous a protection.'

These *Pièces pour le Clavecin* provided one of the great mysteries which have surrounded Handel for two centuries, for the air and variations from the fifth suite is that descriptive melody known as 'The Harmonious Blacksmith'. In Whitchurch churchyard there is a tomb—you will find it a little apart, and defined still to the memory of William Powell, the harmonious blacksmith, parish clerk during the time the immortal Handel was organist of the church. Poor William Powell! Poor Handel! Both of you have been jumbled together in a conspiracy which a couple of upstarts, choristers of the Chapel Royal, named Clark and Wylde, thought the world would never discover.

There never was a harmonious blacksmith! Never in his life did Handel seek refuge during a thunderstorm in a blacksmith's shop and, hearing the even beat of the hammer on the anvil, go out when the storm was over, to compose the immortal melody. Handel never knew a piece called 'The Harmonious Blacksmith', because the piece did not gain that name until 1820, when he had been dead over sixty years. No one ever heard of Handel and his thunderstorm until 1835, when *The Times* first published a letter from an anonymous correspondent provoking the legend of the blacksmith's forge. After that, the story built itself up. A man named Wylde discovered an old anvil in a blacksmith's forge near Whitchurch. Of course it must be Handel's! His friend, Richard Clark, who had posed as an authority on Handel without being found out—a fellow-chorister by the way—came to his aid. They built up a story about Powell, the blacksmith, a Whitchurch parishioner who died in 1780. They gave him a birthday that was not his, they jocularly placed him into an early grave, and they ended by getting up a public subscription to the fellow, so that they could erect a wooden monument, to which they added that it was the result of the efforts of Richard Clark and Henry Wylde.

Once the legend made progress it went from bad to worse. About the middle of last century the people of Whitchurch came to the conclusion that a wooden memorial was scarcely good enough to perpetuate the memory of such an immortal personage as the harmonious blacksmith. So they dragged poor Powell's name into a new scheme. They took away the wooden memorial and erected a stone one, which still remains, and inscribed it to William Powell, the Harmonious Blacksmith, who was Parish Clerk during the time the immortal Handel was organist of the church! Never in his career was Handel organist of the church there. In addition, the new monument was decorated with the musical notes B and E, which were supposed to be the notes made by an anvil on being struck! All blatant imagination!

Thus had the tissue of lies invented by Clark and Wylde grown apace, until it had become difficult to disbelieve it. The title, 'The Harmonious Blacksmith', was also arrived at in equally idle fashion. There was a youth named William Lintern, the son of a Bath bookseller who was apprenticed at a blacksmith's, and was by way of being an average amateur musician. His favourite piece of music was the one in question, which he was always singing until his friends nicknamed him the harmonious blacksmith. Ere long, the title passed on to the piece itself, and it was first published under that name somewhere about 1822. Thus, after many vicissitudes, the piece, which had been written for the cumbersome fingers of a princess, settled down to certain popularity under a title which would have made Handel smile. Still more would he have smiled when the anvil which the smith was supposed to be beating, at the time he took refuge from the storm, came into the auction room, and was knocked down as a treasure of great price, because of the master's association with it!

At the beginning of 1719 Handel composed the twelve anthems which, in honour of the Earl—who had been made Duke of Chandos in April—were called the Chandos Anthems. They were first performed in the chapel at Cannons. How the newly created Duke, ageing, gouty, sitting in his magnificent high pew which was smothered with perfect carving and his dignity, must have tried to understand the wonder of Handel as he listened to 'As pants the hart', or 'O let us sing unto the Lord'. Doubtless he felt not so satisfied with the music as he was with the knowledge that he owned what other rich men lacked—the man who could write these things! Handel must have been equally satisfied with his patron, or he would not have broken out into his paean of praise to the Maker of all things on the occasion of the newly acquired dukedom.

But there were other things which were engaging his attention more closely in the first months of 1719. A rebellion had set in amongst the little circle in London who loved good music, against the sickening stuff that was being offered in the theatres. Something must be done to lift music from the gutter. Something must be done to persuade the King to take a passing interest in music of quality, or it would fade for ever from England. The country had the men in Handel and Heidegger—a wonderful combination of musician and producer—to engage the task. But they must be provided with ample funds. Money at the moment was cheap. Gambling in stocks and shares was going on in fevered fashion, and the South Sea Bubble was swelling before it ultimately broke. Fortunes were being made and dissipated in enjoyment, both licentious and artistic. There were many people who had grown tired of the ceaseless filth of the bawdy comedians, and they readily combined with the genuine music lovers in the new attempt to put music on a proper footing.

The King was approached. He wanted a new diversion, and he was more than conscious that he had of late neglected the musician whom he had once talked about as his protégé. Handel was wasted at Cannons, the King declared. He would give a thousand pounds to start a Royal Academy of Music. A company was formed; it was the hour for companies. Some of the subscribers thought they were going to make big dividends out of promoting music which many of them did not pretend to understand. Five hundred shares of £100 each were sold almost before the ink was dry on the prospectus.

Handel was secured. Heidegger was given a contract as producer to the fledgling Academy. The Duke of Newcastle became governor; Lord Burlington a director of the new venture. The latter, as the result of a journey to Italy, had brought over Giovanni Bononcini, and at Burlington's instigation he was also made a director. The star of this great effort for music rose high. The Duke of Chandos, being a *nouveau riche*, was either not approached, or declined to throw in his weight with the Academy. Nevertheless he could not prohibit the services of Handel since the King was the principal shareholder in the concern.

The importance of the Academy cannot be overrated in the effect its influence had upon Handel's career. Though it afterwards came to a sorry end, it educated a section of the London masses to the brilliance of Handel. When the New Year of 1719 dawned it drew the mentality of the mob away from that which was tawdry and of ill-savour in musical entertainment. Not a moment did Handel rest. He apparently forgot Cannons and remained in London. On 20 February he wrote to his brother-in-law, Michaelsen: 'I find myself detained here by indispensable business, on which it is not too much to say that my whole fortune depends, and which takes much longer than I expected.' His sister had died, and this letter gave his excuse for not crossing to the Continent to share the family grief. 'I entreat you, dear brother, to assure my mother of my obedience,' he continued. Verily his thoughts must have been at the Schlamm house where death had stolen in again. In the same letter he refers to a gift of pewter which he is sending to his brother-in-law, and adds: 'I will ever entertain remembrance of your goodness to my late sister, and my gratitude will last as long as my life.'[1]

Four days later he replied to his old friend Mattheson in Hamburg, who had written seeking a favour: 'You can judge for yourself that it demands more time for consideration than I am able to spare from the pressing occupations with which I am surrounded.' Simultaneously there appeared in the Press the following announcement: 'Mr Handel, a famous Master of Musick, is gone beyond the sea, by order of His Majesty, to collect a company of the choicest singers for the Opera in the Haymarket.'[2]

It was a rushed journey. He first stayed at Düsseldorf, he passed on to Dresden. He went to Halle, and spent a few days with his mother to mourn with her over the family loss of the adorable Dorothea Sophie. Deeper and deeper was the gloom settling over the Schlamm house. Now he was the only child left of the old barber-surgeon's second family. What a fading away of all that holds one to life the years had brought to the woman who, as Dorothea Taust, had come out of the seclusion of the Giebichenstein parsonage to marry the barber-surgeon, and bear him four children—the first a son to die at birth, the second a son who was to carry the Handel name to the far corners of the earth till the end of time, the third a daughter who had married Dr Michaelsen, and the fourth a daughter who had died of consumption just as Europe had begun to talk of the surviving brother.

Deeper and deeper still the burden of grief bore down the old lady. Her years were mounting. Her eyes had begun to fail. Soon she was to know the utter dark which, at this era, so frequently came to the aged. Tante Anna, the little old spinster, was withering up. What could life offer Frau Handel now save that vague intangible thing—the fame of this son? It meant nothing to her; she could not understand. He moved with kings and the nobility; in a vast circle of feckless creatures— was there anything in that? His melody swept through the theatres of Europe—was there anything in that? What could she make of it all? She who had never been thirty miles beyond Halle in her life. Perchance this son of hers sat at the harpsi-

---

[1] His brother-in-law outlived him by more than twenty years.
[2] *Weekly Journal*, 21 February 1719.

chord during his visit and played something that reflected his mood. Even then could the softened notes of the instrument make her understand exactly the meaning of his fame? But if he could have transported her on some magic carpet to a night of *Rinaldo* or *Amadigi*—if he could have perched her somewhere where she could see and hear all and not be seen—the King and his ladies, Society in its soft melting colours under the yellow lights, the hustle, the talk, the excitement, the transcendent music, the voices rising wondrous in their melody as if the stars might hear—then, and only then, could he have made her understand what this art, for which he had wandered far, had meant to him. She was never to learn these things. Only sight, only actual sounds could teach her. His words, his strumming on a weak instrument, could do naught but mystify her the more.

Hearing that Handel was at Halle, Bach walked from Leipzig to meet him. But he was too late. On the day that he entered the town Handel left it to return to England. One must wonder what would have been the effect of a meeting between Bach and Handel. Bach's veneration of Handel, his vain journey over those weary miles is one of the most pathetic episodes in all musical history. It was a pilgrimage to meet a kindred soul. This simple, unspoiled man, searching beyond the thoughts of others, wanting to meet another lonely soul who searched as he!

Handel's quest for singers during this tour was unquestionably a success. This was due mainly to the fact that he happened to arrive at Dresden when the opera season there was in full swing, and a particularly strong company of singers, Italians mainly, was performing. He had no scruples. He promptly engaged the best of them, and, signing the contracts, told them to follow him to England as quickly as they reasonably could. There was Senesino, the famous *castrato*, Signora Durastanti, who had sung for Handel in Venice in *Agrippina*, and who was now to become his *prima donna*, Signora Salvai, and Boschi, the bass, who had previously appeared in *Rinaldo*. The biggest catch of all was Senesino, for, at this period, *castrati* were the rage of London, and Senesino was as fine a *castrato* as ever appeared on the London boards. His voice was a mezzo-soprano, 'clear, penetrating, and flexible, his intonation faultless, his shake perfect. Purity, simplicity, and expressiveness, were the characteristics of his style.'[1]

Senesino took his name from the town of Siena, in which he was born. He had been a street urchin with a divine voice. His singing, the wonderment of a voice 'all sweetness and sadness', made someone take him up. He started his career singing in the smaller theatres in Rome, where he took the part of first 'woman' in an intermezzo performed between the acts of a comedy. Little did Handel foresee when he engaged Senesino the trouble this man was to cause him. He knew not that this tall, overpowering figure was to prove a monument of vanity.

Directly Senesino came to London he developed into a demi-god in Society. Handsome in a coarse fashion, he had the manner of a gallant. His height, his straight figure—and he was head and shoulders above other men—the peculiar sweetness of his voice, whether talking or singing, gave to this sexless creature a lure. It was his singing that brought the women to the stage door, but they came for no other reason than to see him pass out. Women from every grade of Society, peeresses incognito, melancholy wives of respectable city merchants, little wretched courtesans of the streets—they crowded each other there, in dresses of rich silks and satins or rags dragging in the murky pools of rain between the stones, hungry for a look, a word.

For these women who admired him, Senesino had extreme contempt. He was blind vanity riding roughshod over everything, all emotion. He had no sense of humanity. He had no respect for anything that did not directly or indirectly turn again to himself. His rudeness, his coarseness towards women on the slightest provocation was the talk of the town. Once he was so coarse to Anastasia Robinson on the stage that the gouty Earl of Peterborough strode behind the scenes and gave him a sound flogging. This was before the secret marriage between himself and Anastasia had been declared. Poor Senesino, like a vanquished giant, was forced to confess upon his knees that Anastasia was a nonpareil of virtue and beauty.[2] Verily the irascible old peer never had a more justified outburst of temper.

Handel's life in those early months of 1720 knew no rest. He was in no place long. He ate little, slept little. He foresaw, or

[1] Grove's *Dictionary of Music*.
[2] Lady Mary Montagu, letter to the Countess of Mar, February 1724.

thought he foresaw, that this Academy would place him for all time at the head of English music. He anticipated better attention from the King than the Academy ever received, and he believed that the cheap claptrap which was rotting the musical taste of London would be wiped out. In short, he anticipated the greatest musical revival in the history of any nation. He worked ceaselessly, composing between the different tasks of arranging for productions, engaging artistes, discussing scenery. He sat at boards. He moved in the social dining circles of the town, playing the harpsichord after dinner with an ease that would suggest a lack of interest in all commercial concerns. But during the press of the day he had begun to show that snappiness of temper which acute anxiety provoked more certainly in him as his age advanced.

Not that he had forgotten Cannons. Between 1718–20 he had produced on the Duke's stage *Acis and Galatea*, the setting of a piece of thrown-off brilliance by Gay, but a very different *Acis* to that which he was to produce thirteen years later. It was performed by the Duke's chorus and orchestra, and there is some doubt if it had more than one performance. Handel did not set much store by the masque, for he put it away in a drawer, and there it remained for years. What he was busy upon, however, was an opera on the grand scale which should open the first season of the Academy or be its chief production. In *Radamisto* Haym had again provided him with a fine libretto. It was an adaptation from Tacitus, and Handel must have written the music at odd times between his strenuous hours in organizing the Academy. *Radamisto* proved to be one of the greatest operas he ever produced in England.

Radamisto was not ready when the Academy opened at the beginning of April, otherwise there is no doubt it would have been given. Giovanni Porta's *Numitor*, a very indifferent work, was put on and ran six nights. A sorry beginning, but it was, in a sense, no more than a curtain-raiser for *Radamisto*. No one wanted *Numitor*, and apparently few went to see it. Everyone, on the other hand, was talking about *Radamisto*, which was then in active rehearsal, and on 27 April 1720 it was produced.

The *Radamisto* première was the greatest triumph Handel had yet attained. The opera had been well publicized by small talk at dinner-tables up and down Society. All the seats were sold long before the week of production, and people were offering forty shillings for a seat in the gallery![1] The King was there with his ladies.[2] The crush was terrible, and the inconvenience of the stuffy and ill-ventilated theatre must have made it resemble the later black hole of Calcutta.

It was entirely Handel's triumph, for he put on no singers of note, since Senesino had not yet finished up at Dresden.[3] The new opera, with its melodious arias, its tenderness, its martial conceptions, its bold design, carried London. The other theatres, the concert rooms with their ribaldries, which were an effrontery to all decent people, began to empty. The crowds flocked to *Radamisto* like a modern mob to a notorious prize-fight, and the opera had an unbroken run till the season ended on 25 June.

All that had been expected of Handel he had fulfilled. The Academy was established. Music of quality had been restored to the public taste. *Radamisto* was the most popular opera of its epoch, and its success suggested that the public only required good music to persuade its patronage from licentious farces. The airs from *Radamisto* were being sung everywhere. They even reached to the Continent, and a year later Mattheson produced the opera in Germany under the title of *Zenobia*.

The demand for the music compelled Handel to seek its immediate publication. He had left his original London publisher, Walsh. Maybe he was still piqued by the remembrance of the money which Walsh netted over *Rinaldo*. About eight years passed before he went to Walsh again with a score under his arm, and during that time he had plenty of charges of perfidy to bring against him. Walsh pirated music. Handel even accused him of pirating some of the work he published with other houses but there is no proof that he did. Albeit Walsh was a notorious stealer from the productions of the publishing houses of Paris and Amsterdam, which, at the time, were the principal foreign centres from which printed music emanated.

Walsh was also making considerable money by purloining or adapting the work of English musicians as well as that of foreigners. He had done so for a long time. Some years previously he had made a curious admission of the fact in a

[1] Mainwaring, p. 99.
[2] Lady Cowper: *Diary*.
[3] Though Durastanti appeared in the first performance of *Radamisto*, Senesino did not appear in the work until much later.

London paper.[1] Having stolen the work of a composer he had the audacity to call it a reprisal! In an advertisement, dedicated to all lovers of music, he said:

'Whereas in the *Post-Man* of Saturday last Mr Topham has published that I have printed a spurious edition of his sonatas, and maliciously undersell them, now the only true reason of my reprinting these Sonatas is by way of reprisal on Luke Pippard who has lately copied on me the opera of *Clotilda* though in a very imperfect manner. To discourage such practice, I hereby give notice that I have reprinted a second edition of the said sonatas, and sell them for 2/6d. the Set, which is of the same character and more correct than the said Pippard's Edition. The like method of reprisal will be used on the said Pippard, let who will be the author of the Musick. Witness my hand—JOHN WALSH.'

As Walsh had only paid Handel twenty guineas an opera, and had unquestionably made large sums out of him, Handel —when *Radamisto* became a boom—decided that something must be done to protect himself from the fellow. So, while the opera was running, he took out a patent for his music, which would protect him for fourteen years. He had *Radamisto* brought out by a rising music publisher, Richard Meares, who had started in business about ten years before, and had a shop, 'The Golden Viol', at the top of Ludgate Hill. Meares was a popular figure at the concerts in the taverns there, which Handel often attended after playing the organ at St Paul's. It was at one of them that musician and publisher met for the first time.

Handel had yet another reason for publishing his *Radamisto* with Meares. When he brought John Christopher Schmidt from Anspach to London, he not only made him his business manager, but set him up as a music-seller at a shop, the 'Hand Musick Book', in Coventry Street, Haymarket. Here young John Christopher Smith was running about behind the counter selling music to Society's amateur performers. Handel, in publishing *Radamisto* with Meares, must have connived some working arrangement between publisher and music-seller, for both Meares' and Smith's names appear on the title-page of the first edition.

* * *

[1] *The Tatler*, No. 98, 22 November 1709.

When the curtain came down on *Radamisto* on that June night Handel had completed a phase of his life—probably the happiest phase of his life. All these works (*Radamisto* among them) had been the achievements of youth, for, although he was now thirty-five, both mind and body had all the attributes of early youth. That mind which knew no dullness, nor ever lost its brilliance, was to mature; his body, as youth passed, to halt in its freshness. He never studied his health. Only when illness pulled him away from his work did he realize that 'this infernal flesh', as he once called it, was the master of him. He took no exercise save to go from one place to another for business purposes, and he ate far heavier dinners than ever he should have done. He drank a great deal too much beer and coffee, and he was a slave to tobacco. He rode when he could do so, to save himself the trouble of walking. When composing he sat at work all day, on through the night and through the day following. Food was put on his table. He ignored it. Sleep twitched at his eyelids. He forced it away. The claims of his body for rest were always subservient to the demands of a mentality that could neither rest nor be still. He flung all his youth, his physical power, his nerve-force into a sacrifice to his ambition.

He never realized fatigue when it came, because the brain was the exerting force, numbing the body to physical feeling. The wonder is that he did not die before he was forty, for he treated his body as some brute would treat a wretched mongrel that followed at his heels. 'Mr Handel was tired, but he played in a wonderful way,' wrote a Society dame of an after-dinner conversazione. 'They say Mr Handel is ruined so he has begun a new opera,' wrote another diarist a little later. Failures were to come, but out of every failure he drew new strength. When the treasury was empty and creditors were pressing, when enemies herded about him and brought the flail of hatred upon his back, he discovered a new vitality in the silence of his room. His mind had always the power to soar above the pettiness of men, beyond the humiliations of failure.

His music had brought to his feet women in plenty. The women in London Society crowded about to get him to their salons. Old women; young women. He had a peculiar way with them. He loved a battle with a bright conversationalist of the other sex. But he had no interest in the sex as such. What passion he ever knew sought emission in his love-songs at this time. Only on two occasions in his life did the question of marriage ever seriously occur to him. Once he even went so far as to become engaged. There is no record of how it happened, or what was the particular snare that caught him. The episode would not have been later than the *Radamisto* period. This unknown maiden may have been responsible for some of the finest love-songs in his early work. He may have improvised to her on the harpsichord melodies of exquisite worth which the world has lost.

The *affaire* ended abruptly. The mother of the girl in question objected to her daughter marrying a musician. He must give up his music or her daughter. The moment of that decision in Handel's mind might have been one of the world's great losses. Imagine him as a tutor or a clerk earning a pittance to keep a wilful *ingénue*, with all the melodies that were singing in his brain stifled for ever! He decided quickly. His Art was his wife and his mistress. He said so, and he went his way.

A second woman intrigued him. Again music was the difficulty. A musician was only a roving mountebank, was the remark thrown at him. Again he decided as before.

So Youth crept forward and ripened. He matured. He liked the society of women—those women who loved Art. His courtesies, his gentleness to them were extreme. The years passed. He became, by easy stages, the accepted bachelor, sexless, safe. The lure of his music, as a percussion of sex, faded and disappeared from the minds of anxious husbands who, with the habit of husbands, had at first suspected that magic figure of genius that strode through their drawing-rooms, and at whose feet their wives seemed to crouch in indolent adoration. Still later, when years and flesh were crowding upon him, when the world had smitten him hard, and he had come through as a conquering, unsuppressed being, he settled into the place by which he is remembered—that of a man never born for love of women—who gave all the love he knew to the wonderment of his notes. A sort of bachelor uncle, fat, heavy, who had run the gamut of the world's affairs, and come out of it all very experienced and knowing.

The curtain of *Radamisto* in June 1720 was the curtain to Handel's youth. Tomorrow was the day of battle. Senesino, Bononcini, were forms of violence just over the horizon on that June night. For commercialism had never entered his dreams till the formation of the Academy threw him into a world he had not known hitherto.

In June 1720 they should have put him on a desert island with a harpsichord, some paper, and ink. Instead, they tumbled him on to a hotbed of intrigue, of jealousy, and commercialism, which at first he never understood. They swept him into a world of vanity-ridden singers, and cat-brained, sensual women. They flung against him every contraption that would kill the art in the average soul.

It would have destroyed some men, fresh and excited with the world's appraise. It would have destroyed Handel, but for his secret store of courage.

BOOK II

NOON

CHAPTER IX

THE COMING OF BONONCINI

THE first season of the Royal Academy finished in triumph for Handel, and when the curtain came down on *Radamisto* that June night in 1720 London realized that he had created a new and ardent following for good music in the capital. Throughout its run the opera had played to crowded houses. Hundreds of people had been turned away from the box-office, and the shareholders in the Academy were cheered with the prospect of immediate dividends.

At this time London was wallowing in financial frenzy. A fortnight before *Radamisto* finished, the King had given the royal assent to the South Sea Company Bill for redeeming the country's disordered finance. In his speech to Parliament he acclaimed it as 'a good foundation for the payment of national debts'. Instantly the shares rushed up to a thousand per cent.[1] Minor bubbles sprang up everywhere. Endless applications for patents, whereby the exploiters hoped to cadge and catch the public money, were made to Parliament. There was one for trading in hair, another for the universal supply of funerals in Great Britain, one for a wheel of perpetual motion, and one 'for carrying on an undertaking of great advantage, but nobody to know what it is'.[2]

All the shares in the minor bubbles followed those of the great one, to a hectic chorus of fortune-making. All other businesses stood still. Occasionally the gamblers received a mild shock, when a subscription list was opened in the morning in a room taken for the day, and the exploiters of the wildcat scheme disappeared in the evening with the proceeds. But still the public went on. What it lost to an occasional barefaced scamp it hoped to regain on the enterprises of the more plausible scoundrels. Square pieces of card, with the impression in sealing-wax of the Globe Tavern, conveying to their possessors

---

[1] Handel invested some money in the South Sea Company; a receipt form giving instructions of his dividend on South Sea stock, signed by him for money he received therefrom, was sold in a London auction room a few years ago.

[2] Justin M'Carthy: *A History of the Four Georges*, Vol. I, p. 252.

merely the permission to subscribe *some time afterwards* to a new sail-cloth company 'not yet formed', were actually sold in Exchange Alley under the title of 'Globe Permits' for sixty guineas and upwards.[1]

London had gone mad. Music was for the moment forgotten. The only entertainment the public wanted was the farce *The Stock Jobbers*; *or Humours of Change Alley*, to which the mob flocked the doors at every performance. Staid landed gentry in the far solitudes of the country sold out their family heirlooms, and hurled the proceeds into the jobbers' offices. Duchesses parted with their jewels at starvation prices for the same purpose. Any project was good enough. Even the company started for the purpose of 'breeding silkworms in Chelsea Park' had its adherents. Money was made as the shares in these financial swindles rushed upwards, only to be poured out again in a welter of extravagance and profligacy.

The profiteer of the period appeared in the park in his carriage mingling with the aristocracy, and a newspaper of 9 July says satirically: 'We are informed that since the late hurly-burly of stock-jobbing, there have appeared in London two hundred new coaches and chariots, besides as many more now on the stocks in the coachmakers' yards; above four thousand embroidered coats; about three thousand gold watches at the side of their .—— and their wives; some few private acts of charity; and about two thousand broken tradesmen.'[2]

Well may Handel have wondered whether there was room any longer for his art in this Babylon. He did not wait to see, for, with the close of *Radamisto* he departed to Cannons and began preparations for the production of a masque in six scenes and one act, which he called *Haman and Mordecai*.[3]

London, with its hubbub, its closed theatres, had failed to interest him, and Pope's words of this masque—which at a later stage was to be renamed *Esther*—had offered him scope for a setting which would maintain his patronage from the Duke of Chandos. He tried out *Haman* with full scenery and costume in the Duke's palatial theatre, much as one would try

[1] Thomas Wright: *England under the House of Hanover*, 1848, Vol. I, p. 63.

[2] *Ibid.*, Vol. I, p. 65.

[3] No record exists of the actual date of production, but it was certainly before the new opera season opened in November. The Duke of Chandos is said to have paid Handel £1,000 for this masque, but of this, again, there is no record.

out a modern play at Manchester or Birmingham before its production in London. It was a very different work to that which ultimately was to appear as *Esther*. It may have interested the Duke, but it certainly failed to interest its composer, for after this initial performance he put it away in a drawer, as he had done *Acis and Galatea*.

Perhaps it would be correct to say that at this time he was more obsessed by the immediate prospects of opera. When the Academy was founded, Lord Burlington had made a special journey to Rome to discover talent. When he imported Giovanni Battista Bononcini, he had, in fact, brought over a rival to Handel, and a dangerous rival. Bononcini was known in most European capitals. His music was real art, ripe with the full passion of the South.

So important was the intrusion of Bononcini into Handel's life that it is necessary to obtain a glimpse of this strange Italian. He had been born at Modena fifteen years before Handel, and had composed his *opera prima* in the same year as Handel first opened his eyes at Halle. At the age of twenty he was a well-known violoncellist at St Petronio, Bologna, and was studying counterpoint under Colonna. As he grew older he roved from one city to another. Just as the eighteenth century opened he was in Vienna, and was twice on the point of getting married. But he strayed out of these love-affairs as casually as he strayed into them. Maybe, like Handel, his Art was his wife and mistress, for he was sincere in his Art. He continued in the course of the sturdy Modenese Guelphs of the sixteenth century, who never loved one woman only for the space of a whole year, but who gave a month to toying with one, and the next month to fooling with another. He departed, in fact, with Signor Giuseppe Malagodi for a tour through the various countries of the Empire, having left in Vienna a written promise of marriage to a lady of that city, to whom his lavish and princely presents had given hopes of its early fulfilment.[1]

Bononcini continued to rove. He made money easily and was not extravagant. He quickly acquired a vogue which resulted in presents being showered upon him, and then he lost his head. The sweet and impressionable character became that of a *poseur*, a brilliant *poseur*. He was unquestionably amongst the greatest musicians in Europe at the time Lord Burlington persuaded him from Rome. In the main, he has been often

[1] Count Luigi F. Valdrighi: *I. Bononcini da Modena*.

underrated unjustly because he suffered badly in the blaze of Handel's genius. Master of his language as but few, excellent judge of melody as almost none other, he established such harmony between the beauty of sound of the Italian language and that of his music that Bononcini's recitatives and arias stood as the highest point of perfection.[1] He suffered in an unequal comparison with Handel, but his delicacy, the singing of his notes, rose to heights which established him at once as an artist of very extraordinary and abnormal gifts.

If Handel had vanity—and he certainly had of a sort—it was contained within certain excusable limits. It was never aggressive. That of Bononcini knew no boundaries and found no excuse when he came to London. He was impossible, an exotic. He was in the music of his hour what Aubrey Beardsley was in later Art. Like Beardsley, he might have been rather proud of taking peaches in ether, had that been possible at the time.

He feared no one. He was a gallant mariner to the winds of happy chance. He had now reached the age of fifty, and knew half the sovereigns of Europe, and most of its Society. Apparently he loved a joust with royalty. He was in the favour of the Emperor Joseph of Austria to such a degree that the monarch made him extraordinary presents above his salary. Yet Bononcini had the insolence often to refuse to play when requested. At last the Emperor made him come to the Court and asked him: 'Do you consider that it is an Emperor whom you refuse?' Bononcini was quick in retort and as insolent. 'Yes,' he replied, 'but there are many sovereign princes, but only one Bononcini.'[2]

This fit of temper obliged him to leave the Court, and, as the result, he paid a brief visit to England shortly before Handel arrived, but soon hurried out again for the southern sun.

This was the difficult creature with whom Handel had to deal in the autumn of 1720. Burlington had brought him from Rome in the spring, and Bononcini was never the man, with such patronage, and with the rights of his directorship of the newly erected Academy, to sit down quietly and listen to the wonders of Handel, so many years his junior. Certain sections of Society had not helped matters by cleaving to the new importation as the god of the world's music. Most of these

---

[1] Van Kempen: *Georg Friedk. Händel.*
[2] *Earl of Egmont MSS.*, Vol. I, p. 201.

adherents had discovered all they knew about Italian music from the Italian singers who had been flocking into England for the last twenty years, and what they did not know they imagined. So that Bononcini, with his great talents, and, above all, his strict adherence to the art of his land, found himself surrounded by a circle of highly bred and fawning sycophants. They were content to worship, and he was of the opinion that they should be content to worship. He appeared in their salons. They gave heavy dinners that would depress any art so that others should meet him, should listen to the gentle prattle of his Italianized English, and his rather extreme and very technical views about the 'bawdy music of the coffee-rooms'. He was select, a dilettante, a genius, smaller of mind than of genius, who might have stood higher in the world's esteem but for the unfortunate choice of his epoch, and his still more unfortunate liking for plagiarism. He became lazy under the sun of adulation, and, because he was lazy, he eventually stole. Then he fell.

But at that time, before Bononcini had reached the heights of his conceits, the Earl of Burlington decided that definitely he was the man to help Handel in the creation of the Academy. But Handel and Bononcini each went their own way. When the rehearsals of Bononcini's work were going on in London in the autumn, Handel left for Cannons. The wild commercialists who believed they could bring these twain together over the Academy made a mistake that cost them a lot of money. *Astarto* was produced in the late autumn of 1720, and ran thirty nights with Senesino singing in it for the first time in England. Society at once split up into two camps; the Handelians on the one hand and the adherents of Bononcini on the other. The first bitter feud of the Academy had begun.

Something of a compromise was attempted in the spring of 1721. Burlington and others began to perceive that if the heat of the rival factions did not abate the result would be serious for the Academy. Bononcini, Senesino, and Anastasia Robinson were then all living out near Twickenham, where they spent the time, when not at the opera, in giving perpetual concerts, which were attended by all Society.[1] The Bononcini party was as unbending in its attitude towards Handel as the Handelians were towards Bononcini. But, by some means, the Academy directors persuaded the two composers to agree to

[1] Lady Mary Montagu: *Letters*, Vol. I, p. 336.

the extent that they should each write an act to an opera; the first act being written by a third, and more or less mediocre composer, Filippo Mattei, Bononcini writing the second, and Handel the third.

The result was *Muzio Scevola*, and the only success it achieved was to make the battle between the contending factions hotter than ever. It was conceded that Handel's third act was the best of the three, but the controversy had now spread to Society, where the merits of the two giants were discussed *ad nauseam*. The Bononcini adherents were for the most part made up of those who wished to tilt against the German Court, and they included Handel in their invective.

The season reopened in November 1721 with a new Handel opera, *Arsace*. From the night the curtain went up it was destined to fail. It was poor work. It may have been that the violent upheaval of the Bononcini party, which was opposed to everything he said and did, mentally disturbed Handel. Not that he was usually perturbed by violence against him in his later years. He produced a *pasticcio*, *Floridante*, on 9 December and it must be classed as indifferent workmanship. Handel had been provided with a good libretto for *Radamisto*, but that by Rolli for *Floridante* was fatuous, and neither Senesino nor Anastasia Robinson, who sang in the opera, made any impression. Senesino, always ready to blame someone else when he failed to draw, openly declared that Handel had made a fool of him.

Whatever the cause, *Floridante* played only a few nights, and its run was followed by two operas of Bononcini's, *Crispo* and *Griselda*. They were tuneful and popular. The latter was the best of the four operas Bononcini composed in London, and Handel had the mortification of seeing his rival follow his own failure with a couple of works which drew more crowded houses than any seen in town since *Radamisto*.

Some declared that Handel's star had set, but they did not know Handel. He drew aside from the musical circles of the hour. He dropped out of the salons; his swarthy figure was seldom seen in Piccadilly. Not that he was beaten; he had retreated only *pour mieux sauter*. His singers were ill-chosen. Whatever had been the defects of *Floridante*—and he was very frank in seeing his own technical faults—Anastasia Robinson had failed as a *prima donna*. He first set about remedying this by sending to Italy for Francesca Cuzzoni, a brilliant soprano, then twenty-two years of age, who had made her début at Venice three years previously. Although Handel could not have heard her sing when he brought her from Italy and made a contract, her reputation was so remarkable that he was content to give her £2,000 a year.[1]

Before she reached London, Handel had completed a new opera, *Otho*, which, with its big soprano songs, had been practically created for the newcomer. Now she arrived in town with the regality of a queen, but without a queen's appearance. or deportment. She was squat and plain, she dressed badly. She had a vicious temper, which broke out beyond all limits at the first provocation. Her general education, if she had any, was of a crude order. She was flippant and silly. If she had not been born with a divine voice, she would have been passed by as a most uninteresting person.

She came with all the *réclame* of a great artiste. The fact that, on the way over, she had married Sandoni, a harpsichord player whom Handel had sent to fetch her, added to the mystery of her personality, and made everyone turn out to look at her. She put out the record of her daily doings to an inquisitive public as one might throw bits of meat to a dog. Whilst she was trying to make her plain face presentable in front of the mirror, Society was discussing the ways of her daily life. It excused her bad dress, her irritating figure, because she was supposed to be something more wonderful than had ever appeared in London hitherto. Art is not wrapped up in loveliness, it said.

The first thing she did was to quarrel with Handel at rehearsal. He wished a song rendered in a certain way; she insisted on singing it in another. The combat was short and sharp. Handel threatened to throw her out of the window. He had actually seized her by the waist with a view to putting the threat into operation when she succumbed. Although he probably never understood women, he always knew how to master them. He was an apostle of force; not necessarily personal, but mental force. He tamed Cuzzoni in a few minutes. True, she proved troublesome later, but these later conflicts were—from her point of view at any rate—in the nature of a combat against an equal antagonist.

Only a romantic fool like Sandoni would ever have married her. He must have married her for her voice, since there was

[1] W. S. Rockstro: *Life of G. F. Handel*, p. 138.

nothing else about Cuzzoni that would have attracted any man. His marriage was perhaps his single tribute to his art. Even when she rose in London on an instant wave to favour, she had no admirers except those of her singing. She was difficult to explain in the average drawing-room till she sat at the harpsichord.

Sandoni himself was an evil liver, a drunkard, a gambler and coxcomb, who gradually began to pose as the master who inspired Cuzzoni with all the wonders she performed.[1] He was the typical little down-trodden husband, the pet dog that ran and fetched. When later Cuzzoni was brought to bed of a daughter—'it is a mighty mortification it is not a son,' wrote Mrs Delany—

'she sang "La Speranza", a song in *Otho*. Sandoni had been at an extravagant expense to please that whimsical creature. Amongst other superfluous charges, he had bought a fine looking-glass for the child, and a black lace hood for his wife to see company in. In short, there was more talk about this birth than there was for the Princess of Wales when she gave birth to the Princess Louise a few months before.'[2]

On 12 January 1723 *Otho* was produced. Nicolò Haym had provided the libretto, indeed, Haym was destined to be the author of the next five Handel operas. For the first time Cuzzoni was heard by a London audience. This stumpy little person strutting and strolling on the stage, enthralled it by the sheer wonder of her voice. Handel had excelled himself with his music—*Otho* was never surpassed by him in all his English operas—and Cuzzoni bore his notes to the heights of enchantment. All her ugliness, her lack of deportment, her deficient manners, her vanity had fled. The audience rose to her. The boxes stormed her with applause. A man in the gallery, with more enthusiasm than decency, roared 'Damme, she has a nest of nightingales in her belly!' When the house emptied into the winter's night London knew that the Handel–Bononcini battle had ended. Bononcini, with his dainty tunes, his delicious Italian manners in the salons, had been beaten to his knees. His *Griselda* was accounted a playful prettiness. But the real art was here.

[1] Count Luigi F. Valdrighi: *I. Bononcini da Modena*.
[2] Mrs Delany: *Life and Correspondence*, Vol. I, p. 117 *et seq.*

The first night of *Otho* was decisive in its effects. For the performance on the night following seats changed hands at five guineas each. Anastasia Robinson, although she had sung in the opera with Senesino, Boschi the basso, and Berenstadt, was so broken-hearted by the uproar in favour of Cuzzoni that shortly afterwards—at the instigation of the Earl of Peterborough—she retired permanently from the stage. Bononcini, eclipsed, still put up a fighting front. The Handel achievement he judged to be the success of an hour. It worried him but little. He went steadily to work on his opera *Erminia*, which succeeded *Otho* at the end of its run, but proved a poor attraction.

Handel, meanwhile, prepared an even heavier shot for Bononcini. No sooner had *Erminia* ended than he was ready with *Flavio*. He had now reached that stage when he could put out opera after opera with a fecundity peculiar to no other composer. Bononcini began to decline. He withdrew from the Academy, and the Duchess of Marlborough settled upon him £500 a year as her *Kapellmeister*. He had always been in favour with the Marlborough family, and composed the funeral anthem which had been performed at the interment of the conqueror of Blenheim.

Bononcini's story during the next few years was peculiar. There was a club set up by the King's Chapel of vocal and instrumental performers, mostly amateurs, whose object was the cultivation of good music. Steffani had been president of the club, although he did not reside in England, and when he died the members decided to keep the presidency vacant in memory of the great Italian. This annoyed Bononcini intensely, since he considered that the mantle of Steffani was rightfully his. He still continued to be a member of the club, but he sent the committee a composition by a foreign musician which had been printed several years previously, and called it his own.[1] When charged with the fraud Bononcini stormed. The music was his. The club was made up of liars. The argument grew fast and furious, and the only thing to do was to write to the alleged composer at Vienna and discover the truth. Whilst the letter was on the way, Bononcini terminated his membership of the club, a guilty man.[2]

He went down fighting. He crept from salon to salon, a furtive figure, as his popularity waned and his adherents

[1] *Earl of Egmont MSS.*, Vol. I, p. 203.   [2] *Ibid.*

departed in scores. The beauty of his little chansonnettes still kept him a pitied and maligned person in some of the best musical circles of the town. He made out a good case, and he received a good hearing. His personality was half his cause, for he had a charm that bore him far.

All through his later years Bononcini had been a mental crook. He borrowed heavily from other composers, and until his last years in London he was never found out. The ignorance of the English public—even the English musical public— was largely responsible for that. England had at this time a splendid isolation in music, due largely to the conditions then existing, but due scarcely less to her own musical apathy. Handel had destroyed this isolation to some extent by his importation of the best talent from all over the Continent.

Bononcini, with the simple sweetness of his Italian airs, had assisted the movement. But by it he fell; his purloinings were discovered. Eventually, with a view to regaining favour, he presented the Academy of Ancient Music with a madrigal in five voices, but three years later it was revealed that the piece was by Antonio Lotti, and had been published at Venice twenty-three years before. He returned the kindness of the Duchess of Marlborough with sharp practice. After enjoying her £500 per annum for a period of years, he used to entertain her with concerts which she accepted, not imagining that he would bring her in a bill at last to pay the performers, some of whom were promised three guineas a day.[1] The Duchess paid these accounts with demur, and Bononcini aggrieved, his vanity wounded, left her, and got up a scheme to run a musical meeting at York Buildings in rivalry to the opera.

So he came down by chicanery and subterfuge, an artist whose reputation had become threadbare through his own rough usage, a great melodist gone stale. A proud man whom, if he had valued himself less, the world would have esteemed more.

For some time longer he clung to the old haunts. A broken figure, with still some of the vicious Italian spirit left in him. By circular, propaganda, and otherwise, he vainly sought to tear down Handel.

But the glories had departed. Misfortune and melancholy became his constant companions. At one time all things had been in his favour; even Cuzzoni, who carried his banner high,

[1] *Earl of Egmont MSS.*, Vol. I, p. 202.

now also turned against him. In his *Culphurnia*, which was his last London opera, she had been superb. By the simplicity and *finesse* of her singing she made people forget the follies, which had become the scandal of the whole metropolis.[1] Society had fought for Bononcini till he cheated it. Indeed, he had been the soul of Italy in London, where Italy was deemed the fount of all true melody. But he pawned the title for cheap and artless fraud.

A few years still he lingered. Then he went to Paris with Berenstadt, a dead star dropping out in the dark.

[1] Gaetano Berenstadt, Letter in the Liceo at Bologna.

CHAPTER X

ANXIOUS DAYS AT THE ACADEMY

WHEN 1724 dawned, a new apathy regarding music was apparent in London. The Town had of late been spoiled by too many good things. The Academy had raised the level of English music to a height it had never before attained. Europe now turned envious ears to the echoes of melody that came from England. *Radamisto, Muzio Scevola, Rinaldo*, were being given in Europe, and the singers one by one were throwing off the shackles of Venice and Munich, and seeking London engagements.

London grew blasé in a surfeit of rich composing. It needed a sensation to keep its interest primed. The conflict between Handel and Bononcini had offered that sensation, and an advertisement fruitful to the box-office. Now Bononcini had crept away to his little coteries, and his behaviour suggested— even if he would not admit the fact—that Handel was master of British opera.

Not that the Academy was making profits. Its direction had been too extravagant. Heidegger had enjoyed having the money to spend, and he spent it with the zeal of an enthusiast. There was no commercial man on the Board who worried unduly about balance sheets.

Heidegger was doing well also out of his masquerades, which were usually held at the King's Theatre, Haymarket. They had long since developed into rather scandalous orgies, and, as such, were highly remunerative. At a big supper given in connection with the masquerades, Heidegger was challenged on the grounds of his nationality. What right, they told him, had he to come here and set up a carnival of vice and make a fortune out of it when he was a foreigner! Heidegger, as always, was frank and to the point. 'I was born a Swiss,' he said, 'and came to England without a farthing, where I have found means to gain £5,000 a year, and to spend it. Now I defy the most able Englishman to go to Switzerland, and either to gain that income, or to spend it there!'[1]

Heidegger advertised that a sufficient guard was appointed

[1] Theodore Vetter: *Heidegger*.

to prevent disorder both inside and outside the theatre, and orders were given not to deliver any bottles or glasses from the sideboards and to shut them up early.[1] Notwithstanding this, the utmost licence prevailed. Quarrels were frequent and bitter, and duels were constantly taking place within the precincts of the house. Even Heidegger himself was not spared. One day a party of young 'bloods' took him to the Devil Tavern at Temple Bar, and made him very drunk. Not a difficult task with Heidegger. When he was so helpless that he could not move a muscle, a Miss Salmon took a cast of his face. But the joke did not end there. A few days later, when a masquerade was held at the King's Theatre, Heidegger, on going into the room, found a man approaching who was the double of himself in facial appearance. It was Lord Montagu, who had had a mask made from the cast, and now appeared as Heidegger's own double of ugliness![2]

The scandal of the masquerade soon began to stir up trouble. Heidegger remained unperturbed. He was making money heavily, spending it, giving it away. On several occasions, when a masquerade had been particularly successful, he gave several hundred pounds to a friend, with the remark: "You know poor objects of distress better than I do, be so kind as to give this money away for me."[3]

After a while it became obvious that some sort of public action would have to be taken against the indecencies of the masquerades. The Bishop of London was the first to strike. He preached against Heidegger and his works, and he soon set all the clergy doing likewise.

Then the battle began. Heidegger enjoyed it. He was stopping nothing. Instead, he wrote a poem in reply, and circulated it all over the town. It ran as follows:

> 'My Lord, your sermon preached at Bow,
> Came to my hands some weeks ago.
> By which I see you seem afraid
> That harmless pastime, Masquerade
> May spoil the Reformation Trade.'

The battle waxed merrily. Fielding rushed into the ring and wrote an open letter and a poem to Heidegger, which were sold

[1] Lady Mary Montagu: footnote, Vol. I, p. 37.
[2] Rees: *Cyclopædia*.
[3] Theodore Vetter: *Heidegger*.

publicly in the streets at sixpence a copy. It was bitter with that bitterness of which Fielding was a master. It lashed Heidegger with insult. Much of it would be classified today as a blow beneath the belt, as, for instance, when, in reference to Heidegger's ugliness, he wrote:

'I cannot help congratulating you on that gift of nature by which you seem so adapted to the part you enjoy. I mean, that natural masque, which is too visible perfection to be insisted on here, and, I am sure, never fails by making an impression on the most indifferent beholder. Another gift of nature which you seem to enjoy in no small degree, is that modest confidence supporting you in every act of your life. Certainly a great blessing! for I have always observed that brass in the forehead draws gold in the pocket. As for what Mankind calls Virtues, I shall not compliment you on them, since you are so wise as to keep them from the world.'

Fielding's attack came to naught. Heidegger smiled indifference. He did not reply. The masquerades went on. Nothing of abuse ever moved the ugly little fellow, of whom Fielding on another occasion wrote in his poem:

'Monstrous! that human nature can
Have form'd so strange burlesque a man.'

Handel as a commercial proposition was certainly no better than Heidegger. He was in accord with all Heidegger's magnificent staging. He believed that art must lead, and that public inconvenience—the box-office—follow. Handel as an artiste was of course right. But he and Heidegger were the last couple who should have been in partnership, so far as the shareholders of the Academy were concerned. They did things too well; they were not commercialists.

When Handel produced his *Giulio Cesare* in February 1724 he had more or less a clear run before him. Haym had given up his personal tamperings with opera, and had now settled down to provide good libretti. This he certainly did. Handel's next four operas owed their libretti to Haym, but *Giulio Cesare* was the poorest of the set.

Meanwhile, the anti-German element was still strong in London: it derided the claims of Handel as it derided the King.

The monarch, with his lamentable South Sea Company speech, had made London lose faith in him, and it had never had much to lose. He was scarcely regarded as a monarch, but as a spectacle—a splendidly clad figure amidst the wax-lights—growing obese, and a little crippled with gout and other pains, surrounded with a miscellaneous collection of fair ladies, many of whom tried to talk broken English because they had been elevated to the rank of English duchesses. The real English aristocracy, regular in its attendance at Court, rather amused—with no more than an inherited respect for royalty—was derisive in its comments, and wondered what or who was going to be the subject of the next quarrel between the King and the Prince of Wales. King George had to a great extent forgotten his interest in the Academy; he had forgotten that he was supposed to love music. The revived French farces amused him. He lounged indolently in the boxes, laughing at the blatant indecencies, and throwing comment to the beauties about him. He became less staid, more urgent in trying to enjoy life, which, with its sought savours, seemed to lack just that which would make him a happy man. He had become a feckless *abandonné*, who had left his soul behind in the secret rooms and the unmeasured profligacy of the *Herrenhaus*.

Giulio Cesare was fine work, but it failed to evoke more than average attention. Never was Senesino heard to greater advantage. Handel had given him songs which would have made fame for a gutter singer with a good voice. The extraordinary performance by Senesino provoked almost more attention than the brilliance of Handel's music. Nevertheless, this great triumph of composer and artist passed in a few performances, because London was wearying of good music.

When, soon afterwards, Senesino made his attack upon Anastasia Robinson, and received the flogging from the Earl of Peterborough already referred to, interest in him and his work had a swift revival. Forged letters began to fly about, supposed to be written by Anastasia to the Italian. Forged letters from Senesino in return were disseminated like circulars of a modern pill. The town was stirred; the King enjoyed the great joke. These funny little scandals were sufficiently ignoble to be the mainstay of a happy evening in any average Society salon. When, during the singing of his great song 'Alma del Gran Pompeo' in *Giulio Cesare*, a piece of scenery fell down with a crash and an uprising of dust, the wretched Senesino was so startled out of his wits that he dropped in a flood of frightened tears to the stage and Society's ecstasies rose yet higher.

So the ponderous hero who ramped across the stage and sang with the voice of heaven was only a miserable little coward after all! The mysterious personality which had been created about him by the wonder of his singing slipped away like a vanishing cloak of dreams. His heroism stood revealed as so much make-believe, like the stage castle which he had stormed in an earlier Handel opera, to carry away one wing of it on the point of his sword like a trussed fowl. Only one thing was real—as if it were the gift of God left in the wrong body— the magnificent voice that made even an idling King cease his fooling to listen.

Now, in spite of this exhibition, in spite of the fact that, season by season, Senesino became more apparent as a creature with rather second-rate gutter manners and breeding, women still poured upon him their adoration. When ultimately he left England they wept. They loaded him with presents. They crowded about him to get his wretched insincere smile—or even his scorn. They were ready to bear any hurt for him and worship as fiercely as ever.

Such is the power of the human voice. To these many women from the rich villas of Chelsea, from the grandiose mansions of Piccadilly, Senesino was a lone voice singing in a wilderness. Ultimately they let him go like that, and respectable wives of bankers and rich merchants and peers went down to their graves hugging to themselves secret memories of Senesino—memories of nights at the stage door—a glance—a smile. Most respectable wives, all of them. And their more respectable husbands never discovered anything about it.

The god of the whole adventure in the fullness of time went back to his native town of Siena in Italy, and with a good fortune of £15,000—which he had taken from these admirers for seats—built himself a palace. Here he lived with the habits of a prince who had never been educated, sang duets with royalty in public, and settled down to a life of pompous luxury.

With *Giulio Cesare*, Handel had returned to the opera of romance, of movement, of martial airs, and tense passion. Yet the public seemed to have but little liking for it. Had he been such a student of the public's requirements as he is often stated to have been, he would have changed the style of the next work he put out. Handel knew when his work was good, and also when it was bad. The public apathy had been merely an adverse mood in an excitable age. He would not budge an inch from the attitude that he had assumed—namely that he composed for his art and not for the public. He made Nicolò Haym write another libretto for him at once, and Haym produced *Tamerlane*. The opera has a story and a fine one, but Haym certainly did his best to disguise it! He was muddled in his libretto of *Giulio Cesare*, and he was muddled in *Tamerlane*. But Handel's music, and the acting and singing of Cuzzoni and Senesino, smoothed away many difficulties and made *Tamerlane* a coherent whole.

Handel began to compose *Tamerlane* on 3 July 1724 and completed it in twenty days. Like all his greatest achievements it was the outcome of concentration when he lived in one room, ate, slept, worked, existed in an atmosphere that breathed the romance of his notes. *Tamerlane* reflects that concentration. The harmony is brilliant, and it carries some of the most passionate melodies that ever sprang from the master's brain. Cuzzoni's and Senesino's duet: 'I am thine, my only treasure', was one of the greatest triumphs Handel had known till this moment. The intimate sorrow of it, the yearning, carried every man and woman who listened into the heart of a great love story. 'I could die with joy to please you, for my life is only thine.' As these two wonderful voices stole aloft tears streamed down the faces of the people. The hardened from the salons, blasé to all sentiment, who yet went to the opera because it was the thing to do, and who normally used the time as an excuse to laugh and joke in an undertone, were softly crying.

The talk about *Tamerlane* had caused the decaying King to take a new interest in the opera, and the great duet made him cease his idle and disreputable talk to listen. Then the opera had an added interest, because it introduced Handel's new singer Borosini. A curious creature. A man exactly Handel's own age, who had wandered about southern Europe with a tenor voice that created enormous interest for a time, till the repetition of it repelled. Borosini, in the course of these wanderings, had married another singer, Leonore d'Ambreville. When Handel had made his contract with Borosini, who was then singing at Prague, he had to engage his wife also. They were neither of them great singers, but their advent interested people as another Handel diversion. For two years they sang for Handel, then their vogue waned, and they disappeared from the country.

Tamerlane had one virtue above most of the Handel operas —it built up carefully to a tremendous climax. Probably Handel never attained a greater finale than he did in *Tamerlane* until he left opera for oratorio. The close of the work, the dramatic pathos he reached in his notes when the broken Emperor Bajazet passes to death, was the triumph of one carried out of himself by enthusiasm for his task. Bajazet's song, 'Dearest daughter, weep no more', was a masterpiece of attainment. Such a heart-breaking had never been displayed in music before.

Tamerlane sent its audiences weeping into the street when the curtain fell. All through that autumn it held the theatre, and it would have been unquestionably a great financial success but for the extravagance and loose commercial habits of the Academy directors. It was a paying proposition all the time, but money was being poured down the drain in absurd inconsequent ways, because no one cared very much what happened so long as the Academy's doors were kept open.

Handel was probably the only person who had any thought about this side of the venture. Heidegger was too busy with his masquerades. The various governing peers, now that the novelty of the Academy had worn off, sought other novelties to divert idle lives. The King had fallen irreparably to the lure of the wax-lights, the powdered ladies and the French farces. The dull old fellow's days were waning. He was pushing away constantly recurring illnesses as nuisances, persuading himself that a life of eternal pleasure was not taking its toll. In a couple of years more he was to die a heavy, bent up, crying figure in a coach outside Osnaburg. Not a bit regal, not a bit the autocratic adventurer, but very humble when Death touched his shoulder.

No sooner had the curtain fallen on the last performance of *Tamerlane* than Handel was ready with a new opera. He was fighting hard for the falling fortunes of the Academy. If it failed he was conscious that there must come a serious blow to his prestige. Bononcini was like some lowing beast, snapping in frantic frenzy at every Handelian move made by the Academy directors. They were going to destruction with Handel. He told them so. In truth they were, but only because they had not enough commercial instinct between them to keep open the doors of an average shop for a month, let alone a great venture like the Academy.

Handel produced his *Rodelinda* on 13 February 1725. He only composed the last notes of it on 20 January. He knew that the Academy was approaching dissolution unless something important happened to stir the town.

In a way, he gave the town all it wanted to talk about with his *Rodelinda*. Haym's Italian libretto, more human than most of his works, and dealing with the emotions of a deserted Lombardian queen, was sufficient excuse for Handel's emotional songs. Although in *Rodelinda* Handel never reached the powers he displayed in *Tamerlane*, he produced a fine work. It was Cuzzoni who provided the diversion. She appeared in a brown silk dress trimmed with silver that caught the town. None of the songs of Handel brought the audiences to *Rodelinda*; they came to see the brown and silver dress, to talk about it, to copy it. Cuzzoni started a fashion which swept through Society like an epidemic. Though the singer appeared very plump and squat in the brown and silver dress, every Society woman in the audience—with that imagination which is truly a woman's—foresaw what she herself would look like in such a combination of artistic colour. Handel had made an opera, and Cuzzoni a season's fashion. And the odd thing about *Rodelinda* is that the fashion Cuzzoni set on that February night in 1725 has lived longer than the beauties Handel put into that work. Considerably more than a century has passed since the world has seen a performance of *Rodelinda* which was, with its Italian setting, a very beautiful thing. But Cuzzoni's brown and silver dress has run the gamut of empires, has gone out of fashion and ramped through fashion again, and acquired its place as a delicate thought in colour schemes.

The season ended on 19 May. Then for a while Handel was silent. He produced nothing fresh until he began his new opera *Scipio* on 12 March 1726. *Scipio* had a good average run of thirteen nights, but had only one big Handelian number in it, the march which, later on, was purloined by the promoters of *Polly*, the sequel to the *Beggar's Opera*.

He was now forty-one; he had reached what we moderns know as 'mid-channel'. It had not been difficult going thus far, considering his times and the wild and wonderful temperaments of those with whom he had to deal.

But the world was changing. He was changing. All the

melody he had produced in those years was as nothing to what was yet to come. The best of it was to emerge from the vicious and unremitting hurt of the world, driven upon him without flinch or pity. Jealousies, the changing of friends, the foolish quarrels of kings and their spoiled offspring were to bring him wounds which he never sought or deserved. Out of suffering and hidden lament came his sweeter singing. Had it not been for enmities and disappointments he would have been a lesser voice in universal music. Because he was to endure so did he come to discover the world's grief, its tenderness, and by his divine gift change it into a song of hope.

CHAPTER XI

THE GREAT QUARREL

HANDEL had now been in England sixteen years. The question of his naturalization had not troubled him; it is doubtful if he ever thought about it. London had accepted a German Court. It possessed a King who even now could talk only execrable English, and who hectored in rapid German his wife and his suite in public at all times. There seemed no reason, therefore, why Handel, whose mode of speech confirmed his German origin, should assume a nationality with which his speech was inconsistent. In everything else he had become English. He had assimilated the characteristics of the English people, which the monarch had never attempted or wished to do.

The Bononcini quarrel had, however, changed matters. The Italian had, by astute propaganda, worked up a case against the German Handel. The knowledge of his German origin had been inconsequent to the London which prided itself on having captured the greatest musician of Europe. But the stock of the German Court was falling. The King was becoming more and more unpopular. His German mistresses were considered less and less necessary in the salons. The quarrels between the King and the Prince of Wales had reached the stage of vulgar discourtesies in public. Nevertheless, it was mainly the Bononcini propaganda that compelled Handel to apply for naturalization.

At the beginning of February 1727 (modern calendar) he made his petition to the Lords, and it ran as follows:

'To the Right Honourable The Lords Spiritual and Temporal in Parliament assembled.

'The Humble Petition of George Frideric Handel sheweth That your Petitioner was born at Halle, in Saxony, out of His Majesty's Allegiance, but hath constantly professed the Protestant Religion, and hath given Testimony of his Loyalty and Fidelity to His Majesty and the Good of this Kingdom.

'Therefore the Petitioner humbly prays That he may be added to the Bill now pending entitled "An Act for Naturalisating Louis Sechehaye". And the petitioner will ever pray, etc.

'GEORGE FRIDERIC HANDEL.'

On 14 February Handel went to the House of Lords and took the oath of allegiance. Six days later the King put his signature to the Bill that made him a British subject.

He pursued his work. Before him was the hopeless task of saving the Academy. But in the midst of it all his thoughts went back to Halle. He had planned a visit to his mother the previous summer, but the endless harassing of business claims kept him in London. No letters reached him now from the Schlamm house. All the news he received of his mother came from his brother-in-law, Dr Michaelsen, who had since married again, a Fräulein Dreissig. Amidst all the upheaval of opera we find Handel writing to him: 'I cannot be so ungrateful as to pass over in silence the goodness you have shown to my mother in her advanced age, for which I offer you my very humble thanks. You know how interested I am in all that concerns her.'

The affection of Handel for this simple German woman, who had borne him, increased with the years. She was the only woman who ever held any real place in his heart. His sisters were dead. He was mildly interested in his nieces, but the old lady of Halle had supreme command of that solitary affection he had for one of the opposite sex.

Meanwhile, the state of affairs at the Academy urged the directors into a desperate move. There had sprung up in Italy a brilliant young singer in Faustina Bordoni, who, at the time, was performing at the Court Theatre in Vienna. She was precisely the same age as Cuzzoni—twenty-six. Indeed they had both made their début at Venice the same night in 1719, an odd coincidence in view of the great part they were to play in each other's lives.

The directors of the Academy decided that Faustina must be secured at all cost. She must be brought as a supplement to Cuzzoni in a wild scheme to hold up the languishing exchequer of the Academy. From beginning to end it was a mad proposition, and it was entrusted to Handel to fix the contract. The Academy did not require two such singers. Faustina was a mezzo-soprano who ranged from B to a little above G. If anyone had thought about it at all, he would have realized that to bring two ambitious young artists to the same theatre was inviting all the trouble at the bestowal of the god of mischief. But the directors in their colossal wisdom declared that the Academy wanted a diversion, and Faustina would provoke the diversion. She did.

She was sent for, and a handsome contract made with her, which is said to have been on a level with Cuzzoni's £2,000 a year. Whether or no, it was big money. She soon proved to be the exact opposite of Cuzzoni in every way. She came simply. There was no proclamation of her likes and dislikes, her daily doings, her fads, her moods, as had been the case on the arrival of Cuzzoni. She was short and pretty. Cuzzoni was short and plain. She had a figure; Cuzzoni never possessed the ghost of one. She was witty and bright in conversation. Cuzzoni only posed, and her talk, when she discussed subjects other than herself, was heavy and dull. She had elegance; the manner of a Venetian lady of quality, vivacity, a sparkle, not so much Italian, but the product of a distinct and different personality. Cuzzoni had a voice of few notes, but those all sweet, even and sonorous. Faustina, on the other hand, had a voice brilliant in every part, and of inconceivable agility, so that she drew the gouty and infirm from their beds to go and hear her.[1] Whilst Faustina was generous—generous to the point of self-sacrifice—Cuzzoni had a small-souled meanness—a meanness towards her friends, and a greater meanness towards her fellow-artistes.

As Cuzzoni before her, Faustina was late in arriving. Billed with her advent, the town began to talk. A coarse pamphlet was issued branding her as a voluptuary, which she never was. Carey the poet received her with a poem called 'The Roman Singer; a satire on the effeminacy and voluptuousness of our Time'. When Faustina arrived she had not a shred of character left. How Cuzzoni must have laughed, for she was to drink the bitter dregs of jealousy to the end.

The Academy put these two warring temperamentals down in the theatre and left the rest to Handel. If Handel had been of sound intelligence in the understanding of women, he would have bought Faustina a return ticket to Venice and packed her off. But he did what few other men in the history of music could have done so successfully. He composed an opera—*Alessandro*—in which the soprano songs were so arranged that neither Cuzzoni nor Faustina had a greater part than the

[1] Vincenzi Martinelli: *Lettere familiari e critiche*.

other. He had so arranged his melodies that sometimes the voice of Faustina interlaced with that of Cuzzoni, then fell, whilst that of Cuzzoni rose to the heights. *Alessandro* was produced on 5 May 1726, and the extraordinary phenomenon of these two singers in a work that had been created for them, and which showed them in contrast, yet apparently left them both friends, drew the Town.

Only for a time, however. The possibility of human frailty exerting itself was too good for the Town to miss. The rival singers split the patrons of opera into two belligerent factions. They fought their battles out in the salons long before the singers themselves knew that a storm had begun. Faustina began to be accepted in certain salons for her generous nature, apart from her powers. The Countess of Burlington, Sir Robert Walpole, Lady Cowper, drew her into their family circles to the exclusion of Cuzzoni.

Faustina was not mercenary. Where her art was appreciated she would sing without fee or reward, and her liberality towards young and struggling artistes went to the verge of prodigality. Once, a young virtuoso, whom misfortune had deprived of all means of existence, called upon her for assistance. 'To receive alms,' Faustina told him, 'would be degrading to you, but you shall be heard and properly rewarded. I shall recommend you to some of the first houses in town.' She gave him letters of recommendation, and asked him to acquaint her of the result as soon as possible. Her proud confidence had deceived her. The young man found all doors closed to him.

When he returned he found Faustina finishing her toilet to go to a grand reception. He told her the story and she was silent. Then without a word she took off her valuable diamond bracelets, and handed them to him. The youth groped for words and found none. 'Take these!' she said. 'I have promised to help you. They are not charity, but the well-meant gift of one artiste to another!'[1] And she slipped from the room before he could reply, leaving him with the gleaming gems in his hand.

Faustina was a born actress, which Cuzzoni never was. That lumpish figure could not get away from being—just Cuzzoni. Moreover, Faustina's gifts had been in good protectorship for training. Gasparini, the great theoretician, had given her a full

[1] A. Niggli: *Faustina Bordoni-Hasse*.

musical education at Venice. Later, Bernacchi brought her
general equipment to perfection, and the Bolognese singing
master, Pistochi, taught her the art of simplicity and directness
of expression.[1] Such was her singing that she had the art of
sustaining a note longer than any other singer, by taking her
breath imperceptibly.[2] Her début in Italy had brought her a
storm of applause. Venice was conscious that a new singer had
arisen, though the musical firmament of the time was alive
with stars that might blaze into sudden constellations or drop
out. But when Faustina had made this successful first appearance she returned to her studies, a woman self-critical, disappointed with herself perhaps. Not all the temptations of
operatic managers could get her on to the stage again for a
year.

Before *Alessandro* had been running a few days the storm
broke. Cuzzoni's followers wildly hissed the new singer whenever she opened her lips. The confusion looked like jeopard-
izing the success of the opera, but it played to full houses till
7 June, when the season closed. None too soon for Handel's
peace of mind, since, in the quarrel of these two women, he
was faced with a problem more difficult than he had ever
known.

During the summer of 1726 Society was a camp divided.
Cuzzoni's followers became so bitter that sometimes they
threw aside those friends who dared to support Faustina.
Cuzzoni, who was living a very immoral life—her wretched
little husband could do no more than wring his hands—was
the paragon of purity in the opinion of those who met at
Society's dinner-tables to discuss the invented immoralities of
the rival Faustina. The Town went into hysterical controversy
over these two women. Race-horses were named after them;
'Cuzzoni' and 'Faustina' ran against each other at Newmarket.
Duchesses wore Cuzzoni or Faustina favours, and were derided in Piccadilly by rival supporters.

Whether the commotion was responsible for the opening of
the next season being delayed cannot be said. The King's
Theatre doors were closed until 7 January 1727, to be reopened
with a poor opera by Ariosti, *Lucio Vero*, a production which
survived but a few nights. Only Handel seemed able to keep the
opera going these days, and when Ariosti failed, he was ready
with his *Admeto*. On the last day of January he produced it

Ibid.   [2] Burney: *History of Music*, Vol. IV, p. 308.

with the rival singers, now apparently reconciled, singing together. Where he obtained the libretto from is unknown. It may have been Haym's, but it was better work than Haym had provided hitherto. It was the story of Alcestis, a great story of passion, and it drew from Handel some of the best melody he had ever given to London.

Admeto was a brilliant success, but the theatre was turned into a pit of revolution. The followers of Faustina and Cuzzoni came night by night to cheer their respective heroines and hiss the rival, much as a tenth-rate prize-fight would produce howls and cat-calls from the crowd. What nights of exasperation and pain must this unholy babel have brought to Handel! How his temper, so easily roused on occasion, must have leapt almost beyond control when, at each performance, his melodies were lost in a hubbub raised by a rabble which, in the main, was drawn from a Society that had forgotten its manners.

It is surprising that he did not impetuously close *Admeto* down. In his later years he would have done so. But he kept the opera going until, on 6 May, it was succeeded by Bononcini's *Astyanax*. The Handel–Bononcini controversy fanned up yet again, and made confusion worse confounded.

Astyanax had a hectic life of one month. It is doubtful if any member of the audience ever knew what the opera was about, for it played to continual disturbance every night. To go to the opera now had become a form of merriment far removed from love of music. Street roughs began to assemble there for sheer enjoyment of the nightly upheaval. Gangs of them gathered in the streets outside the theatre and attacked other gangs who represented the rival favourites. Heads were cracked, windows smashed, carriages overturned, dowager duchesses 'thrown out in the filth like sacks of corn'. Some declared that if the two singers were not put in bags and drowned in the river they would soon cause a civil war!

The crisis came on 6 June. When Faustina appeared on the stage the rabble that represented Cuzzoni rose up and shouted her down. A battle began in the auditorium and finished on the stage by Cuzzoni setting upon Faustina, and the two women tearing out each other's hair. Some of the audience rushed the stage and joined in the fray. Smashed scenery—a pandemonium of struggling humanity! And the Princess Amelia, very scared, in the royal box!

This sensation killed Bononcini's opera—or so he declared,

and possibly with truth. A deluge of pamphlets, descriptive in coarse language of the two singers, came down on London. The best of them, *The Devil To Pay At St James's*, was attributed to Arbuthnot, of whom Swift wrote to Pope that if the world contained a dozen Arbuthnots he would burn his *Travels*. The Arbuthnot pamphlet gained fame as far away as Italy. 'Which of the two is the aggressor,' he wrote of Faustina and Cuzzoni, 'I dare not determine, lest I lose the friendship of many noble personages, who espouse some the one, some the other party, with such warmth that it is not now, as formerly, i.e. Are you High Church or Low, Whig or Tory; are you for Court or Country; King *George* or the Pretender; but are you for *Faustina* or *Cuzzoni*, *Handel*, or *Bononcini*?' Meanwhile, the comedy of the 'fighting cats', as Faustina and Cuzzoni were called, was so widely discussed that Colley Cibber produced a farce *The Rival Queens*, which drew the Town by its satire and coarseness.

In the late summer Handel revived *Admeto*, but Faustina would have none of it. She pleaded illness, and went off to Paris with Senesino, where she met with an overwhelming reception. The Continent had been well stirred by the news of the quarrel in London. Even the Duke of Bedford had crossed to France to fight a duel with the Duc d'Orléans in order to prove that Faustina was 'an angel and Cuzzoni a devil', and came back with royal blood on his sword. Never perhaps in the later history of London had the community been so stirred by what had begun as a private quarrel. Yet, as Faustina declared when she reached Dresden, 'Not one of those who lavished money on me, and fought and quarrelled about me had a real appreciation of what I consider to be my true merit in art. They quarrelled about me, because they had nothing else to do, and *wanted* to quarrel.'[1]

Free from the jealousies of the foul-mouthed but sweet-voiced Cuzzoni, Faustina went south. She passed through her native Italy on wings of song, a woman unspoiled, a very great artist. She threw her money this way and that in a trail of benevolence. Cuzzoni hoarded hers, and carried it about with her in a bag, fearful of trusting it to English banks. At Venice Faustina was hailed as the finest soprano the city of the lagoons ever bred. The great palaces needed her; crowds gathered to watch her splendid gondola pass. No Doge ever had the in-

[1] A. Niggli: *Faustina Bordoni-Hasse*.

fluence over the Venetians that was Faustina's in the autumn of 1727. She was the uncrowned queen of the lagoons.

At the time a young man of twenty-eight, named Johann Hasse, was professor of music at the Scuola degl' Incurabili in Venice. Porpora, who was shortly to be Handel's opponent in London, had trained him. Hasse was clever, and when Faustina returned to Venice he was easily the most popular composer of the day. Maybe it was a sense of pride as a true Venetian that made Faustina refuse to meet him. She would have nothing to do with the Saxon, although he called at her house to pay her homage.

Impetuous hot-headed Faustina! How easily Fate brought her to her knees! She went to a big social function. Hasse was there in the capacity of a performer. He drew into the background, snubbed, resentful. Presently he sang. Faustina, a little smile of derision playing about her pretty lips, listened, certain that this young man whose *Miserere* at the Scuola had been so much talked about, was only an imported Saxon, mediocre as most of those imported Saxons were mediocre. But as his voice rose she was stirred. The petulant pucker of her lips smoothed away. Very cautiously, and without his seeing, she drew a chair near the harpsichord behind him. What a voice, what a song! It was a song of his own composing, sung in a clear tenor voice of superb expression. She was entranced—she who thought to mock. The twinkling of the harpsichord ceased. Then again it sounded as he broke into one of Domenico Scarlatti's most difficult sonatas.[1]

Faustina had found a master. She said nothing, but she set out to win him, silently, earnestly. Once she threw to the embarrassed young man a flower from the scatter of blooms which admirers in the boxes had cast on to the stage. But the Saxon she had snubbed drew farther and farther into the background until Faustina achieved, as she always achieved. She married him.

It was a romance which, sudden as it had been, endured against all the batterings of chance and time. They were received at every Court, the finest pair of musicians of their day. Dresden knew them, Paris, London. The Electress Maria Josepha of Saxony made them her personal friends, which affection from her was proof enough of their moral rectitude, a compliment Handel's biographers have generally withheld

[1] A. Niggli: *Faustina Bordoni-Hasse*.

from Faustina. Never once did Faustina lose her self-assertiveness on justified occasions. Whilst she was playing in *Zenobia* at Dresden the Elector engaged in animated conversation with a Polish lady of the Court, when suddenly Faustina exclaimed: 'Silence! I command you!' The words were uttered with such majestic force that the conversation in the box of the Elector stopped abruptly and was not taken up again.[1]

Just as they had been opposite in their artistic temperaments, so were Faustina and Cuzzoni directly opposed in their matrimonial ventures. Never did Faustina swerve in her unfailing fidelity to Hasse, for she lived with him without a break for upwards of sixty years. Rich and titled philanderers, fascinated by her voice and attractive personality, kings and peers endeavoured to intrigue her into dishonour. Their blandishments did not even disturb the surface of her deep and settled affection. She moved amongst great men, she was fêted at every Court. But the greatest man of them all, as she judged greatness, was Hasse. In a personality that was impulsive and often difficult to understand and as easily wounded, there remained an unbroken and unbreakable fidelity to her husband. Not so with Cuzzoni. Her lovers openly entered her house, while Sandoni could do no more than hang about like a kept dog. In the end she poisoned him, and was condemned to death in consequence. Yet so marvellously did they contrive these things in those days, that she slipped out of the sentence somehow and charmed audiences with her singing for years afterwards.

The adventure of these two women tried the patience of Handel, and well-nigh drove him to distraction. When it was ended he laughed about it. He called them a pair of hussies. Cuzzoni he declared to be a she-devil, and Faustina Beelzebub's spoiled child. Nevertheless he had a profound respect for them to the end of his days, and a quite impersonal regard.

They had never been to him any more than rather perfect instruments in his orchestra.

[1] *Ibid.*

CHAPTER XII

THE FALL OF THE ACADEMY

ONLY eight days after the battle royal between Faustina and Cuzzoni at the opera, Sir Robert Walpole, sitting at dinner at his house at Chelsea, received the news that King George I had died at Osnaburg. The monarch who had changed the whole life of London—and not for the worse, if little for the better—had perished miserably on the highway like some humble wayfarer on his last journey. An end not bereft of pathos, without the trappings of ceremonial which he loved, and without a woman near him—he who had always loved women.

What a wretched and humble death! What a picture it weaves of the simple process of dying! The King, talking in the coach to the Private Secretary and Privy Councillor who alone accompany him, when a stroke paralyses his right side. He falls forward, his mouth agape, they clutch him, hold him up. 'Drive on! drive on!' moans the crumpled-up figure, as heavy and inert as a sack of corn. They stop the coach, try to pull him out to the road. Then, as they bend over this unregal figure, his wig awry, his eyes wide-staring and frightened, his mouth twisted with pain, the cry, like a little muffled scream, is repeated: 'Drive on! drive on!'

So they drive at a mad rate, over ruts in the road, over cobbles and obstacles, bumping and shaking out the pitiful flickering flame of his life, till they clatter into the Bishop's courtyard at Osnaburg, and hammer with frenzied impatience at the doors closed against the night. And all to no purpose. The hunched-up figure in the chaise is a corpse by the time they make someone understand that they have a king there. The Secretary and Privy Councillor crouch over him, peer into his face, lift the dead hands—scared out of their wits, both of them, and wondering what they are to do with a king's body thrust on their responsibility in a foreign land.

The news, when it reached London town, was as staggering as it was unexpected. No one had believed that he would die, not yet at any rate. He was so happy with his mistresses, his beer, his little funny Court. And he had gone out stupidly in a strange county without the hand of his last favourite to even

THE FALL OF THE ACADEMY

straighten his pillow. Walpole leaps from the table as the news is borne to him, shouts for a horse, dashes into the saddle, clad in the easy *vêtements* of the evening as he is, and rides hell for leather to Richmond, where the Prince of Wales is living in sensual luxury. Such is the pace he makes that he kills a couple of horses on the journey, short as it is.[1] The following day the Prince is proclaimed King of England in London. He is assumed, as his father was assumed before him, with no particular welcome, yet no positive antagonism. His chief virtue is that he is a change.

Whatever plans Handel had for the immediate future were upset by the Osnaburg tragedy. His relations with the Prince had not been so cordial as they had been with his father. Certainly there was no open dislike, but their intimacies had been seldom and a little forced. Anything might happen now.

Handel took the step that healed any breach there might have been. He set to work and composed the four beautiful Coronation anthems which were performed at Westminster Abbey on 11 October 1727, when the crown was placed on the brow of the second George. Indeed, he not only composed the music but selected from the Bible the words which he set.

Apropos of Handel's achievements with these anthems, it may be remarked in passing that there has been brought to light in the British Museum a copy of Mainwaring's life of the composer which came from the Royal Library, and is covered with notes made in ink in a handwriting which is very like that of George III.[2] If it was indeed the King—whose love for Handel's work extended throughout his life, till, in his childish senility, he used to wander aimlessly round the bedroom droning Handel—who had these notes, then they are of peculiar interest. In writing of Dr Maurice Greene, organist and composer of the Chapel Royal, he says:

'That wretched little crooked ill-natured insignificant writer Player and Musician, the late Dr Green, organist and composer to King George II who forbad his composing the Anthems of his Coronation Oct. 22nd 1727, and ordered that G. F. Handel should not only have that great honour, but, except the 1st choose his own words. He had but four

[1] *Walpoliana*, p. 104.
[2] The Mainwaring copy with notes was discovered by Mr William C. Smith, late of the British Museum.

weeks for doing this wonderful work which seems scarcely credible; as to the first (anthem) it is probably the most perfect if possible of all His superb compositions.'

The Coronation was a scene of magnificence, the like of which had never previously been witnessed at the Abbey. The richness, the display of wealth inseparable from the Georges, was manifest to the fullest degree. The dress of Queen Caroline was as fine as the accumulated riches of the city and suburbs could make it; for besides her own jewels (which were of great number and very valuable) she had on her head and on her shoulders all the pearls she could borrow of the ladies of quality at one end of the town, and on her petticoat all the diamonds she could hire of the Jews and jewellers at the other.[1]

The glory of the Handel anthems, wonderfully performed as they were by Handel's own selected choir of nearly fifty singers, gave the new King an opportunity to show the public that his neglect of the musician in the past, and, in some respects, his mild animosity towards him, was a phase that had gone for ever. He promptly decided not only to continue the pensions which his predecessors had settled upon Handel, but to make him an additional grant of £200 a year for his services as musick-master to the Princesses Amelia and Caroline. It was the pledge of peace. George II had many a battle to fight on Handel's behalf, during the coming years, but from the day of his Coronation he remained as faithful to Handel as Handel was faithful to his Court. The hot-head Prince of Wales, with his hectoring and bluster, only made George II more stubborn in the cause of Handel. George had a poor sense of music, but he realized that to throw over Handel would be to alienate himself from the musical coterie which was so firmly rooted now in the town.

The influence of the Coronation and the new monarchy shaped the pleasures of London in the autumn of 1727. Even French farces dropped out of favour for the nonce. Handel rose to the occasion and produced his *Richard I* at the King's Theatre in November. He had not composed the work hastily, for it was begun immediately *Admeto* finished its run in May. The libretto had been provided by Rolli, who admitted that he had borrowed considerably from other sources, a detail in those days. Not that he even gave the authorities he borrowed

[1] Mrs Delany: *Life and Correspondence*, Vol. I, p. 140.

perhaps it is too little to fay, that the work was anfwerable to them. But let the grand *Te Deum and Jubilate* speak for themfelves! Our bufinefs is not to play the panegyrift, but the hiftorian.

The great character of the Operas which HANDEL had made in Italy and Germany, and the remembrance of RINALDO joined 'with the poor proceedings at the Haymarket, made the nobility very defirous that he might again be employed in compofing for that theatre. To their applications her Majefty was pleafed to add the weight of her own authority; and, as a teftimony of her regard to his merit, fettled upon him a penfion for life of 200 *l. per Annum.*

This Geo.III. agrees with Handel that the De Kingu Te Deum is far superior; it has more effect from the Subject being treated with a degree of force approaching to Inspiration, and even the Hallelujah Chorus in the Messiah and if possible Worthy is the Lamb, and the unexpected Amen at the Close.

A PAGE OF MAINWARING'S LIFE OF HANDEL
From the Royal Library. Having the footnote criticisms of Handel and his associates, believed to be in the handwriting of George III.

from the credit of mention. Handel thus had ready an opera which, by remarkably good fortune, exactly suited the mood of the hour in extolling the greatness of a former English king.

But opera was on the wane in London, and even Handel could not revive it. His *Richard* had but a modest run of eleven nights. He had disregarded the warning from all sides, that if he ever put Faustina and Cuzzoni into the same opera again, he was a fool who might understand music but certainly did not understand the feminine temperament. Both the singers did well in *Richard*, and Senesino had some of the best songs. But the opera faded away almost without even passing interest. The clash of arms, the storm and stress of battle in some wonderful orchestration left London unstirred. The quarrel of the two singers drew warring forces afresh to the theatre—but forces led by a meaner public. The noise and commotion of continual interruption made Society—now grown more staid as it waited for the social plans of the new king to unfold—stay away from the opera. Those who attended withdrew directly the babel began. The theatre thus became the meeting-place of noisy crowds that journeyed from slumdom and disreputable suburbia for the sheer delight of creating a diversion.

No opera could survive under such affliction. Moreover, the social gaieties in honour of the succession were also attracting more attention from moneyed circles than was Handel's music. The Academy was going down, and, only because he believed that its closing would destroy the structure of good music in town and complete the surrender of all melody to the French bawds, did Handel fight so hard for it. He openly declared that, but for the Academy, his disgust at London audiences would have driven him out. But he was not prepared to draw away from a losing battle. The failure of *Richard* hurt him, but he disappeared from the Haymarket only to compose a fresh work against time.

He had obtained the libretto of the opera *Siroe, King o, Persia*, from Pietro Metastasio, the Italian poet. But it was too long, and he gave it to Nicolò Haym to cut down. Metastasio was a curious young man, who had had an equally curious upbringing. He was now thirty years of age, and had been born in Rome, the son of a papal soldier. His godfather was Cardinal Ottoboni, and herein was the first link that brought him in the end to Handel. It was the Abate Gravina who adopted and well educated him and discovered his talent as a

poet. Metastasio was destined for the priesthood, but at heart
he had no regard for the Church. He lived a life of never-
ending dissipation. Gravina had died and left him a fortune
of 15,000 scudi, a house and a mass of valuables, and with this
assistance he was content to go the pace. He flung his money
away in debauchery, and moved in the decadent underworld
of the Church.[1] But he was a poet of quality. His *Siroe* was the
product of a man only on the threshold of his career. Handel
was pleased enough with the work, although after Haym had
cut it considerably, he proceeded to reconstruct portions of it
to suit his music. Of this Metastasio was unaware at the time,
or his hot blood and quick temper would undoubtedly have
brought him speedily to England, where he would have created
a greater diversion at the King's Theatre, when Handel produced *Siroe* on 17 February 1728, than ever the querulous
factions of Faustina and Cuzzoni had done.

Siroe was almost Handel's last effort to save the Academy,
and a great deal of it was recast music from his *Flavio* of 1707.
But the mood of London had changed. The Academy had
already come to be looked upon as a scheme as unstable in
conception as any of the wild-cat schemes for which the reign
of the first George had been responsible. Those who had put
their money into the Academy already regarded it as lost. The
shareholders had not received any dividends for a long time;
the titled directorate had almost faded away.

Handel's final stroke of bad luck came with the production
on 29 January of *The Beggar's Opera* at the Little Theatre in
Lincoln's Inn Fields. It preceded the première of *Siroe* by
three weeks and completely took the wind out of Handel's
sails. Gay and Pepusch between them had devised the very entertainment for which the town languished. They had borrowed
the most tuneful melodies in the national airs, and adapted
them to Gay's words in such a way that they had produced
what was the parent of our modern form of musical comedy.
Or, what is more likely, Gay wrote his words to the airs.
Pepusch had assisted Gay in selecting the music; he adapted
the tunes and he composed the overture. He brazenly com-
mandeered from Purcell and Handel. The latter, at the very
moment when he was needing all the force of his reputation to
make a success of *Siroe* in a losing battle, found his grand
march from *Rinaldo* purloined and set to the loud bawling of

[1] Vernon Lee: *Studies of the Eighteenth Century in Italy.*

highwaymen in 'Let us take the road'. True, it was a great air for a highwayman's son, and soon it was all over the town. Whatever reputation it had in *Rinaldo*, it immediately earned far wider notoriety under the ægis of its thieves. The spirit of it, the strident adventure in every note, made, it is said, more vagabonds and pickpockets than any decadent song in English history.

When Gay showed *The Beggar's Opera* to his patron, the Duke of Queensberry, the latter remarked: 'It is a very odd thing, Gay. This play is either a very good thing or a very bad thing.' Moreover, Quin, the famous actor, who perhaps knew more about the public taste than any man of that period, refused the part of the rascal Macheath, because he believed the piece would be a failure. It was therefore given to an actor named Walker, a sound actor but a weak singer, and he had the privilege of being the original creator of Macheath.[1]

The Beggar's Opera stormed London. Gay's brilliant satire, his gibes at Society, his broad immoralities drew to Lincoln's Inn all the pleasure folks in town. The opera ran a lurid course of ninety nights. Swift, who was really the originator of *The Beggar's Opera*, for he had suggested a comedy based on prison criminals to Gay some years before, proclaimed it. Society, blushing at its lewdness in the murky recesses of the boxes, returned to see it again and again. 'I desire you will introduce *The Beggar's Opera* at Gloucester,' writes Mrs Pendarves to Mrs Ann Granville.[2] 'You must sing it everywhere *but at Church*, if you have a mind to be *like the polite world*.' Rich, who was running the Lincoln's Inn Theatre, sat down quietly to be worthy of his name. And the end of it all savours the later romances of the Gaiety of our time, for Lavinia Fenton, the first actress to play the part of 'Polly', eventually married her patron, the Duke of Bolton. Oddly enough she lived happily with him ever after.

This was the mood of London when Handel produced *Siroe* in February. It was given only eighteen performances. Not even Signora Mignotti, who had discarded the corsage for the doublet and created a wild sensation in male attire, could keep the opera going against *The Beggar's Opera*. Yet it had its ardent supporters. 'May your Honour leave as soon as she can her work looms, and, having concluded a truce with

[1] *Life of Quin.* Anon.
[2] Mrs Delany: *Life and Correspondence*, Vol. I, p. 163.

embroidery, come to hear this beautiful opera,' wrote one of them to Lady Newdigate of Arbury. 'I am sure that Jove in his Olympian feasts has not such an elegant diversion.'[1]

It was useless. The counter-attractions of *The Beggar's Opera* were too strong. *Siroe* concluded its run of nineteen performances, yet such was the beauty of Metastasio's libretto that it was continuously reset by other composers for nearly a hundred years. At the end of April, Handel produced his *Tolomeo* (Ptolemy). It was the last shot in his locker for the Academy, and at best a hasty work based on as hasty a libretto by Haym, though not without a singular beauty in some of its airs.

Tolomeo survived seven performances, then the Academy curtain came down for the last time. The money was all gone; mismanagement and extravagance had caused an endless succession of losses. Even Handel with certain commercial acumen could not see that singers paid at the rate of £2,000 a year—which was the remuneration of Cuzzoni and Faustina, and certainly Senesino could not have been much cheaper—gave the shareholders no chance. The failure provoked a scream of joy from Bononcini in the shape of a widely circulated and anonymous brochure giving advice to music producers! The venomous Italian had his little crowning hour.

But, all things considered, the Academy had been an influence, and, in failure, left an influence. It had achieved more to establish sound music with the English people than any musical movement of the eighteenth century. It had declared the mastery of Handel to those who, ignoring partisan creeds and petty quarrels, remained faithful to their convictions. If for no other reason, then, the shareholders did not lose their £50,000 in vain.

[1] Vincenzi Martinelli: *Lettere familiari e critiche.*

CHAPTER XIII

THE PARTNERSHIP WITH HEIDEGGER

THE Academy to which Handel had devoted his thoughts and hopes in those gay spring days of 1720 had fallen down like a pack of cards. Senesino, after a last wild burst of temper, had left Handel and taken Faustina and her husband to Venice. Cuzzoni and Boschi had followed. All the stars adorning the firmament of Handel's imagining had slipped away in the dark. After the nine days' wonder of the Academy's failure and a general clamour, in which everybody was blamed—the directors, the singers, Handel himself—Society came to the conclusion that Italian opera had been an expensive experiment in London which nobody wanted, and Handel an equally unnecessary attachment to a very German and unpopular Court.

He was isolated. He seemed to disappear from the town. Occasionally he was seen going slowly along in the gardens with that swaying, ambling walk so characteristic of him. His broad figure, his German jargon, his deep chuckling laughter vanished from the concert rooms, from the little coteries of true music lovers. Some said he had gone to the Continent and would not return; others that his heart was broken, and he would never be seen again. There were still some who found in his absence from those circles that had been his life a cause for laughter as at the fall of a giant.

He composed nothing. During the months that immediately followed the Academy's collapse, all interest in composition seemed to have forsaken him. Not that he was beaten. He had made money, and had saved money. In the late autumn he concocted a scheme with Heidegger whereby they would both put £10,000 into the King's Theatre, and run it themselves with a new opera of Handel's making. Gay and Pepusch had put up a sequel to *The Beggar's Opera* in *Polly*, for which the Duchess of Queensberry was banished from Court, because she strove to sell some seats to the King, *Polly* being a most vicious and tuneful satire on those circles that moved about the throne. The Lord Chamberlain arose and smote *Polly* and its would-be producers, which made the scandal more scandalous, for everybody wanted to read the opera if they could not see it.

These two efforts of Gay's were heresies which proved to Handel that, given the entertainment it required, London was still prepared to fill any theatre. Heidegger had made his thousands out of his masquerades as Handel had done in the past out of his music, so they got together a puppet board of directors, but were quite clear in their own minds that they alone would direct the theatre.

The project opened a new vista to Handel. Not that there were any singers of sufficient merit left in the country to draw Society out after its heavy dinners. So he set off for Italy in January 1729 in search of artistes, in spite of the fact that he had written nothing as yet for them to sing.[1]

He wandered from Milan to Rome, to Venice, mixing in musical and operatic circles, and became a constant patron of all the theatres. The opera had changed enormously since last he trod the dust of Italy. It had become more popular, and, to a great extent, held the place in public favour later occupied by the music-hall. The poorer classes deprived themselves of the necessities of life in order to buy tickets of admission; even mendicants got in somehow, and crouched in the corners, in the corridors or anywhere, so long as they could see and hear. In Rome no women were allowed to perform in the theatres; the female parts were taken by *castrati*, who usually sang well but acted badly—especially in grand opera—without feeling. The result was that the opera-goer had to be generous in his licence, as for instance, when the part of a pretty vivacious girl was played by a heavy man with big feet and hairy arms, and a thick, black beard. Young boys took the parts of female dancers, and there were police regulations in force by which they had to wear black breeches.

As for the spectators, they wandered about in casual fashion during the singing. The performance being long, and composed of at least two-thirds recitatives, it was the usual thing to visit people of one's acquaintance in their boxes, especially the ladies whose conversaziones one had been in the habit of attending. That was an obligatory attention, and the conversation was carried on openly and loudly.[2] Not that there seemed

---

[1] Handel's biographers declare that he went to Italy in the autumn of 1728, but the *Daily Post* of 27 January 1729 says: 'Yesterday morning Mr Handell, the famous Composer of Italian musick, took his leave of Their Majesties, he being to set out this day for Italy.'

[2] Abbé Jerome Richard: *Description historique de l'Italie.*

to be the slightest consideration for the other members of the audience or the performers. In Venice, for instance, where the theatres were named after the churches, and were the property of noblemen of the city, it was customary to spit out of the upper boxes, and to throw therefrom the parings of oranges and apples upon the company in the pit, without any regard as to where the refuse fell, 'though it sometimes happens upon the best Quality', who, though they had boxes of their own, had gone into the pit to hear better.[1]

In excellence the operas were below the level of those which Handel had given in London. Like the comedies at the lesser theatres, they were coarse and lewd to the worst degree. Addison declared them to be more lewd than any he had seen in other countries. 'Their poets have no notion of genteel comedy,' he said, 'and fall into the most filthy double meanings imaginable when they have a mind to make their audience merry.'[2] Indeed, the whole state of the theatre in Venice, as Handel found it, must have sickened him.

The new adventure was stirring within him the wildest emotion for action. Success: he thought of nothing else. All the life of the southern cities that did not trend to musical achievement left him unmoved. Society attempted to fête him; he spurned it. The sycophants of the Ottoboni Court came out to clamour to him, for was not he a product of that Court? So they said. But he kept out of the reach of pomp and the shallowness of the social scale, searching, travelling, insensitive to fatigue.

In Venice he found Signora Strada, a soprano and in some respects one of the best artistes he ever had. She was troublesome, even more troublesome in the end than Cuzzoni had been. When Handel brought her to London they nicknamed her 'The Pig', so unprepossessing was her appearance. Like Cuzzoni, she was heavy and awkward in her movements, and, like Cuzzoni, she had not the knowledge or the taste to dress in such a fashion that the repellent movements of her body were modified by the beauty of the clothes she wore. When she first came on to the stage to sing, people openly laughed at her quaint waddling figure till the magic of her voice held them silent, yet at first she failed utterly to attract. People could not

[1] Edward Wright: *Some Observations made in Travelling through France, Italy, etc.*, 1730.
[2] Addison: *Travels through Italy and Switzerland.*

forget her ugliness, her uncouth manner, and were repelled by these defects, even though they were charmed by her singing. 'Her person is very bad, and she makes frightful mouths,' wrote Mrs Delany. 'Strada weeps all day because she is so plain that she is afraid to consult her mirror,' declared a diarist, while another remarked that her ugliness was a fitting match for Heidegger's. The jest caught the town. A lampoonist distributed a brochure wherein was described her marriage to Heidegger, 'Which ceremony was attended by the Beauties of all the Ages, from Beelzebub downwards!'

In the face of this onslaught, Handel had some difficulty in getting Strada accepted, but the injustice of the attack made him fight with that desperate courage which he always put up against foul antagonism. Strada was a great artiste; beyond that he had no interest in her, and, as he always judged by the standards of art, it was enough for him. He wrote melodies for her, so composed as to prove the beauty of her voice in every branch of singing. Gradually he worked her into the salons. He took her here, he played her accompaniments there, smiling inwardly perhaps, at the shallowness of a Society that was content to be led by the nose, as he led it in this instance.

Strada was the pick of the singers Handel engaged in Italy, and he secured all his principals before leaving Venice. The best *castrato* at the time—in Italy at any rate—was Bernacchi, who had made a single appearance in London twelve years before, and, on receiving a cold douche for his enterprise, had returned to Italy sentimentally opposed to all things English. But he had made great progress as a singer since 1717, and somehow Handel persuaded him to accept a contract and return to London in the autumn. He also secured Fabri the tenor, and his wife, who used to play male parts, and Signora Merighi, 'a woman of fine presence, an excellent actress and a very good singer with a counter-tenor voice'.[1] As it chanced Handel had bagged a fine batch of Tartars. They were quarrelsome, vain, they worried him continually from the moment they came to London, and when adversity knocked at the door, Strada was the only one who did not leave him in the lurch at once.

To Handel, the immediate future appeared bright in that spring of 1729. He had now at his call a company of singers which, given a good opera, would achieve where the Academy

[1] Mrs Delany: *Life and Correspondence*, Vol. I, p. 184.

had failed. Not that he had yet considered the question of the opera: he had neither written a note nor chosen a libretto. He was on the threshold of some glorious chance. That placid German temperament, with all its English influence and fashioning, was ruffled by excitement and nervous disorder. He rushed wildly from place to place. He accepted invitations to big houses, and as suddenly forgot them. There was not a theatre of any consequence in the cities of Italy with whose company he was not familiar.

In all this turmoil, this pleasure in the prospect of the new conquest of London, one thing alone perturbed him—the state of his mother's health. In March he wrote from Venice to his brother-in-law Michaelsen, and asked him to send news of his mother from time to time. 'You have only to address your letters to Mr Joseph Smith, Banker, at Venice (as I have already explained), and he will forward them to me in whatever part of Italy I happen to be,' he added. In the same letter he avowed his intention of meeting Michaelsen in July, which suggested that he proposed to return to England by Germany, and so visit Halle and his mother on the way.

But things were not to take the order he had planned. His letter to Michaelsen brought a reply which urged him to journey to Halle in hot haste. Frau Dorothea was in grievous distress from a paralytic stroke.

Not a day, not an hour did he wait. He packed himself, bag and baggage, into the stage-coach bound north. His forthcoming adventure in London was forgotten; his newly engaged singers became a mere set of ciphers in his mind. He wrote no letters to London. Heidegger for weeks was without news as to what had become of his partner. Slowly the lumbering coach bore him towards Leipzig, by roadway and rut, past plain and pass ablaze with the wonderful flowers of early summer, their gentians and German lilacs. In early June the coach ambled into Halle, and released a wretched traveller, a morose personage, who had been 'uncommon surly on the journey'.

He scarcely knew what he would find at the Schlamm house. The impossibility of receiving news of any kind made it easy to conceive that Frau Dorothea might have followed her husband to the great Halle vault. Instead, as he entered that house of his birth, he found an aged woman, blind, just creeping stealthily from room to room with the aid of a stick. All else about the house had stood still; the dust of years, tender as the memories that were provoked, lay over the heavy Saxon furniture. The same simplicity everywhere, the same frugality so typical of the Tausts and the old barber-surgeon. The simple, midday meal; the simpler supper. The same streets that had not changed, and their quaint houses lolling against each other like old cronies. No change since that morning when, in the full spirit of rebellious youth, he had set out for Hamburg. No change—save in old Frau Dorothea, that once quiet, pious mother, who had watched him go with grief and tears.

This was the last occasion on which Handel was to see his mother alive. Some foreboding of the fact must have been present in his mind, for he refused all attentions elsewhere. In vain did Bach send his son Wilhelm to him, inviting him to pay a visit to the Bach household at Leipzig. All time that Handel could spare from the pressing call of affairs in London was spent with Frau Dorothea; the last duty he was ever to pay her.

At the end of June he left Halle. On 1 July he reached London, having passed through Hamburg, where he engaged a bass singer named Riemschneider, who, however, rendered such a poor account of himself before English audiences, that he quickly returned to Germany. Preparations for the forthcoming season proceeded with feverish haste, but, apparently, the last thing Handel bothered about was the composition of the opera which was to open his season, and he only completed it on 16 November for presentation a fortnight later. A librettist, Matteo Noris, provided him with a rehashed version of an earlier opera, and on 2 December *Lotario* was given at the King's Theatre.

The opera was a failure; it failed from the first night. If Handel had proved a disappointment he had not, at least, betrayed the public, for the tenor songs in the opera should have saved the work. But he had neglected to observe that the public taste in music was changing, or, if he had observed it, then he had resolved to set that taste at defiance. The liking for Italian opera was rapidly on the wane. London audiences were also getting a little weary of a long string of foreign singers either performing in their own tongue or in a mixture of Italian and English. Strada, too, who made her début in *Lotario*, had yet to live down the attack made upon her personality. In addition, the King had gone to Hanover on a two years' sojourn, leaving his Queen in town to lead Society in the way it should go. She, having little interest in good music and no understanding of it—despite her zeal in having her daughters trained to musical efficiency—did not bother to patronize the Court music-master's new venture. George, with his ladies at Hanover, his cards, his French theatre, was entertaining himself, oblivious to the struggle which Handel was making to sustain good music in his English capital.

Yet another factor shortened the life of *Lotario*. The success of *The Beggar's Opera* with its English songs had completely captured the taste of the public. Imitations of Gay's adventure sprang up in all directions, and were put on at the theatres and concert rooms. Some of them, such as *The Beggar's Wedding* met with a little success, others with none. Nevertheless they all contrived to draw away the audiences which, ten years before, would have crowded the theatre doors to a Handel work. Handel must have noticed these signs or he was supremely dull to his own interests. But since he was ever an opportunist where the public taste was concerned, it is the more surprising that he persisted in giving his audiences what they certainly showed no desire to see and hear. When, at the end of February 1730, he produced a successor to *Lotario* in *Partenope*, he copied his own mistakes, or else he deliberately tried to force upon London the very type of opera it least wanted. Again he rushed his music, and only completed the last act twelve days before the opera was produced. So once more a work of full Italian flavour, and written by an Italian, Silvio Stampiglia, was given to London.

The public shrugged its shoulders, growled at Handel and his Italian antics, and kept aloof. The critics told Heidegger in so many words that he was partnered by an idiot. When the season ended in June, Heidegger, with his passion for money, must have begun to think over the warning. A considerable portion of the twenty thousand pounds they had put up had gone. As critic, Heidegger was on easy ground, for certainly he had produced both the operas well.

The Haymarket partnership was openly sneered at after this brace of obvious failures. Handel was advised by the critics to return to Hanover and create melodies for the King's joy-making at the *Herrenhaus*. Heidegger, on the other hand, was informed that he could only make money by vice—a gibe at the irregularities of his masquerades—and the ugly rascal began to believe it.

The only man who made anything out of this ill-fated start at the Haymarket was John Walsh, the music publisher, who ended his lengthy quarrel with Handel when *Partenope* was produced. He arranged a new contract with Handel over this opera, by which he became his publisher till the end of the musician's life. Handel proved a good client, his best client. Walsh, senior, had made large sums by reprinting other composers' songs in various editions as a set-off to Handel, when the latter took his publishing to Cluer, in addition to a mass of music stolen from Amsterdam. It was his son, who succeeded him when he died in 1736, who was to make more out of the master than his father had done, for he sold edition after edition as rapidly as his presses could produce them. When he followed his father into the same vault at St Mary-le-Strand Church, he left savings to the extent of £40,000, just £10,000 more than his father had accumulated. Verily the pair of them made more out of Handel's music than did Handel himself.

The failure of *Partenope*, and the losses of the season, at last became clear evidence to Handel that the opera as he had constructed it was radically wrong in its appeal. Not for a moment did he believe his music to be the cause. He was probably right. The London audiences were as delighted as ever with his composing. Had he secured a librettist who would have transposed the scene of the book to anywhere on earth except Italy, he might have played to crowded houses. London was tired of Italy, tired of Italian music, tired of its singers with their abnormal habits, their vanities, their silly quarrels. An English libretto at this stage would have saved Handel and established him in management. It is not unreasonable to suppose that this notion was put up to him at the time.

At no period of his life did Handel exhibit the same unyielding 'pigheadedness' as in 1730. He was sore—bitterly sore —at the sucess of Gay's melodious hotch-potch and the trivial French unmusical 'mixed grill', which had come swiftly in its wake. English singers of mediocrity began to earn incomes in these plausible trumperies which kept them from starvation. It was their success—and success of quite a lesser degree—that made Handel seriously consider whether English singers ought not to be introduced into his productions. But the mood which led to the introduction of John Beard and Mrs Cibber was not yet. Handel was stubborn and he had to pay for it. He believed in Italian opera, he was the sworn apostle of Italy as owning all the soul of opera.

He fought Heidegger over the point. The king of masquerade threatened to withdraw from the Haymarket and leave Handel to 'his fantasticks'. He declared that he would withdraw the balance of his ten thousand and cut his loss. It was not the loss of his money so much as the loss of Heidegger that perturbed Handel. He could not do without Heidegger, for he never professed to have the instinct of a babe at production. He wanted the stage set, he wanted to sink on to his stool at the instrument, wave his hand, jerk his wig, sweep his singers to heights which only he had explored before, cry 'chorus' and reach that great antiphony which he had dreamed, careless of all the work of production that had created the atmosphere. Society or paupers might flock the boxes, but the audience was to him just something that listened.

After the failure of the first season he had to act very quickly. Bernacchi, the Venetian *castrato*, had been a dismal failure for no other reason than that he was a newcomer.[1] He had drawn Italy, had pleased Austria, but London would have none of him. Handel dismissed him when the curtain fell on *Partenope*. Riemschneider went back to Hamburg of his own accord, thoroughly convinced that opera in London was a fool's game. Strada was the only singer to whom Handel adhered as worth salvage. By the time *Partenope* had failed, she had become established as a singer in the salons. Mrs Delany wrote of forming parties to hear her sing. Later she unbent, and declared that Strada was the 'draw' of the evening. This unhappy wobbling woman with the voice of gold! Society would have sent her back to Italy, but Handel made it accept her, till she became the one foreign singer remaining in London who carried the public.

The catastrophe of the opening season had been mainly one of singers. The public was violently hostile to half the singers

[1] Manuscript note on the page which deals with *Lotario* in the copy of Mainwaring's life of Handel from the Royal Library (see p. 173), the note may have been written by George III: 'Bernacchi was a good singer, far superior to any we now hear at the Haymarket Theatre, but not equal to either Senesino or Farinelli; had party and fashion not made all mad at the time, Handel's operas must have been full, yet solid and good sense cannot always hold (?) its proper place, though folly and extravagance for a time may prevail.'

Handel had engaged in Italy. Prejudice was the factor that governed this antagonism. Handel, therefore, set to work to sort his principals. He wrote to Mr Colman, British Envoy at Florence, giving him powers to engage Italian singers on his behalf. This man, who, it seems, had no experience in music, was given a commission to engage artistes according to their repute, a foolhardy proceeding only accounted for by Handel's inability to take a further journey to Italy. Senesino, whose hostility to Handel had been obvious from the time that he first set foot in London, the man of a thousand vanities, coarse speech, dirty in living, so that he fed himself with his fingers, was re-engaged by Colman. 'I learn the reasons that have determined you to re-engage Sr Senesino for the sum of fourteen hundred guineas, to which we agree', Handel wrote to Colman in October 1730 on behalf of himself and Heidegger. He was content to sink the old feud, and to subject himself—as he knew he would be subjected—to fresh annoyance and irritation from this fellow, rather than that the future of the opera should suffer. Senesino's vogue had been tremendous; with the aid of this rapscallion Handel believed that the popularity of opera might be restored.

The season opened on 3 November. Handel had become cautious, he was not risking any more money nor quarrelling with Heidegger over new productions till the box-office took to itself a healthier appearance. Accordingly he opened with a revival of *Scipio*, with Senesino back in his original part. Once again the old enthusiastic crowds began to roll up to the doors. All through the winter he made money with revivals of his own and other operas. And no composer of any time ever loved making money better than Handel, not for money's sake, for he lived simply enough, but because it was a form of vanity derived from the knowledge that his work was successful. The partnership was prospering. Society came down to the Haymarket in their chairs and coaches. Handel was sought after with fresh zeal. Society had suddenly remembered him.

At the beginning of February 1731 he produced his new opera *Poro*, though Heidegger would have continued revivals till the end of the season. The book was Metastasio's, and as usual was hastily composed. Handel completed the second act in a week. *Poro*, with its background of Oriental romance, was instantly a success. Never did Senesino in all his London singing rise to a greater height than with the air 'Se possono tanto'.

He had never been out of favour, now he attained in one night a far greater popularity than ever. In a week all London was humming the airs, and, to meet the demand for the music, Walsh rushed out edition after edition. It was obvious that Handel had lost none of his magic. Many declared that *Poro* was the best opera he had given London.

When *Poro* had finished its run *Rinaldo* was revived with the addition of some new songs, because it was an opera of the same romantic category. But the revival was short. A terrific heat wave descended on London at the end of May. It became impossible to sit in the ill-ventilated theatres, though the doors were kept open throughout the performances. Crowds assembled in the street, to the obstruction of all traffic in the narrow thoroughfare, in order to hear the music without the onus of having to pay for seats. But no production could stand against this onslaught of humidity. The concert rooms closed down, the theatres followed, and Handel was the last to shut his doors.

The partnership was prospering; not a single performance had been played at a loss throughout the season. When opera in England had sunk to its lowest ebb Handel lifted it up again. Society was attracted from the lewdness of the French farces, and flocked to his boxes. Even Heidegger began to think that perhaps there was something left in legitimate entertainment after all.

CHAPTER XIV

THE BIRTH OF ORATORIO

A season of triumph, and yet in the midst of it—disaster. On the 27th of the previous December Handel's mother died: on 2 January 1731 she was laid beside the old barber-surgeon in the Handel tomb at Halle. Handel was just completing the score of *Poro* when the news came to him.

Frau Dorothea had been the only woman who ever stole beyond the fringe of Handel's affections. He never understood women: he never cared for them, save with a distant friendship. Faustina, Strada, Mrs Cibber, and the two frail creatures to whom he had once paid attention and who had occupied a few hours of his thoughts, had sped out of his life again as might some trespassers in a world that was never theirs—all these people were no more than moods or points of interest.[1] Handel had ever been, and continued to be, a sort of sexless creature. Only one woman ever influenced his life, ever put the meaning of womanhood into a soul that sang most sweetly of the feminine sex. Quaintly enough, his great understanding of his mother came, not from her presence, her ready influence, but from her distance. She always seemed to reach out to him, in Hamburg, in Italy, in Hanover, in London. When he was soaring, or when in the grip of adversity, she was ever there. He had deserted her, and was always conscious of this desertion. Frau Dorothea might have lived her later years in greater comfort if he had never left Halle, and had developed, not a being who was to sing through the centuries, but a very able organist at the Liebfrauenkirche, with fixed and constant wage, who kept a respectable and quietly ordered life com-

[1] The copy of Mainwaring from the Royal Library which contains manuscript notes supposedly written by George III (see p. 173) has the following scribbled on p. 108: 'G. F. Handel was ever honest, nay excessively polite, but like all Men of Sense would talk all, and hear none, and scorned the advice of any but the Woman He loved, but his Amours were rather of short duration, always within the pale of his own profession, but He knew that without Harmony of Souls neither love nor the creation could have been created (?) and Discord ends Love as certainly as the last Trumpet will call us from our various . . . to the all merciful Seat of a merciful but at the same time Righteous Judge.'

patible with the Handel repute. Instead, he had marched away one gay morning out to the vagueness of a strange quest, to rise to something beyond the reach of her simple mind, to sit with princes and kings, great men and rogues, in a world of his own fashioning. But in some mysterious manner she impressed herself upon Handel where every other woman failed.

He was conscious of this influence in Hamburg when he sent her money from his first earnings. He continued the remittances in Italy; in London, even when his banker was pressing. He gave her what time he could spare from his activities; in the midst of his greatest failures he never omitted to write his regular letter. It is necessary to consider this extraordinary link between them carefully, because it was not a filial relationship so much as the benevolence of a friend, a great mastering influence that was distant, yet ever present—an influence that stood for the entire understanding of a sex in the rather lonely mind of Handel.

A few days after he had produced *Poro* he wrote with the full bitterness of his loss to Michaelsen: 'I cannot yet restrain my tears. But it has pleased the Most High to enable me to submit. Your thoughtfulness (over the burial) will never pass from my remembrance until, after this life, we are once more united.' A little later he wrote again and thanked Michaelsen for his 'arrangements on the occasion of the interment of my dearest mother'.

In the spring of 1731 Handel was a solitary figure in the world. The Halle vault hid his two parents, the sisters had gone. Michaelsen, his brother-in-law, whom he only saw once, had married again and raised a new family. Michaelsen had become a rather prominent figure in German political life; if he had ever heard a Handel air played he would not have recognized it, for he had no interest in music. All the German ties were now to Handel as things of the dust. In England he had his queer assortment of friends: Burlington and Newcastle, who never really understood him. Chandos, who had long since gone down in the melancholy magnificence of his own creating. Heidegger, with his brain pulled by seven devils, steeped in licentiousness, a commercial materialist. A few singers, a few cronies who gathered with him in the concert rooms, wild, kindred souls, when he yearned for real understanding; Christopher Smith, who alone was more to him than these others, because he had an understanding of his humanity.

The success of the season of 1730–31 had brought to Handel new friends. The merit of most of them had little savour of friendship, and they dropped away as quickly as they came, when the shadows began to slowly fall. Among them was James Quin the actor—Jimmy Quin, that quaint, disgruntled Irishman, who would fight a duel with anybody, and sit with hands crossed in reverence at a Handel first night. *The Beggar's Opera* pushed Quin into the friendship of Handel. He told Handel frankly that he did not agree with his operas at all, that Handel might have achieved something had he possessed a sense of humour. If Handel would introduce real comedy into *Poro*, said he, then he would play in it, but he had never been born to play the mute at a funeral. He might even sing, as he had done more than once upon provocation.

Under the veneer of high spirits Jimmy Quin possessed a smarting soul. He had refused Macheath in *The Beggar's Opera* and an engagement worth a few thousands. Handel was the only man who could combat 'this vilely dangerous concoction', as he called *The Beggar's Opera*, and Quin clove to him. Quin was an opportunist. He had started in the Law and been led astray. He spent a very hectic youth. Heidegger caused him to be thrown out of his masquerades more times than he could count. He drank; he trifled in the dovecotes. He was brilliantly clever. He had a supersensitive soul easily aroused to a queer sense of provoked dignity. Soon after he found success on the stage he fought a duel in Hyde Park over Lavinia Fenton, the actress, who played the part of Polly in *The Beggar's Opera*. Any quarrel he could pick over *The Beggar's Opera* was good enough for Quin. As it happened, Lavinia Fenton was sitting in the upper boxes to see a new play when an Army officer made some remark to her which she construed into an insult, and he was rebuffed. Some nights later, the Captain, a little inebriated, hissed her on the stage. This was enough for Quin. He challenged the officer. They met in Hyde Park, and Quin, very nervous, fired his pistol and grievously wounded his antagonist in the tail of his coat!

Poor Jimmy Quin; he had a big soul, but a most disreputable temper. It was his vagrant disposition alone that drew him to Handel, and often the pair could be seen walking up the Haymarket, Jimmy expostulating, Handel grunting and 'God-damning-the-rascal'. Handel was staid in his behaviour; Quin petulant. He had a difference with Bowen, an actor, at Drury

Lane, and promptly shot him in the stomach. Bowen died three days later, and Quin somehow escaped after a brief retention for manslaughter. Just like Quin! He shot another actor in the throat and was playing the next night as if it had never happened. All this was too much for Handel, who told Quin that he had never understood the buffoonery of pistols! But Quin loved it. He lived on the froth of a wave of women, of adventure and independence. He told Handel that he was a god of music and believed it, and he fought a duel for some common little strumpet the same night. He was one of those strange adventurers with a streak of art in their compounding, who steal like vagrants into history, and are really very fine fellows when one has a proper sense of their proportion and romance.

During the rest of 1731 Handel remained in the background. He produced no new work in London. In the late autumn he revived *Poro* for a short run, but the lure of it had passed. He cut out practically all his social engagements. Sometimes he was seen at the Court, sombre, unnecessary, his thoughts miles away, forgetful, preoccupied. He inevitably walked alone, and he would pause in the street and rattle out a mixture of German and English about someone or some new irritation. He became conspicuous by these strange manoeuvres, and many who did not understand thought him mad. In Bond Street and Brook Street he was a familiar, lumbering figure. He prowled through the streets; he browsed through them. Unconscious of outward happening. None of the sounds about him meant anything until he heard a note, a call, that started a theme running in his mind. He was not posing, and he disliked being considered eccentric. But he drifted away in the sway and surge of an imagination of sounds—an imagination that shut out all the influence of sight and feeling.

On 15 January 1732, the partnership made a fresh bid for favour by the production of Handel's new opera *Ezio*.[1] Handel had gone again to Metastasio for his libretto, but the poet's work had been cut and altered out of all recognition. Handel had small regard for poetry or prose; lover of art as he was, he held the opinion that a libretto was merely a hook on which to hang the garment of his melodies. It is true that he often com-

[1] It is not known when Handel began or completed the composition of *Ezio*, because, contrary to his habit, the manuscript of the first two acts is undated, and the last page of the third act is missing.

plained bitterly about the libretti he had to set, and apart from grumbling he took the law into his own hands and sub-edited them at will. Very few had the courage to take him to task for it. Jennens alone did so with any result over *Saul* and *Messiah* in the later years. Certainly Handel ultimately became more cautious in his mauling of the libretti offered to him. Though he held Metastasio and his work in high esteem, he had no mercy for it when he set *Ezio*.

Probably he had some doubt of the opera's success, for he was far advanced on the composition of *Ezio*'s successor before the former was produced, and he was right. *Ezio* ran for a few nights only, and was not at all to the liking of the town. He completed the composition of *Sosarmes* less than three weeks after the première of *Ezio*, and, when the latter failed, he took it off quickly and produced *Sosarmes* on the 19th. Walsh had not been able to get the *Ezio* music cut, and so lethargic was he in this respect, that the widow of Cluer, Handel's late publisher, stepped in and stole it. Very typical of publishing morals when the publisher was deemed respectable, even though he was a prowler who plundered where he liked. Undistinguished as *Ezio* was, it had nevertheless brought about the début in a new Handel opera of Antonio Montagnana, a remarkable bass, who had been sent to London by Handel's agent in Italy. Montagnana was a success, for the greatest merit of *Ezio* was the fine bass songs which Handel had composed for him, and for years to come the Italian was to be one of the musician's best singers.

All the promise of the previous season was absent from that of 1731–32. It was not entirely Handel's fault. *Ezio*, if it was not greatly to the liking of the Handel following, contained some fine work. *Sosarmes*, on the other hand, was hampered by its foundation on an absurd libretto by Matteo Noris, which had been originally set and produced in Venice in 1694. Such silly stuff was it, that the wonder is that any composer, let alone two composers of great standing, ever troubled to set it at all.

There was apparently not much life in the season. If *Ezio* and *Sosarmes* did not lose money for Handel and Heidegger, they certainly did not make much, though they were patronized by that small circle of Society that really understood good music. 'I went to the Opera *Sosarmes* made by Handel, which takes with the town, and that justly, for it is one of the best

I ever heard,' wrote the Earl of Egmont in his diary.[1] Moreover, the two operas had to combat a rising tide of melody, which was being given in the principal music rooms. Private musical societies were also springing up all over London at the instigation of the musical members of rich families. One went to a musical club to sing or play on an evening a week, much as the froth of Society went to the clubs to gamble, and this led to musical gatherings taking place in the homes of Society in greatly increasing numbers, thus luring away those who would otherwise have patronized Handel.

On Handel's birthday, 23 February, an event took place which was the cause of the musician's ultimate change from opera to oratorio. The Chapel Royal was then under the control of Bernard Gates, himself a singer and composer. Gates was an enthusiast, a disciple at the feet of Handel, and he had sung in the Chapel Royal choir as far back as 1702. Ultimately he became a member of the Abbey choir. He was one of a little band of the Academy of Ancient Music, who fought hard for the maintenance of real music in London at a time when lewd and tuneless songs threatened to swamp Handel and all his works. Gates had also been one of those responsible for unmasking Bononcini's thefts and had conducted much of the correspondence with Lotti. He had two daughters, both of whom he named Atkinson, after a Mrs Atkinson who had been laundress to Queen Anne. Mrs Atkinson made money over the dirty washing from the palace, and she spent some of it in bringing up the girl who was ultimately to becomes Mrs Gates. There was therefore some reason for Gates thus honouring the wash-tub by condemning his two children to endless confusion by giving them the same Christian name.

In spite of his few peculiarities, Gates was a zealot, and he decided to spring a surprise upon Handel. As a young man he had sung in the master's performance of his *Haman and Mordecai* at Cannons, so probably possessed a copy of the score, although no print of the work at that time existed. When Handel's birthday arrived he was asked by Gates to attend a performance of the masque by the children of the Chapel Royal at Gates's house in James Street, Westminster.[2]

[1] *Earl of Egmont MSS.*, Vol. I.
[2] The first two performances were held at the Crown and Anchor Tavern.

Handel was delighted with the performance, and considerably touched by the sentiment which had prompted it. A little later further performances were given at the Crown and Anchor Tavern in Arundel Street, Strand, by the Academy of Ancient Music.

Gates may have been responsible for the second performance; certainly Handel's biographers have invariably credited him with the enterprise, but there is little evidence that he was, that the children of the Chapel Royal performed in it, or that Gates was ever there at all. We have contemporary evidence that the second performance was an achievement. 'From dinner I went to the Crown and Anchor,' wrote the Earl of Egmont in his diary, 'where the King's Chapel boys acted the *History of Hester* writ by Pope and composed by Handel; this oratorio of religious opera is exceedingly fine, and the company was highly pleased.'[1] There was obviously a coterie of kindred souls like Gates that was prepared to appreciate Handel in this revolution in musical production.

The two performances set Handel thinking. As *Haman* was appreciated there was no reason why it should not be put on at the theatre. His pupil, Princess Anne, who had missed the performances, desired it above all things, and her enthusiasm decided Handel. At any rate, it was a change from *Ezio* and *Sosarmes*, both of which lacked the ingredients of signal successes.

If Heidegger had aroused a storm from the Church by the excesses of his masquerades, it was a mere breeze compared with the storm that swirled about Handel when his intention was known. To put a Bible story on the stage, played by common mummers, was the text for Church sermons up and down the town. 'What are we coming to,' wrote one prelate, 'when the will of Satan is to be imposed upon us in this fashion?' 'Handel always mixed with the lost; now he had become their slave,' declared another. But Handel, who found in the beauties of Church music, rather than in sermons, his approach to the God of his creed, went quietly on with his preparations, and the impious Heidegger, if he thought the project a little mad, at least was a party to it.

The storm burst in full measure when Dr Gibson, Bishop of London, forbade the performance, and, since he was Dean of the Chapel Royal, the children there were put out of Handel's

[1] *Earl of Egmont MSS*, Vol. I.

The Mattr Eburn
Most Celebrated
SONGS
in the
ORATORIO
call'd
QUEEN ESTHER
To which is Prefixt
The Overture in Score
Compos'd by
Mr Handel.

London. Printed for & Sold by I. Walsh Musick Printer & Instrument-maker to his Majesty at the Harp & Hoboy in Catherine Street in the Strand
N.º 288

By courtesy of the British Museum

THE TITLE-PAGE OF THE FIRST EDITION OF *ESTHER*

reach. The obstacle only stiffened Handel's resistance. He acknowledged no Bishop as he acknowledged no King, as dictator of his performances. Nevertheless, the Bishop's edict originated the oratorio. Finding it impossible to produce *Haman* with dramatic representation, Handel made Samuel Humphreys write some additional words, although Pope had been responsible for the words of the masque, and, instead of the masque in six scenes crowded into one act, it became a full-length work, which Handel renamed *Esther*.

Esther was the first oratorio, and the Bishop had caused it. On 2 May 1732 it was performed, but without costume, scenery, or action. Four days later the Royal Family attended *Esther* in state, and the success of the oratorio was assured. The advertisement in the *Daily Journal* of 19 April best describes it.

'By His Majesty's Command. At the King's Theatre in the Haymarket on Tuesday the 2nd Day of May will be performed

The Story of Esther

An Oratorio in English. Formerly composed by Mr Handel, and now revised by him, with several additions, and to be performed by a great number of the best Voices and Instruments.

'*N.B.*—There will be no action on the stage, but the House will be fitted up in a decent manner for the Audience. The musick is so disposed after the manner of the Coronation Service.'

So small a thing can cause a revolution! Bernard Gates, a diligent little person, not far removed from mediocrity, striving to be different. Keen on this choir. Worshipping that mighty genius that soared so far above. Plume-hunting perhaps, but at least sincere. And a prating Bishop, pious, outraged, shocked. A strictly conventional Bishop who is remembered, not for his good works, but because he stormed across the path of Handel. Officious, hectoring creature—if only he had known that he was going to get the credit of turning the tide of Handel's notes so that the world was given *Saul, Israel, Judas Maccabaeus, Messiah*. Or that, because of it, Time would remember him for his prating, when the recollection of all his good works had gone down into the dust of a forgotten tomb.

Esther was achieved. The first oratorio was an established form of music in England. And Handel had started on that dreaming which found the path to the stars.

CHAPTER XV

THE VISIT TO OXFORD

WHATEVER obstacles Handel had encountered in the past, bad management, the vanity and quarrelling of singers, the hostility of Bononcini and others, had been surmounted by his genius and the strength of his personality. He had not cared. The gibes, the propaganda of enemies had never seriously wounded him. When people did not agree with him he declared it was because they were ignorant. When they attacked him it was because they were jealous. When he had been called 'a German nincompoop' he had commented on the insular mentality of the average Londoner. His work had been too serious an occupation for him to ruminate unduly over these things. A sudden explosion of anger, a flood of invective, and the affair was over. He was lord of his walk; and he kept his dignity.

So far, no concerted powers had come against him. His enemies, by acting singly, had hurled blows which had no more effect than stones against metal. But now the great onslaught was near.

The success of *Esther* set the pirates busy, and the times were early enough for any pirate to jump the law. The first open act of war came from a Covent Garden furniture-maker named Arne—a tradesman with distinct musical qualities, who, if he rendered little service to humanity besides making its beds, at least bred two notorious children—Dr Arne, the composer, and a girl, Susanna Maria, later known as the famous Mrs Cibber, the actress. But Arne *père* was an opportunist. He realized that in resurrecting *Haman* in the guise of *Esther*, Handel had not achieved all the resuscitation of the work he had put in for the Duke of Chandos at Cannons. He therefore coolly set about producing the Cannons version of *Acis and Galatea* at the Little Theatre, directly opposite the King's Theatre in the Haymarket, under the very eyes of the composer, and without the intention of paying him an oat for the theft. He billed the play as Handel's, and even employed Handel's cook, Waltz, a bass of quality and an instrumental player above the average, to play in it!

Arne's first performance took place on 17 May 1732, and it set Handel in a fluster. Here was warfare brought to his very doorstep, and the enemy was smiting him with his own weapon. Arne had put his daughter Susanna up in the part of Galatea, though her contralto voice, never very strong, was quite unsuited to such a part. As an actress Susanna was superb, and she might never have been seriously considered as a singer but for the bold adventuring of her father with another person's property, and the fact that the few deficiencies of her voice were more than balanced by the intense feeling in her singing which became more beautiful with the years.

Handel, storming down the Haymarket, must have raved at the little hussy's name when he found the town crowding to Arne's doors. He cursed Arne, he cursed his daughter, he cursed everyone who supported a policy of 'damned robbery' by going to the theatre. He cursed London. The old firework temperament, the same explosion, and afterwards the same lull and kindliness! Ultimately Arne's Galatea, Susanna, after her domestic infelicities as Mrs Cibber, and the fretful fever of her stage life, became one of Handel's warmest friends. He went to her house in the solitude of his later years, sank heavily and goutily into her arm-chair, and cracked jokes with that rapscallion Quin in the chair opposite. He played for Susanna while she sang, played to her some of the best pieces of his uncompleted oratorio—and really paid attention to what she said about them—told her that she was pretty that night, or plainer than usual, and turned away while she smiled or pouted, to extemporize on the harpsichord, his fat hands dimpled like a baby's. Little did he care about the girl who had pirated his Galatea when, hammered on the anvil of life, she was hostess to him, and he and Quin grew old together. 'His hands are feet and his fingers are toes,' said Quin after one of those Susanna evenings. But if he had revealed his affections he might have added that there was no one he cared more about than the old bachelor perched at the harpsichord.

Nevertheless, Susanna at the Little Theatre was another creature altogether. Her later virtues were not suspected by Handel in 1732. This brigand Arne had stolen a march on him, and had done it rather cleverly. Handel piled enough invective upon him to send him back to his furniture-making, and then solemnly set himself to think how he could circumvent the fellow.

He soon discovered a way. Arne had less than a month's clear run with *Acis* before Handel produced a new version of the work at the King's Theatre. It was a rushed production, put together anyhow. He drew heavily upon his *Acis and Galatea* composed at Naples in 1708, and pushed the excerpts haphazardly into the Cannons version. Signs of the confusion which absorbed him, of the makeshift policy of accommodating his singers to the work in order to cause no delay, are apparent from his scribblings on the score. His Galatea at Cannons had been a contralto, now he gave the part to Strada a soprano. Senesino was his Acis, although at Cannons a tenor had sung the part. He marked on the manuscript a song to be sung by one singer and when the piece was produced it was sung by another. Reinhold, Beard, and others, are marked in pencil to sing songs which they never sang at all.

There is no doubt that Handel was stirred deeply by this production of Arne's, and realized that, unless he could protect himself by producing what might be termed an official version of his own work, there was no reason why all his successes could not be revived against him one after another. His *Acis* of 1732 was a successful but polyglot affair. The songs he had taken from his Naples creation were sung in Italian, those from the Cannons music in English. There was no action on the stage, but a set rural scene of rocks, groves, and shepherds. The production was therefore a novelty. It was not an opera, it was scarcely an oratorio. Interest in the work which had been stirred by the quaintness of the production, and the brazen effrontery of Arne in purloining Handel's work, brought crowds to the King's Theatre. What had seemed a disaster became a triumph.

Not but that *Acis* found as many enemies as it had friends, indeed, a pamphlet which appeared at the time may be quoted as representing the common criticism of many,[1] both on *Esther* and *Acis*. The following was the criticism of *Esther*: 'In this opera Miss Arne an undertaker's daughter appear'd in a most amiable light' writes the pamphleteer.

'I left the Italian opera, the house was so thin, and crossed over to the English one (Arne's) which was so full I was forced to crowd in upon the stage, and even that was

[1] *See and Seem Blind, or a Critical Dissertation on the Publick Diversion*, London. Printed for H. Whitridge.

thronged. Is not this odd, I say, for an English Tradesman's Daughter to spring up all of a suddain to rival the selected singers of Italy?

'This alarm'd H——l, and out he brings an Oratorio, or Religious Farce, for the deuce take me if I can make any other Construction of the word, but he has made a very good *Farce* of it, and put near £4,000 in his pocket, of which I am very glad for I love the man for his Musick's sake.

'This being a new thing set the whole world a-madding. "Haven't you been at the Oratorio?" says one. "Oh, if you don't see the Oratorio you see nothing," says t'other; so away goes I to the Oratorio, where I saw indeed the finest assembly of People I ever beheld in my Life, but to my great surprize, found this sacred Drama a mere Consort, no scenery, Dress or Action, so necessary to a Drama; but H——l was plac'd in a Pulpit (I suppose they call that their oratory). By him sat Senesino, Strada, Bertolli, and Turner Robinson, in their own Habits. Before him stood sundry sweet singers of this our *Israel*, and Strada gave us a Hallelujah of Half an Hour long;[1] Senesino and Bertolli made rare work with the *English* Tongue, you would have sworn it had been *Welsh*. I would have wished it had been *Italian* that they might have sung with more ease to themselves, since, but for the name of *English* it might as well have been Hebrew.'

Acis ran till the early summer, and then London received a fresh surprise to talk about. Hardly had the piece been withdrawn than on 24 June there was produced a pastoral play by Bononcini. The Italian, his career in England almost finished, the enemy who had for years pursued Handel with a viciousness of real Italian intensity, blossomed out at the theatre run by Handel and Heidegger. The enemies of Handel declared that at last the German—by his enemies Handel's naturalization papers had never been acknowledged—had yielded to the public demand for a master greater than he. Handel's friends, on the other hand, retorted that Handel had been generous in allowing Bononcini to use his theatre, but such generosity was the act of a madman. Perhaps Handel may not have been opposed to the concession of the theatre. He gave Bononcini

[1] *Esther* was played at the King's Theatre, May 1732, and contains the Hallelujah referred to.

plenty of rope with which to hang himself, foreseeing the failure that would follow. Finding Handel successful with *Acis,* Bononcini had compounded a weak, ineffectual, rustic opera, hoping to scoop up some of the patrons of the master.

Bononcini was now living a wretched life, deserted by his friends for his plagiarisms, a discredited musician, dissolute and alone. At his best he was a great singer—there was a delicacy and loftiness in his music which probably Handel in his lighter composing never reached. But his vagabondage destroyed the art in him. How this wretched production of his ever gained possession of the King's Theatre in June 1732 one cannot conceive. Handel had his great moments of good nature, but they must have been greater still if he did actually tolerate Bononcini there after the piled-up abuse, the studied propaganda of hatred, the thefts of which the Italian had been proved guilty, even apart from consideration of the fact that the Bononcini production was a futile copy of his own success.

Strada was asked by Bononcini to sing in this work, but her husband published a notice in the newspapers that on no account would she do so, and reserved his reasons.

Heidegger, on the other hand, had had his rough moments with Handel. He was far removed from being a sleeping partner. His purse was his art, and, seeing that Handel was a little befogged by Arne's manoeuvres, and not ready with his next opera *Orlando*,[1] he must have let the theatre to Bononcini to get some return for the summer. It is just the kind of thing Heidegger would do.

Heidegger was the most calm and suave personage that ever strolled through early eighteenth-century London. No one ever saw him in a temper. He smiled at insult, smiled at life. He had a clever cupidity that never could be swindled, and so generally had the last laugh. As for Bononcini and his production, the heat of the summer, and the lack of interest in him and his works, soon killed it. Guests at the Marlborough table were allowed to listen to no other music than that of Bononcini; and it was so rare now for the Italian to discover a melody in his notes that he was his own enemy. The season closed Bononcini down, the Lotti dispute[2] became too hot for him, and the Duchess died—the Duchess under whose social 'pull' he had sheltered his own pettiness, his thefts, his little broken

[1] Handel did not complete *Orlando* until 20 November that year.
[2] See p. 154.

vanities so long. He was left a proven impostor and disappeared.

Handel, in his life's ordering, was seldom clever. He was too impetuous, too flamed to the opportunities of the hour, too ready to throw in all his powers against failure when it loomed up mighty and overwhelming against him. He answered neither Arne nor Bononcini with any new work. He let the season run out; London could talk as it might. He quarrelled with his partner Heidegger; he made it up again. He eluded the Court except for the music lessons and his royal pupil. He became a law unto himself. He was not certain as yet that there was a distinct and sufficient public for oratorio. His conservatism kept him to opera, and only hard hitting and failure eventually drove him out of it. The King had told him that 'these Italian discords' were finished in London. Society tried to teach him his business, so did a falling treasury, but he clung to his creeds.

His new opera *Orlando* was produced on 27 January 1733, after a postponement from 23 January, and its success made him more adamant than ever as the champion of Italian opera. This work is unquestionably one of the three greatest operas that ever came from Handel's imagining. It was based upon an old libretto by Dr Braccioli, which had been originally set and produced in Venice as far back as 1713 under the name of *Orlando Furioso*. The motif of the libretto appealed in turn to every side of Handel's composing; its pastoral simplicity, its love scenes, its storm, its riot of madness. The awakening of *Orlando*, and the great triumph of the finale, gave Handel better opportunities than any other writers had done hitherto. Seldom had Senesino had such songs as *Orlando* provided for him. Yet, as soon as the work had completed its run of sixteen nights, he left Handel and went over to his enemies. Strada, who had been as well served as Senesino in the matter of songs, now reached her greatest popularity in London. Her plainness was forgiven, her uncouth manners, which had softened somewhat under the influence of town, were no longer a bar to her in select circles.

It is very doubtful if the partnership made much money out of *Orlando*. Brilliant as it was, it had not been so well patronized or talked about as *Esther* or *Acis*. It is not surprising, therefore, that Handel decided to temporarily abandon opera for oratorio. He persuaded Samuel Humphreys, who had written the additional words for *Esther*, to compile a libretto from the Biblical story of Deborah. Handel actually completed the composition on 21 February, and put the work into immediate rehearsal.

On 17 March *Deborah* was given for the first time, and, had conditions been normal, it would have proved unquestionably a great financial success. The King, Queen, and the Royal Family were present, with the exception of Frederick, Prince of Wales, who had begun to show his open hostility to Handel for no other reason than because his father was loud in his praise. Mrs Delany declared that *Deborah* was charming. 'Went in the evening to see *Deborah*, an oratorio made by Handel,' wrote the Earl of Egmont in his diary.[1] 'It was very magnificent; near a hundred performers, among whom about twenty-five singers.' In the majestic double chorus that follows the Overture, Handel rose to a height he rarely attained.

Deborah was one of Handel's offspring that had everything against it from the very beginning. The patronage of the Court gave it no additional favour, for never had the Court been so much at variance with the public. The King's recent long sojourn at Hanover had confirmed the suspicion that all his interest was really in Germany. The greatest mistake of all was made by Handel himself. He increased the prices of admission all round. The boxes were a guinea; seats in the gallery half a guinea, so that only 120 people paid for admission to the first performance; the others forced themselves in.

Handel could not have made a greater blunder, for increased prices were at that time the principal topic of conversation. Sir Robert Walpole was floundering in a morass of the national excises, and, to save the Government from bankruptcy, he had revived the salt tax the year before, and now was about to impose a tax on tobacco, and two shillings on spirits and wine. The people were flaming. The muddle had been brought about by Walpole's reduction of a shilling off the land tax, which benefited, of course, the moneyed classes. Therefore he was now taxing the multitude to release those who had money enough and to spare for taxation purposes. National hatred against Walpole surged up at once; there should be, the mob declared, no taxation of the commodities of life. For Handel to put up his prices on top of the commotion, meant adding fuel to fire. They could not do without salt, tobacco, or wine, but they could do without Handel. Such was the import of the outcry.

Instantly, all the bitterness of the town was turned full blast upon Handel. A pamphlet letter was circulated in the Press which hurt him terribly. His regular patrons made resolutions among themselves to ban his theatre. Senesino and others had left him, declaring that they would never sing for him again, and, as a matter of fact, most of them never did. In vain did Handel and Heidegger declare that the increased cost of the seats had been made necessary by the large sum they had first expended on re-illuminating the theatre. People laughed at the excuse and kept away.

Stung by the attempt to crush his work, his temper became violent. At times those about him thought he was demented. Even his singers were afraid of him; Strada alone was the only person who could provoke any docility in one they called a savage beast. He turned upon all and sundry at the slightest cause, rattling out torrents of abuse which stung and cut, but were never intended to wound. Paolo Rolli, who had written the libretti of some of Handel's earlier operas, published a letter in which he spoke of Handel as having been thrown into a fit of deep melancholy, 'interrupted sometimes by raving fits, in which he sees ten thousand opera devils coming to tear him to pieces; then he breaks out into frantic incoherent speeches, muttering *sturdy beggars, assassination*, etc.'

An unfortunate incident occurred about this time which did more than all else to cast Handel into ill repute. Goupy, the artist, had painted the scenery for *Admeto* and several of Handel's later operas, and was famous for his cartoons, often bitter and more often vicious. He was also drawing-master to the Prince of Wales. During the *Deborah* upheaval Handel met Goupy and asked him to go to his house in Brook Street for dinner. Whilst they were walking there Handel carefully explained that he was losing all his money over the theatre, that he was already as poor as a church mouse, and that Goupy must not expect more than the simplest fare. This Goupy received and no more. When the meal was over, Handel excused himself on the plea that he had some writing to do. He had, as he explained it, got an inspiration, and wished to commit it to paper. Time passed and he did not return. Then Goupy, looking out of the window, saw Handel in the next room, which was diagonally opposite, enjoying himself with some Burgundy, a case of which had just been sent him by a well-known peer. Goupy, who had considerable veneration for his cups, left the house in high dudgeon. When Handel returned to the room he found that his guest had vanished without an explanation, and the next knowledge he had of him came from the publication of two infamous cartoons. One of these, called 'The Charming Brute', represented Handel as a hog seated at the organ, surrounded with all the delicacies of the table.[1]

The cartoon spread to all towns of the country with amazing speed. The shops openly exposed it for sale. Society laughed over it. Handel's enemies fêted Goupy as if he were a David who had a slung a stone and struck Goliath. The picture fanned up all the enmity against Handel; it was the most telling propaganda ever issued against him. Ultimately the original came into the possession of Horace Walpole, was eventually sold by auction, and only a very few prints of it remain.

Fine as *Deborah* was, it could not endure against the concentration of adverse circumstances. Its failure helped to bring about the breakdown of the partnership between Handel and Heidegger, which was actually dissolved the following year. Together they had produced some of Handel's best operatic work, and, given time, their treasury might have righted itself. Handel's enemies nevertheless had found the joint in his armour.

The feud between the Prince of Wales and his father had flamed up more furiously than ever, owing to the Prince having thrown himself into the battle against Walpole. The coxcomb now flattered himself that he would become a figure like Sir Robert Walpole by attempting to re-establish the defeated Excise scheme.[2] The King had refused to pay his debts, and had openly excommunicated him from the Court. The Prince, in return, declared that his pet aversion in life was the music of Handel. As his sisters Amelia and Anne were faithful in their worship of Handel, the Prince found this an excellent excuse for quarrelling with them as well. Cut off from the Court—for the Queen above all others was intent on his absence so long as he consorted with the King's enemies—

---

[1] The date of the original pastel is not known, but the two engravings of it date from March 1754.
[2] Horace Walpole: *Memoirs*, Vol. I, p. 70.

the Prince, in the secrecy of St James's Palace, connived at the downfall of the musician. He openly declared that the music of the nation should no longer lie in the hands of 'this impostor'. Being something of a musician himself—he played the violin and composed sonnets, which he not infrequently set to music—he believed that he could hoist himself as the leader of London's Arts. Immaculately clad, he strode down Piccadilly most mornings, accompanied by all the young bloods he had gathered around him in the course of his very hectic youth, vowing the destruction of Handel. There was only one thing that absorbed his thoughts more than women, and that was his hatred for the master. Aware that the Handel–Heidegger partnership would shortly terminate, he saw in this, and the failure of *Deborah*, his opportunity.

A preliminary meeting was held at the behest of the Prince at Hickford's Room, in Panton Street, Haymarket, on 15 June. The Duke of Marlborough gladly arrayed himself beside the Prince as his principal supporter in the coming attack. They had money in plenty, for, if the Prince was not in funds, he certainly had the call on all he required from his colleagues. Their first act was to engage the Italian, Porpora, as composer to this so-called 'Opera of the Nobility'.

Porpora was to lead the onslaught on Handel, and they could not have chosen a better man for the task. He had in him all the venom of a Bononcini. He was a year younger than Handel, a restless individual, who had wandered through half the Courts of Europe pursuing his own shadow. He cherished old hates, and gave them his reverence as a man of honour. For instance, when Hasse, the husband of Faustina, arrived in Naples in 1724, he became a pupil of Porpora, till, happening to meet Alessandro Scarlatti, he transferred his allegiance. Porpora carried that wound as a thing of memory, and well did Hasse pay for its gift in his later life.

But Porpora had a clientele who knew a greater fidelity than Hasse was prepared to give. An instance will suffice. In his later years he came in contact with a Venetian gentleman named Cornaro, who had been sent to Vienna as ambassador of the republic. Cornaro had a mistress who lived for music, and she took singing lessons from Porpora. This woman insisted that her lover should take Porpora with them to Vienna and refused to be separated from him.[1] Porpora was packed up

[1] Fétis: *Biographie universelle des Musiciens*.

like some chattel in the baggage of this elegant lady. He was maintained in plenty, studied like some imported monarch, and paid a fine salary into the bargain in return for the music lessons. All for the freak of a woman. Yet that Vienna visit was to yield something that was to be of use to the world. It was at Vienna that Porpora began the musical tuition of young Haydn.

Handel had met Porpora in his Venetian days, and had complimented him on his three-act opera *Berenice*, unsuspecting that this man, whose ability he extolled, was to be launched against him in London not a quarter of a century later. But Porpora was a creature of nerves and vanity, and the greatest teacher of music of his age in Europe. Royalty were taught by him. A Porpora education was the greatest musical gift one could bestow. Humble people with talent poured big fees into his coffers for the same service. Yet he could never keep money, for he had no knowledge of money values. When the Prince of Wales and his circle selected him as the instrument to use against Handel, they had him at his prime. He was then making considerable money, and living in indigence. He could not help it; it was his way. He went through life like that, and he finished his life in the same fashion. He lived some eight years longer than Handel, but the old habits remained. Signor Corris, who had studied under him for years, was his disciple at the time of his decease, and he said that, though his friends paid him a considerable sum, not only for his instruction but for his board, Porpora kept so miserable a table that he was frequently driven out of the house by hunger to seek a dinner elsewhere.[1]

The selection of Porpora as the leader in 1733 of this 'Opera of the Nobility' was without question a move of cleverness. Europe was ringing with the name of Porpora at the time; he was a figure of importance. As soon as he was given power at the meeting in Hickford's Room, he set to work at once. The Prince's apostles had put up a large sum of money, and, even if the Prince himself could do no more than shake his stick and breathe venom against Handel, he was an enthusiastic leader for a crusade. Porpora's first act was to buy off Handel's singers one by one. Senesino, who is credited with having been present at the Hickford's Room meeting, was the first. Cuzzoni followed, with Montagnana hard in her wake. Handel

[1] Fétis: *Biographie universelle des Musiciens.*

found his organization falling to pieces.

Disaster waited on the steps of the King's Theatre. Hot and frequent must have been the conferences between Handel and Heidegger. The game was up, yet they refused to admit it. Each had lost the £10,000 put into the partnership, and was well loaded with active debts besides. It meant a financial finish to both of them, for, whereas Heidegger had squandered the thousands he had made over his masquerades in loose living and a whole seraglio of mistresses, Handel, if he had made profits, had sunk the greater part of them in the King's Theatre. But he had never secured the profits which should have been his, bearing in mind the fact that it was his work that brought the crowds to the theatre. He had ever borne the blows, with but a small share of the treasury.

But why did he now suddenly throw up everything and depart for Oxford? Was it mood? Was it some inducement which the annals have failed to record? He had no association with Oxford; he knew no one there who could exercise any persuasive influence over him. Moreover, he was on the verge of his great battle with the 'Opera of the Nobility', which should have been sufficient reason to keep him in town. He must have been fully aware that it would be a battle of hard blows and no quarter. Yet he suddenly rushed out of London at the behest of the Vice-Chancellor of Oxford University, just after his best singers had left him for the rival stage. He packed up what remained of his company, and appeared in the university city prepared to give at least a couple of performances a day, to rehearse, with all the hindrance which rehearsal away from one's base entailed in the eighteenth century, and generally put in more work in one week at Oxford than he would have devoted to a production before royalty.

The circumstance was the more peculiar because he had just been annoyed by the Oxford people. It is said that they had asked him to become a Doctor of Music, and, coming at a time when his German birth was constantly hurled in his face, the invitation was accepted. Then he discovered that the honour would cost him nothing short of £100 in fees for the patent. He was furiously angry. They had tricked him. The honour which cost them nothing to bestow was a trap to bag his guineas. So he reasoned. 'I will not throw my money away for what the blockheads wish,' he declared. He refused to pay a farthing, and he never received the title.

There is little doubt but that the offer was a trap to get Handel to Oxford—a trap laid by a few enlightened souls who wanted the prestige of his company and his music. For when he refused to go forward with the honour, they gave him an invitation to take his company to the city.

Without doubt they paid him very well indeed for it, as is suggested in a document recently discovered for the author at Bologna. The narrative is better told in the writer's own words.

'The author of this narrative having forgotten a circumstance of about the year 1738, which helped not a little to re-establish Handel's credit and to put his affairs in order again, I may be allowed to mention it, as it brought both honour and gain to Handel, and among a very numerous company of Strangers I was present there. Having decided to celebrate the Public Art with great solemnity, and thinking there would be a much greater number of people if it were accompanied by some popular entertainment suited to the ladies and others who would be little pleased with the usual scientific proceedings, the University of Oxford invited Handel to come and give a performance of an Oratorio or some solemn music on that occasion for a very generous fee though not pretending to say generally what it should be. But they say it was sufficient for the transport of the whole orchestra there and back, as well as the pay of all the musicians, who were little short of 100, for all the time they were away from London, which was about a fortnight. They say the lowest player received a pound a day, and the singers much more according to the pay they require. Handel was so scrupulous in his choice of virtuosi for this performance that there was not a single poor performer; and for their part they competed so to shew their respect for the Master for being chosen on this occasion according to their merit and not by their engagements, that every one of them appeared so well dressed that it looked an orchestra of cavaliers. The success of the Oratorio matched completely the work of the virtuosi and the splendour of the performance, and it was said that Handel took back to London £4,000 clear of all expense.'[1]

[1] *Compendio della vita di G. F. Händel*, in the library of the Liceo Musicale at Bologna.

It is evident, therefore, that Handel's main object in going to Oxford at all was to replenish his depleted coffers, while the University authorities induced him to come purely with the notion of making a celebration of what was in the ordinary way a very dull proceeding.

So Handel with his company reached Oxford on 4 July, and immediately went into rehearsal. On the following day he listened to the speeches all the morning, including an oration in lyric verse on 'The Praise of True Magnificence' from Lord Guernsey, a student at the time, and a son of the Earl of Aylesford. His relative was Charles Jennens who, a few years later, provided Handel with some of the best libretti he ever had.[1]

At five o'clock the same day Handel opened his programme with a performance of *Esther*.

Oxford, which was the home of the arts, knew little of Handel beyond the copies of his music which Walsh poured into the city. It is doubtful if a dozen people in the place had ever seen him. Rumour had dragged his name, his very genius, this way and that. Yet Handel's arrival at Oxford might have been the triumphant entry of a king. The crowds were tremendous, all the roads leading to the city were packed with dusty, eager travellers bent on the same errand. Even the accommodation at the hostels ran out, and people slept in the streets. 'The Persons of Quality and Distinction who are come hither on this occasion,' wrote the local paper, *Read's Weekly Journal*, on 14 July, 'make a very grand appearance, and are greater in number than ever was known before; the little hutts of the neighbouring villages are mostly filled with the Gentlemen of Cambridge and Eton, there being no accommodation in this or the Towns within five or six miles about us.'

Handel had brought down in his pocket a surprise for these people of Oxford in the shape of a new oratorio, *Athalia*. Samuel Humphreys prepared the libretto from Racine's story. Apparently Handel had composed it quietly without any intention of producing it at the King's Theatre. By chance, he

---

[1] On the death of Handel, Christopher Smith, his amanuensis, gave to Jennens a set of the Master's concert scores, numbering over a hundred volumes. These Jennens passed on to the Earl of Aylesford, whose son, this same young Lord Guernsey, in due time owned them on succeeding to the title, a happy souvenir of his oration before Handel. These volumes are now in my Collection.—Author.

finished the composing just a month before he went to Oxford, from which it is scarcely imagination to suppose that, in return for the honour of a Degree, he intended to give the University people a new and special work. Even when the question of the fees he would have to pay annoyed him so much that he told Oxford politely that it could keep its honour, he still presented the city with *Athalia*. But he made the city pay for it. He sold the seats at 5*s.* each, and came back from Oxford very considerably richer than he went there. A true Handelian stroke!

His intention was to produce *Athalia* at Oxford on the ninth, but as 'the ceremony of conferring the Degrees on the gentlemen engag'd the Theatre to a very late hour of that afternoon Mr Handel's new Oratorio call'd *Athalia* was deferr'd till this day (10 July) when it was performed with the utmost applause.'[1] As well it might, for *Athalia* contained some of the richest jewels of his composing. The opening lines sung by Strada were a wonderment in melody such as that newly built theatre had not known earlier. Then followed the chorus 'The rising world Jehovah crown'd', which was the greatest triumph in oratorial chorus Handel had yet reached.

> *'He lent the flow'rs their lovely glow*
> *And breath'd the fragrance they bestow'*

sung by a chorus of virgins, moved many in the audience to tears.

Handel gave *Athalia* five times in Oxford during the visit, and packed the theatre to the walls on each occasion. He performed *Esther* three times, *Deborah* once, a *Te Deum* twice. Never had Oxford heard the like in music; it pressed him to return. And yet how some of them hated him for no other reason than because he was of German birth! Thomas Hearne of St Edmund's Hall wrote that Handel 'and his lousy crew, a great number of foreign fiddlers' had come down. He resented any foreigner in the place, and he resented more than anything Handel charging 5*s.* for a seat; for he referred to it in his diary day by day, and ended up with a note 'His book (not worth 1d.) he sells for 1/-'. Not that Hearne was alone. Pamphlets attacking Handel and 'his foreign crew' began to appear. All this upheaval was, nevertheless, mere turbulent froth, a prejudice against his foreign singers. In a short time the city was seething with a controversy that might have been

[1] *Read's Weekly Journal*, 14 July 1733.

as spirited as that which had surged around Faustina and Cuzzoni if Handel had not gone back to town at the end of the week. What would have happened if he had paid their fees and taken his Degree it is hard to say. There would have been a university scandal; they would have burned his effigy and carried his head—or a masque of it—on a pike. The oddest thing about the visit, when all is said and done, is that Handel, being short of a bass—Montagnana having now deserted to the 'Opera of the Nobility'—dug out his cook Waltz, forgave him for ever performing in Arne's pirate version of *Acis*, and took him to Oxford to sing a leading part.

When Handel reached London again he arranged with Heidegger that their partnership should continue for another season. Colman, who wrote the words of the next opera, *Ariadne*, which Handel began composing in October, had received a letter from that rolling-stone Owen MacSwiney, then at Bologna with Walpole, that he had discovered a fine *castrato* in Giovanni Carestini, who might very conceivably fill the place left by the secession of Senesino. Carestini's voice, originally a soprano, had fallen to the fullest, finest, and deepest contralto perhaps ever heard. Oddly enough, he had first appeared on the stage in a performance of Bononcini's *Griselda*, and he came to London now to try to save the Handel ship from foundering. Like all the *castrati* whose perfections of singing brought admirers to their shrines, Carestini had his conceits. If he was not so great a monument of vanity as Senesino, he was scarcely more generous in his loyalty to those who employed him.

Handel completed the setting of Colman's *Ariadne* in October, but did not produce the opera until the end of January 1734. Meanwhile, every difficulty was flung in his way to prevent his producing a new opera at all. The 'Opera of the Nobility', sponsored as it was by the Prince and the 'bloods', who surrounded him, and led by Porpora, had opened in Lincoln's Inn at the end of December with an *Ariadne* of Porpora's composing. Handel's opera, following a month later, was therefore a counterstroke in the shape of a duel between two composers, who stood alone in Europe at the moment. Very certain of himself, Handel stepped into the ring. If he had inferior singers—only Carestini and Strada remained now to head his bill—he at least had the strength of his own work against Porpora's.

But it was never a battle of merit, but one of personal bias. The Prince sat nightly at Lincoln's Inn with his complement of ladies. The King and Queen, infuriated beyond measure with the insolence of their son, lounged in the royal box at the Haymarket, a little dismayed by the poor house.

Handel was going down; the empty theatre was the visible sign of it. His wretched singers could scarcely maintain the beauties of the songs he had given them. Not that *Ariadne* was Handel at his best. His worries, the increasing cohorts of the enemies against him, the falling away of friends who, in fat years and lean, had followed his fortunes and patronized his work, his treasury thin and starved for want of new capital just when his enemies had money in plenty to burn, coloured his composing. But for a few fine songs and a wonderful minuet, his *Ariadne* was a collection of rather masterful sounds.

The giant strength of the man was breaking. The sedentary life, the constant strain of working all through the day and night, often without food had begun to tell. He had his hours of placidity shut up in Brook Street, with naught to jar him save the rumble of a horse vehicle, or the scuffle of the chairmen carrying the denizens of these streets to the haunts of glamour, and back again. Then followed the hours of nerve-racking activity at the theatre—hours that spoiled his temper and threatened to warp his great spirit. He slept little when production was driving him. Only when the mood was failing, when the first grey slabs of daylight began to dim his candle, did he creep up that broad staircase (which still exists) to his couch in the front room above. The growing years, the turmoil of increasing combat with enemies and anxiety, were sapping the physique of the giant whose brain still leapt as if to the pulse of some retarded youth.

For a period the fight between the two *Ariadnes* was balanced. The competition of the one helped the other. Antagonists of the Court supported the Prince's exploit, only to find themselves left out of the controversy because they were unacquainted with Handel's version. The struggle, bitter as it was, and carried on without quarter on either side, assisted the finances of both parties. But the clamour of politics and political hatreds soon claimed the louder voice.

On 6 July 1734, Handel and Heidegger separated. The partnership, which had produced some of the best work Handel had composed, failed in the end as dismally as did the Academy. The closing of the theatre was, as one paper declared, 'a triumph for the debtors of a brace of madmen!' Heidegger had dipped into art and burnt his fingers; Handel, too, had lost his money, but his prestige remained undamaged.

Then, before he had time to consider his plans, his enemies stepped in and took the lease of the King's Theatre ere he could protest. Handel was thrown into the street. His money was gone, his partner had left him. Society shed some crocodile tears and exclaimed: 'Poor Mr Handel', but was rather pleased that the Prince of Wales had been able to score an achievement off that horrible Court.

They said that Handel was finished. The Prince bragged about it. Porpora declared himself to be the music-master of London. But, while they were talking, Handel decided to go into management on his own account.

CHAPTER XVI

THE CRASH

THE disappearance of Handel from the King's Theatre was the beginning of a new and desperate phase in the conflict with the 'Opera of the Nobility'. His enemies had won the first bout. They had beaten him out of the theatre which had been associated with so many of his productions, and of which he loved every brick and stone.

He was now a solitary figure. Most of his friends had deserted him. Among his singers Strada alone remained. There was nothing left for him to do but to take the theatre in Lincoln's Inn Fields from which his enemies had launched the attack which culminated in the capture of the Haymarket. The lessee at Lincoln's Inn Fields was Rich so, although Handel was his own manager, he had become associated with the very man who had done more than anyone to ruin his operas with *The Beggar's Opera*.

Rich was a creature of opportunity. His father, a theatrical manager, had built the theatre at Lincoln's Inn Fields, and died in 1714, just before it was finished. On the night the theatre was opened it was therefore draped with crêpe. At his father's death John Rich found himself, at the age of twenty-two, in possession of a respectable fortune and a new theatre. Within six weeks of the descent of the last curtain on old Rich, his son had opened the theatre he had inherited as a going concern. There was no art about Rich—he ran his theatre to pay. Although he was popular, he had had very little education, and his language was vulgar and ungrammatical. He was a very good talker, and loved a private party where he could gather his cronies about him and regale them with the latest anecdotes of the town. He had an irritating habit of calling everybody 'Mister'. It clung to him all his life, and it was commonly said that he would call the undertaker 'Mister' when he came to measure him. This habit drew a sharp rebuke from Foote in later years. Rich had called Foote 'Mister', whereupon the actor asked him why he did not call him by his proper name. 'Don't be angry,' pleaded Rich, 'for I sometimes forget my own name.' 'That's extraordinary indeed,' Foote retorted. 'I knew you would not write your own name, but I did not suppose you could forget it!'[1]

Rich produced masquerades, pantomimes, cheap farces—anything that drew the guineas; he even played harlequin himself. Moreover, he got together as disreputable a set of actors and actresses as ever herded in the green-room of a London playhouse.

To come down to this in the autumn of 1734 must have been, for Handel, the descent to the pit. The gang that clustered about Rich used the theatre as a sort of club whether they were employed or not. Some actually slept on the premises because they could not afford common lodging. The whole neighbourhood stank, the narrow streets that led to it were a drift of mud, garbage, and filth, that lay rotting for weeks on end. Footpads made play in the alleys. Not infrequently they overturned a chair on its way back from the play and calmly robbed the tenant thereof. Into this wretched atmosphere Handel, ill and overwrought, was pitchforked with the broken remnants of what had once been a great company of singers. His health was against him, the town supercilious now that he had fallen from his high estate, and was using a theatre which was the home of mediocrity, lewdness, and discomfort. But not for long. Rich, with the money made out of his cheap productions, and *The Beggar's Opera*, had been busy building a new theatre in Covent Garden.

Handel's last act before joining Rich had been the production of a serenata called *Parnasso in Festa*, to celebrate the marriage of Anne, the Princess Royal. Not that he had been in any mood to compose music for rejoicing, since the marriage took place in March—only four months before the dissolution of his partnership with Heidegger. But his position at the Court made it necessary that he should compose for the event, though Anne was not his favourite pupil, and she had done a great deal to set the Prince of Wales against him.

It was a peculiar marriage. Her husband, the Prince of Orange, was a good-looking humpback with plenty of audacity and no money. His income was less than £12,000 a year, and his debts would have taken a king's income for years to repay. He was a happy-go-lucky nincompoop. His fiancée despised him before she was married to him. George

[1] Thomas Davies: *Life of Garrick*.

and his Consort disliked the very sight of him; the Prince of Wales was openly rude to him. The marriage was now persisted in because it would assure the Protestant succession. So the town said. But the true reason for the match was that there was no one else in Europe for the Princess to marry. She had to choose between marrying this piece of deformity in Holland, or dying an old maid immured in her royal convent at St James's.[1]

So Handel, tired and buffeted by ill-chance, put *Parnasso* together. He can scarcely be said to have composed it for the occasion, since so much of the music was taken from the *Athalia*, which he had produced at Oxford the summer before and never given in London. But *Parnasso* was deemed of sufficient importance to draw all the Royal Family to the first night, including the Prince of Wales, who could scarcely keep away from what was a state function.

When Handel opened his season at Lincoln's Inn Fields on 5 October he put on *Ariadne* again. There was still some excitement left in town about the rival *Ariadnes*, and he was sure of a certain audience. But he soon found that the crowd he could draw at the King's did not want him at Lincoln's Inn. The treasury takings were meagre; at no time was he able to sell more than half his seats. The better places were all but unfilled. He therefore revised *Il Pastor Fido*, with a few additions, including some dances for a French dancer called Mlle Sallé and her satellites, a company of performers whom Rich had imported from Paris before Handel's arrival. They were not of the class of artistes whom Handel usually associated with his work. They were licentious, but not wildly so, as the broad minds of the age accounted them. But the battle was going against Handel; he knew it. Furthermore, he appreciated very keenly that if he were beaten out of Lincoln's Inn as completely as he had been from the Haymarket, all chances of recovery were lost.

To understand the reckless gambling of Handel at this period, the irresponsible things he did, the manner in which he allowed his art to be profligated and abused for the first and only time in his life, it is necessary to realize what was forming against him. He appears now partly demented, a wild, hunted figure, throwing reason to the winds. For, in

[1] Hervey: *Memoirs*, Vol. I, p. 233.

addition to capturing his theatre, the 'Opera of the Nobility' had the greatest army of talent against him that has ever been engaged for consecutive performances in a London theatre. And they were now negotiating with Hasse—the husband of Faustina and a composer of considerable merit, who would have shone as one of the brightest stars in the Georgian firmament had he not been overshadowed by a group of greater men than himself.

The Prince's band of titled marauders bought up Hasse. They bought up Senesino, for a while at any rate. They had Cuzzoni, although ere long she disappeared mysteriously one morning without a farewell to any of those who still clung to her wretched personality. They had secured Montagnana. All the people whom Handel made in England. And now they produced their master-stroke in the discovery of Farinelli.

Farinelli, whose real name was Broschi, was brought hurriedly into fame in London at a wave of Porpora's magic wand. Porpora knew his game, every move of it. He knew where to find the chinks in Handel's armour. He knew the sheer emptiness of the Prince, of Marlbrough, of all the titled idlers who had set out to ruin a man who, from his generous soul, had thrown the honours of praise to Porpora in another country. Porpora read the public like a book, but he was mistaken in his reading of Handel. He thought he had broken Handel when he forced him out of the Haymarket.

The Farinelli connection had really begun in 1720; so do the simple episodes, scarce worth remembering, bring their harvest in the passage of years. It was at Naples in the house of a famous singer who had been acclaimed at the opera—La Romanina. Metastasio was there. Porpora was there. And Farinelli, then a boy of sixteen or seventeen, 'too tall to be hidden behind the stumpy Porpora'. Farinelli was shy, with that common self-consciousness of youth, and La Romanina tried to draw him out. She endeavoured to make him sing. He protested. Yes, he would sing, but only with her. She sat at the harpsichord and struck a few notes. When she began to sing, the boy following timidly, subduing his voice, till the ecstasy of the music seized him, and he was nervous no longer. The voices soared together, Farinelli's, pure, true—so true that all those who listened waited breathlessly—a voice that rose all-glorious above that of his companion. La Romanina ceased singing. As if unaware that she sang no longer, Farinelli went on.

When this song bore to its close, when the last faint notes of the harpsichord tinkled away and were lost in the sweetness of the boy's singing, those in the room could endure the tense passion of it no longer. They rose up; they embraced him. They cried: 'Bravo, Farinelli!' Metastasio jumped from his seat, ran to the harpsichord, seized hold of Farinelli and cried: 'I am honoured by this applause; we belong to each other, we are fellow pupils, twins, born together for the World—you in song, I in verse. Remember it in later years, twin brother.'[1]

When Porpora came to the King's Theatre he remembered Farinelli, who was then performing at Dresden, and his first act was to sign a contract with him to come to London. Truly Porpora was earning his money from these titled backers, who lacked a single note of music between them, but whose sole mission was to destroy Handel.

Porpora, cunning, soaring on the wings of vanity, introduced Farinelli at the King's Theatre three weeks after the opening of Handel's season at Lincoln's Inn Fields. He had put on Hasse's *Artaxerxes*, an opera of considerable merit, and far better than Porpora's own *Ariadne* with which he had first attacked Handel. Farinelli with his faultless soprano, and the wonderful singing of Senesino in the same opera, killed all interest in Handel and his works. Nevertheless the singers had never met till they came face to face on the stage on the first night. Then, as Farinelli finished his first song, the great Senesino, overcome with his singing, ran up to him and embraced him.

Farinelli was a new sensation—the greatest sensation since the arrival of Senesino, years before. He was the perfection of all *castrato* singing. He was a magician of that delicate singing which has in it all the beauties of a woman's voice, and greater wonders than any woman's voice ever discovered. The applause of the town heartened the 'Opera of the Nobility'. How the Prince raved, and the little dangerous mouse-eyes of Porpora closed in vicious exultation! What could Handel's Carestini do against these—Senesino and Farinelli—the most perfect combination of voices possibly in the story of the world's music? 'I went to the Opera where I heard the

[1] Vernon Lee: *Studies of the Eighteenth Century in Italy*.

finest voice that Europe affords—Farinelli lately come over,' wrote the Earl of Egmont in his diary.[1]

If Farinelli had the voice of a divine flute, he certainly could not act. Senesino, on the other hand, was an actor as well as a singer of superb grace. A critic of the time who knew both of them, wrote thus about Farinelli and his singing:

'What a Pipe! What modulation! What ecstasy to the Ear! But heavens! What Clumsiness! What Stupidity! What offence to the Eye! . . . If thou art within the environs of St James's thou must have observed in the Park with what Ease and Agility a cow, heavy with calf, has rose up at the command of the milkwoman's foot: Thus from the mossy bank sprang up the divine Farinelli. Then with long strides advancing a few paces, his left Hand settled upon his Hip, in a beautiful bend like that of the *handle* of *an old-fashioned caudle-cup*, his Right remained immoveable across his manly Breast, 'till Numbness called its Partner to supply the Place; when it relieves itself in the portion of the other *handle of the caudle-cup*.'[2]

However great were Farinelli's shortcomings as an actor, he immediately became the craze of the town. He was fêted everywhere. For a long time he kept Porpora's theatre crowded at every performance. Society, which had conceived an aversion to Italian singers, decided to take Farinelli to its bosom, in spite of his nationality. When Farinelli was singing the theatre was always crowded. Lines of carriages, stretching down to Pall Mall, waited at the theatre doors; flunkeys, an army of flunkeys, hung about in multicoloured liveries.

One day while the Farinelli craze was at its height, a wag who was fond of music appeared at the gallery door, where the porter demanded the name of his master. To this the wag replied: 'I am the Lord Jehovah's servant,' and with that he was admitted, one of the doorkeepers saying to the other: 'I never heard of that man's master before, but I suppose he is some scurvy Scotch lord or other.'[3]

The Duchess of Portland, writing of a birthday party six months after Farinelli's arrival said: 'There was about *forty*

[1] *Earl of Egmont MSS.*, Vol. II, p. 122.
[2] *Reflections upon Theatrical Expressions in Tragedy.* Anon., 1755.
[3] John Taylor: *Records of My Life*, Vol. I, p. 331, 1832.

gentlemen that had an entertainment, and Farinelli made a magnificent suit of clothes, and charmed the company with his voice as Orpheus did (and so kept them from drinking).' Verily, he must have been a brilliant fellow, if his fascination was able to restrain a Georgian Society gathering from its cups! It can no longer be denied that the conceited little man had his points, which were of some service to humanity.

Presents were showered upon him. His salary was £1,500 a year, but he never made less than £5,000 a year during the whole of his London engagements. The Prince of Wales was so carried out of himself by Farinelli's singing that, although his friends could not afford it, he gave the singer a gold snuff-box set with diamonds and rubies, inside which were some diamond knee-buckles, and a purse of one hundred guineas.[1]

No wonder that Farinelli grew rich, for the example of the Prince was followed by all Society. But the days were to come when the Italian was to sing in London to a house containing only £34. 'He received', wrote the critic of his singing, whose comment is quoted above,

'from some of the fairest hands in England, Boxes ennobled with those expensive Productions of Nature (jewels) and render'd more valuable by including notes from the Bank for £1,000 each. Such were the offerings of that day to the *tuneful see-saw Clumsiness* of this Divinity. At the same time, on the *same* stage, and in the same Operas, shone forth in full excellence of Theatrical Expression, the *graceful*, the *correct*, the *varied* Deportment of Senesino. Farinelli had *stole* the Ears, but Senesino was the *Eyes* of the House: that part of it, I mean, that were not musick mad. Twice in a short interval of time have I seen this masterly Actor in the Opera of *Artaxerxes*. And eighteen years have not obliterated the memory of that great, but natural manner of his Deportment in a scene which called for the exertion of almost *every Passion*.'[2]

Under these attentions, Farinelli's conceit soon became appalling. He strutted through Society like a little bantam-cock, till, in spite of his singing, the town became bored with

[1] R. A. Streatfeild: *Handel*, p. 135.
[2] *Reflections upon Theatrical Expressions in Tragedy*. Anon., 1755.

the presumption of the fellow. He was coarse and patronizing, and his temper unspeakable. An episode which occurred at the Prince of Modena's levee at St James's Street, to which all the best people in town had been invited, must have reminded Farinelli that he had rather overestimated his importance. The singer had taken it upon himself to attend the ceremony without an invitation. He strolled into the crowded room, believing that he would be hailed by everybody. In his gorgeous velvet and brocade he passed from one group to the other, expecting conversation to cease as he approached.

Then the Prince of Modena saw him. He flamed with indignation. Quickly he edged his way through the crowd towards Farinelli, and when he reached him he exclaimed in a voice not loud, but full of portent: 'Get out, fellow! None but gentlemen come here!'[1]

Whilst the Farinelli storm was in full blast Rich moved into his new theatre at Covent Garden, and Handel with him. This was just before Christmas 1734. The satirical pen of Hogarth could not be restrained at such a house-moving, and he published a print showing Rich's triumphant entry into the new theatre with a long train of actors, authors, and scenery; Rich clad in the skin of a dog—one of the personages in the harlequinade of *Perseus and Andromeda*—is seated with his mistress in a chariot drawn by satyrs. The diminutive figure of Pope is seen in one corner treating *The Beggar's Opera* in the most contemptuous manner, from which it may be supposed that the poet, jealous of his old friend, had expressed an unfavourable opinion of the production.[2]

Directly he had installed himself at Covent Garden, Handel prepared to give more violent battle to his enemies by producing two new works in rapid succession. He opened the theatre with a *pasticcio* based upon his former operas, and entitled *Orestes*. But it was only designed as a makeshift while he rehearsed his new opera, *Ariodante*, which he ultimately produced on 8 January 1735. The Handel of *Ariodante*, and the operas that immediately followed it, is a different person from the composer of *Rinaldo* and the kindred triumphs. He had begun to realize that the public no longer desired serious

[1] *The Political State of Great Britain*, October 1737, p. 390.
[2] *Caricature History of the Georges*, p. 87.

Italian opera, or, if it did, then Hasse—a master of this form of craft—could give all that was required at the King's Theatre.

Handel was changing. He was introducing a lightness into his work which remained henceforth in all his operatic composing till the end of his days. He could no longer please himself, as his finances became alarmingly low. Now he was groping to find a halfway-house between the opera that was his real form of expression, and that music which had developed from the changing mood of the people. *Ariodante* is slight, with only a few moments of tense drama, and he concluded each act with a ballet in order to accommodate those French dancers, Mlle Sallé and her supporters.

The offerings of the new theatre and a new opera failed to attract. *Ariodante* had but a brief run, and could not have paid expenses. Yet Handel, just fifty years of age, was full of fight, just as his body was becoming full of rheumatism. At times he could scarcely move for the pain that racked his right side. The act of playing an instrument gave him intense agony. Sleeplessness was beginning to worry him. Great moods of depression assaulted him like grim overhanging clouds, and lasted for days. His temper became violent; some of his actions almost brutish. Then as suddenly the rheumatic pains would depart, he would sleep for a couple of days like a dog, and, waking, eat heavily, and enjoy again his wine, his beer. The scowls on his face, that kept those about him from approaching unless driven to do so by actual necessity, departed with the other ills, and the kindly smile would reappear like sunshine after rain. Then would he crack his jokes, fling his repartee across the table at his colleagues like darts of fire, and go on working more furiously than ever, careless of what his body would have to pay for it. The enemy of which he had the smallest fear was pain.

By means of working in frantic periods of haste, which periods were followed by others of suffering and inactivity, he had his new opera *Alcina* ready to go into rehearsal at the beginning of April. It was based on a libretto by Antonio Marchi, and must remain for all time one of the most exquisite of his lighter works. 'The best he ever made,' wrote Mrs Delany. Its superb ballet music, for which doubtless the Mlle Sallé troupe was the provocation that led to its composing, shows Handel in his richest moods. Even before the new opera was through its rehearsals he had trouble with Carestini who was to carry the principal part. Carestini, with that conceit without which no singer of the period was complete, sent back to Handel the beautiful song in *Alcina*, 'Verdi prati', as unworthy for him to sing. Handel could ill afford to risk a quarrel with Carestini, but he did not hesitate. He called a carriage and drove to Carestini's rooms. He hurried in upon the singer with all his fury raging. 'You dog!' he cried, 'don't I know better than yourself vat is good for you to sing? If you will not sing all the songs vat I give you, I vill not pay you ein stiver!' The sight of the outraged master storming up and down the room impressed Carestini. He had nothing more to say. He sang the song.

Alcina was produced on 16 April, and Handel ran it through to the end of the season. Amongst his singers in both *Ariodante* and *Alcina* was Cecilia Young, who afterwards married Dr Arne. Cecilia Young was a high soprano,[1] but Susanna Arne— by now Mrs Cibber—was a contralto. Cecilia Young was considerably talked about, and Strada was so jealous that she resented the coming of this new soprano. Otherwise the company appeared to be happy enough.

Directly *Alcina* finished the season, Carestini created a disturbance. He was still smarting from Handel's rebuke over 'Verdi prati', and he now announced that he was going to leave the company. The loss of Carestini meant a desperate blow to Handel at the time. The company was none too strong, and there was no prospect of obtaining a successor, even if one existed, ere the autumn season opened. It was useless for Handel to reason; the blood of the Italian had been fired, and it would never be cooled in England. Within a few days of the season's close he left London for ever. Verily, Handel had to pay for his rebuke and London also, for thereby was lost one of the finest singers of the Handelian epoch. The outraged man returned to Naples, and for a quarter of a century afterwards sang all over Europe, soaring from triumph to triumph. But he had finished with Handel and with the English. Mlle Sallé also departed, piqued by a demonstra-

---

[1] Burney in *The History of Music*, IV, p. 653, describing Cecilia Young, says: 'This lady, afterwards the wife of Dr Arne, with a good natural voice and a fine shake, had been so well taught, that her style of singing was infinitely superior to that of any Englishwoman of her time.'

tion that had been made against her nationality at one of the last performances of *Alcina*, and returned to Paris, where she joined the French Academy of Music. If her loss was in many ways a good thing for Handel, since she was becoming very unpopular, she had brought out of him some of his greatest ballet music.

After the close of *Alcina*, Handel, subject to more frequent recurrences of illness and lengthening moods of depression, began to be disturbed about his health. If a break came now, complete victory lay with the Prince and Porpora at the King's Theatre. Stories began to circulate that the Haymarket management was in trouble on account of increasing expenses and a diminishing treasury. Several of the Prince's supporters had tired of the venture; the novelty of running opera had worn off, and they were putting up no more money. A smash at the Haymarket seemed possible at any time.

The break, when it came, would leave Handel master of the field. He knew it, and fought against the tiredness and pains of his body. Soon after *Alcina* closed he went to Tunbridge Wells, and stayed there some weeks, drinking the waters. He walked about, a lonely figure, moody, speaking to no one. But if the waters drove the rheumatism from his joints, they could not ease his mind. He was worried about his singers, his finances. The next season—if he would ever reach a next season—seemed too dark for the mind to explore. He wrote to Charles Jennens, the librettist, who at a later stage was to be so closely associated with him: 'There is no certainty of any scheme for next season, but it is probable something or other may be done, of which I shall give you notice.'

The future was vague; the stars in their courses seemed set against him. He returned from Tunbridge Wells better physically, but mentally in a state of storm, and immediately began to look round for singers. Further importations from Italy were impossible—he had neither the time nor the funds. But there was a boy he remembered—a boy who had sung with the Chapel Royal children at Gates' house at Westminster, when they gave their performance of *Haman* for his birthday. That boy, John Beard, was now nineteen years of age, and had developed a clear tenor voice which, if it had no outstanding sweetness, possessed certain strength.

Handel engaged Beard as his leading tenor. It was an

experiment—a daring experiment—but it was a case of the devil driving. He then set about a composition of a version of Dryden's Ode, which Newburgh Hamilton rearranged for him, and he completed the scoring of the oratorio *Alexander's Feast* in twenty days. A prodigious performance! Bearing in mind the state of his health, the anxieties that were crowding in upon him, and the everlasting irritations of his enemies, it was the work of a giant—work that was rewarded by the most extraordinary first night he had had for years, when the oratorio was produced on 19 February 1736.

The theatre was crowded; the *London Daily Post* declared that there was over £450 in the house, an extraordinary sum even for a Handel 'big' night. When Beard sang the first song:

> '*Happy, happy, happy pair*
> *None but the brave deserves the fair,*'

London knew that Handel had discovered a great singer. Little did Beard realize that from this February night he was to be associated with the master through most of the triumphs of his later years, and many of his failures. If he had to go down to the depths with Handel he was to rise also to the heights in his company.

Alexander's Feast was in most respects the greatest triumph of Handel's middle life. The grandeur of his music, the majestic choruses, reflective of all the pomp and richness of the story, the beautiful words of Dryden—and never before had Handel set so fine a 'book'—Strada at her best, Cecilia Young at her best (for was not her lover, Dr Arne, who was to marry her before the season was out, watching her from a box?), to say nothing of the 'hit' made by young Beard—all these circumstances bore upward to success. The rapture of the audience, the vast applause, 'such as had seldom been heard in London', must have fired the blood that was growing slothful in Handel's veins. He took to himself a new youth, and worked harder than ever. But it was a false strength, born of excitement.

The approaching marriage of the Prince of Wales compelled Handel to consider the demands of the Court with regard to music. If the Prince had done more than anyone in an attempt to ruin him, he could only shut his eyes to it. Apart from the slight to the Court which taking counter-action would involve, his own dignity would never have per-

mitted it. If the Prince had accumulated against him a formidable arsenal in the shape of ample funds from a group of
worthless lordlings, Handel accounted his Art something
greater than all the money of the Prince's collecting could ever
buy. So he sat down and composed his 'Wedding Anthem'
with a good grace. When the Prince married the Princess of
Saxe-Gotha at nine o'clock on the evening of 27 April, the
Anthem was played so well that the Prince, moved by the
sublime crashing chords of the organ, declared his delight to
those about him, but he spared Handel any expression of his
praise. Not that Handel was dismayed. He promptly composed
his festive work *Atalanta*, and made it his next production.

The marriage of the Prince was a farce, threaded with
tragedy. None knew it better than the Prince; none less than
the English people who acclaimed it. It was a mere passing
scheme in the ordering of kings. On 12 February, George II
had sent five cabinet ministers to the Prince of Wales at St
James's to suggest that if His Royal Highness liked it, he
would demand the Princess of Saxe-Gotha for him in marriage. The Prince knew nothing of her, had never seen her.
Was marriage so necessary? His idle life, his secret suppers
were more to his liking. But he returned the obedient reply
that 'whoever his Majesty thought a proper match for his son
would be agreeable to him!'[1]

Happy hypocrite! With only a short time of celibacy left
to him, he delved more deeply into the hidden life of the
profligate. As for His Majesty—he would send for the lady,
but the Embassy declared that there was a certain procedure
which must first be carried out. Papers must be prepared, endless noodles in this country and in Germany must be acquainted officially with the King's decision, before it could be
accomplished. The King became impatient; he was going to
Hanover to Madame Walmoden when Parliament was up,
and would stay for nobody. If they could not hurry this
marriage business, he would depart and leave it to them.

Some ministers became scurried. The Princess was sent for,
and the wretched girl—no more than seventeen years of age—
arrived at Greenwich without a companion of any sort, save
a man, on Sunday morning, 25 April. They took the news to
the King in chapel, and he went on with his prayers. No one
worried about the girl, who had not the first idea where she

[1] Hervey: *Memoirs*, Vol. I, p. 112.

was to go. She might fuss around with an accumulation of trunks, jabbering German, and everyone sublimely unconscious and casual as to who she was, or why she was there. She spoke no English and only a few words of French. But what was the need? Her mother had assured her that as the Hanover Family had been over twenty years on the English throne, to be sure, most people in England spoke German (and especially at Court) as often and as well as English.[1]

The Court left the unhappy girl in that plight till Tuesday, the twenty-seventh. And this was her wedding-day! Then they brought her in the royal coach to Lambeth, took her, white and trembling, across the river in the royal barge, and thence to the palace. By this time she was half-dead with fright; so much so, that when she was shown into the room where the King and Queen were awaiting her (round which room the King had stormed and sworn for an hour, because of the Princess's late arrival, while Queen Caroline sat in meek suffering at the excitement of her lord), she tripped and fell prone on the floor at the feet of her future father and mother-in-law. It was a happy accident. George liked this humility; it spoke volumes. So when the man she married ill-used her, left her in constant tears, George II never forgot that pathetic figure lying on the floor. He helped her. When her miserable husband died, it was on George she relied, and he never failed. With all his infidelities to his own wife—and no better Queen ever served an English King—he possessed still that peculiar streak of gallantry, of kindliness, which made life bearable to this girl from Germany.

They married her at nine o'clock that night while the strains of Mr Handel's music filled the air. They supped an hour and a half later in the royal apartments, when the Prince, with his whirligig conceit, declared that his sisters should sit on stools, while his bride and himself had chairs. But the new Princess remonstrated: chairs were to be brought for all, and they were brought.[2] It was the first family jar. Then the Prince retired to his dressing-room, donned his gown of silver stuff, his cap of the finest lace, and the *quality* were afterwards admitted to see the bride and bridegroom sitting up in bed.[3]

[1] Hervey: *Memoirs*, Vol. I, p. 115.   [2] *Ibid.*, Vol. I.
[3] *Ibid.*, Vol. I, p. 118.

It was for this farrago of nonsense that Handel made his 'Wedding Anthem'; for this sacrificing of an unhappy Princess that he composed his *Atalanta*. He produced it on 12 May with the utmost splendour, just a fortnight after the royal marriage. It carried the spirit of love, of the open air, of nymphs, of passionate music, and tender cadences. The effect was magical; the Prince now began to ruminate. Was this man worth destroying who would produce such music for the wedding of his enemy? He sent for Handel. Of what he said there is no record, but the old feud was ended. The Prince withdrew from the King's Theatre enterprises, and seemed to find more favour in attending Covent Garden.

The King was annoyed. The Prince was his enemy. The Queen had refused to see him; he was forbidden the Court. Verily Handel found himself between the devil and the deep sea.

But the action of the King soon decided matters. He withdrew his subscription from Handel's theatre, and with the ladies of his favour he kept away. 'Where the Prince goes,' he declared, 'I am not seen.'

So he went off to Germany. To Hanover. To Madame Walmoden. . . .

To Handel the breaking-point was near. He spent the autumn of 1736 trying to recuperate, to call back those energies which this great war, waged against a single soul, had drawn from him. He drew into utter seclusion, in the belief that, without the stir of social affairs, his old strength would return. He had spent his youth on his art and now he was not aware of it. For those great nights of triumph, of mastership, when the shake of his wig told people he was pleased, he had paid and paid again, and the bill was still undischarged. Though he believed he was resting by keeping in seclusion, he was composing. He had two operas completed and another half done before the winter returned. He was concentrating all his faltering strength into the effort of a giant, and told himself he was recuperating. Money was running out. True, *Alcina* had paid him, but the heavy mounting of *Atalanta* did not pay its expenses. The future was dark and menacing.

He strode round his room in Brook Street like a penned-in fury. He was living on dreams, hopes. Page after page of score was turned, and he still seemed fresh. Fatigue, when it came, was a visitor of uncertain intervals; he knew no time for sleeping. The night was the day—just some working space.

Ugly rumours that he was dying began to spread about town. It was the 'Opera of the Nobility' that was dying, worn out, spent and moneyless in the unholy fight. Whilst they counted the meagre contents of their coffers down there in the Haymarket, Handel sat in that front room of his Brook Street house composing, heaping up, as he believed he was heaping up, all the weapons for a new battle. Pain stormed at his right hand, swept with raging torment down his right side, but he pushed it away. He talked to himself, to the empty room, addressed imaginary people . . . composed a little . . . still talked. The daylight came and he thought it was sunset. . . . He worked on. Then, when autumn was dying, he arrived at the theatre as if he had just returned from a holiday.

He had two operas ready. The first, *Giustino*, he had begun and finished in three weeks. Only eight days after he had completed *Giustino* he began *Arminio*, finished the first act in four days, and completed the whole opera in eighteen days. To have argued with him that work capable of saving the lost fortunes of a theatre could not be produced in this hurry, would have brought a storm of invective. In the case of Handel, too, it would have been exceptionally incorrect.

He produced the second opera first, on 12 January, and it failed. Mrs Delany wrote that when Handel played the overture to her before the production, she found it charming. But *Arminio* never realized but a small portion of his expenses, although Handel had put up some attraction in Conti, who elected to be known as Conti Gizziello, after D. Gizzi, the maestro who had trained him in Naples. Conti first appeared in a small part in *Ariodante*, and then again in *Arminio* and *Giustino*. The *Daily Post* said he was one of the best performers in the kingdom, but he certainly could not save Handel.

The desperation of Handel is visible in his actions of the next few months. *Arminio* failed in January, and he put on *Giustino* in February. It played to empty houses, yet the King's Theatre in the Haymarket was papered from boxes to the pit. He took off *Guistino*, since it was a hopeless project

from the first night, and completed the opera *Berenice*, based
on some unknown libretto. The days were gone when he
could have his libretti prepared for him; he must obtain his
words where he could. *Berenice*, with its beautiful minuet and
the elusive haunting melody of its songs, was produced in
May, and taken off the same month. Handel was breaking,
but he fought on. He revived his *Triumph of Time*, one of the
first fledglings of his Italian sojourn, and put it on in the
early summer. It too failed.

The giant was falling. The singers at the theatre were upset
by the constant failures, the continual new parts. They
drifted away one by one, the Italians to return to their country
in the belief that opera as such was dead in London. Debtors
were pressing. The balance of the £10,000 saved, with which
Handel had come out of the King's Theatre debacle, had
disappeared. He was piled with debts. Of what use now was
the favour of the Prince of Wales, since the Prince and his
moneyed friends had destroyed him?

The pain in his arm increased, until his right side was
partially paralysed. In vain did the *London Daily Post* publish
a notice in May that 'Mr Handel who has been suffering from
rheumatism is recovering'. He was not recovering; he was
becoming rapidly worse.

He closed the doors of Covent Garden Theatre on 1 June
1737. He was broken. The debtors then began to assail him
in shoals; they threatened to send him to prison. He must
have reasoned with them very effectually, for, instead of casting him into the debtors' penitentiary, they all accepted his
bills. With one exception—del Pò, the husband of Strada,
refused to accept any settlement but that of cash.

Ten days later the King's Theatre closed down with
admitted debts of £12,000, two thousand more than the total
claims against Handel. If Handel's fortunes were obscured
for the moment, they were not beyond recall, but Porpora,
whose music had never been popular in London, was finished.
He went to Venice, composed, sank step by step into extreme
poverty, till, when pleurisy killed him, a public subscription
had to be organized to pay for his funeral. He went to a
pauper's grave as Handel in due course went to the
Abbey, which perhaps was one of the comparisons of
greatness.

Meanwhile, his mind unhinged, his body tormented by

tortures unspeakable, Handel travelled to Aix-la-Chapelle. He was bowed, and walked painfully with a stick, but his eyes, that ever saw beyond tomorrow, perceived with certainty the things that were to come.

CHAPTER XVII

THE DEATH OF THE QUEEN

HANDEL remained at Aix-la-Chapelle until November. He had no plans for the future, and, if he dreamed about further productions, he had no money to carry them out.

But now the road was clear for him in London. Porpora had disappeared. Senesino was in Italy creating a new furore. Farinelli had returned to the same country with a fortune made out of his three London seasons, and forthwith began the building of a palace which he named 'The English Folly' as a compliment—a rather back-handed one—to those who had filled his pockets and snuff-boxes with guineas. The London operatic world had tumbled to pieces.

Aix, with its quiet, its waters, soon produced a cure in Handel. The pain disappeared from his limbs, the curtain of despair from his mind. So complete was his cure before the summer waned, that he is said to have left the baths and gone straight to the Cathedral, and to have played upon the organ with all his old fire, whereupon some nuns who chanced to be passing declared that a miracle had been performed.[1] The glamour of those victorious nights in London was a lure with him still, and refused to be shaken off. He returned to London through Flanders, with the opening of a new opera in his pocket.

Back in Brook Street he was idle no longer; he began to work feverishly on the new opera. He discovered, too, that his old partner, Heidegger, had taken the King's Theatre, and opened there at the end of October with a *pasticcio*, called *Arsace*, which had not the strength or life in it to keep the theatre open for more than a few nights. He had taken the theatre hurriedly, without properly considering the question of productions, only to find that there was no one to compose for him. Therefore he was about to defy the churches and revert to his old scandalous masquerades, when the blinds were drawn up in Brook Street, and the heavy swaying gait of the musician in Bond Street told London that Handel had

[1] Mainwaring, p. 115. n.

returned. Heidegger lost no time. He urged Handel to finish his opera that he might produce it.

Handel was not yet free from trouble. Directly his return was announced in the *Daily Post*, Strada's husband, del Pò, pressed for the settlement of his debt, and threatened to put Handel into prison. Only the knowledge that he was composing a new opera for the King's Theatre made him stay his hand for the moment.

Affairs at the Court also hindered Handel in his project. On 9 November, Queen Caroline, sitting in her new library at St James's Park, was suddenly taken ill. She was hurried home. They dosed her with the prescriptions of this and that quack. Bent with pain, she played her part at the drawing-room that night, only to be reprimanded by the King because she had forgotten to speak to the Duchess of Norfolk. She went to bed, grew rapidly worse as the days passed. Doctors buzzed here and there, surgeons talked, shook their heads, grew hopeful and despondent by turns, and could do nothing.

The Queen's increasing agony decided them at last to operate. Once, twice, thrice did they cut this unhappy woman, and all the trouble she gave them was to groan violently during the process, for which she apologized fulsomely to one and all when the operation was over.

The news spread that the Queen was dying. She *was* dying. The Prince of Wales made vain efforts to see her, but she refused him admission because he still consorted with the King's enemies. With some hypocritical affection for his mother, he implored the King to permit him to visit the sick chamber. 'If the puppy should, in one of his impertinent affected airs of duty and affection, dare to come to St James's, I order you to go to the scoundrel and tell him I wonder at his impudence for daring to come here,' the King told Lord Hervey.[1] 'His poor mother is not in a condition to see him act his false, whining, cringing tricks now.'

The King was terrified by the Queen's condition. He forgot his kingdom, even his seraglio, in his fears. For the truant who philandered and lived for the pleasures of the hour was, after all, a homing creature. He had always leaned on the Queen; although frequently rude to her in public, his rudeness had brought only a weak smile. He told her frankly about his infidelities, wrote to her about them from Hanover, and

[1] Hervey: *Memoirs*, Vol. II, p. 499.

grumbled because she had written only nineteen pages in reply.[1] Mrs Selwyn, one of the bed-chamber women, was wise in her generation when she told the King that he was the last man with whom she would have an intrigue, because he always told the Queen![2]

And now the Queen was sinking towards Death. He passed from violent temper to abject fear. When Dr Hulst told him that she could not live, he promptly boxed his ears.[3] The Queen had once said that no woman had a right to live after fifty-five, and it was obvious that she would not live. Only her courage made her dying so slow. They dragged in old Paul Bussière, the aged surgeon of ninety, and asked him what could be done.

Again the knife. Again the wretched Queen, distorted in agony, faced the horrible ordeal. Old Bussière held the candle while Ranby performed the operation. For a moment the Queen smiled up at Ranby, when he was about to begin, then, remembering that he had but recently divorced his wife, she said: 'What would you give to be using your wife in this manner!'[4]

The flicker of a smile crossed the grim, clean-shaven face of the surgeon, and he went on with his work. Then came a diversion, which shows the strength of this woman. Ranby was stooping over his task, and Bussière bent nearer with the candle when, in doing so, he set his wig on fire. The incident was a little alarming. Now to show her contempt of the pain the Queen told Ranby to stop awhile, as he must let her laugh![5]

Nothing could save the tormented woman. Imagine the scene of that Sunday night, 20 November. The King weeping furiously, and kissing the lips he had so often left for others. The Queen opening her eyes awhile and urging him to marry again, and then his historic reply: '*Non, non, j'aurai des maîtresses.*' The King choking out sobs in the hot heaviness of the room. Presently the Queen seemed to sleep a little, and the King, worn out with his grief, crept on to a bed on the floor and, for all his sorrow, fell asleep. Princess Emily was

[1] Walpole: *George II*, Vol. I.
[2] *Ibid.*
[3] *Earl of Egmont MSS.*, Vol. II, p. 445.
[4] *Ibid.*
[5] *Ibid*, p. 446.

on the couch-bed in the corner. Then, rousing herself and all those in the room, the Queen suddenly exclaimed 'Pray!'[1] In a few minutes she who had borne so much from the puckered-up figure by the bedside, and never revealed her burning hurt to another, passed quietly out. In vain did Princess Caroline hold a looking-glass to her mother's lips in search of some tiny breath of mist on its surface that would still betoken life. Her little startled cry came too soon for the waiting King. ' 'Tis over!'

What a panic seized the miserable man! So affrighted was he lest the spirit that had just passed should return, that he ordered a menial to stay in his bedroom for the rest of the night.

But the King's grief was no more than a surface storm that never reached the depths. He became wildly demonstrative in his sorrow. He gave funeral orders; he countermanded them. He ordered mourning, but, strive as they might, they could not find mourning deep enough for his display. In his perturbation he snubbed Walpole. He wanted an imposing funeral, so that the Queen should not be buried till such time as was necessary to prepare her obsequies in all their magnificence. He wanted great music; he wanted Handel. He then ordered a new vault in Westminster Abbey to be made just big enough to contain the Queen's coffin. Then he ordered it to be made twice as large, because he said he would be put in the same vault when he died, and they were to see to it that his dust mingled with that of his Queen.

Therefore, in the process of time, they did see to it. He was buried in the same vault, and the side of his coffin and the adjoining side of the Queen's coffin were withdrawn before the vault was filled in. For years the withdrawn sides of the two coffins stood on end in Westminster Abbey, leaning against the wall. But long before George II went there he had forgotten all about this odd freak of fancy that had given such an order.

He soon brought Madame Walmoden to England and made her Lady Yarmouth. How easily she made him forget. He had grown too puffy and fat and gouty, and ever pursuant of bright eyes, to care very much where they left him when that ignoble nuisance, Death, put an end to what had been a caper better pursued than attentions to the State. Perhaps

[1] Hervey: *Memoirs*, Vol. II, p. 538.

he did not care what the People thought. There was still the prerogative of Kings. But the People did think, and immediately after the Queen died someone printed an epitaph and pasted it up on the Royal Exchange. It ran thus:

> '*O Death, where is thy sting*
> *To take the Queen and leave the King!*'[1]

The calamity at the Court—and it was recognized as a dire calamity, since the Queen had always maintained the dignity of sovereignty, which George profligated so insistently —stirred the town. It stirred Handel. The Queen had always been his friend. George, on the other hand, had supported him in a vagrant fashion, in such spasmodic moods of energy as one not inured to the Arts could bestow. Handel realized at once that the Royal funeral, which was fixed for 17 December, made certain demands upon him which could not be ignored.

He immediately threw aside his opera, and set some words from the Bible, which were selected for the purpose by the Sub-Dean of Westminster. With these words in front of him he composed one of the greatest anthems that has ever been put to paper for the passing of a soul.

All the pomp and majesty of sovereignty was in that service. The King was there, heavy, prominent in his grief; the Princesses, softly crying in the Royal pew with the grief of those who had lost a real mother, and possessed a father whom they never respected. Let one who was there describe the ceremony. The Bishop of Chichester wrote to his son:

> 'I came to attend the funeral which was performed last night in great order, and was over two or three hours' earlier than I thought. The procession went into Henry VII's chapel. Princess Amelia was the chief mourner. Before seven the service in the Abbey was actually begun, and the whole was finished before nine. The funeral service was performed by the Bishop of Rochester, as Dean of Westminster. After the service there was a long anthem, the words by the Sub-Dean, the music set by Mr Handel, and it is reckoned to be as good a piece as he ever made; it was about fifty minutes in singing.'[2]

[1] *Earl of Egmont MSS.*, Vol. II, p. 458.
[2] *Hare MSS.*, Vol. 91, Appendix IX.

Handel must have been conscious on that December evening of the great power and grandeur of the chords which his brain had produced. There must have been a sense of pride, achievement, in this his first public performance after the great break. One can see him, searching this face and that, dreaming and wondering if into those crude souls the melancholy, the mourning, had been borne by his music.

'*She that was great among the nations, and princess of the provinces!* . . .
Their bodies are buried in peace, but their name liveth evermore.' . . .

The great uprising chords seemed to expel Death and the swirl of Death's wings. Many of those who had reviled this woman, laughed at her, gibed at her tame, German *Hausfrau* simplicity, at her questioning, sensual husband, at her little reverences and morning prayers, of which the whole life of the Court made a mockery; who reviled her for her heartlessness in keeping the Prince of Wales from her death-chamber, when he was no worse than a gay dog, and a merry fellow; who were genuinely amused by her quaint habit of having fresh-plucked flowers put up beside her bed, as if to remind her of a summer she had lost—many of these people were moved to tears. Handel brought those sycophants closer to this ill-fortuned woman than they had ever been.

For the grandeur of his anthem had in it all sympathy, all understanding. The burst of chords seemed to draw back the curtains that revealed a soul. This Queen, this misunderstood person! She who had tried to carry through a difficult part, and in spite of all her wounds had played the game to the end.

She played it so well that her husband with his crocodile tears was afraid lest her ghost should come back.

CHAPTER XVIII

'AS SOME LONE SHIP'

THERE were times when Handel stood exalted in the favour of the town; others when the town seemed to lose interest in his work, and remember only that he had been born a German. Not that his qualities were at any period challenged, save by active enemies who had axes of their own to grind. The real thinkers of the day, Pope, Steele, Hogarth, Fielding, and their cult, declared unceasingly that Handel was the greatest genius in music that had ever trodden the soil of England. Only Swift stood aloof in a splendid isolation of spleen.

The Royal obsequies over, Handel returned at once to his new opera *Faramondo*, the composition of which he completed on Christmas Eve. He produced the work on 3 January 1738.[1] The town acclaimed him as a giant refreshed. The 'Funeral Anthem' had impressed the public with the amazing versatility of this man who, after being broken on the wheels of chance, his health smashed, had turned from light opera to a masterpiece of sorrow, which held in its majesty all the mourning of a nation.

Nor had his great fight against the overwhelming forces at the King's Theatre been forgotten. These forces had been dissipated, but Handel had come back, and, if his health was insecure, he had at least the courage to seek the old battle-ground. A third factor in Handel's favour was that the Prince had withdrawn his hostility. The Prince—the town said—had seen his mistake. Therefore, in the shadow of the Prince, Society hurried to support Handel afresh.

Faramondo was not a good opera. From Handel it was indifferent work. The libretto was foolish, and the music at

[1] Streatfeild, Rockstro, and others give 7 January as the date of production, but the Augustus Harris cuttings, which are invaluable and very reliable in their information, give 3 January, and the fact that the notice of the publication of *Faramondo* by subscription appeared 7 January, points to the earlier date being correct as regards the *première*. The date is only important as showing with what alacrity Handel completed the opera and produced it after the funeral ceremonies of December, on the music for which his whole energies had been expended.

few points reached his accustomed height. His health still worried him, and his debtors plagued him yet more. Not that he would have offered these nuisances by way of excuse. When the public applauded the opera on its production it is possible that the sight of its composer back in his old place inspired much of the sentiment, for the takings of the box-office failed to reflect this enthusiasm. The Press acclaimed the work. 'Last night the new opera of *Faramondo* was performed at the King's Theatre to a splendid audience,' declared one journal on 4 January, 'and met with general applause. It being the first time of Mr Handel's appearance this season, he was honour'd with extraordinary and repeated signs of approbation.'

A new singer had been imported from Italy for the opera, a *castrato* named Caffarelli, and possibly he helped considerably as a draw. Was he a new Farinelli? All London wanted a new Farinelli. It desired a Farinelli with a smattering of manners. A creature to lionize who had legitimate gifts and the breeding to carry rather than intrude them. The public had not forgiven the Prince and Porpora for the wild-cat schemes at the King's so recently. True, they had produced Farinelli out of revolution, but had lost him again, and for ever. Handel himself was tired of *castrati*, and had distinct leanings towards Beard as his principal male singer. But he hesitated to cut out the *castrato* part altogether so soon after the glories of Farinelli. He therefore wrote several songs in *Faramondo* for Caffarelli, and waited for the public to call when it had had enough of such singers.

Not that London ever approved Caffarelli in full measure, for after he had sung in *Faramondo* and Handel's succeeding opera, *Serse*, he went back to Italy a disappointed man. He began a career of extraordinary brilliance which made his name a byword in every city of the Continent. He was fêted. They flooded him with money. He was carried to the theatre in a carriage hidden in a garment of flowers. He accumulated an enormous fortune, with the aid of which he built a great palace, as Farinelli had done before him. Indeed, the size of one's palace on retirement from the stage was the best indication of one's quality as a singer in those years.

Porpora had found Caffarelli years before—many years before Handel had heard his name. For Porpora with his ugly habits, his vanity that would not allow him to sit down to a meal with any of his singers except his principals, who talked to the Prince of Wales as he might to a scene-shifter, and addressed him intimately by his Christian name, was, at the back of it all, the greatest impresario seen in London for a hundred years. He had a most uncanny flair for discovering genius. Caffarelli was a case in point. He had been a peasant's child—his real name was Gaetano Majorano till the composer Cafaro took him up and taught him music, whereupon the boy adopted a form of his name. Caffarelli was sent to Naples. To Porpora. For five to six years Porpora kept that youth to the study of one page of exercises, then he told him to depart. 'Go, my son,' he is reported to have said. 'I have nothing more to teach you. You are the greatest singer of the age.'

If this incident was not like Porpora, so sure a product of his mixture of eccentricity and genius, it would be easy to disbelieve it. When Caffarelli originally reappeared on the stage at Rome at the age of twenty-one, he had a voice of beauty that seemed to sing from the stars. He played a woman's part, and Rome went tumbling out of the theatre into the night, conscious of a great discovery. Caffarelli was thirty-five when *Faramondo* was produced, and yet London had never heard of him. But the London of Handel was only self-contained in its musical knowledge, in which perhaps lies the reason for that ultimate change coming upon Handel himself. A change which made him compose music such as could never have been a product of the Continent.

Neither Handel nor Caffarelli could save *Faramondo*. After a few performances it was taken off. Heidegger had lost money over it, and Handel's creditors were more clamorous than ever. In a frantic fit of desperation he produced a *pasticcio* of his own works on 25 February 1738, under the title of *Alessandro Severus*. It failed more dismally than *Faramondo* had done, and his plight became extreme. Del Pò was not only forcing his claim for settlement of his debt, but was vicious, ready now to go to the fullest limit of the law, so that Handel was threatened with a new bankruptcy and the debtors' prison. Yet he asked for no favours, called for no mercy as he might well have done, seeing that he had made his creditor's wife, Strada, all she had become.

Some friends forced the issue that saved the situation. Handel was fifty-three, and if his intellect was only just on the threshold of the great maturity which gave his best-remembered works to the world, his physical powers were sinking. Rheumatism, the product of his absurd neglect of his health, had been fought down once, but was beginning to recur. He drew more and more into himself, his pride smitten by his inability to force a way by settlement with those who held him in thrall. His friends suggested that a benefit concert should be given for him. He scouted the idea. He was angry—violently angry. He had not come down to beggary, he declared, and such affairs were the bald admission of a flat purse. This at fifty-three, when he had written more notes—and better notes—than any man for many epochs. He let off salvoes from his mingled English-German vocabulary. He swore. He stormed. Ultimately they made him accept the concert.

It was given on 28 March 1738. Far from being considered in the nature of a charity, Society looked upon it as a special affair that should not be missed. The theatre filled, and still Society poured in. 'Over five hundred persons of rank and fashion were discovered on the stage.' And the profit to Handel for that one night, when he secretly hugged to himself his pride, was a record figure. Society, all London, told him, in that spontaneous honouring, that if he were in the throes of penury he was still Handel. The concert gave him something over a thousand pounds with which he paid del Pò, and condemned him to the Shades with all the other creditors to keep him company.

His financial worries at an end for a while, he completed *Serse* and produced it at the King's Theatre on 15 April. It was the second of the two operas for which Heidegger had offered him £1,000. *Serse* is one of the big mysteries in Handel's life. No one knows where he obtained the libretto, or why he should suddenly adopt broad farce and expect to make a success of it. He may have had it in his mind to cut into the success of *The Beggar's Opera*, but *Serse* was about the last work that would do so. Certainly he could have been in no mood for farce after the anxieties on the grounds of health and finance through which he had passed, and from which he had not as yet escaped. In spite of all the incongruity of *Serse*, it produced the air which, through the two centuries that have since elapsed, has been far better known to the public at large, and more frequently played, than any-

thing Handel ever composed—an air about the shadow of a
plane-tree, and better known as the famous 'Largo'. Out of
this absurdity, *Serse*, which had no *raison d'être*, no beginning and no end, Handel in a mood conjured a piece of
melody which, now, as then, holds a theatre audience when
it is played, and remains one of the master melodies of the
world. Not that *Serse* could succeed on a single air. Before
the season had ended the King's Theatre had closed down,
and Heidegger had decided that, for the time at any rate,
Handel was an expensive form of speculation.

But one man, at least, had made a lot of money out of
Handel whilst the theatres had been losing on him. This was
Jonathan Tyers, who ran Vauxhall Gardens as an evening
pleasure haunt for the better classes of Society. Tyers was a
queer mixture of artistic inclination and hard commercialism.
He had opened the Gardens six years before on a stretch of
ground he leased from Elizabeth Masters at the cheap rental
of £250 a year. It had been a great opening. The Prince of
Wales had been present, with a guard of one hundred soldiers
with fixed bayonets. Tyers arranged all possible demonstra-
tion for the pomp-loving Frederick, and the hundred bayonets
was the finishing touch, for only four hundred persons paid
for admission! Frederick, with his little army, was disgusted;
all this would make him appear a coward to a handful of
people. If something had occurred to provide an excuse for
the use of this armed might, things would not have been so
bad. The ceremony lasted from nine o'clock in the evening
until four o'clock in the morning, and the only unexpected
incident was that a drunken waiter put on a masquerading
dress, and a pickpocket stole fifty guineas from a visitor, and
was caught red-handed.[1]

In spite of the fiasco of the opening, the Prince remained
a constant visitor to Vauxhall Gardens till his death. Its open
immoralities appealed to him. One bought a silver season
ticket, a beautiful trifle designed by Hogarth, or paid a guinea
to mingle with the select for the evening. Tyers ran the Gardens to pay, and he made them pay by appealing to the passions on the one hand, and the artistic senses on the other.
Vauxhall Gardens after dark held the cream of the night life
of London. Everybody went there. One dined there, met the
ladies of the town, and listened to Handel-music, played by

[1] Warwick Wroth: *The London Pleasure Gardens*, p. 286 *et seq*.

the finest orchestras obtainable, whilst they supped. For Tyers had always run Handel on his bands. He may have had no sense of music, he may have had Handel played just because people were in the habit of going to hear his music. Whatever was at the back of his mind, he was faithful to Handel.

Vauxhall Gardens soon came into high favour. One went there usually by boat, and at Westminster and Whitehall Stairs barges and boats were always in waiting during the evening for the hire of intending visitors. Despite the loose morals of the place, bishops visited it, and somehow managed to retain their characters. City men took their families, attended by a footman carrying provisions. The scene at the landing-stage was unlike any other in London, for, although Tyers had beadles placed there to keep order, the commotion was beyond description. All boats were mixed up in hopeless confusion, there was a mob of people in wonderful dresses shouting and swearing and quarrelling, and a parcel of ugly fellows running out into the water to pull one violently ashore. Then the crowd streamed through a dark passage into the glaring splendour of a thousand lamps.[1]

Tyers, canny fellow, looked after his patrons well. The food was of the best; the wines—there were no wines in London like those that figured on Tyers' carte. And the prices, like the food and the wine, were extremely select. In consequence, a great many brought their own food. Not that this bothered Tyers. The people with money to burn gave him all the profits he wanted.

Then he pandered to the Prince and opened a rotunda, which he named after him, and the Prince, with his mob of night-fellows, repaid him for the compliment. The decorations were wonderful, and Hogarth allowed some of his pictures to be copied for this purpose. There were cunning little boxes, artistically decorated, where one supped in sinister secret to the daintiness of a Handel minuet played with perfect understanding. One danced to a number from *Alcina*. There was an absorbing operatic dreaminess in an excerpt from *Acis and Galatea*, whilst the cool winds came flooding into the boxes, fresh with the scent of the massed flowers in the flower-beds which the army of gardeners employed by Tyers had planted. Rich merchants went there

[1] *Ibid.*

after the turmoil and heat of the town. The quality forsook their heavy tables and port decanters for the soothe, the intimacy of Vauxhall Gardens, its string of lights, its half-hidden boxes with some crazy swinging lantern throwing splashes of light and shadow into them; its delicate dinners, and the glamour which thinly veiled sin brings to an indolent life. One ate and drank, one gambled and danced, and met people, and met other people, and Tyers was a good fellow It was all very wonderful.

Originally Tyers issued a thousand guinea tickets for the season. Later on he raised the price to 25s., and ultimately to two guineas. Certain patrons, like Hogarth and Handel, had special tickets of their own; most of them with Hogarth's elegant design engraved on silver. Handel's ticket showed an Arion riding on a Dolphin. Hogarth went one better, and had a ticket that had been struck in gold, and which bore the words 'Hogarth. In perpetuam Beneficii Memoriam'.[1] This may have been a special gift from Tyers in recognition of what he had done for the success of the Gardens with his designs.

In the summer of 1738 Tyers decided to carry his Handelian proclivities further. He commissioned Roubillac, the principal sculptor of the time, to cut him a statue of Handel for £300, and Handel actually sat for the purpose. Handel was then put up in marble, a sitting figure playing a lyre, and the queue to the Gardens grew more dense than ever. The fame of the statue passed to the Continent, and Mattheson, Handel's old friend at Hamburg, now possibly a little jealous, wrote a letter pointing out that England had honoured his compatriot by this manoeuvre. That it was merely the trick of a glorified restaurant-keeper to pander to the mood of his patrons, did not occur to him. For no one benefited from the statue except Tyers, and, of course, the sculptor, and the former proved once more that fame is a profitable commodity to trade upon.

At no time in his life were the changing moods of Handel so obvious as in this year 1738—moods due, no doubt, to his health and anxieties. The man with strong opinions from which he would never depart, who forced his will on the public and gave them what he wanted whether the public liked it or not, began to hesitate. He seemed uncertain of himself, more

[1] Warwick Wroth: *The London Pleasure Gardens.*

uncertain of the public taste. What else could have urged him to waste his energies on such a silly affair as *Serse*? And now, realising when the summer came that he had made another mistake, he switched right over again and composed *Saul*.

His energy during the late summer and autumn was stupendous. He compiled two of his greatest oratorios in four months. *Saul* was begun on 23 July and finished on 27 September, and four days later he began *Israel in Egypt*, which he called *Exodus*, and of which he wrote the second act first.[1] He completed the masterpiece in twenty-seven days. This change from musical farce to oratorio may have been in a measure inspired by the great approbation he had received from the public for the 'Funeral Anthem'. Two things suggest that this was so. Firstly, because he introduced into the original score of *Saul* all the greatest work from the 'Funeral Anthem', and then crossed all or most of it out. Secondly, he had been in possession of the libretto of *Saul* for a considerable period. Three years previously he had written to Charles Jennens the author: 'I received your agreeable letter with the enclosed oratorio. I am just going to Tunbridge, yet what I could read of it in haste gave me a great deal of satisfaction.' This libretto could have been none other than that of *Saul*, for it was the first Jennens ever offered to Handel.

Charles Jennens must ever remain one of the most remarkable figures that crossed Handel's path. Where they met no one knows. Jennens was a brilliant man, even if he did some absurd things in his time. Also, he was a rich man and a man popular in cultured Society, and it is not unlikely that they met in some London salon. Jennens was fifteen years younger than Handel, so that he would be thirty-five when he sent him the words of *Saul*. Rich in his youth, particular, careless of expenditure, he ultimately became a disciple of Croesus, because his ancestors left him a fortune, which they had made in Birmingham industry. When, eventually, he succeeded to the carefully invested thousands of the family's savings, he started by spending a great portion of it in building the palatial residence at Gopsall in Leicestershire, which, since then, has been the home of Jennens' descendants, the Earls of

[1] Handel termed this work *Exodus* in places in his autograph. It was announced and produced as *Israel in Egypt*. The book of words was also published under this latter title.

Howe. In laying out the grounds alone Jennens spent £80,000.
But this was not until 1747. Meanwhile, he was writing Latin
poetry and mixing in a circle of thinkers, writers, musicians,
and painters, who had like cleverness to that of himself.

Certainly, of all Handel's associates, Jennens more re-
sembled him than any other. He was big and heavy, he was
a bachelor, and, like his partner in art, he died one. He was
quick-tempered. His conceit far surpassed anything Handel
ever knew. He loved pomp and display; he knew a pride of
purse for which Handel had no use whatever, and at which he
openly laughed. Yet there was a link between these two which
brought them very closely together in art, if not in their
private lives.

When Jennens lived in Great Ormond Street, London, he
would drive down to his publishers in a magnificent carriage,
drawn by horses with plumes; with a lackey sitting up behind,
whose duty it was to get down and sweep the pavement free
of rubbish before his master got out. Handel, on the other
hand, walked everywhere until his rheumatics made it impossible to walk. Jennens spent money; Handel saved it. The
neighbours called Jennens 'Solyman the Magnificent'.[1] He
dressed magnificently. His table was ever laden with the
choicest foods. It had always been so.

Many have declared hitherto that the libretto of *Saul* was
not the work of Jennens at all, but of Newburgh Hamilton.
But there has been discovered recently a letter from him which
confirms beyond all dispute that Jennens did write *Saul*. The
letter is important because of the light it throws on Handel
in the summer of 1738, when the two collaborated over the
creating of *Saul*. It is written from Queen's Square, London,
to the Earl of Guernsey, the son of Lord Aylesford, whose
performance at Oxford during Handel's visit to that city, has

---

[1] Jennens acquired this nickname owing to Dr Johnson showing
to a friend an article on Shakespeare which Jennens had written.
The friend asked: 'Who is this conceited gentleman who lays down
the law so dogmatically?' To this Dr Johnson answered: 'A vain
fool crazed by his wealth, who, were he in Heaven, would criticize
the Lord Almighty; who lives surrounded by all the luxuries of an
Eastern potentate—verily an English "Solyman the Magnificent";
who never walks abroad without a train of footmen at his heels, and,
like Wolsey, with a scented sponge 'neath his nose, lest the breath of
the vulgar herd should contaminate his sacred person.' From that
time Jennens was always called the 'Gospall Solyman the Magnificent'.

been referred to in an earlier chapter. It is dated 19 September 1738, and runs as follows:

'Mr Handel's head is more full of maggots than ever. I found yesterday in his room a very queer instrument which he calls carillon (Anglice, a bell) and says some call it a Tubalcain, I suppose because it is both in the make and tone like a set of Hammers striking upon anvils. 'Tis played upon with keys like a Harpsichord and with this Cyclopean instrument he designs to make poor Saul stark mad. His second maggot is an organ of £500 price which (because he is overstocked with money) he has bespoke of one Moss of Barnet. This organ, he says, is so constructed that as he sits at it he has a better command of his performers than he used to have, and he is highly delighted to think what exactness his Oratorio will be performed by the help of this organ; so that for the future instead of beating time at his oratorios, he is to sit at the organ all the time with his back to the Audience. His third maggot is a Hallelujah which he has trump'd up at the end of his oratorio since I went into the Country, because he thought the conclusion of the oratorio not Grand enough; tho' if that were the case 'twas his own fault, for the words would have bore as Grand Musick as he could have set 'em to: but this Hallelujah, Grand as it is, comes in very nonsensically, having no manner of relation to what goes before.[1] And this is the more extraordinary, because he refused to set a Hallelujah at the end of the first Chorus in the Oratorio, where I had placed one and where it was to be introduced with the utmost propriety, upon a pretence that it would make the entertainment too long. I could tell you more of his maggots: but it grows late and I must defer the rest till I write next, by which time, I doubt not, more new ones will breed in his Brain.

'My humble service to all Friends; I am, my Dear L'd etc.

'C. JENNENS.'[2]

[1] A cursory examination of the autograph of *Saul* suggests that Handel carried out the advice which Jennens gave him with regard to the position of the Hallelujah.

[2] The late Countess of Aylesford discovered this letter, now first published, when going through the Aylesford family papers for material that would assist the writing of this book. Jennens was the cousin of the wife of the second Earl of Aylesford.—Author.

Handel and his maggots! What a happy notion, coming as it does from Master Jennens, who had more maggots than anyone. The subtlety of its suggestion that he knows more about the making of an oratorio than Handel! He always held that opinion, even over *Messiah*. And here, too, he pricks Handel a little with being 'overstocked with money', when only six months before they had to organize a charity concert to save him from the debtors' prison.

Handel was still in severe penury. The discharge of his old debts had drawn from him all the money he had raised by his operas for Heidegger, and the proceeds of the charity concert. Yet in the midst of his own anxieties he went out to help others who were even less fortunate. A 'Society for the Support of Decayed Musicians and their Families' was organized. They made Dr Arne interested in the scheme, Edward Purcell, son of the composer, Pepusch, Handel, and others, and gave a performance of *Alexander's Feast*, which put the Society on a sufficiently safe footing to enable it to go forward. All his life Handel continued to support this Fund; in fat years and lean, he was ever ready to give or to compose for it. When they wanted money they performed his operas. When they wanted something new, he wrote them something new. The Fund was his hobby, and out of that hobby, which helped more lame dogs over stiles than ever Handel was aware of, came the Royal Society of Musicians.

Handel completed *Saul* in September and *Israel in Egypt* a month later, but he did not produce either at once. For the time being he seemed to have dropped his old habit of rushing a work on to the stage almost as soon as the notes were dry on the score.

In the autumn of 1738 he had difficulties to encounter which held him up. Heidegger had failed. After advertising for two hundred subscribers to enable him to carry on the King's Theatre, he closed down, and Handel was left with the task for the first time of finding the money to produce *Saul* on his own account. He sought no friends; borrowed no money. His faith in himself was still strong enough to urge him to risk a season. He took over from Heidegger the remainder of his lease of the King's Theatre, and produced the oratorio there on 16 January 1739.

Saul was a very poor success, for although it was played six times during the season, it failed, in spite of its grandeur, to impress the town. The solemnity of its Dead March, for which Handel had borrowed kettle-drums from the Tower, passed almost unobserved.[1] The extraordinary overture, which he marked *organo ad libitum*, and for which he sat at the instrument at the first performance and extemporized most of it, might have been some music-hall jangling, for all the attention it received. Probably the oratorio was a fine form of music for which the public was not yet ready, and that the lack of patronage was due to lack of understanding. At all events, *Saul* achieved more success when it was revived time after time in the later days of Handel. Mrs Delany wrote of it: '*Saul*—one of my beloved pieces'. And in the fullness of time the oratorio found a constant public long after other works of Handel, such as *Radamisto*, which had been highly successful when produced, were forgotten.

The reception of *Saul* disappointed Handel, whose financial position was not in a state to stand failure, and, if he did not lose much money over the work, he certainly did not make any. The reception of *Israel in Egypt*, which immediately followed, was even more heartbreaking. The public dismissed it as unwanted, from the first performance. A few lone critics acclaimed it, but the boxes remained empty. Handel, in a fit of desperation, lost his nerve to some extent. After its cold reception at the first performance he began to pull the work about; he introduced secular airs from his Italian operas without reason. Still the public failed to respond. It did not understand. The oratorio was withdrawn, a failure, before April was out.

Yet in *Israel in Egypt* Handel produced some of the greatest pictures of natural happening he ever achieved. His choruses and double choruses were directly designed to attain this result. In the double chorus 'And there came all manner of flies and lice in all their quarters', there is to be found, clear and unmistakable from the instruments, the buzzing of flies. Much of this effect which Handel prepared with such success, has been lost in later years by the predominance of the singers over the orchestra in point of numbers. In 1739 Handel had on an average from twenty-five to thirty-five singers in his chorus, and precisely the same number in his orchestra. Thus the voices and the instruments had an even balance, which enabled him to get the effects required from each at their

[1] *Wentworth Papers*.

appointed time. But, as the years moved past, it became customary to sacrifice the beauty of his instrumental music to big effects in the double choruses. The numbers of the singers grew till, in their preponderance, they drowned all orchestration. Thus, at the Westminster Abbey celebration in 1784, the chorus had grown from the 25 to 35 of Handel's day, to 275, and the orchestra to 250. But at one of the last Handel Festivals, the chorus had swollen to 3,500, and the orchestra, being only 500 strong, was hopeless to cope with such a volume of sound so that much of the beauty of Handel's instrumental work was only heard in the solos. This defect is always noticeable in *Israel in Egypt*, for with such a volume of singers, swept to all energy by the ecstasy of Handel's conception, it is almost impossible to hear the buzzing of the flies which the composer so expressly designed for the instruments, in order to obtain his dramatic picture.

Israel in Egypt teems with such imitations of nature impressive in their realism. 'He gave them hailstones', is one of the greatest replicas of storm in the history of music. In 'He sent a thick darkness', is all the heaviness of profound and pressing night, and again in 'He led them through the deep' one hears the rolling of great waters. Yet so lacking was the imagination of the time that this complete mastery of the effects obtainable in music passed unperceived. Save for a single performance the year following, Handel did not perform *Israel in Egypt* again for seventeen years.

John Beard was the only person who really profited by *Israel in Egypt*. He was now Handel's principal male singer, and the master had written several of the best songs in the work specially for him. Moreover, the day of *castrati* was passing, and this oratorio brought Beard great prestige. At that time he had a rapidly growing popularity, and had completely taken the place of the Italian singers in the public favour. 'Beard did more justice to sense than any of our performers,' wrote Horace Walpole to a friend at a later period, 'for though he laid a stress on every syllable, yet at least the audience, such as were capable, could suppose the right accents.'[1] He had also a remarkable knowledge of music, for there was little else that had ever interested him in life save singing. He could sing any song at sight, and in a voice more powerful than sweet.[2]

[1] Pohl: *Mozart und Haydn in London.*   [2] Rees: *Encyclopaedia.*

It so happened that when these two oratorios were passing through their brief and troubled lives, Beard was one of the most widely discussed men in London, owing to his domestic affairs. Society execrated him, for he had committed a wanton act against all its proprieties. A few months previously he had married a young Society woman, Lady Harriet Herbert, who had been a widow for four years, after a previous married life of only as many months. For a member of Society to marry a singer was a scandal almost past forgiveness in the salons. Society's gallants might intrigue with the ladies of the theatres without besmirch, for were not the latter common prey? But for a demure little creature of twenty-two, as was Lady Harriet, to marry one who lived the promiscuous and unstable life of the stage, was another matter.

The affair was discussed for weeks, written about, made fun of. Lady Mary Montagu wrote in one of her letters:

'Lady Harriet Herbert furnished the tea-tables here with fresh tattle for the last fortnight. I was one of the first informed of her adventure, by Lady Gage, who was told that morning by a priest, that she desired him to marry her the next day to Beard, who sings in the farces at Drury Lane. I told her (Lady Gage) honestly, that since the lady was capable of such amours, I did not doubt if this was broken off, that she would bestow her person and fortune on some hackney coachman or chairman; and that I saw no method of saving *her* from ruin, and her *family* from dishonour, but by poisoning her; and offered to be at the expense of the arsenic, and even to administer it to her with my own hands, if she would invite her to drink tea with her that evening.'[1]

In marrying Beard, this unhappy little widow, therefore, brought a hornet's nest upon her head, and Society, if ready to pay to hear her husband sing, forbade her the drawing-rooms. She was ostracized. She went dolefully here and there seeking this friend and that, only to find the closed door. Her name was bandied about with those of the women of the town, than whom the superior people thought her no better. It was a slow gliding from the heights she had known, a social decay. Ultimately, driven by the need of some feminine society, she began to consort with actresses. It was social

[1] Lady M. Montagu: *Letters*, Vol. II, p. 38.

suicide. If she had been shunned before, she was now made an outcast, and those to whom she had given the deep affection of a simple soul—a soul that lives on affection because it knows naught else for sustenance—heaped upon her all the spite and terror that only women can give to another. And so ultimately they killed her socially, such was the senseless prejudice of the time.

Israel in Egypt had failed and the season was ending—a season which had been replete with disaster. A circulated pamphlet which poked fun at Handel's misfortunes, and rejoiced in the fall of 'a great bear', cut him to the quick. He had the courage, but little else, to enable him to continue. Funds had practically run out. Former friends were falling away in such numbers, hoping to escape from the cloud which had fallen over him, that he 'found consolation in being undisturbed in his thoughts by the accosting of his acquaintances when he walked down Piccadilly'.

On the very day that the theatre doors closed on *Israel in Egypt*, he completed another work, which he named *Jupiter in Argos*. It had two performances, 1 May and 5 May in 1739. He may not have had the money to go on; he may have decided that the mood of the town was so dangerous that he would only risk further disaster if he attempted further productions that season. *Jupiter in Argos* therefore has never been produced on the stage, and is to a great extent a mystery work, for there is apparently no complete copy of it in existence.[1]

---

[1] Only a very small portion of the autograph is in existence at the Fitzwilliam Museum at Cambridge, together with a portion of Christopher Smith's transcription. I have in my collection Christopher Smith's transcription of all the songs in *Jupiter in Argos*, which are as follows: *Gia sai che l'usignuol cantando geme*. (Thou knowest already that the nightingale sighs singing.) *Svenate il Genitor, perduto il Regno*. (The father killed, the Kingdom lost.) *Iside, dove sei?* (Isis, where art thou?) *In braccio al tuo spavento ti lascio*. (In the arm to thy terror I leave thee.) *Priva d'ogni conforto*. (Deprived of all consolation.) *Non é d'un alma grande*, etc. (It is not in the nature of a great soul to murmur against fate.) *Al gaudio, al riso, al canto*. (To joy, to laughter, to song, etc.) *D'amor di Jove al canto*. (Of Jupiter's love to song.) *Non ingannarmi cara speranza*. (Dear hope do not deceive me.) *Vieni, vieni O de viventi*. (Come, come O of the living.) *Deh! m'ajutate, oh Dei*. (Ah! aid me, O gods.) *Taci e spera ti basti cosi*. (Be silent and hope.) *Se portessero i sospir miei far*. (If I could make my sighs)

There is in the British Museum a copy of these songs, made at a later stage of the eighteenth century and by another hand. But there

There seemed no hope for Handel. All the circumstances of the time were against him. He knew that he had given of his best in *Saul* and *Israel in Egypt*; his subsequent revivals of these two oratorios is proof of his faith in them—faith that was ultimately justified. But at this stage anything he produced would have failed, however great its beauty, for the cabal of his enemies was too strong for him.

He was on the verge of breaking. Solitary, yet still content to strive. 'As some lone ship——'

And then came the war.

---

is ample evidence that this copy was made from that by Christopher Smith in my possession, because in my copy the ink from the notes on the pages has come through, and the copyist, mistaking these stains at times for dots, has put them in. My copy was part of the Aylesford collection, and a broadcast of an arrangement of it was made a few years ago. The same volume, by the way, contains also a Hornpipe 3/2 in D major, in three parts, 'compos'd for the concert at Vauxhall, 1740'.—Author.

CHAPTER XIX

THE LAST OPERAS

THE trouble with Spain had been long a-brewing, and now it boiled up, owing to an international quarrel over somebody's ear. Jenkins, a mariner of sorts, had been caught by the Spaniards and subjected to the indignity of having his ear torn off. That was his story. Not that Jenkins was above reproach. He had been a bubble on the flood of chance, tossed here, tossed there, making money by very questionable methods, losing it, spending it, till enthusiasm compelled him forth to a new adventure.

Jenkins declared that the Spaniards had his ear, and since the quarrels between the English and Spaniards in South America had become a continual sore, Jenkins was believed. He became at once a gentleman, a maltreated hero. On account of this fellow, England went to war with Spain.

The war fever smote London with a sudden blast. Crowds gathered, howled, and were dispersed. Bells clashed throughout the city. Any person with an ounce of Spanish blood in his veins, and known to possess it, ran like a fox to earth. Shares dropped like plummets. Young bloods bought up merchant ships and began to pile them with arms with a view to carrying out a little privateering against the Spaniards. A peace-weary people rejoiced.

To produce an ordinary opera under such conditions would have been madness. Handel, with his constant flair for recognizing opportunity, set Dryden's *Ode for St Cecilia's Day*. He completed it in nine days, and produced it at the theatre in Lincoln's Inn Fields in November. It was an attempt to catch the interest of the public at a time of upheaval. He had cut his expenses at the Haymarket by moving to the smaller theatre, and the Ode, reflecting the mood of the hour, promised success. Its sublime choruses drew attention when those of equal beauty in *Israel* had been passed by. The chairmen slouched through the mud to Lincoln's Inn Fields with their aristocratic burdens, when they had never been required to go to the Haymarket.

In the early winter of 1739 it seemed as if Handel's fortunes might return. The *Ode for St Cecilia's Day* was played to crowded houses. He revived his successful *Alexander's Feast*, his *Acis and Galatea*, and still the tide of fortune, moving if at all, was certainly tending in his direction. But the Fates connived against him. In mid-December a wave of icy weather swept over London. Broken clots of ice floated down the Thames, met at the bridge-piers and froze. The surface water, brought to a halt by the obstruction, froze into sheet ice.

The Thames became a frozen field. The poor died like flies in their crazy dwellings, fell and perished in the streets, but the solid Thames was covered with revellers who lit fires and roasted oxen on the ice. The river became a hurly-burly of horseplay and noise.

The weeks passed and the cold went on. In January it became worse instead of breaking. Places of entertainment shut down because the means to warm them were lacking. Handel fought against the onslaught of this new enemy with all the frenzy of despair. He warmed his theatre, shrouded the doors with thick curtains and advertised the fact in the London Press. Still his audiences continued to diminish, since the average citizen who possessed a fire had little desire to leave it.

It was a battle now as to which could hold out the longer—Winter or Handel. To close down meant a loss on the season. So he applied himself to the setting of a version of Milton's *L'Allegro*, which Charles Jennens had prepared for him, and he completed the work in less than a month. During that time he had to watch his theatre growing more and more empty. The boxes were deserted, and most of them 'papered'. Not only was the weather fighting hard against him, but a new cabal had been formed in social circles, for which there appeared to be no reason. There was a very definite section of the public out to force him again into bankruptcy. They put noisy ruffians outside the theatre to cause commotion; chairs were overturned, stones thrown. Those who had such love of music that they dared to brave the cold, were intimidated by disorder around the theatre, which the beadles were powerless to restrain. Even the posters announcing Handel's performances were torn down from the theatre walls.

He was rapidly losing money. But he produced *L'Allegro* in February, and, as had so often been the case before, did not even get his expenses back. *L'Allegro*, which has all the rustic charm of *Acis*, wonderful in its symphony, glad and restful in those scenes of communing with Nature, failed utterly to draw. Still, the attacks on the theatre and those who frequented it continued. He was almost beaten. There was nothing for him to do but close the place down. Nevertheless, one of his last acts before doing so was to give a performance of *Acis* and *St Cecilia* for the benefit of the Decayed Musicians' Fund—this at a time when there was practically nothing between himself and penury.

But, if the public had failed to be drawn by Handel during those winter months, the Cibber scandal had diverted the town. The sloe-eyed beauty who, as Susanna Arne, had sung in her father's stolen version of *Acis and Galatea*, and filled the theatre exchequer under the very nose of Handel, had given the town all the savour it wanted in a salacious age. What a pitiful creature! Not all her beauty nor her talents, which were of high order, could change that particular destiny which the sovereignty of a splendid womanhood held for her. No wonder Handel found in her a kindred soul; no wonder that at a time when the world was using him as badly as circumstances— mostly of her own making—were using Susanna Cibber, he delighted in her company, with Quin and a few other cronies, who had very little care for the bother of outside things.

If Mrs Cibber had been plain and untalented she would still have been one of the picture-women of history. Her personality was a lodestone. She drew all men to herself, all women too, and she seldom quarrelled with either. She swept into a room where royalty kept the floor and held it to silence at once. 'This woman—she is the devil!' exclaimed George II on one occasion. 'She would hush the King!' Her preparations for this work of conquest were magnificent. She boasted that it always took her three hours to do her hair. A woman all moods. Her affections were extreme and genuine, and when a few fellow-creatures of her own choosing were in her rooms she would rush into the kitchen, hustle the maids right and left, while she prepared some dainty dish of her own imagining —for she cooked divinely. Quin once ejaculated that the chocolate she had given him was a drink from heaven, but it had killed her dress. It had. In preparing this one cup for him she had smeared the ingredients all over a dress which must have cost a very large sum, and the emerald-green silk was daubed with brown. She smiled. If the sacrifice of the dress had helped Quin to the ecstasy of his chocolate she was glad. 'There are others', she laughed, with that amazing lure which was hers.

Handel's friendship with Mrs Cibber, and it matured into a great and clean friendship, began about 1738. It may have been the blows of the world that brought them together, and art linked them in that intimacy they were to know. The marriage of Susanna Arne was all wrong to begin with. She married a reprobate, and there was trouble about the dowry.

Colley Cibber had no forgiveness for his son Theophilus if he married a young actress from the Covent Garden furniture shop without sufficient wherewithal. The young actress very soon proved that she could fend for herself. Shortly after her marriage to the dissolute Theophilus she made a hit in *Zara* at Drury Lane. They gave her £100 for the season, and she made another £100 in presents. The next season they gave her £200, and a benefit. Susanna then became avaricious. She wanted a larger salary than any other player in the house, and left because it was denied to her.

Even a headstrong woman like Susanna could not prevent her marriage being a failure. She could not keep Theophilus Cibber faithful, she could not keep him sober. The tie of children might have achieved it, but both their children died at birth. Theophilus began to sink to the society of those gutter-denizens as truly lost as he. One morning at dawn, waking to the consciousness of an empty married life, to a future that held nothing beyond her art, Susanna crept from her bed as the sun was beginning to pick out the roofs of London, and, with all the warmth of life in her heart, slipped away silently to Burnham in Bucks. To a rather faithful and love-sick young man named Sloper. It was as if she were pursuing some dream that had absorbed her in the darkness.

The result was sordid upheaval; a thorough washing of the Cibbers' dirty linen in public. Theophilus brought a case against Sloper for £5,000 damages. They fought it out at the end of 1738, to the great diversion of the town. How it roared with laughter over the evidence of Hayes, the Cibbers' land-lord in Leicester Fields, who had bored holes in the wains-coting, through which he surveyed hour after hour the love-making of the ardent young man Sloper and the actress! Cibber lost; had he not been a party to the whole affair? He then went into hiding, whilst Susanna threw up her stage engagements out of sheer panic of him. He discovered her hiding-place, broke in, and stole her valuables like some miserable footpad.

It all seemed like a pretty farce that is going to have a happy ending. He rushed to Florence with the proceeds; in the farce he would have been arrested at Dover. But, after a hectic year at Florence on the pawned chattels of his wife, he returned, full of courage and audacity, and brought an action for ten thousand pounds damages. The failure of his last suit had made him reckless, for he doubled his claim—and the jury gave him £500. Heaven knows why. Possibly because—for the Georgian epoch—he had been so considerate in keeping away for a year.

Susanna was more frightened of him than ever. Again she went into hiding. Again she departed from the stage out of fear of this wandering madman. Handel and a few others knew of her hiding-place, and they came like happy visitors out of the dark, to find some comfort in their lives by meeting. Mrs Cibber lived in constant fear of Theophilus. The months passed, but the fear, like an enveloping shadow, continued. Some roughs followed her home, and she believed they were the spies of Theophilus, but directly she reached her house they turned and ran, for they were no more than night vermin. Her life was becoming narrowed and warped by terror. Goaded by fear she ultimately rushed out of London, out of England. Theophilus would never follow her to Ireland, so she went there. And that is how it came about that she sang in the first performance of *Messiah*.

Handel spent the summer of 1740 in Brook Street, and in the society of but a few friends. The taverns knew him no more; he had dropped out of public life as if death had claimed him. Only after dark did he go out to the houses of his intimates— Mrs Cibber, Sir Hans Sloane, Mrs Delany. At Mrs Cibber's he played his new music before the world heard it, because she was frank in her criticism.

Or he would stroll up to Bloomsbury Square, to the house of Sir Hans Sloane, that fidgety old *poseur*, hiding in a surfeit of wonderful books in still more wonderful bindings. It was one of these bindings that caused a rift in their friendship. Handel was taking tea with him one day, and Sir Hans was showing him his volumes. Very pompous and purse-proud was Sir

Hans. Handel placed his buttered muffin on the volume he held in his hands. The horrible silence of Sir Hans did not impress him at all with the sense of tragedy. But the rift had come. 'To be sure it was a careless trick,' declared Handel afterwards, 'but it did no monstrous mischief; yet it put the poor old bookworm terribly out of sorts. I offered my best apologies, but the old miser would not have done with it.' Sir Hans had finished with him. A man who could put a buttered muffin on a book!

Above all others, Mrs Delany had the truest sense of his genius. He came to her table an exalted person. She wrote about him, she gloried in every note that he put to paper. She was one of the few people of his time who understood him. Small wonder then that when London killed *St Cecilia* and *L'Allegro* he went to her house a proud figure still, unbroken, but a little ruffled by his treatment.

By the end of September he had completed the composition of an opera *Imeneo* (Hymen), which he had begun two years before. A month later he had completed another, *Deidamia*, from a libretto by Rolli, who had so foully attacked him. Neither had any outstanding merit, but Burney was enthusiastic about the latter. Handel produced *Imeneo* in November, and it ran for two performances. The town howled it down. It was effete, no more than a stir in the mud of mediocrity. *Deidamia* was produced on 10 January 1741, and ran three nights. If it had been a Handel triumph, which it was not, it could not have succeeded. He had no singers. He had only Reinhold and La Francesina, very average people, who lacked any drawing power whatever. All of the others were, as Lady Bristol wrote, 'a set of scrubs'. His management was bad, his publicity was bad; he had, in fact, no business organization whatever. He flung a new piece at London, and expected London, without proper advertisement, to understand. He was, by sheer muddling of business affairs, killing his own reputation, pouring out work of quality that never had a chance, and condemning himself thereby to the Bankruptcy Court.

The two operas drew from him in their failures what few savings he had. They drove him down. With all his powers at their greatest, Handel could not at this stage have made a success. Society had isolated him. They talked of him much as they had done in a former year as a burnt-out fire. The salons that had wanted him, when he came fresh from the Continent

with all the laurels of achievement, had strayed to the lures of
the constantly revived *The Beggar's Opera* and *The Dragon of
Wantley*. Young, half-fledged actresses found favour among
the gouty peers, who, a few years ago, had declared Handel,
with his wild Zoo of Italians, the music-maker of the world.
The flesh and the devil had enslaved them while the master
now drifted to poverty.

Handel's last Italian operas were dead; they had never lived.
Deidamia contained fine work, but it was spent upon deaf
ears. If Handel had not created a diversion at this period, he
would never have been heard of again in his lifetime. His
diversion was *Messiah*. But when the spring of 1741 came he
was broken. London had successfully buried him. He had only
the remnants of a following. His health was beating him down,
and he slept but little. He was shunned in the street. He
decided to leave London. Opera was dead. And—to London—
he was dead.

It is difficult to conceive and analyse the mood of Handel at
this hour, the grandeur of a spirit unbroken when all the forces
of Man and the Elements had combined to crush it. In *St
Cecilia* and *L'Allegro* he had conceived melody which had no
trace of a suffering soul, no cry for pity in an endless throbbing
pain. He seemed to have passed beyond these things, to have
subdued feeling and forgotten hurt, to have dwelt with themes
of music which came like jewels to his paper only to be cast to
crowds that ignored them. Handel ever sang the sweeter in
suffering. He reached the heart of the world when the world
was against him. He most truly understood the place of Man
in the universe, when the hatred of Man would have torn him
down.

It softened him, this sorrow. He crept away, stirred but
secret in his old pride. He no longer broke into oaths and
violent fits of anger at each and every provocation. The certainty, the superiority of Youth had gone. Suffering had
driven it out. He mellowed to a greater kindness. He was one of
the founders of the Society for Decayed Musicians at a time
when he was enduring the torment of poverty and indignity.
As the world passed him and hurt him so he grew to love it
more; to bend down to the midgets beneath, and to know
anxiety for their stressful little lives. His simple living became
more simple as his demands upon Life decreased. Friends left
him and he sealed his lips. The pains of an unhealthy body tore

him, tortured him, but the beauty of all things never faltered in his notes.

His life had been like a river, so gusty and noisy and certain in youth. Forcing its way. Driving. Then broadening out in discovery. And now deep and slow moving; hiding all its secrets beneath a placid surface, quiet and imperturbable. Passing onward and outward towards the waiting sea.

CHAPTER XX

'MESSIAH'

WHEN Handel closed the theatre on *Deidamia*, his fortunes had reached their lowest ebb. And yet out of this welter of suffering came the glorious *Messiah*.[1]

He withdrew entirely from public life between February and November 1741. If he remained in London during that period no one was aware of it, for he shrank into greater seclusion. Again London repeated its old belief that Handel was finished and would be seen no more. He was not missed at Court. For all the thought the King gave him he might have been some starveling tradesman who had put up the shutters after a valiant struggle to live. The King hated failures, or anything that suggested lack of comfort, and Handel had failed.

It was at this juncture that Charles Jennens came boldly into Handel's orbit by sending him the selected words from the Scriptures which were to be the basis of *Messiah*. Jennens has come down in fame through the centuries for the compilation of the words; his pride in the achievement was colossal. All the success of the great oratorio was his; he knew it. 'I shall show you a collection I gave Handel, call'd *Messiah*, which I value highly,' he wrote to a correspondent at a later stage, 'and he has made a fine Entertainment of it, tho' not near so good as he might and ought to have done. I have with great difficulty made him correct some of the grossest faults in the composition, but he retained his overture obstinately, in which there are some passages far unworthy of Handel, but much more unworthy of *Messiah*.'

---

[1] This oratorio is frequently called *The Messiah*. This is not strictly correct. The autograph is styled *Messiah*, and both Handel and Jennens referred to it as such in their correspondence. Only twice was Handel known to call it *The Messiah*; once in a letter written to Jennens from London on 9 September 1742, when he said: 'I shall send the printed Book of *The Messiah* to Mr J. Steel for you', and again in a letter dated 19 July 1744, when he wrote: 'Be pleased to point out these passages in *The Messiah* which you think require altering.' In the letter quoted above Jennens also calls it *Messiah*.

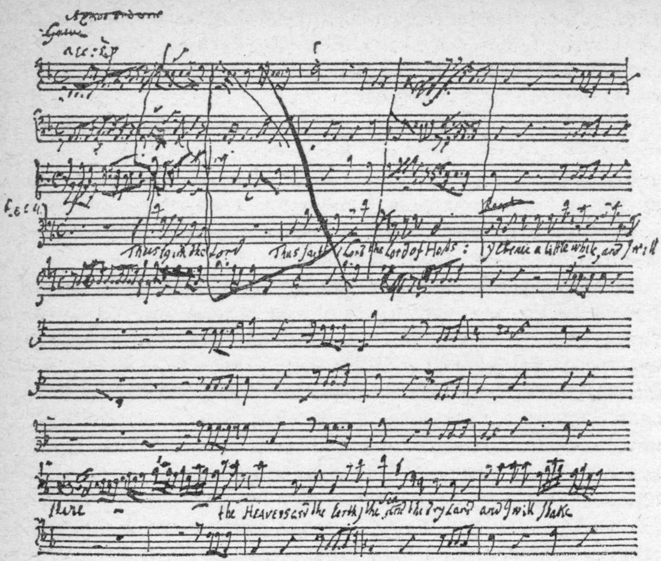

As Handel wrote it, and—

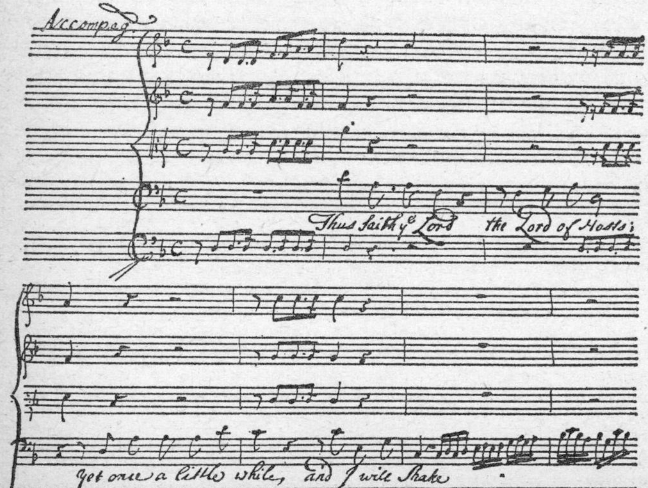

As Christopher Smith translated it.

'Is it not curious,' asks David, 'that Jennens speaks of gross faults in the composition of Handel? Ah, but who would remember a poem by Jennens today if Handel had not immortalized it with his *gross faults!*'[1]

The delightful patronage of Jennens! One can imagine more horses with funeral plumes than ever were required to draw his carriage up Great Ormond Street after *Messiah*, and two lackeys instead of one being engaged to sweep the oyster-shells from the street before this Colossus of intellect emerged, haughty and serene, from his carriage.[2]

Jennens was now having an ugly battle with the Shakespeare commentators, whom he declared to be 'twaddling antiquaries without taste or talent'. He followed up this attack by rewriting and publishing *Hamlet*, *Lear*, and *Othello*, and others of Shakespeare's tragedies. Instantly there came down upon his head a storm of abuse which hurt him severely. But, if wounded, Jennens was in fighting mood. He wrote with his own hand a pamphlet in reply, which he published. Dr Johnson, George Steevens, Malone, Warburton—they had one and all attacked Jennens for his audacity in tampering with the sacred work of Shakespeare. After the issue of his firm reply Jennens 'looked over the newspapers every day to see if the severity of his retort had compelled them to hang themselves'. The joke grew; everybody was laughing except Jennens. Steevens and his gang of wits revelled in it, and baited the pompous gentleman the more. Presently they put out an epi-

---

[1] E. David: *G. F. Handel et Sa Vie*, p. 278.

[2] Jennens has been credited through the length of the years with the compilation of the words of *Messiah* from the Scriptures. But when researching for this book I found that Hone, in his *Table Book*, Vol. III, col. 650, of the period, gave the credit to a man named Pooley—a half-starved curate who was secretary to Jennens, and he declared that it was the Pooley selection of words which Jennens took to Handel. Consequently, in the earlier editions of this book, I passed on Hone's tribute to Pooley.

But in the course of further research for this edition I have come to doubt the story. Since this book was first published, and dragged Pooley from the dust of the eighteenth century, he has appeared in a film and in B.B.C. broadcasts. I have found no evidence beyond Hone that Pooley ever existed. The clergy lists of the period do not include him, and there is no record of him in the Jennens era. Therefore I think Hone's story must be regarded as a myth, and that it was Jennens who made the libretto of *Messiah*.

gram which, though credited to Steevens, is not clever enough for his pen.

'After Mister Charles Jennens produc'd his Defence,
He saw all the papers at Martyr's,
To learn if the critics had had the good sense
To hang themselves in their own Garters,
He thought they could never outlive it! The sot
Is ready *to hang himself,* '*cause they have not.*'[1]

This was the mood of Jennens when, with the manuscript of the libretto of *Messiah*, he saw Handel in the summer of 1741. That the selection was a fine one all posterity has agreed, and Handel certainly believed that the genius of Jennens had given him a wonderful libretto, for in subsequent letters to him he refers to 'your Oratorio *Messiah*'.[2]

At the end of August, Handel, with the Jennens words in front of him, sat down to the work of composition in the little front room of the house in Brook Street. He completed the first part in seven days, the second part in nine days, the third part in six days, filling in instrumentation in two days. The whole of *Messiah* from beginning to end was set upon paper in twenty-four days. Considering the immensity of the work, and the short time involved, it will remain, perhaps for ever, the greatest feat in the whole history of musical composition.

It was the achievement of a giant inspired—the work of one who, by some extraordinary mental feat, had drawn himself completely out of the world, so that he dwelt—or believed he dwelt—in the pastures of God. What happened was that Handel passed through a superb dream. He was unconscious of the world during that time, unconscious of its press and call; his whole mind was in a trance. He did not leave the house. His manservant brought him food, and as often as not returned in an hour to the room to find the food untouched, and his master staring into vacancy. When he had completed Part II, with the 'Hallelujah Chorus', his servant found him at the table, tears streaming from his eyes. 'I did think I did see all Heaven before me, and the great God Himself!' he exclaimed. Of a certainty, Handel was swept by some influence not of the world during that month—an influence not merely visionary.

[1] Hone: *Table Book*, Vol. III.
[2] Letters of 29 December 1741 and 9 September 1742.

Never in his life had he experienced the same emotional sense, and he never experienced it in the same measure again. For twenty-four days he knew those uplands reached only by the higher qualities of the soul.

He finished *Messiah* on 14 September 1741. On 29 September he completed the first part of another oratorio, *Samson*, from a libretto which Newburgh Hamilton had based upon Milton's 'Samson Agonistes'. Yet he did not complete it until October of the following year. Music—and music that was on a scale of grandeur not often attained—was rushing from him like a flood.

He had no thought for production. The work as it was completed was put away. *Messiah* went into a drawer for seven weeks. It is doubtful if he ever intended to produce it in London, for the sickening experiences of the last few years had decided him to leave town at the first opportunity. Had an invitation not come to him in the autumn from the Lord-Lieutenant of Ireland, and the Governors of the three charitable institutions in Dublin, to go to that city, it is not improbable that he might have returned to Germany, if only for a period. In which case *Messiah* would never have been first produced within the realm of the King.

The mood that was upon Handel responded immediately to the call from Dublin. If London no longer wanted him, he was at least a prophet not without honour elsewhere. Moreover, the principal charity for which his services were sought was the Mercers' Hospital in Stephen Street, which looked after the wretched prisoners in the debtors' prison—prisoners who were either fed by charity or left to starve. The fact that he had nearly been thrown into a debtors' prison so shortly before may have had some influence on a great soul to which charity never appealed in vain.

He left London at the beginning of November, and broke the journey for some days at the 'Golden Falcon' at Chester, where he held private rehearsals with the company he had taken with him. Not till the eighteenth did he reach Dublin, for heavy seas were running in the Channel, and all the packets were late. The Irish Press acclaimed him. *Faulkner's Journal*, the news-sheet of the day, announced that 'the celebrated Dr Handell' had arrived by the packet-boat from Holyhead, with an insistence on the 'Dr', which must have reminded Handel—if he saw the paper—of the Oxford exploit, and the

Oxford professors who wanted his hundred pounds!

His principal singers began to reach him one by one. Mrs Cibber, who had renounced her acting at Drury Lane and her continuous playing of 'Polly' in *The Beggar's Opera*, had joined him, more to escape from a worrying husband than for the joys of an Irish début. One can imagine how she and Handel had contrived a scheme in the Cibber drawing-room, with Handel at the music-stool.

Mrs Cibber is supposed to have been in Dublin at the time of Handel's arrival, but on this point authorities differ. Signora Avolio arrived in a yacht soon after Handel. Handel's company was now complete. He took a house in Abbey Street and set about his affairs. William Neal, a music-publisher, had built a new music-hall in Fishamble Street, and opened it but a few weeks previously; now as Secretary of the Charities' Commission which had summoned Handel from his seclusion, he placed the building at the disposal of the master.

A new joy in life began to surge through Handel. A rosy tinge crept across the world as he knew it. The whole social life of Dublin was disrupted by his coming. People peered through the Abbey Street windows and swore that they had seen him composing a vast and new work, which was to be a gift to the Irish nation. They called upon him at all and every hour, only to be told that Mr Handel was busy. Composing, of course. One veteran declared till the grave claimed him that he had actually seen the master composing *Messiah* at Abbey Street.

Events followed each other in rapid succession in Dublin. Mrs Cibber was flown as a kite. She appeared in a play at the Theatre Royal called *The Conscious Lovers* to test out the attitude of the Irish towards the invaders. She captured the people; they thronged her carriage and smothered her with flowers. What can her success have meant to Handel? Some winnowed recollections of the days when he hustled up the Haymarket cursing wholesomely the little girl, Susanna Arne, who was drawing the crowds to the stolen version of his *Acis and Galatea*. Susanna Arne—Mrs Cibber—the prophetess of the new day. What a whirligig was life! London caught the echo of her triumph a few weeks later, and the *Gentleman's Magazine* appeared with a laudatory poem about her Dublin acting.[1] The stars were set in their courses. Yesterday was for-

[1] March 1742.

gotten. The hurt, the struggle had been no more than the blemish of an hour.

Handel opened his season with a performance of *L'Allegro* two days before Christmas. The piece which had failed in London was acclaimed in Dublin. 'Without Vanity,' Handel wrote to Jennens, 'the Performance was received with general Approbation.' The moral effect of this success was soon evident in him; it proved that his work had failed in London, not because of its quality. These crowding Irish people, the insistence of the Duke of Devonshire that he should repeat the performance, the demonstrative populace that hailed him as a god of music when London had forgotten him through sheer surfeit of the beauty he had given it, stirred him, excited him.

The old despairs departed. Never had he known such ecstasies at the organ. The whole spirit of the man was uprising as a root may yield new and freshened life after the surge of winter. 'The music sounds delightfully in this charming Room,' he wrote of Neal's music-hall to Jennens just before the New Year, 'which puts me in such excellent Spirits (and my health being so good) that I exert myself on the Organ with more than usual success.' The tide had begun to run again. Not for many years had Handel loved his life so much.

He followed *L'Allegro* with *Alexander's Feast*, and, after a temporary delay caused by the illness of Mrs Cibber—he revived *Imeneo*. There was no break in the crowds. *Imeneo*, which had run its two nights to poor houses in London, was now hailed in Dublin as a triumph. So great, indeed, was the number of people seeking admission that Handel had to issue an apology through the Press because he had had to turn away all members of the public who had not purchased subscribers' tickets for the season.

It was not until March 1742 that any announcement was made regarding *Messiah*. The work had been kept as great a secret in Dublin as in London. But on the twenty-third an advertisement in *Faulkner's Journal* made it known that a ticket for the rehearsal of Mr Handel's Grand Oratorio on 8 April would be given gratis to anyone who purchased a ticket for the first performance, which was billed for 13 April. The *Dublin News-Letter* published a separate announcement with the addition that 'Books are also to be had at a British sixpence each'. On the morning of the first performance the Dublin papers issued a notice that the doors would be open at eleven, and that the oratorio would begin at twelve. They added a note requesting 'the Favour of the ladies not to come with hoops this day to the Musick Hall in Fishamble Street. The gentlemen are desired to come without their swords.'

Seven hundred people crowded into the music-hall on that Tuesday when *Messiah* was first given to the world. Hundreds more waited in the street. 'Words are wanting to express the exquisite Delight it afforded to the admiring crowded Audience,' wrote *Faulkner's Journal* next day. Dubourg, the violin *maestro*, who had for years resided in Dublin, was in charge of the band. The choirs of two cathedrals had been trained to the greatest perfection in the choruses. If the male singers, Baily and Mason, were weak, the beauty of the voices of Signora Avolio and Mrs Cibber more than made up for their deficiencies.

Mrs Cibber as an actress had no equal in London. But her voice, if meagre, was beautiful with intense feeling, born of those emotional qualities which had made her so great an actress. There was a quality in her singing which Signora Avolio, with all her superb training, her certain precision, never obtained. Mrs Cibber put more than the art of the singer into her part in *Messiah*. She understood, perhaps no less than Handel, the meaning of every note he had written. So wonderful was her rendering of 'He was despised', that Dr Delany, who was present, exclaimed: 'Woman! for this thy sins be forgiven thee!'

With all her frailties, Mrs Cibber reached more nearly to the intense ideal of Handel in this air than those who followed her. Perhaps it was because her life was all tragedy—tragedy broken by large patches of sunlight and colour that brought her happiness, and made her believe that these things would go on for ever. So impressed was Handel that for long afterwards he wrote all his contralto songs for her. In this performance of *Messiah* she shared the songs with Signora Avolio.

Each of the three charities received £127 from this first performance of *Messiah*. But, in spite of the sensation which the oratorio had aroused, it was not given again till June, during which time Handel gave concerts composed of extracts from his other works, the *Water Music*, *Scipio*, *Saul*, the chorus in *Atalanta*. On 3 June, *Messiah* was again given to a crowded house. The weather was tropical. Lest any should be frightened away by the heat—Handel had had this experience before—he stated in his advertisement of the performance that 'in order to keep the Room as cool as possible, a Pane of Glass will be removed from the top of each of the Windows'. There was no need for these fears. The crowd that gathered at Neal's Music Hall was prepared to submit to any vagaries of the weather.

With this second performance of *Messiah*, Handel's public performances in Dublin came to an end. He was present at the two benefit concerts given in July to his singers, Signora Avolio and Mrs Arne (Cecilia Young),[1] at which excerpts from *Esther*, *Faramondo*, were performed, but he was eager to return to London. There was no need for him to prolong his stay, for, by creating this diversion in Ireland, he had reminded London of its need of him.

He left Dublin in August with every intention of returning the following year, and on his arrival in London he wrote to Jennens:

> The report that the Direction of the Opera next winter is committed to my care is groundless. The Gentlemen who have undertaken to meddle with Harmony cannot agree, and are quite in a confusion. Whether I shall do something in the Oratorio way (as several of my friends desire) I cannot determine as yet. Certain it is, that this time twelve-month I shall continue my oratorios in Ireland, where they are going to make a large subscription already for that Purpose.

But that which he had planned never took place. His nine months in Ireland had been a triumph for which London yet intended to make him pay.

Even now his enemies were waiting for his return.

[1] Dibdin wrote of Mrs Arne (Cecilia Young): 'She was deliciously captivating. She knew nothing in singing or in nature but sweetness and simplicity. She sung exquisitely, as a bird does, her notes conveyed involuntary pleasure and indefinable delight.'

At one of these concerts Dubourg the violinist is said by Burney to have extemporized with his instrument to such an extent that he lost his way, but at long last came back to the right key, whereupon Handel shouted out, so that all could hear: 'Welcome home, Mr Dubourg!'

CHAPTER XXI

THE RETURN TO LONDON

HANDEL had a great love of London. He should be included amongst the greatest of Londoners. London persecuted him as it persecuted few men, but he always came back to it. Ripe with all the favours of his Dublin visit he returned to London unannounced, rather like a child that has had its little hour of life, and goes back to the discipline of a hard school.

There was no announcement of his return to Brook Street. He did not appear in public; he gave no concerts. But London was in a mood to receive him. Dublin had clustered with laurels the man whom London would not stir beyond its door to hear. Pope had published the fourth volume of his *Dunciad* in which he extolled the greatness of Handel, and spoke of him as the man to save music from the serfdom of the Italian opera. He wrote of the wonder of his choruses, of his sense of sound which made him project new instruments into a chorus to gain effect. He even declared that Handel had used cannon in a chorus, which Handel never did—except in the *Firework Music* later. Only once, when dissatisfied with a chorus, Handel had exclaimed, 'Oh, that I had a cannon'.[1]

Pope had, in fact, changed that weathercock thing—public opinion—into an appreciation of Handel such as he had never received in London before. He made London, with the dust of Handel's German origin in its eyes, forget that he had ever come from Germany. He cleverly forgot Handel's association with a German and unpopular Court. He convinced London that in Handel it had a genius. Such praise from Pope caused Handel's enemies to think again. To pursue their venom too far might place them on the wrong side of the fence. The storm of hatred lulled.

Handel had completed *Samson* before going to Ireland, with the exception of 'Let the bright Seraphim' and the following chorus, 'Let their celestial concerts'. He made these additions immediately on his return from Dublin. But as the work was so near completion, why did he not perform *Samson* in Dublin? Was not the lure of London, as claiming in that age as

[1] Horatio Townsend: *Handel's Visit to Dublin*, p. 103.

now? Did not the old gentleman who scuffled down Bond Street and Piccadilly, very aloof, his eyes on the ground, vision these things? He had become forgetful of the London life he had known. 'I had,' declared an intimate friend, 'to stop him and make known to him who I was.' He had forgotten, not only friends, but all the bitterness London had given him. His thoughts sailed over the Bond Street roofs, like fledglings that sought the great currents and the lure of speed and freedom.

He produced his *Samson* at Covent Garden on 18 February 1743. He had Mrs Cibber as 'Micah', Beard as 'Samson', Mrs Clive and Signora Avolio, who sang the glorious air 'Let the bright Seraphim'. No longer Senesino and Faustina and Cuzzoni—that bag of troubles. So far as the artistes, the *Samson* cast could not compare with them. These others who dreamed in song were securing enormous fees on the Continent. But he had a workable cast. Beard was displacing *castrati*, though when Horace Walpole heard him in *Samson* he declared that he had only one note in his voice. But he added that Handel was setting up oratorio against opera and was succeeding.

Then the King stepped in. He went to the second performance of *Samson*, in all the glory of his blue satin, with his ladies, his show, his pompous patronage. A most diverting night, for they bagged a gang of rogues who had looked upon *Samson* as a great opportunity for their craft. Most dishonourable fellows, who had worried the beadles, and plundered the best houses without let or stay. Consider their names. John Price, known as 'The Pigeon', captain of London's pickpockets. William Cole, known as 'Stink-and-End'. And William Meredith without a nickname, but the best snatcher of purses in all Town. What a night they meant to make of it! Right under the King's nose too! Nevertheless that excellent person, Holden Bowker, High Constable for the city, became aware of the premeditated *Samson* robberies. He put his police at the doors. They intimidated gentle ladies, and innocent individuals who were particularly sensitive about the ladies at their sides, but 'The Pigeon' and 'Stink-and-End' were up before Colonel de Veil for judgment in the morning.[1] And the King, knowing nothing at all, went quietly home, 'humming *Samson* in his carriage as if it had been some new imported tune from Paris'. George all scent and romance. Handel went back to Brook Street, very conscious that *Samson* had borne him home

[1] *Daily Post*, 25 February 1743.

to the heart of that recalcitrant London.

All Society was at *Samson* that night. The presence of the King had flung the Handel star loose in a new firmament. Burlington, Middlesex, floundering along with his Italian opera and losing the guineas which he denied his wife, 'that vain girl, full of Greek and Latin and music and painting, who was very short, very plain and very yellow, and the mistress of the Prince of Wales'.[1] Wortley Montagu, decorative, spruce, well-bathed. A dandy in lavender. Scented, select, cultured to an indolent display, which later singled him out as the leader of fashion—as the one superior person. A little later Thomas Brown wrote of him to Philip Gell at Hopton:

> 'To-morrow I dine with Wortley Montagu who is *merveillement débarqué*. He has robbed Paris of everything that is rare or elegant. He went to Martin's (where they make the varnished boxes) and bought the whole shop, which cost him 600 louis d'ors; his diamond buckles cost him 1,000 louis. In short, he is computed to walk £2,500. His wigs surprise everyone, they are made of wire; literally and truly there is no hair in them.'[2]

And upon the mood of these fanatics Handel's success depended.

Handel had attained a new triumph. He had sounded his trumpets afresh outside the walls of Jericho, and they had collapsed at his feet. He became once more a living fibre of London life. He was sought after, acclaimed. What had London yielded in the way of entertainment while Handel was away? A muckle of Italian opera and offending lewdness. Lord Middlesex was plagued with endless worries at the King's Theatre—he and his wobbling satellites, Lord Brooke, Lord Conway, Lord Holderness, Mr Conway, Mr Frederick, and the others. There was a diminishing treasury, scurvy singers, stormy Board meetings. They had burnt their fingers badly. They were all grumbling at each other. The Windham letters are rather eloquent on this point.

> 'Lord Middlesex, it seems, is the chief manager in the affair: the men of penetration give hints that his Lordship's sole aim is to make his Mistress, the Muscovita, appear to

[1] Horace Walpole: *Memoirs*, Vol. I, p. 76.
[2] MSS. by Chandos Pole Gell, Hopton Hall, County Derby.

great advantage upon the stage. With this intent, say they, he has taken care to hire singers with voices inferior to hers, and hers is not worth a farthing. Lord Brooke is quite easy in the matter. I believe he would pay a thousand pounds more rather than have anything to do in it in the character of manager. . . . Lord Brooke is surely the sweetest man alive, if he kept not Symmer in the house with him, and such a crowd of servants to pick one's pockets after one has dined with him.'[1]

Samson was sung eight times, and was without question a money-maker for Handel. It attracted the town, chiefly because he had produced music which provided mental enjoyment after the prolix inanities of the King's Theatre opera under Lord Middlesex. Mrs Cibber, too, as a singer in religious oratorio was a novelty for London.

Handel then decided to produce *Messiah*. But the difficulties with the Church, which had proved such a stumbling-block with *Esther*, broke out again. It would be the act of a madman to put *Messiah* on a play-bill. So Handel was told. Ten years before he would have laughed. But his experience had taught him that he could no longer laugh at public opinion. He gave *Messiah* the title of *A Sacred Oratorio*, but the latter title very soon fell out in favour of that of *Messiah*.[2] The complete work was not published until 1767, when Randall and Abell—the successors of Walsh—produced it at a guinea a copy by subscription, plus another half-guinea on delivery of the book.

London did not want *Messiah*. It was sung only on three occasions that season. The religious controversy kept many people away. They argued that any work about the Omnipotent should never be performed in a playhouse. A few hailed it as a masterpiece in religious thought, but they were lone voices crying in a wilderness. The King attended one performance, and was so moved by the fervour of the 'Hallelujah Chorus' that he rose to his feet and remained standing till the last chords had dropped to silence.[3]

---

[1] *Windham Letters*, p. 203.

[2] The title 'Messiah' was used in the notices for the performances in Ireland in 1742. 'New Grand Sacred Oratorio called "Messiah" ' and 'Messiah' is the title of the libretto.

[3] It is said that the custom of the audience rising to its feet at the singing of the 'Hallelujah Chorus' began with the King's action on this occasion—the audience being unable to remain seated while the

For years the storm about performing a work of this nature in a playhouse rolled on. The clergy called the oratorio sacrilege and Handel a heretic. All leaders of religious thought were at one in their efforts to shut the theatre. There was nothing about *Messiah* that appealed to the age. It was outside the rut of eighteenth-century musical comprehension. No one really understood it. No one wanted to understand it. Yet an expert recently calculated that if the lowest royalty payable on a musical work had been paid on *Messiah* since it was first sung in London, over two million pounds would have been paid for performances in Britain alone on an oratorio which London at that time despised.

The few who did understand it failed to convince the others. At a later revival a letter in the Talbot-Carter correspondence proved how sure was the opinion of a faithful minority. Miss Talbot wrote:

'The only public place I have been to this winter, was last Friday, to hear the *Messiah*, nor can there be a nobler entertainment. I think it is impossible for the most trifling not to be the better for it. I was wishing all the Jews, Heathens, and Infidels in the world (a pretty full house you'll say!) to be present. The Morocco Ambassador was there, and if his interpreter could do justice to the divine words (the music anyone that has a heart *must* feel) how must he be affected, when in the grand choruses the whole audience solemnly rose up in joint acknowledgment that He who for our sakes had been despised and rejected of men, was their Creator, Redeemer, King of Kings, Lord of Lords! To be sure the playhouse is an unfit place for such a performance, but I fear I shall be in Oxfordshire before it is heard at the Foundling Hospital, where the benevolent design and the attendance of little boys and girls adds a peculiar beauty even unto this noblest composition. But Handel who could suit such music to such words deserves to be maintained, and these two nights, I am told, have made him amends for the solitude of his other oratorios.'[1]

King was standing. This may be so, but it is hard to imagine a seated audience during the rendering of such a paean of praise to the Maker of all things. The honour rendered to King George as the originator of the custom I think should be attributed to the decency of a thinking people.

[1] Carter-Talbot Correspondence.

One questions whether Handel believed he would make money from *Messiah*, and, since London did not seem to want it, he withdrew it.[1] He associated it with all his later charity for the Foundling Hospital, and, during his lifetime, he raised eleven thousand pounds for the Hospital by its performance. Perhaps those days of its composition still bore their vivid impress. At any rate, when the Foundling Hospital wanted to get a Bill through Parliament to authorize the regular perform-ance of *Messiah*, Handel rose in his wrath as if the Governors had trodden on sacred ground. They were going to steal his rights—so he argued, and properly so. 'What for they take my music to Parliament!' he exclaimed in his anger, and had the Bill withdrawn.

He ultimately declared that 'He saw the lovely youth' in *Theodora*—that later oratorio of ill-fortune—was the greatest chorus he ever wrote. The 'Hallelujah Chorus' was his second favourite. But, as a work apart, *Messiah* was his one creation that ever pleased him, and which he never altered, except in small measure. His final oratorio *Jephtha* remained fragrant to him till the end, because, as a complete work, it was the last offering of a fruitful life. *The Triumph of Time and Truth* was performed through his years, and was altered and re-altered, until the work of 1708 would scarcely compare with the version of his later life. But *Messiah* remained to him the one beautiful thing that held in it all those vagrant thoughts he had ever had of religion and its influence.

After *Messiah* had been produced in London, he happened to call upon Lord Kinnoul, who had heard the work, and who complimented Handel upon it as a great entertainment. 'My lord,' replied Handel, 'I should be sorry if I only entertained them; I wished to make them better.'

Happy soul! He knew, as few creators do, that he had done something for humanity. At least he realized what he had given.[2]

---

[1] *Messiah* was performed three times in 1743, not at all in 1744, twice only in 1745, and not again until 1749.

[2] The autograph of *Messiah* was in the private Royal Music Library at the British Museum and has now been given to the nation by Queen Elizabeth. After the death of Handel, the King of Prussia offered Christopher Smith £2,000 for it. To this, Smith [the Elder] made the rejoinder that, as Handel had been so well treated in England during his many years in London, he would not sell the

manuscript. He left it to his son who in turn presented it to King George III.

The manuscript remained at Buckingham Palace—latterly in the ballroom— but during the War of 1914–18 it was moved to the King's private room in the British Museum.

At St. Michael's College, Tenbury Wells, Worcestershire, there is a conducting score made to a great extent by John Christopher Smith, but it contains several numbers in Handel's autograph.

What is now called the 'Tenbury' Copy was used by Handel at Dublin, when, on 13 April 1742, he gave his first performance of *Messiah* there.

At a later stage he seems to have presented this copy to the City or to the Dublin Musical Society. Ultimately it came into the hands of Mr William Young Ottley on whose death in 1836 it was put up for sale with his effects, and bought in by his nephew, Edward J. Ottley, for £1! He gave it to Sir Frederick Ouseley, Bart., in 1867. Thus it came to rest at Tenbury Wells Museum.

CHAPTER XXII

THE SECOND FAILURE

As soon as the season closed, Handel began the composition of a secular oratorio, *Semele*, the words of which had been adapted from Congreve. He composed the first bars on 3 June, and finished the work on 4 July, probably with every intention of producing it at the beginning of the autumn season.

But, as had so frequently happened, the affairs of the nation intervened, and caused him to lay aside this oratorio based on mythology, in order to take an active part in the nation's rejoicing. On 27 June the battle of Dettingen had been fought at the little village on the River Main, and resulted in an English victory. King George himself had led the English troops into battle.

The conflict had been so unexpected, and the news of the King's valour more unexpected still, that London was thrown into a fever of excitement. This unsympathetic King, who lolled about in the salons, who talked an improvised English to all the best ladies of the town, this miserable figure, afraid even now of some phantom return of his wife, had shown courage no one believed him to possess. There was no martial bearing about George. He had no liking for things military, nor the breath of cannon. He only sallied into war from some certain sense of duty—a sense more oddly developed in him than in any of the Georges—sitting his horse very badly, till the horse, alarmed by the firing, ran away at Dettingen, and nearly bore him into the enemy's ranks. At least he tried to look the part, and to take his war experiences seriously. When he regained safety he dismounted, and, finding his feet firm on the good earth, exclaimed: 'Now I know I shall not run away!'[1]

George and Dettingen completely changed the attitude of the English people towards the Court. *Quel courage! Quelle bonne chance!* His retinue, safely housed in the Palace while the Royal master was away and nearly getting killed, covered him with compliments when he returned at the head of his troops, very smiling and tired of campaigning. The obese little man

[1] W. M. Thackeray: *The Four Georges.*

loved the fêting better than he had loved the smoke of Louis' cannon. He held receptions. He held more receptions. There must be a proper celebration—crowds, the sound of cannon—a procession—of course, a procession—and martial music. He sent for the Court musician, Handel.

On 17 July Handel began his *Dettingen Te Deum*, and on the thirtieth he began the *Dettingen Anthem*. Many of Handel's biographers declare that for the *Te Deum* he adapted some of the composing of an Italian priest named Urio, who had lived in the seventeenth century. But no definite proof of any kind has ever been discovered. These charges of plagiarism have constantly recurred in the Handel biographies.[1] That Handel, more gifted with originality than most of the composers the world has known, should prowl about looking for the indifferent work of lesser and unknown people is a foolish charge. His brain was always fertile with more melody than his pen could put to score.

When the *Te Deum* was performed at the Chapel Royal on 27 November it was declared to be one of the most majestic works that ever came from the master. It took rank beside the *Funeral Anthem* as the greatest composition for public occasion he had produced. Every kettledrum and trumpet that he could press into service had been secured. The music was martial, stately. It moved the King deeply. Could any man, save Handel, have put into the rattle and rumble of drums the glories of Dettingen? What pomp! What clamour! What majesty! And what thoughts passed through George's mind as he listened. The field and the smoke wreaths . . . the bolting, foolish horse, and his own silly plight—why had he ever come? . . . The break of the French across the river . . . and the howling mob in the streets when he returned! Perhaps he had never really appreciated Handel till now. Even the *Funeral Anthem* had not moved him so much, since he had never understood death.

Handel produced nothing further in 1743. He kept *Semele*, complete to the last note and phrase, in his drawer for eight

[1] Mr P. Robinson, in his admirable work, *Handel and His Orbit*, adequately deals with, and largely disproves, the charges of plagiarism brought against Handel by his enemies. It is not proposed to introduce a technical survey of these points into this volume since Mr Robinson has given proof that Handel was not a plagiarist—except on himself.—Author.

months. Illness had begun to attack him again. 'Mr Handel has a palsy and cannot compose,' wrote Horace Walpole at this season. He remained in London, but the old antagonisms against him were springing up afresh because he had, by his concerts, drawn patrons from the bastard Italian operas which Lord Middlesex was now providing at the King's Theatre. The competition did not affect Middlesex alone. The pick of Society had backed the noble entrepreneur with their money. Handel was therefore helping to keep the dividends expected from the King's Theatre out of the pockets of those who, in earlier times, had been his hosts.

The cabal against him grew in strength as the winter progressed, and when, on 10 February 1744, he produced *Semele*, he had an angry Society ranged in line against him. If *Semele* was rather foolish in its story, Handel had at least given it some glorious airs. 'Where'er you walk', had a grace which has held it high in popularity for two centuries, since it bears all the delightful atmosphere of some of the best themes in *Acis and Galatea*. 'O Sleep, why dost thou leave me?' is a little jewel, clean cut and haunting. 'Now Love, that everlasting boy' is the essence of all living and all happiness. But *Semele* was only performed four times and is little known in this country, in spite of the fact that, from beginning to end, it is Handel at his best, both in chorus and aria. Its comparative failure in 1744 was due mainly to the attitude of Society. 'There was no disturbances at the Playhouse,' wrote Mrs Delany after her visit to the theatre, a remark significant in its suggestion.[1]

Mrs Delany remained one of Handel's strongest supporters. Lady Brown, on the other hand, was conniving with her social set to ruin Handel by giving concerts and functions, graced by wanton extravagance, on the very nights chosen by Handel for his concerts, in order to keep people away from his theatre. Lady Brown was merely a rich person without any musical knowledge whatever. But, like some people of these times, she imagined that riches are the true road to accurate criticism of any subject pertaining to Art. Mrs Delany was talking about Handel, always talking about him. He spent evenings at her house, brought his singers and entertained her guests. She was never patronizing; on the contrary, she yielded the patronage to Handel. She went to the extent of compiling a libretto,

[1] Mrs Delany: *Life and Correspondence*, Vol. II.

which she hoped that Handel would set, for just after the production of *Semele* she wrote to Mrs Dewes:

'How do you think *I have lately been employed*? Why, I have made a drama for an oratorio out of Milton's 'Paradise Lost', to give Mr Handel to compose to; it has cost me a good deal of thought and contrivance. . . . I begin with Satan's threatening to seduce the woman, her being seduced follows, and it ends with the man's yielding to the temptation; I would not have a word or a thought of Milton's altered, and I hope to prevail with Mr Handel to set it *without having any of the lines put into verse*, for that will take from its dignity.'[1]

If ever she gave the libretto to Handel, he successfully buried it without taxing her susceptibilities unduly. His amanuensis, John Christopher Smith, produced a version of *Paradise Lost* after Handel's death, for which parts of Mrs Delany's libretto may have been used.

The comparative failure of *Semele* found Handel with another work ready in *Joseph*, an oratorio based on words by James Miller. Was it some portent that the opera circle at the King's Theatre was breaking, or a premonition of disaster to himself, that made Handel work so feverishly? Something drove him from one work to another with an endurance that could never last. *Joseph* was not a success, although it contained a few beautiful arias, for some of which Handel had secured a new contralto in Signora Galli, who had made her début in Italian opera at the King's Theatre shortly before.

What a meteoric life was Galli's! *Joseph* was merely a prelude to what she was to achieve in London. When later Handel produced his *Judas Maccabaeus* she was encored every night. She was a thin Italian figure when she came; her singing had a natural beauty and little cultured execution. Under Handel, she rose to become one of the best contraltos London possessed, and she stayed with him up to his last oratorio, *Jephtha*. She sang the old warrior out. But she grew fat. She became waspish in temper till only Handel could manage her. The few good looks she possessed betook themselves off and left a hulking, heavy figure that lumbered on to the stage, and lumbered off again. She publicly snubbed duchesses and 'the

[1] Mrs Delany: *Life and Correspondence*, Vol. II, p. 280.

quality', who wished to honour her socially, a woman once cultured and careful, who flung money away on whims and fancies, believing that her voice of gold, and the lure of it, would last for ever.

Such was Galli. Ultimately she lived with Miss Ray the actress, and was with her when some ill-conditioned lover, named Hackman, shot at and killed her, and then turned his pistol upon himself so slightly that he lived to be hanged for murder. Then Galli gravitated downhill. The old Italian pride would not break even under the lash of poverty. She tried to sing, and when the public laughed at a voice that had withered with the years, she crept away broken and hurt, yet ready to make a fresh attempt to get back. She was one of those slaves whom music treats too hardly. In her later years she sang 'He was despised', and the Earl of Mount Edgcumbe records that her voice was cracked and trembling, but had in it all the dying suggestion of good quality.

But the public was kinder than usual to this woman it had made a toy. 'It was pleasing to observe the kindness with which she was received and listened to,' wrote the Earl about that performance,

> 'and to mark the animation and delight with which she seemed to hear again the music in which she had formerly been a distinguished performer. The poor old woman had been in the habit of coming to me annually for a trifling present; and she told me on that occasion that nothing but her distress would have compelled her to so expose herself.'[1]

The glorious contralto whom Handel made, dropped slowly to beggary, her voice gone, and only a few friends left to toss to her some occasional charity. A piteous tragedy that death ended in the same miserable fashion in a London slum.

When Galli appeared in *Joseph* her day was at its dawn, though the oratorio from its first performance was a failure. It was played but three times, and then it dropped out of English music.[2] Handel was again faced with serious losses at Covent Garden; malignant whispers got abroad that he was about to fail for the second time. Pure invention—yet they proved to be

---

[1] Earl of Mount Edgcumbe: *Musical Reminiscences*, 1834.
[2] Germany had never heard *Joseph* until it was first performed at Halle in 1910.

right. Handel heard them and said nothing; he worked more furiously than ever. It was Lord Middlesex and the King's Theatre with its Italian operas which was breaking. The company collapsed in June, and its members dispersed. Not a coin remained in the coffers; they had, in fact, lost money from the commencement. Middlesex found around him a host of titled people in the drawing-rooms, in his clubs, who had lost money over his unintelligent productions, and were not so disposed to crack jokes and bottles with him as freely as of yore. My lord was distressed. He spread the Handel calumny far and wide, he was even more active than Bononcini had been in his hatred of Handel. Then, finding that it eased Society's hurt not a whit, he quietly went abroad for his health, and lived a dissolute life in Paris and elsewhere till the thrall of Piccadilly and clubland lured him back again. He found his circle broken, and his erstwhile splendid friends by no means anxious for his society.

If Handel did not openly rejoice over the failure of Lord Middlesex in the Haymarket, it can have been but a lean source of sorrow to him. He answered the critics as to his own stability by walking in at the front door of the King's Theatre as Middlesex went out by the back. He engaged the theatre for the ensuing season, and, early in June, was in correspondence with Jennens with regard to a new libretto. 'I shall be glad to receive the first act, or what is ready, of the new oratorio with which you intend to favour me,' he wrote to Jennens on the ninth. On 19 July he wrote again: 'I immediately perused the act of the oratorio with which you favoured me, and the little time only I had it gives me great pleasure.'

In August he declared himself to be greatly pleased with the second act. He urged Jennens to send him the third. He was hard on Jennens' heels, composing faster than the maker of words could put his lines together. Jennens continued to write on and on, and Handel became nervous. The oratorio, as Jennens was constructing it, threatened to take a whole day to perform. 'It is really too long,' Handel wrote to him in October. 'I retrenched already a great deal of musick that I might preserve the poetry as much as I could.'

But Jennens was not accustomed to being stopped by Handel or anyone else. *Belshazzar*, or *Belteshazzar* as it was then called—the name being changed just before the first performance—reached a length beyond the capacity of any oratorios. Jennens, therefore, insisted that the book of the words sold at the theatre should contain *Belshazzar* as he wrote it, with the passages that had been omitted from Handel's music specially marked. By his perversity and conceit over this libretto Jennens certainly spoilt the oratorio. It was far too prolix, even as Handel had set it. Bombast ran riot throughout the whole creation. The author rode on the high clouds. But there was drama in the theme which gave Handel the opportunity for some of his most sublime choruses. The arrogance of Jennens had been overcome by the nobility of Handel's composing, but not sufficiently to carry the work to popular favour.

Handel opened his season at the King's Theatre in November, but contented himself with revivals till 5 January 1745, when he produced his secular oratorio *Hercules*. He had composed Thomas Broughton's adaptation of Sophocles whilst waiting for Jennens to send the acts of *Belshazzar* to him. But *Hercules* was never for a moment in favour, and after a few performances it was withdrawn.

On 27 March, *Belshazzar* took its place, and was thought so little of that, in order to keep faith to some extent with his subscribers, Handel had to revive *Semele*, *Joseph*, and *Saul*. But the whole season failed to recoup his bare expenses, and he closed the theatre on 23 April, having given only sixteen out of the twenty-four concerts for which he had contracted.

The future was black in the extreme. It is doubtful if Handel, in those days of 1745, could imagine any future, the whole town seemed to have turned once more against him furiously. 'I went last Friday to *Alexander's Feast*,' wrote the Countess of Shaftesbury on 13 March, 'but it was such a melancholy pleasure, as drew tears of sorrow to see the great, though unhappy, Handel, dejected, wan, and dark, sitting by, not playing on, the harpsichord, and to think how his light had been spent in being overplied in music's cause.'[1]

As soon as he reopened the King's Theatre the cabal broke out afresh. Every form of social entertainment was purposely held on the nights of his concerts, to lure his patrons away. They tore down his posters. His theatre was picketed with rowdies who caused the same disturbances as they had done when he occupied Lincoln's Inn Fields. Young bloods thought it the height of good sport to go down to the theatre doors and roar like maddened bulls when the chairs and carriages were arriving.

[1] Malmesbury Papers.

Whatever mental torment Handel endured at this period he kept to himself. He wrote no angry letters and gave no rebuke to the libels that were turning the town against him. If he passed his friends in the street it was not in pique, but because he would walk for hours with his thoughts, seeing nothing beyond them. The world was spinning about him like a crazy top, but he kept his balance. His bank account was nil, his singers clamouring for money, yet he knew no plaint, no call for quarter. The big, ambling figure was seen coming down Piccadilly—a little bent the giant had become now—with the same pride and his courage still unbroken. No genius of any age could hope to achieve against such a concentration of enemies.

Then came the inevitable result. His head was going. Rheumatism—or more probably, neuritis—tore at his limbs. He did not sleep. Every movement brought to his lips a smothered groan of pain. Some said he was going mad, and his enemies knew that he was finished. When Handel vanished from London to the seclusion of Tunbridge Wells, they realized that they could search about for a new victim as sport for their loose sense of humanity.

Handel had crashed for the second time.

CHAPTER XXIII

THE TIDE TURNS

HANDEL was seen again in London in August 1745, and the Town was astounded.

He appeared in Brook Street as if he had risen from the dead. But what astonished London still more, was that he had leased Covent Garden for the ensuing spring. How had he done it? Whose money was he going to waste now? So they asked across the dinner-tables. Not that he had recovered. But the first urge of the new life, which the enforced rest had given him, was to bring him back to his work. He was still disordered in his head, and not until October was he clear of the trouble.[1]

Yet the old warrior was full of battle. His veins warmed to a slow passionate heat. Though he talked about his ailments with the inquietude of an ageing man, they in no way impinged upon his desire to work.

The salvation of Handel at this stage was—as it always had been—complete belief in himself. That belief alone kept him from drawing away, a finished broken figure, at various crises in his career. That is where the man was as great as his music, and so few of the masters have possessed a courage equal to their chords. They dropped into dissolute existence, starved and gloried in a vagrant art, and died of empty stomachs, some of them, because they did not possess that complete mental courage which fought for survival. They struggled; a few died miserably, like martyrs. More gloriously than some martyrs. But Handel never meant to be killed. Hudson, in his portraits of Handel, has put in the severity of that underlip. They could smash his health, shun his music, but not by endless manoeuvre could they change his fighting personality an iota. He was sixty years of age, and a game sixty. Not the sixty that acquires a gentle indolence by looking at its birth certificate, and slides, fruitful no longer, into that calm inertia which is an unspoken invitation to Death.

Hardly had Handel returned to London than Prince Charlie, the Pretender, landed in Scotland with hopes of an

[1] Malmesbury Papers.

army. He became a personified rumour. He swept through the towns, the lowliest villages—a rumour. He would storm the country—for was not this fellow bound for Westminster? He would flick the Hanoverian George off his throne like a fly from a paper. Jacobitism was a secret creed which, at his word, would stir in the people like a soul returning to a life-less body.

The rumours frightened London. The Guards were turned out and sent to Finchley. There would be siege, starvation. There was a run on the shops; a greater run on the banks. Many of the aristocracy departed as far South as they dared. To Exeter; to Cornwall. London never knew such upheaval. It had no order, no organization which would be of any service on the arrival of an armed force against the capital. And that foolish fellow, the invader, was trying to swing his magic personality across a few glum Scotsmen.

The King exclaimed: 'Pouf!' He held more receptions. Had not the mischievous horse at Dettingen nearly pitched him into a worse mess than this would ever become? If he had still possessed a Queen he would have walked up and down the room—as he always did when talking to her—and de-claimed on the vanity of the upstart. Instead, he told his lesser queens all about it, and was supremely content. But when the danger came nearer, he packed up all his valuables into endless crates and prepared to depart to Hanover. His son's defeat of the Pretender alone made him alter his mind.

The rebels reached Derby. Then the change in the plans of the raiders kept the King firm to his capital. London liked his courage, and a wave of confidence in him passed through the town. Hysteria disappeared like mist before the late sun of a February morning. There would be no raid, no siege, no plundering, no George trussed like a skinny fowl beneath a Jacobite thong. The verve of the people caught Handel. He composed, with that magic quickness so truly his own, *The Occasional Oratorio*. Some of it was borrowed from his failure, *Israel in Egypt*, and he interwove in the new work a few of his best moods from the *Coronation Anthem*. For the rest, he composed over thirty new numbers, one of which was a song, in which he used the opening bars of Arne's 'Rule, Britannia'. He produced the complete work for three per-formances in February 1746, giving free tickets to those of his patrons to whom he had not fulfilled his obligations in the matter of the number of concerts held during the previous season.

His tremendous overture in *The Occasional Oratorio* was a worthy sop to throw to his faithful adherents, and it repaid them for their loyalty. Even George was regaled by the strident call of victory in this paean of thanksgiving. If it had not been too late to turn from the errant little dancers, the bright eyes lifted to his beneath the high coifs in the salons, he might even yet have tried to live up to Mr Handel. But his day was too far spent. The first dim evening had begun to steal across those sweet pastures of his life which his fretful feet had found so often.

If *The Occasional Oratorio* made no loss, the free seats Handel had given to those subscribers of the previous season to whom he felt himself to be honourably in debt, precluded all possibility of profit. The work, however, brought to him fresh interest from the nation. This man at least could understand the joy of the people, and could put it to chords. The enmities began to die down automatically. The man who had composed a nation's thanksgiving could not be dragged through the mud any longer.

Scarcely had the work been forgotten than the overthrow of Prince Charlie at Culloden on 16 April roused the nation to fresh frenzy. The young Duke of Cumberland, said London, had acquitted himself well. He had shattered the forces of the Pretender beyond all reconstruction; he had removed for ever that menace that had once threatened the homes of London. He had done his work valiantly, the glorious victor; he had butchered every living thing that might have been in contact with the Pretender! There were no half-measures with him; he was taking no risks. He had gone on slaughtering for days, and many of the people killed up in the Highlands knew no more about the Pretender than they knew about Handel. The Duke of Cumberland held the firm opinion that if they had had no truck with the Pretender they might have had, and forthwith drove a sword through them. A very excellent thing to do according to the view of the town at the time, and of the King in particular.

As for George, he preened himself with pride at the exploits of this cub of his, who had got himself perpetually into scrapes in town for trying to steal other men's mistresses. A worthy successor to the conqueror of Dettingen. The Duke of Cumberland's brother, the Prince of Wales, was so mightily pleased about the whole butchering, that he approached and requested music for his brother's home-coming, which should be as glorious as had been *The Occasional Oratorio*.

Handel at this time—the summer of 1746—was living in very respectable poverty. He was making no money, and, apart from such investments in city companies as remained untouched, and they were few, he had but his Crown pension. True, his expenses were small. His house in Brook Street cost him only £35 per annum, and he had two servants. In his dress he was careful, but not extravagant. He wore a gold-laced coat, ruffles, and a three-cornered hat. He kept up appearances in his dress. It was his business to keep up appearances, and at no time in his life did he adopt that shoddiness and grime which so many associated in that age with real Art. His dress was really very expressive of his character. He never wore old garments, and he disliked new. Even when he had not a guinea in his pocket, he preferred the style of a man who might not be rich, but whose art at least was sufficient to save him from any bother with the bills of tailors. When he was in funds he never dressed richly: when he was poor he never dressed poorly. His garb was, in good times and bad, always that of a man whose income was certain, whose art was a staple thing one did not have to dress up to, as Bononcini and Farinelli and others who had dropped out of the battle, had felt it so necessary to do.

It was in the summer of 1746 that Handel met a divine named Thomas Morell, D.D., a worthy person given to writing execrable poetry. Morell had written a libretto called *Judas Maccabaeus*, and on 9 July Handel began to set it to music. On 11 August he finished it, and then for some reason put the work away. The Duke of Cumberland did not return from Scotland till the autumn, and it may have been impossible to fix a date for a production associated with battle and victory till the youthful butcher could impress London with his greatness and his bloody sword.

Morell was a bad copy of Jennens. With all his vast pomp, Jennens was clever. Jennens, if he never reached the clouds, was conscious of those secret clefts in them where the real poets forgathered. Morell, on the other hand, was an irritating person with no real gift. All his libretti for Handel bore the heavy stamp of the amateur. His name is only preserved instead of being forgotten as it deserved, because Handel set his words. In a letter written some years later, Morell complained of the things an author must submit to,

'if the composer be of an haughty disposition, and has but an imperfect acquaintance with the English language. As for myself, great lover as I am of music, I should never have thought of such an undertaking had not Mr Handel applied to me when at Kew in 1746, and added to his request the honour of a recommendation from Prince Frederic. Upon this I thought I could do as well as some who had gone before me, and within two or three days carried him the first act of *Judas Maccabaeus*.'

Handel could not answer these words when they were written; he had been buried in Westminster Abbey. But one can imagine this pompous little parson's conceit, when, after the man who had made him had gone to the kingdom of all melody, he furtively acclaimed himself as the veritable source of inspiration of *Judas Maccabaeus*—so great a source that, on their coming together, Handel had to bring a recommendation from royal hands in order to secure his libretto!

Further in his letter, Morell narrated that when he called upon Handel with the manuscript of the first act, the composer wished to proceed with the oratorio on the spot.

'I will bring you more tomorrow,' said Morell.

'No, something now,' said Handel. ' "So fall thy foes, O Lord", that will do. And he immediately carried on the composition as we have it in that most admirable chorus,' Morell continued.[1]

Handel produced *Judas Maccabaeus* at Covent Garden on 1 April 1747, and from the first night it was a success. By accident rather than design, Morell had chosen a Jew for the hero, and immediately all the Jews in town began to crowd the theatre. A Jew on the stage as a hero rather than a reviled figure was a thing practically unknown in London, and Handel at once found himself possessed of a new public. If his old supporters in Society still kept aloof, dreaming of ancient enmities, the Jews of London more than made up for them. *Judas* was played six times that season, whilst

[1] *Hodgkin MSS.*

three performances of *The Occasional Oratorio* were given, and three of *Joseph*. In the later revivals of *Judas*—and Handel performed it in all some thirty times—he made additions which ultimately brought the work to the form in which we now know it. For instance, not till the following season did he introduce that famous chorus 'See the conquering hero comes', which was originally part of *Joshua*. Years elapsed, too, before the chorus 'Sion now her head shall raise' appeared in *Judas Maccabaeus*. It was the last chorus of Handel's composing, and not until his eyes were blind and he could not see its effect upon the audiences, did it become part of his orattorio.

Handel was unquestionably now making a good deal of money from his concerts. What was more important, *Judas Maccabaeus* carried him completely back to popular favour. Those who had lost their money over Lord Middlesex and his adventure at the King's Theatre had begun to forget their grievance against Handel as the cause. One by one they were coming round to the view that they had backed the wrong horse, and that success had attended the one who by merit deserved it. Handel now had the complete support of every member of the Royal Family. Then Society, like a flock of sheep, began to dribble back to his theatre as if they had never known aught but complete friendliness for him.

'The plan of *Judas Maccabaeus* was designed as a compliment to the Duke of Cumberland upon his returning victorious from Scotland,' continues Morell in his letter. 'I had introduced several incidents more apropos, but it was thought they would make it too long, and were therefore omitted. The Duke, however, made me a handsome present by the hand of Mr Poyntz.' Then, concludes the smug little amateur —'The success of the Oratorio was very great, and I have often wished, that at first I had ask'd in jest, for the benefit of the 30th night, instead of the 3rd. I am sure he (Handel) would have given it to me; on which night there was about £400 in the House.'[1]

Altogether Morell did very well out of Handel. Certainly he made more from the partnership than he could have earned by his writings in any other form if one may judge by their quality. But he criticized Handel freely and often, not

[1] *Hodgkin MSS.*

only in letters to his friends, but even to Handel's face. One day, like Jennens before him, he told Handel frankly that he considered an air in *Judas Maccabaeus* was not worthy of his words. Now, if Handel had a high respect for Jennens, and was prepared to submit to criticism from him, he had not the same sentiments towards Morell, whom he recognized as being but a poor versifier at best. Morell's rebuke stung him to anger. 'You teach me musick, sir!' Handel exclaimed. 'Mine musick is good Musick. It is your words that is bad. Hear the passage again. . . . Now go and make words to that Musick!'

Although Handel had been so reviled, and had only now begun to return to favour, there were plenty of hawks ready to sweep down and bear away the prize that was his. Directly *Judas* became successful, he had to submit to a *pasticcio* made up of songs from his operas being performed at the Italian theatre. *Lucio Vero*, as the work was named, had quite a modest success, and Handel had to run the gamut of competition from his own compositions, out of which he received nothing. Moreover, they stole his *Ottone* and produced it at the Haymarket.

Among the singers in *Lucio* was Giulia Frasi, who had come to London at the same time as Galli, a woman of some prettiness, who had, according to Burney, 'a sweet clear voice and smooth and chaste style of singing, which, though cold and unimpassioned, pleased natural ears and escaped the censure of Critics'. Frasi proved to be the only recompense Handel received for the theft of his work in *Lucio*. He promptly engaged her for the following season, and she remained one of his favourite singers till the end of his days.

The season's success had put Handel on his feet again. His health was fairly good. With the lure of a new prosperity in front of him, he worked even more fiercely. Attempts to draw him back into Society were unavailing. Handel had departed from Society for ever. The friends who had turned from him were not re-accepted. He was courteous, with that studied civility which put the stamp of a gentleman upon all his letters and conversations, but he remained aloof. Instead, he drew further and further into his shell as the years pressed him, and his work demanded all the energy his troubled body and mind had still to give. Mrs Cibber, Mrs Delany, Frasi, and a few hundred kindred souls claimed him. The heavy, stooping figure shuffled through their drawing-rooms, and, in the home of each, monopolized a favourite chair. His laugh was as joyous as ever; his wit as quick. His brain, which had been ceaselessly worked throughout the years, was yielding the same riches as it had ever done. Only his body was weakening. Handel at this stage of his life was not a spent mental force; he was never stronger.

As soon as the season concluded, Morell came to him with a new libretto, *Alexander Balus*, based on the story of the love of the King of Syria for Cleopatra, daughter of Ptolemy. Handel began its composing on 1 June 1747, and completed the last notes on 4 July. Even then he was not content, nor would he pander to his increasing age by taking a rest. Instead, he began to compose *Joshua* at the end of July, and completed the work on 19 August. In two and a half months he had scored two full oratorios, sound testimony of his mental strength at the age of sixty-two.

For *Joshua* as for *Alexander*, Morell had supplied the libretto. Seemingly he had become rather more tractable, for he refers to Handel insisting on his adding certain lines. 'I will step into another parlour and alter them immediately,' Morell told him, and concludes, 'I went down and returned with them altered in about three minutes; when he would have them as they were, and had set them, most delightfully accompanied.' Sufficient proof surely of the miraculous speed at which Handel could compose.

Handel opened his season at Covent Garden on 23 March 1748 with *Alexander Balus*, but the Jews were not attracted to this Jewish story in song as they had been to *Judas*. The oratorio was only performed three times that season. It was strong in chorus, and a particularly beautiful piece of Handel's composing, but it failed to draw. It fell down between the middle classes which had thronged to *Judas*, and Handel's social patrons who were not enthusiastic over work that emblazoned the Jews. Nevertheless, Handel was ready with *Joshua* as soon as *Alexander Balus* ceased to draw. When he asked Hawkins what he thought of 'See the conquering hero comes', the latter said he did not care for it, which drew the retort that Hawkins would live to see it, 'more popular with the people than my other fine things'. Handel was right and Hawkins was wrong, for when, shortly afterwards, Handel transferred the chorus to *Judas* he gave it a certain place for posterity.

The season might have been unfruitful, but six performances of *Judas Maccabaeus*, sung to crowded houses, made good the deficiencies of the new oratorios. *Alexander Balus* and *Joshua* were then relegated to the limbo of forgotten things, each of them carrying jewels of surprising beauty, such as the great chorus in *Alexander* 'O calumny', the glorious aria 'Convey me to some peaceful shore', and the exquisite air, 'Hark! he strikes the golden lyre'. But so rich was Handel's life in melody that the ages have been content to leave these two oratorios amid the dust and memories of a forgotten epoch, in spite of the ripeness of his composing which they bear.[1] Germany alone has had its occasional performances of *Joshua*.

Before the season had closed, Handel was engaged on new work. He had reached his sixty-third year, but the powers of endeavour showed no sign of halting. The burly figure shuffled down Brook Street daily. One met him in the park, alone, always alone. Talking to himself. Stopping at times, looking at nothing, and talking, then going on heavily and bent, with the aid of a thick walking-stick. People heard wild scraps of conversation as they passed him. One is recorded: 'The devil! The father was deceived, the mother was deceived, but I was not deceived. He is ein damn scoundrel, and good for nothing.'

All the summer of 1748 Handel spent in composing. He did not leave town. From the beginning of May till mid-June he worked on *Solomon*, the libretto of which is supposed to have been supplied to him by Morell, but of this I have some doubt. If Morell had been the librettist of so splendid a work he would scarcely have refrained from mentioning the fact in the survey of his associations with Handel, which he included in his famous letter.[2] *Susanna* occupied Handel from 21 July till 24 August, and there is no record of the person who provided him with the libretto; his name is

---

[1] *Alexander Balus* has never been revived in proper fashion since Handel's death, until lately. Performances, usually by amateurs, have been given at Scarborough, Darlington, Sunderland, and elsewhere, and some of the finest numbers were sung at various Handel festivals during the last century. Apart from this, the work has been little known in this country, as it was in Germany before the last war. I have Christopher Smith's copy of this work which Handel used at his concerts.—Author.

[2] *Hodgkin MSS.*

lost. When autumn came, Handel had two of his greatest works ready for production, and Christopher Smith busy completing his concert copies.

He produced *Susanna* on 10 February 1749 and gave it for three performances. On 17 March he followed it with *Solomon*.[1] He still clung to his fetish of the Jews, for *Susanna* dealt with the Jewish captivity in Babylon, and *Solomon*, of course, was Jewish throughout. He had thrown open his theatre now to all and sundry. He had as much regard for the pit as the boxes. Indeed, he had reached the conclusion that the fidelity of the pit could balance the infidelity of the boxes. He began at this stage to earn a ripe treasury by giving the people what they required. He had done with the quality. The freaks and moods of the salons were a matter for despair rather than hope. And at best the salons had very little real musical instinct. It might be said that they had attended his performances in the past at the instigation of some vague sense of duty. Society usually talked through the performance while the pit listened. The former made a Handel concert a meeting-place for re-telling the new scandals, for settling bets, for gibing and jesting at the expense of some unfortunate who had wilfully, or otherwise, departed from a social creed; they preened themselves and peered from their boxes at somebody's coif. It was diverting; it was life. It assisted Handel's treasury and spoiled his concerts. He shook his wig in distinct disapprobation and was angry. But they talked and gossiped in the dark hiding of the boxes louder than ever, and without concern for anyone.

Since *Susanna* and *Solomon* carried no special appeal, Handel revived *Samson*, *The Occasional Oratorio*, and *Hercules*. He drew his crowds, his talkers, his disciples, and they fed the till, even if so many of them did not understand the fare for which they paid. *Susanna*, one of the longest works of Handel's devising, passed over the heads of a mob that was quite ignorant of its beauties. All the purport of his music through the years sang in *Susanna*. But it was pushed aside;

[1] Schölcher assumes that because Handel composed *Solomon* upon all sorts and sizes of paper he was still in debt, and that this was a form of economy. This is surely a shot in the dark, and a bad one, considering that he did not compose in this fashion his other work subsequent to his bankruptcy. Indeed, there is every evidence that Handel was pulling out of the slough of debt when he composed *Solomon*.

it dropped into immediate neglect.[1]

Susanna and *Solomon* occupied but seven performances between them in 1749. Handel made money, but he made it out of revivals. The old war-horse was becoming staid, more accommodating to the will of the people. His years were waning. He had no desire to enter into a fresh battle. The old pugnacities had dropped away from him, and in 1748 he showed for the first time that he had become a servant of the people to the point when he would give them such of his work as they liked. He cared little for revivals; to him revivals were the stale nights of yesterday. But if the public wanted revivals there was still his wonderful repertoire.

Nevertheless, he would go on creating. There was nothing left in life if he could not go on creating. This new work at least provided an outlet for the melodies that ran continuously through his mind. He must go on creating. The years remaining were so few. And still there seemed so much to give.

[1] When *Susanna* was performed at the famous Dom at Halle in 1922 it was accounted one of the greatest musical revivals in Germany of modern times. I was present at this performance and saw 3,000 people deeply moved as but a small portion of the world's musical repertoire could ever move them. Yet *Susanna* has been unknown in this country, probably because of its length.—Author.

CHAPTER XXIV

THE 'FIREWORK MUSIC'
AND THE FOUNDLING HOSPITAL

ONE of the chief factors in the success of Handel's season of 1748–9 was the conclusion of the war, and the signing of peace at Aix-la-Chapelle in October 1748. The peace, even though it was destined to be but short-lived, had a magical effect upon the whole community. Money, which had been 'tight' since '45, became liquid again. A strong Government was in power, and soon after the peace was signed it proved its power by reducing the Bank rate to three per cent and succeeded in getting the money. Such a rate had not been heard of before. The cautious merchant who lent his savings 'neither to Jew nor Gentile, but only to the Government', held up his hands in horror. His whine passed unheard; three per cent remained the Bank rate after the peace, for more than a hundred and fifty years.

It was not until the better conditions of life, which the peace secured, reminded the people that the cessation of hostilities had not been celebrated, that a day for national rejoicing was decided upon. The populace had taken but little notice of the war, a war which had only impinged upon the life of the community at odd times with a jarring note. After all, it was remote. News was tardy, so that the peace had to prove itself a public benefactor before London recognized that a new and better influence had fallen over the national life.

The King demanded that the Peace of Aix-la-Chapelle should be celebrated. He may have wished to cover the be-littling conditions which the treaty involved, and in February 1749 preparations were begun. They were trying to whip to life a corpse. The Government lent its aid. Had not the French given up Madras, and the British Cape Breton Island? But so far not the voice of a single cannon had hurled re-joicing to the winds.

Handel was sent for by the Court, and instructed to prepare music immediately, for what was to be the greatest cele-bration of peace in the history of the nation.

In the centre of the Green Park an enormous wooden building was constructed, and a hot-headed Italian, Chevalier Servandoni, was given the task of designing the fireworks and letting them off. The excitement of London grew as the building in the Green Park assumed enormous proportions. No one knew what was going to happen. Then, presently, when they had run the unsightly affair to a height of over one hundred feet, and built wings on to it extending north and south, the crowds that gathered to watch this modern Babel in its forming became more inquisitive still. For now the carpenters began to put upon it the elaborate arms of the Duke of Montagu, since he had probably footed the bill. They constructed a huge musicians' gallery, and erected over it a crude figure of Peace attended by Neptune and Mars—or so the crowd was left to surmise from the atrocities in wood which leered down from aloft. Then, greatest triumph of all, they crowned the whole contraption with a great bas-relief showing King George handing out peace to Britannia, a portrait no more like George than it was like Heidegger. At the summit of that was a great pole uplifting a vast sun which, on the night of celebration, burst suddenly into flame after several abortive efforts to light it, and blazed with such power that the whole Park was lit as by the light of day.

Handel, with his speed of composition, was ahead of time with his music. True, the autograph bears no dates, but he was able to give a full rehearsal in Vauxhall Gardens on 21 April, six days before the celebrations were to begin. Twelve thousand people went to that rehearsal and paid 2s. 6d. each for admission. So great was the press of carriages that all traffic was held up on London Bridge for over three hours. Nothing but the music was to be rehearsed at Vauxhall Gardens. There were to be no fireworks, no decorations, and a mob of this calibre went to hear it. This fact proves the grip which Handel had begun to acquire anew on the people.

The Vauxhall rehearsal was merely a suggestion of what was to follow on Tuesday the twenty-seventh. Not only were all the entrances to the Park thrown open on that day, but a breach, nearly fifty feet in length, was cut in the park wall to enable the crowds ample entrance and exit. One hundred and one brass cannon had been installed near the huge wooden building to thunder out a Royal salute that should start the firework display; eighteen more smaller ordnance were under the musicians' gallery to fire single shots during Handel's music, and so give colour to the wild rejoicing in his notes.

The King was enchanted. Why had he not thought of this after Dettingen? He had the men—the guns—Handel. His excitement was intense. He changed his uniform twice in the first two hours. He appeared in the crowd, with a kingly smile of approbation. He inspected the huge wooden building, the galleries, the engineer's arrangements, and found them good. He changed his uniform again. He gave a heavy purse of money to be distributed among those who had achieved the construction. He reviewed the Guards from the garden wall. For three hours he reviewed Guards. He went on reviewing Guards. . . .

With the coming of night the crowds grew more dense, and the air for April was close and dust-laden, since there had been no rain for many days. Coaches struggled through the masses in the side streets or were turned back. Thieves enjoyed a wild orgy without let or hindrance. The town was let loose.

Handel had prepared a fine band, worthy of the occasion. He had forty trumpets, twenty French horns, sixteen hautboys, sixteen bassoons, eight pairs of kettledrums, twelve side-drums, and flutes and fifes. For the first time he introduced that forgotten instrument, the serpent, into his band; indeed, he put it into his score but took it out again. Perhaps he was not enamoured of the instrument, for when he first heard it he declared that it was not the serpent that seduced Eve. *In toto* he had for that night as fine a band as he had ever conducted.

The *Firework Music*, as he called it, though it may lack the sublime beauty which characterizes his *Water Music*, was nevertheless a great achievement. The King, the Princesses, and the Duke of Cumberland, together with the Duke of Montagu, Master of the Ordnance, the Dukes of Bedford and Richmond, were in the Royal Library, the windows of which were only five hundred yards from the ungainly construction which the dusk had slowly concealed. And now its entire outline was limned with strings of fire. A fine setting for Handel's music, which leaped and dropped like tongues of flame. But little of it was heard by the Prince of Wales, for, engaged as he was in a fresh quarrel with his father, he kept aloof from the royal party, and witnessed the fireworks from the house of the Earl of Middlesex in Arlington Street.

The music ceased. The crowd, splayed like a black carpet in the flare of the lights, roared. . . . A rocket stole up, exploded, drifted away in sparks. A surge of excitement spread with a dull muffled murmur over the crowd. It was the signal for the fireworks, and the hundred and one little brass cannon roared in unison.

But the fireworks were muddled. They went off in fits and starts. The giant sun alone blazed nobly from the head of the pole. Little serpents of flame sped up the staging, fizzled and spluttered and went out. Men climbed like monkeys with torches, and lit things, lit them again. Thus hours passed with fitful display, followed by intervals of irritating failure.

Then came the climax. The great building was set on fire; in a few minutes it was a mass of beating, roaring flame. The crowd began to stampede, to shout, to hustle. Women were trodden down, and the heat became terrific. George giving Peace to Britannia dropped, with his head aflame, into a cauldron of fire. It was ignoble, humiliating. And so hysterical became the gallant little Italian Chevalier Servandoni when he witnessed the failure and destruction of all his organization, that he drew his sword upon the Duke of Montagu, and was promptly arrested.

The only success that had come from this national celebration had been Handel's. The King was very conscious of it. Apart from the music, the affair had too much of the damp squib about it for his liking. He realized that Handel had saved some dignity for him from what might otherwise have been a complete fiasco involving the royal person. The burning George dropping with a clatter and a cloud of uprising sparks into the fiery furnace below had been pitiable. It might have been the work of some demon of mischief, prodding and poking under the cloak of vanity and pose which the King had worn all day, with complete success, as he believed.

The King's esteem of Handel was warmed to new life by the events of 27 April. When in May the composer gave a performance of the *Firework Music* for the benefit of the Foundling Hospital—that institution which the big-hearted Captain Coram had organized nine years before out of the profits made from his trading vessel—the King subscribed two thousand pounds. As for the Prince of Wales, he attended the performance in person, since his father's subscription had relieved the monarch of the necessity of being present. Thereby another family jar was avoided, and the prestige of royalty for supporting all charitable things suffered not at all.

Handel's performance in May 1749 for the Foundling Hospital, or, as it was then called, 'The Hospital for the Maintenance and Education of Exposed and Deserted Young Children', is memorable, since it marked the beginning of his rich patronage. It also strengthened the friendship between himself and Hogarth, for the painter, with all his whims and fancies, his loves and hatreds, never wavered in his devotion to the cause of these lost children. Ultimately, both he and Handel were Governors of the Hospital together. It was this concert of 27 May which brought to Handel the offer of the Governorship, since not only did he perform his *Firework Music*, but gave extracts from *Solomon*, and concluded with a composition he had specially prepared for the occasion, 'Blessed are they that consider the Poor', now known as the 'Foundling Hospital Anthem'. The Foundling Hospital was a continual source of pleasure to Handel in these later years. He never ceased to work for it.

In studying the character of Handel one can appreciate how natural it is that this charity should appeal so warmly to his great heart. He who had suffered and been buffeted about, who had given his best only to have it flung back in his face, who had been hounded into bankruptcy by a cabal for no reason at all, who had climbed out painfully and unaided, only to be hounded in again. Is it not certain that this man, whom the world tried to break, should understand better than most the great battles in small lives that were taking place when deserted children were brought up to the Hospital, and the great iron bell at the inner door clanged? Could he not realize the poignancy of the waiting while a woman balloted with balls out of a bag as to whether the child should be admitted or thrown back upon the world? Now that London had set aside its temper, and, at long last, had definitely acclaimed his genius, there was no venom left in him. His heart was full of tenderness which had sprung from gratitude. He had mellowed into a warming kindliness with the years. Certainly, he had given hurt in plenty as he had received it, but the fits of temper, the sharp words so often undeserved, bore no trace of malice. Faults Handel had in profusion, but his worst enemy could never write malice down as one of them, and there is no recorded instance of his having treated an enemy with spite.

Shortly before he was made Governor of the Foundling Hospital, he presented the charity with an organ. Very little is known about the instrument, except that it was made by Dr Morse of Barnet, doubtless the same person whom Jennens refers to as 'Moss of Barnet', when in his letter to Lord Guernsey[1] he refers to Handel buying a new organ. Handel's organ seems to have served the Hospital until a larger one was erected there in 1768.

He opened the organ in person on 1 May 1750 with a performance of *Messiah*. All the tickets, and they cost half a guinea apiece, were sold out at Batson's Coffee House and White's Chocolate House (later White's Club) days before. The Hospital Chapel could accommodate a thousand persons, but more than that number were turned away at the doors. The press and confusion was terrible. Many distinguished persons who had neglected to purchase tickets in advance, drove up to the doors believing that they would obtain seats without difficulty. Some of these were subscribers to the Hospital funds—could they be turned away? The result was inevitable. They were sold seats which had already been sold to someone else, and, when the real owners of the seats arrived, they had perforce to go home again.[2]

This haphazard method of doing things displeased Handel who had never yet issued tickets for a concert which he had not honoured sooner or later. He soon discovered a way out. He announced a second performance for 15 May at which every ticket sold for the first concert, and as yet unhonoured, should take precedence. It was an act of grace, which brought further funds to the Hospital and enabled Handel to keep faith with the public. The second performance of *Messiah* in the Hospital Chapel was as successful as the first. From that year onward Handel gave *Messiah* for the Hospital once every year, and brought in £500 to £600 net for the charity with each performance; one concert (May 1753) realizing as much as 925 guineas.

His colleague, Hogarth, too, gave of his best. He painted a portrait of Captain Coram and presented it to the Hospital. Later on, when he painted his large picture, 'The March of

[1] See p. 52 *et seq.*
[2] *General Advertiser*, 4 May 1750.

the Guards', he decided to raffle it. He sold all the tickets except a few, and these few he gave to the Hospital. As not infrequently happens on these occasions, one of the unsold tickets drew the picture, and that is why it hangs now in the court-room of the Hospital. Worth—who shall say? I believe ten thousand pounds has since been refused for it.

Meanwhile, Handel had completed a new oratorio in the previous July, but, for some reason known only to himself, he held it over for production till March 1750. *Theodora* was perhaps the worst libretto Morell ever prepared; it lacked character. Its poetry in the main was mere amateur stuff, which must have taxed Handel's patience to set it.[1]

Theodora from its inception was a failure, in spite of the fact that it contained a few of the most remarkable numbers of Handel's composing. Handel had told Morell that he regarded 'He saw the lovely Youth, Death's early prey' as the greatest chorus he ever composed, but there are probably few people in this country who are familiar with it. 'Angels ever bright and fair' from *Theodora* has alone remained in the memory of the populace. The chorus 'Oh Love Divine, Thou Source of Fame', is in many respects equal to the best choruses in *Messiah*. No less can be said for 'How strange their ends'.

The London public killed *Theodora* on the night it was produced, and because of its failure then it has ever been accounted one of 'those dull works' which Handel flung off to make money. Morell himself knew the work to be a failure, though he would never have blamed himself as the cause of it, for he wrote:

'The next I wrote was *Theodora* (in 1749) which Mr Handel himself valued more than any performance of the kind. . . . The second night of *Theodora* was very thin in-deed. . . . I guessed it a losing night, so did not go to Mr Handel as usual; but seeing him smile, I ventured, when 'Will you be there next Friday night,' says he, 'and I will play it to you?' I told him I had just seen Sir T. Hankey,

[1] I have Morell's autograph copy of the words of *Theodora*, which belonged to Handel and which he used for his setting. It bears Handel's inscription in his own hand on the first page: 'I intend to produce this Oratorio at the Theatre Royal, Covent Garden, GEORGE FRIDERIC HANDEL.' The neatness of Morell's writing is in quaint comparison to the ageing scrawl of the composer.—Author

and he desired me to tell you, that if you would have it again, he would engage for all the Boxes. 'He is a fool.' [It is presumably Handel speaking.] 'The Jews will not come to it (as to *Judas*) because it is a Christian story, and the ladies will not come because it is a virtuous one.'[1]

He was quite right. If the Jews supported his oratorios when they had a Jewish interest, the Christians certainly had no interest in the only Christian oratorio—apart from *Messiah*—Handel ever composed. But the forces of the elements were again working against him. *Lotario* had been killed by a heat wave. *Il Penseroso* had perished beneath the awful blast of a terrible winter. *Theodora* was killed by earthquakes. The earthquake shocks began on 5 February, and when *Theodora* was produced five weeks later, the town was at the height of the scare. Society departed out of London in droves. Those who remained were frightened to go out after dark lest they should be killed by the falling tiles from house-roofs, and equally frightened to remain at home in case their homes should collapse over their heads.

'The madness of the multitude was prodigious,' wrote Mrs Montagu on 20 February after a visit to the oratorio. 'Nearly fifty of the people I had sent to, to play cards here on the Saturday following, went out of town to avoid being swallowed. . . . The Wednesday night the Oratorio was very empty though it was the favourite performance of Handel's.'[2]

Was ever a man so dogged by Nature conniving at his destruction? A winter such as did not occur once in a century had shut his theatre; now an earthquake—almost an unheard-of event in London—destroyed *Theodora* before it was produced. Not that the earthquake shocks, continuous as they were for some days, were of serious portent. A few people were killed by falling masonry, others injured, but it was no more than the edge of a general shock which had spread through Europe.

Nevertheless, the conscience of the town was smitten as with a wasting disease. A wave of licentiousness and drunkenness had risen to a height hitherto unknown. Crime was on

[1] *Hodgkin MSS*. Historical Manuscripts Commission, Report XV., App. Pt. II, pp. 92, 93
[2] Elizabeth Montagu: *Correspondence from 1720–61*, Vol. I, p. 274.

Sir

Js on five hundred What Ever my Dividend pounds South Sea Stock that
the South Sea Company pays att the Opening
of their Books next August pray pay it
To Mr Thomas Cartonnel or order and
you will oblidge

Sir

London this 9 June 1716

Your &c. Servt.
George Frideric Handel

204

350

15

Sir

J having received the Permission of the
Artillery Kettle Drums for my use in
the Oratorio's in this season ;
J beg You would consign them to the
Bearer of this Mr Frideric Smith

Jam

Saturday
Febr. 24
1750 .

Your very humble Servant
G F Handel

TWO HANDEL LETTERS

(1) The signature on the top of the document shows Handel's handwriting when he first came to London; and (2) His handwriting at the age of 65.

the increase; sobriety was ebbing out as a forgotten virtue from the upper reaches of the social life. The people were pulled up rudely by the shocks. This London, then, was Babylon. They would escape from it before the vengeance of God descended. The churches were crowded with worshippers. The rich and the poor trembled sleepless in their houses by night, watched walls that seemed to move beneath the dancing shadows of the lights. Only when the sun rose in its accustomed place beyond the chimney-pots, did they believe that God had not singled out London for vengeance. With the coming of nightfall again the old fears returned, and, in the dreadful shades, frightened figures slunk past with the palsied steps of fear. London forgot all else save the earthquakes. It forgot Handel. It forgot *Theodora*. It may have been that under other and better circumstances *Theodora* would have risen triumphantly, as it should have done, by the brilliance of its music. Never indeed had the elements shown any pity for Handel; the old mythical gods were bent on rending him in their own fashion, long after London had buried its hate.

Morell at this period was a close personal friend of Handel. His little conceits had been shed through the certain knowledge that Handel would have none of them. After Handel's death he wrote two librettos for Christopher Smith, *Nabal* and *Gideon*, which, when the Master's hand had passed to the dust of the tomb, Smith dressed up with music. 'The music of both are entirely taken from some old genuine pieces of Handel,' wrote Morell in 1764.[1] Which, being so, it is surprising that these words should have been lost.

Yet the prattling of this Doctor of Divinity is not without interest, in so far as it gives us pictures of Handel which otherwise would have been lost. 'I heard him (Morell) say,' wrote John Taylor,

'that one fine summer morning he was roused out of bed at five o'clock by Handel, who came in his carriage a short distance from London. The doctor went to the window and spoke to Handel, who would not leave his carriage. Handel was at the time composing an oratorio. When the doctor asked him what he wanted, he said, 'What de devil means de vord billow?' which was in the oratorio the doctor had

[1] *Hodgkin MSS.*, Historical Manuscripts Commission, Report XV. App. Pt. II, p. 93.

written for him. The doctor, after laughing at so ludicrous a reason for disturbing him, told him that billow meant wave, a wave of the sea. 'Oh, de vave,' said Handel, and bade his coachman return, without addressing another word to the doctor.'[1]

Theodora was only played four times, and then to practically empty houses. If the failure disturbed Handel, he did not show it; the veteran had become accustomed to pushing away his griefs unnoticed. He lost money over the *Theodora* performances, and decided to attempt no more productions that year. Not that he ceased to work. Rich was going to produce Smollett's *Alceste* at Covent Garden, and Handel was engaged to set it to music. He completed the work during the earthquake scare. The scenery was painted; the production put in hand. Then presumably Rich changed his mind, and, finding the music left on his hands, the composer put some of the *Alceste* music to some words of Spence's *Polymete*, and, adding new composition, called the work *The Choice of Hercules*.

But there was no question of production, and *The Choice of Hercules* was put away. The days when sheer ardour made him rush a work on to the stage had gone, never to return. If his brain answered to the same vigour of youth, his body was slow and ageing. He was frequently in considerable pain. His eyes had begun to trouble him, but as yet there was no suggestion of blindness. He complained bitterly when he found himself unable to do the things to which he had been accustomed, as if he had deluded himself that he would never grow old.

In May there came to London a ghost of those glorious years he had lost. Cuzzoni, quarrelsome no longer, but a spent force and well-nigh destitute, arrived on the scene of her old triumphs and begged for benefit. She was only a shadow of the Cuzzoni he had once called the 'She-devil', but, with his typical generosity, he allowed her to sing in a performance of *Messiah* on 18 May. Her performance was a farce. Cuzzoni could no longer sing. She did not look even

[1] John Taylor: *Records of My Life*, 1832, Vol. I, p. 334 *et seq*. *Note*.—This John Taylor was the grandson of Chevalier Taylor the oculist who, at a date later than that of the above episode, operated on Handel's eyes.

Theodora.

An
Oratorio.

I intend to perform this Oratorio at the Theatre Royal in Covent garden
George Frideric Handel

The words of 'Theodora' in the autograph of the writer, Thomas Morell, which Handel used for setting, with his autograph on the title page. In the possession of the Author.

the Cuzzoni London had known. She had become thin, with a lined face and skinny limbs. Those who heard her piteous attempts on that May day must have thought they dreamed when they remembered the Cuzzoni to whom the man in the gallery had called out 'Damme, she has a nest of nightingales in her belly'. Never beautiful, she was now hideous. The old arrogance of manner which had so ill become the fat waddling creature she had formerly been, had departed.

Now the voice—the voice that had once carried the thoughts of her audience up to the very gates of heaven—had gone and left the croak of a raven.

Poor Cuzzoni! She was as much a thing of the past as was the brown and silver gown that had caused such a sensation when she wore it in *Rodelinda*. They laughed at her. There were cat-calls. The pride that poverty had compelled her to suppress was wounded to the quick. She rushed from the stage, hurried out of London, and in Holland was arrested for debt and thrown into prison. Here she might have spent the rest of her days, but the Governor of the prison used to permit her to go out on occasion in order to give a performance, and by this means she got together enough money to pay off her debtors, and so gain her release. The world had broken her. She made her way back to Italy, and there we take leave of her, a factory hand making buttons to earn the coppers that would keep her in bread. Everything about Cuzzoni except her body, her voice, her pride, aye, probably her memories, had gone down as dead things pass, whilst this shell of a once famous woman plodded painfully to and fro at her button-making. When she died they pitched her away, like so much carrion, in a pauper's grave, forgetful that she had once been a queen in Europe.

What a revelation to Handel must have been Cuzzoni's performance in *Messiah*! This youthful vixen he had once known. . . . Where had gone the years? . . . Was he, too, passing like that, and yet so unaware of it?

In August he left for the Continent. Between The Hague and Haarlem his coach was overturned and he was badly injured. London was unaware of the accident till the *General Advertiser* of 21 August announced that he was out of danger. He passed on to Halle. The city of his childhood was now a place of strange people. A city of memories. Strangers were in the Schlamm house. Sebastian Bach, who had walked in vain those weary miles from Leipzig to see him when he was at Halle in 1719, had now died but four weeks previously, and his son, Wilhelm Friedemann Bach, reigned in the place of old Zachow at the Liebfrauenkirche organ. The place was changing. People were changing. Passing on. Passing on and leaving him. . . .

He turned his steps and came back to London. He had been to Halle for the last time.

BOOK III
EVENING

CHAPTER XXV

THE YEARS OF BLINDNESS

WHEN Handel returned to London in the late autumn he had changed. The vigours of his life were passing; he knew they were passing. The shadows had begun to gather; the sun to seek the hills.

He was no longer seen walking in the streets, or in the Park. When he appeared at all he was driven in a hackney carriage. His mind remained clear. The eyes, more deeply set, still reflected the old fires. It was only his body that was failing—his body that made the task of going up the broad staircase at Brook Street an act of pain. His flesh hung heavily like some hindering garment.

He attempted no fresh work that year: he gave no more concerts. January, however, brought Morell with a new libretto. The theme pleased him. No sooner did the libretto come into his hands than he pushed aside the lethargy of the past few months and sought his harpsichord. *Jephtha* was to be the last great work of his life. Its composition entailed pain from his eyes, so that he produced it only by great suffering.

It would seem that Handel's return had urged Morell to provide a new libretto for him, since upon his own showing he did not write *Jephtha* till January 1751, and Handel began its composition at the end of the month. Writing of his libretti Morell said: 'My own favourite is *Jephtha*, which I wrote in 1751, and in the composing of which Mr Handel fell blind.'[1] Handel completed the first act on 2 February; eleven days later he had almost finished the second act.

The old feverish haste he had always known with the inspiration upon him was no longer possible. The autograph of *Jephtha* tells its own story of what was happening. At the end of the opening *Largo* of the Final Chorus of Act II he had written in German: 'Reached here on Wednesday, February 13. Prevented from proceeding on account of the relaxation of the sight of my left eye.' He then crossed out the

[1] *Hodgkin MSS.*, Historical Manuscripts Commission, Report XV. App. Pt. II, p. 93.

Facsimile of Handel's score of *Jephtha*.

Another piece of the *Jephtha* score, written ten days later.

word 'relaxation' and wrote in English 'so relaxt'. On the next page he wrote 'Saturday, 23 February, feeling rather better. Resumed work.'

The greatest of all his enemies had loomed up suddenly and without warning. Blindness. Was there any power remaining that had not striven to destroy him? The malice of enemies, many of whom he had never known, senseless personal feuds and petty spites; then heat shutting down his theatre, frost, earthquakes—Jove with his thunderbolts ever ready. He had endured them all. At this hour, with London docile at his feet, life had seemed to take to itself a new attraction. A sweeter lark sang in the skies now that the storm had gone. He had come to recognition, definite recognition.

The menace to his eyes frightened him with its threat of darkness. All the bludgeoning that Circumstance had given him in the past had been as naught compared with this. He stopped his work. He hurried off to Cheltenham and drank the waters. As if the waters could restore that which, by the laws of human decay, was so swiftly passing! He visited Bristol. With the old enthusiasms in him he extemporized on the wonderful organ then in the city's possession.

After a few weeks he returned and consulted Samuel Sharp, the principal oculist of Guy's Hospital. A brief examination told the oculist all he wanted to know. Handel was going blind. He had *gutta serena*. An immediate operation was recommended, but nothing could be done. The sight of his left eye had already gone.

Not all the accumulated hatred of his enemies produced the despair in Handel which then came to him. 'That fortitude which had supported him under afflictions of another kind now deserted him,' declared Hawkins. If Handel had no actual terror of the coming dark, he had the utmost dread of the termination of his work. The knowledge crushed his heart. It broke his spirit. He went back to Brook Street, and remained there, supine, but working at odd intervals on *Jephtha* with short-lived spasms of feverish energy, then drifting away swiftly, suddenly, into great deeps of despondency.

In March, Frederick Prince of Wales died. The event must have stirred Handel deeply, even though he laboured under a greater affliction than the Prince ever bestowed upon him. The nation was in mourning almost before it knew that the

Prince was indisposed. On the twelfth he had followed his father to the House of Lords after a slight attack of pleurisy. He grew hot, returned to Carlton House to change, and, later, lay for three hours on a sofa in a room opening onto the garden. He caught a fresh cold and took to his bed. No one showed any great concern. Three doctors and a surgeon came to look at him and thought him better. But a week later he began to cough violently. Doctor Wilmot told him that in a quarter of an hour he would be better. The cough continued. Only one doctor—Hawkins—had the sense to see that he was dying. He went out of the room and said: 'Here is something I don't like.' But the Prince knew. He put his hand on his stomach and exclaimed: '*Je sens la mort!*'[1]

What a scurry those words produced! If he had only urged the same impatience when the little German Princess waited for him at Gravesend! He felt the coming of death, and they knew now that he was dying. Parvonarius, his German valet de chambre, lifted him up. He felt the long, quick shudder of death pass like a shock through the Prince's body 'neath his hands. 'Good God!' he exclaimed, 'the Prince is going.' In his horrible fear the fellow had forgotten the title of 'His Royal Highness'. The Princess snatched up a candle, hurried to the bed . . . the Prince was dead.[2]

So passed the man who had hindered, had hurt, the greatest musician of his time more than any other. What did he know of music when he would have destroyed music? What had he learned of the tenets of sovereignty since all women were his spoil, all measured progress that did not include his indolent figure, so much retrogression? He died, said Horace Walpole, resembling his pattern, the Black Prince, in nothing but in dying before his father.[3] Snuffed out in a stuffy room, without pomp and the awed silence of a nation. And with a large moth, born too soon, fluttering stupidly up and down the window-pane. . . .

Did the man whom he had persecuted, and who was now fighting his coming blindness, figure in these dreams when, his life, his vanities paling, he hung between the hemispheres? Or did the conscious fragments of his mind linger lovingly over those sweet moments of earth, when life had been so

---

[1] Horace Walpole: *Memoirs*, Vol. I, p. 71.
[2] *Ibid.*
[3] *Ibid.*, Vol. I, p. 72.

dear, those other eyes so bright, and the future stretched out before him as some rich flood, warm and inviting? That night, for instance, at Carlisle, when, at his big supper, he and the maids of honour had bombarded a pastry mould of Carlisle Castle with sugar-plums.[1] Or did he dream again the bitterness of that hour when his mother had him turned from the palace gates lest his insincerities should spoil the calm of her dying?

Handel had made anthems for royal weddings and funerals, for victories and peace treaties, but he was not allowed to prepare a funeral theme for the dead Prince. The King hustled the body away to Henry VII's chapel without music, and in the most secret fashion he could. Maybe he had a sense of satisfaction that he had done with this renegade son of his for ever. Then he visited the widow—ignored the chair of state she had placed for him, and sat on the couch with her, wept more of his crocodile tears, and counselled her children to deserve the fortune to which they had been born.[2] It was all very droll.

Handel struggled through to the end of *Jephtha* with amazing fortitude, and completed the work on 30 August. But he was able no longer to score scene after scene with the rapidity he had always found possible, even so recently as in the composition of *Theodora*. That he worked wearily is evident from the erasions and alterations throughout the autograph of *Jephtha*. 'Waft her, angels', one of his most serene inspirations, was worked over and recomposed in part. At times he was compelled to break off through sheer physical suffering, as his annotations on the score bear evidence. His hand shook, his lines had begun to wave and dodder like those of a blind man. So scrawled are the words that they are almost unreadable. He must have worked with his eyes close against the paper.

Jephtha was produced on 26 February 1752, and its reception pleased Handel. The work brought to him a great many hundred pounds before the coming of death. He would have continued his concerts throughout the remainder of the season, but that depression, caused by fluctuating hopes and disappointments with regard to his sight, wrapped him as in a shroud. In May, William Bromfeild,[3] surgeon to the Princess

[1] *Ibid.*
[2] *Ibid.*, Vol. I, p. 83.
[3] In other Lives of Handel the name of William Bromfeild is given as Bromfield or Bramfield. The above is the correct spelling.

of Wales, operated on his eyes. At first it was believed that the operation had been successful. He was able to see better, but not for long. The dark drew in more closely. So slowly that at first he scarcely noticed it. At last he ceased all work. He groped his way from room to room. Sitting alone. Ever alone.

Since Sharp and Bromfeild had failed to restore his sight, he gave himself into the hands of Chevalier Taylor, who was then oculist to the King, and, indeed, oculist to nearly every monarch in Europe. The Chevalier travelled extensively, and spent a great deal of time between one European Court and another. He was particularly well known, too, at Tunbridge, where he moved about among the rich invalids who migrated there, and relieved them of heavy fees and not much sickness. There was a very great deal of the quack about the Chevalier. Skilled he certainly was, but he posed as being able to cure anything. He was a tall, good-looking man, very popular with the ladies. He dressed in great splendour, and could not exist without the most lavish expenditure in his household.[1] Eventually he wrote his memoirs in three volumes, in which he described his adventures with women in the most blatant fashion, and associated them with his achievements in his profession. Verily, the Chevalier must have been so magnificent that to be attended by him was a luxury for which one could never hope to get off cheaply. He made his very large income by trading in the main on the credulity of the suffering.

The Chevalier himself described his attempt to restore Handel's sight. He wrote:

'I have seen a vast variety of singular animals, such as dromedaries, camels, etc., and particularly at Leipsick, where a celebrated master of music, who had already arrived to his 88th year, received his sight by my hands; it is with this very man that the famous Handel was first educated, and with whom I once thought to have the same success, having all circumstances in his favour, motions of the pupil, light, etc., but upon drawing the curtain we found the bottom defective from a paralytic disorder.'[2]

Handel's case was hopeless.

[1] John Taylor: *Records of My Life*, Vol. I, p. 13.
[2] *The History of the Travels and Adventures of the Chevalier John Taylor, Ophthalmiater*, 1761, Vol. I, p. 25 *et seq.*

It was about this time that Handel had his quarrel with Smith the elder. The twain had gone together to Tunbridge Wells, and were walking in the street when an altercation sprang up between them. Handel's temper was fiery; his affliction had not helped matters. He never minced his words, and, it is probable that on this occasion he was particularly unjust, for nothing else would explain Smith's behaviour. Smith, well aware that Handel could not see without him, turned sharply on his heels, and, leaving Handel standing in the street, returned to London.

It was a storm between old men, stirred up, no doubt, by their age and infirmities. But nothing can excuse Smith for this wanton act of cruelty to Handel, who, if he had often been difficult and unreasonable, had at least saved Smith from poverty. Few things in Handel's life hurt him so much. The callous cruelty left an open wound. He refused to have any further knowledge of Smith. He struck his name out of his will.

The sequel came shortly before his death. Handel told Christopher Smith the younger, who was then making his manuscript copies, conducting his affairs, and looking after his concerts, that he intended to put his name in the will in place of that of his father. Smith was horrified. What would the world say? The idea was impossible. He would accept nothing. He besought the master to make his peace with his father before it was too late. That two lives, so closely linked through bad days and good, should be separated by bitterness at the close was a tragedy, the weight of which was better perceived by the younger Smith than by either of them. Probably Handel had long since forgiven the elder Smith, for he had no sense of malice. Now it was the son who brought the two veterans together again. The name of Smith the elder went back in Handel's will, and, not only was the original legacy of £500 restored, but an additional sum of £1,500 added to it! Could the master have stooped more graciously, or forgiveness have been made more sublime?

The announcement that Handel had now completely lost his sight appeared in the *Theatrical Register* of 27 January 1753. The most formidable enemy of all his life's garnering had beaten him. Yet he showed no inclination to draw away into seclusion and so hide his hurt. The fever to work pressed him when the calmness of resignation followed the first rebellion against his affliction. He had a dread of idleness, a dread of being helpless in a corner and waiting for death. He began to try to accommodate his life to the new order of things. He sent for the younger Smith, who was travelling on the Continent, to return at once and organize the season's concerts. Moreover, he still gave performances for charities, including one which he had never helped before.[1]

There was no bending to the yoke of oppression. If he could not compose with the old strenuous fervour, he could still play. He practised for hours a day. He sat at the instrument and extemporized from the dreams that came to his mental vision, his chords as brilliant, his melodies as sweet as they had ever been. On Sundays he still appeared a regular worshipper in St George's, Hanover Square.

With the assistance of Christopher Smith, Handel gave a full season's concerts at Covent Garden in 1753, the master performing his concertos from memory, but ultimately he extemporized. Had he not been able to work at this period, even in this modified degree, his life would have become unbearable. It was the atmosphere of his concerts, the knowledge that he was still an important figure in them that eased his affliction. If he was not completely blind at this period—and on this point there is a little doubt—it was quite impossible for him to see anything unless it were held close to the eye. He was to all intents and purposes, a blind man. Once more Fate juggled with him. Though he was helpless, he began to make money more rapidly by these concerts than he had ever done before!

Handel's position in London was now quite clearly defined, he was the absolute master of English music. His rivals had gone; their music had been forgotten. His enemies had dispersed or buried their hates, save that in 1753 one of them put an anonymous announcement in a London newspaper to the effect that the Foundling Hospital was preparing an elaborate funeral service for the day following the musician's decease. It was an act as wanton as that of Smith at Tunbridge Wells. The fury of the Hospital Governors knew no bounds. The Secretary was sent to convey personally to Handel their disgust at such a heartless trick, and to assure him that they

---

[1] On 7 May 1753, Handel gave a performance of *Judas Maccabaeus* for the Lock Hospital, which brought to this charity £84 2*s*. 6*d*. When he promised this performance of his Oratorio he was made a perpetual Governor of the Hospital.—*Records of the Lock Hospital*.

hoped he would live for many years. Handel received the messenger and the message. If the former had expected a burst of anger against the malcontent he was mistaken. He received only a laugh. 'It was,' declared Handel, 'very bad farce!'

Christopher Smith was now in the position of absolute manager, and he remained so till the end. Only in 1753 did John Stanley, a brilliant organist of the period, who had been blind ever since he was two years old, conduct a performance of *Alexander's Feast*. It was Sharp the oculist who first suggested to Handel, on losing his sight, that Stanley would be of great assistance to him, which drew the trite answer from Handel: 'If the blind lead the blind, shall they not both fall into the ditch?'

The years crept past Handel and still he lived. London became accustomed to the blind figure sitting beside the organ at the later revivals of his oratorios. *Susanna* was repeated, *Samson*, *Jephtha*, all of them with new songs added. The giant had not spent his force though he had lost his sight. He worked steadily, dictating his new work to Christopher Smith, since he could no longer score the notes himself. He would not rest, no one could induce him to rest, for his mind was as active as it had ever been. His hands were swollen with gout, he moved about with the greatest anguish and difficulty. In every way he was a law unto himself in the matter of what he did, and any attempt to thwart him, even for his own good, brought forth the quick whip of temper.

He was still making money fast. Before he had been blind two years he had not only cleared all his debts, but had considerable funds in hand. He stood now without a creditor, a happy position unknown to him since the days of his beginnings. A beggar in 1746, and in 1759 he died worth £20,000 in savings, and all his debtors satisfied in full! Most of the money had been made by giving London revivals of the work at which London had scoffed when it was first produced in the heyday of his enthusiasm. How he must have laughed at London!

In 1757 he entirely revised *The Triumph of Time and Truth*. The words by Panfili, which he had set in all the ardour of youth in 1708, were translated by Morell. Indeed, it was Morell who alone collaborated with him in his later years. Jennens, having inherited untold wealth, had withdrawn to the anxieties of spending it. But Morell, the queer little

parson with his high cheek-bones, half-fed expression and
furtive eyes, would come to Brook Street with the honour of
being one of the few people welcomed within that door.

At least half of the 1757 version of *The Triumph of Time
and Truth* was new work, laboriously produced through the
instrumentality of Smith. But it was so fresh, its melody so
true, that no waning of Handel's powers can be detected.
The public liked the work, for it was given to crowded houses
four times that year, and twice in 1758. Nevertheless, the
body of Handel was dying. Only his brain lived on.

But the sun had reached the hills. And yet, to Handel,
how short had been the day!

CHAPTER XXVI

NIGHT IN THE HILLS

THE sands were running out. Handel knew at the end of 1758 that he was dying. His strength was sinking like the sap from a tree in autumn. Only with the greatest difficulty was he able to get about. He craved for solitude. More solitude. Visitors to Brook Street found that he was not receiving. Only four or five people found it possible to get beyond the stout janitor, de Bourke, who guarded the door. What little energy remained to Handel he stored, jealous lest it should be given to any project other than his concerts.

They missed him in the streets. The ambling figure with the big stick that had for so many years walked almost daily through the Park, was seen no more. From Marylebone Gardens, where he used to go and sit on one of the seats to listen to the excellent band that performed there and to criticize its music, he had gone for ever. The regular *habitués* of the Gardens missed his shuffling step. He was never seen except at his concerts, or in his pew at St George's, Hanover Square, on Sundays. The Handel of the old Haymarket nights, the Handel who for more than forty years had been astir in the life of London, had passed. When they caught a glimpse of him in his hackney coach as he went to and fro to his concerts, it was as if they had seen a ghost go by. They talked of him as one who, like some gorgeous comet, had swept across the sky almost before London was aware of it. More and more did London wish to forget that it had ever striven to destroy him.

His life at Brook Street in these closing days was simple in the extreme. The pleasures of the table, with his health broken, lost their appeal: at the close of the year his appetite failed altogether. Food became a nuisance. Very often Christopher Smith watched the bulky figure perched up at the table, eating scarcely sufficient to keep a bird alive. His body no longer needed nourishment, for it was will-power alone which kept him going.

There was no luxury and very little comfort in those Brook Street rooms. The ease that might have helped a man, afflicted as he, to bear his suffering, was entirely absent. More probably he would have rejected it had it been provided. Every room betrayed his character; his hard, rugged simplicity. Plain furniture—almost bad furniture, and certainly worthless. A few good pictures on the walls. His Rembrandts, his Denner portrait of himself, some landscapes—the pictures he had loved so much.

Step into the room in which he worked and look at its contents. An oval table, a square block table, half a dozen old matted chairs, a chimney-glass in a gilt frame, his harpsichord, a wall desk, five china coffee-cups and six saucers. Or pass into the dining-room—quietly, lest the still figure should hear—and look at the humble shoddy things. An iron hearth, seven matted chairs, two round card-tables, a leather stool, a broken chimney glass. Or into his bedroom—where is the majesty of greatness here? The queer white tester bed, the crimson haritten furniture, an old stove, six matted chairs much the worse for wear, a wicker firescreen, a glass in a frame.[1] Were these things luxury? These tawdry little belongings of the man who had been the pride of kings? But to Handel they *were* luxury. In a room redolent of riches his home life would have been spoiled. The old bachelor had loved these things. They were part of him. They were simple and he had found his way to the heart of the world by the understanding of simple things.

At the end of 1758 he had ceased to compose. He knew that the end was not very far away. He spoke of it openly, and not with fear or regret. Then would follow a mood of energy, or rediscovered life, as if he had pushed Death aside even as it waited at his elbow. He played with Death, appearing at times to invite it as he lay with lulled senses in a kind of dream. A few hours later he was hustling Christopher Smith about his coming concerts.

When the oratorio season opened in March he announced a series of twelve concerts. He gave *Solomon* once, with additions and alterations; *Susanna* and *Samson* three times, *Judas Maccabaeus* twice, *Messiah* three times. He seemed to have sprung out at London suddenly as a man, believed to be dead, might spring from the shroud. It was amazing. The curiosity of seeing him, like some wonderful wraith, at the performances, helped the season to a great success. The entire town began to

[1] From the inventory of his effects made at the time of his death, when his furniture was sold to his principal servant, John de Bourke.

talk of Handel anew. A new generation was taught that the master still lingered, like some brown clinging leaf after winter has swept the tree.

Handel conducted all the concerts without the first trace of any waning strength. He would go on, the town said, for many seasons yet. There was some mystic cloak of invincibility about him. He had beaten adversity, he would beat Death till, without warning, he suddenly dropped in the concert room, or in passing up his own stairs. They knew he would go like that. They said so. Nor could they imagine oratorio without Handel.

He was now seventy-four. His birthday came; March passed. The season went on, with every seat sold for each performance. The clamour of spring swept with green gladness across the trees in the Park. The performance of his *Messiah* at Covent Garden, on 6 April, was to be his last. He carried it through to the final Amen without fatigue. Who associated Death with Handel at this hour? *Messiah* had never been given better. The packed audience dispersed into the night entranced. Handel had been wonderful; he was always wonderful these days. But even as they talked he was lying in a faint at the theatre.

They hurried him home to Brook Street, put him to bed, and called in his friend, Dr Warren. They did not know he was dying. So they spoke of his illness as a return of the old strain, due to the heavy season. Twelve concerts in little over a month, and at the age of seventy-four! Some day the veteran would learn his lesson.

Handel had no illusions as to the imminence of death. He said so with a certainty which they disregarded. He lay there, his sightless eyes fixed on the ceiling for days. A few friends called, those special friends whose step he knew, whose voices were the only sounds he cared to hear—James Smyth, the perfumer of Bond Street, Christopher Smith. Dr Warren was with him for some hours every day. Handel told them that he had one great wish—to die on Good Friday, and it was now Holy Week. It was a peculiar sentiment which haunted him, just as another dying man might cry for a glass of port, or some little fanciful thing that had not mattered very much in life, but which, with Death waiting by the bed-curtains, became so necessary.

London knew nothing of his illness, for not a single paragraph had appeared in the papers. Whilst Handel lay dying in its midst, London was absorbed that week by other things— the movements of warships at Deal—the patent four-wheeled carriage that went without horses, and was shown at a shilling a head at Cock's auction-rooms—the hanging of five young rapscallions (one of them, only eighteen years of age) at Salisbury for highway robbery and sheep-stealing—the fate of the noblemen who were going to be placed in the brand-new dungeons built in the Tower of St Julian at Lisbon, dungeons four feet square—the boom in Jesuit drops sold by Mr Rock, the chemist at the foot of Ludgate Hill. These were the topics which made London chatter that week, whilst the greatest musician in English history slipped slowly from life.

Throughout Holy Week Handel lay as if waiting, immune to the passing of time. He seemed like the hulk of a ship help-less in a sea that tossed it, wave by wave, towards a harbour it was so powerless to reach of its own volition. He remained in that waiting-place which Death and Life have contrived be-tween them, so that the passing from one sphere to the other never seems to be a real happening. His consciousness only left him at odd moments, when he appeared to dream. He knew people; he felt the kindliness of them about him. Then the mind would stray a little, as a wharfed boat might slip to the limit of its rope at the heave of the tide. When they crept into his room, they knew not if he slept or heard them. The open, sightless eyes, that knew neither sunrise nor sunset, were still turned to the ceiling; the coverlet still heaved with slow, slight movement.

At times his mind seemed to drift away from the room. Broken sentences from his lips, told those at the bedside that he had stolen away on one of his secret adventures, as if the mind had temporarily left its earthly abode, to probe pre-maturely into those infinite mysteries it was so soon to know.

Whence travelled his thoughts during those days, whilst he waited for Good Friday? Did they, in the quiet of that room, return to the old beaten trails? Did his dreams bear him again to past Haymarket triumphs, so that he heard once more the exquisite singing of Cuzzoni and Faustina? Did he step like a wandering ghost into the theatre whilst they performed his first English opera *Rinaldo*, and see himself, the youth acclaimed, joyous, sweet with the love of Life, before those years when they had tried to break him? Or did his memory drift back to Italy, when, on the first night of *La Resurrezione* the world seemed but a gilded ball in his hand? Or to Hamburg—to the battles with Keiser, to those first ambitions shared with Mattheson, to the secret hopes, the little hidden poverties? Or, did his mind in those last hours, call up his life in judgment, sift it and bring back, as being greater than all else, the memory of an old lady groping round the room with a stick at Halle? Or did visions of the old barber-surgeon pass across the eyes of his mind—of his own funny fingers flustered by the organ notes at Weissenfels—of Aunt Anna—the organ at the Liefrauenkirche—old Zachow . . .? Perhaps in the weary waiting he found these things again, and knew these people better—they who figured so largely in the pageant of his life.

Only three days before he died he added a codicil to his will, clear, concise, and without any confusion as to his earthly affairs.[1] Then, when the morning of Good Friday arrived, he bade farewell to all his friends in turn. He told his servant not to admit any of them again, for he had, he said, now done with the world. Only Dr Warren and the apothecary remained. Presently the latter, too, crept away, and left the doctor alone.

The day bore to its close, and the silent figure on the bed still breathed. There was quiet in the chamber where the wings of Death waited to bear a great soul to the infinite. Handel's sun had set. Darkness came in through an unlit window. There was night in the hills.

Before the daylight was fully come his soul had passed. No man knew the precise hour of that passing. No man witnessed that slight change in Handel which revealed that a joyous voyager had gone upon his way. . . .

The news hurried through the Press.

'This morning, a little before eight o'clock, died the deservedly celebrated George Frederick Handell Esq,'

said the *Whitehall Evening Post* of 12–14 April. The *Scots Magazine* for that month said:

'He was perhaps as great a genius in music as Mr Pope was in poetry; the musical composition of the one being as

[1] The last codicil, like the three former, is not in Handel's handwriting, but only signed by him.

expressive of the passions, as the happy versification of the other excelled in harmony.'

Three thousand people gathered in the Abbey to see Handel buried on 20 April—a tribute from the London that had scorned him. The funeral took place at eight o'clock in the evening. One journal—the *London Evening Post*—declared that he was to be buried at the Foundling Hospital, near Captain Coram. But Handel, by his will, had left £600 to pay for the monument over his resting-place in the Abbey.

The *Whitehall Evening Post* (19–21 April 1759) said:

'Last night about Eight o'clock, the remains of the late great Mr Handel were deposited at the foot of the Duke of Argyll's Monument in Westminster Abbey; and though he had mention'd being privately interr'd, yet from the Respect due to so celebrated a Man, the Bishop, Prebends, and the whole Choir attended to pay the last Honours due to his Memory; the Bishop himself performed the Service. A Monument is also to be erected for him, which there is no doubt but his Works will even outlive. There was almost the greatest Concourse of People of all Ranks ever seen upon such, or indeed upon any other Occasion.'

Rockstro[1] laments the absence of information as to the music performed at the funeral. The *Public Advertiser* (20 April) made this quite clear.

'This Evening the Remains of Mr Handel will be buried in Westminster Abbey. The Gentlemen of His Majesty's Chapels Royal, as well as the Choirs of St Paul's and St Peter's (Westminster Abbey) will attend the Solemnity and sing Dr Croft's *Funeral Anthem*.'

The points are important, for they prove that Handel was not buried midst a great concourse of people in haphazard fashion, as some of his biographers have suggested. A more elaborate ceremony could not have been ordered for a king, and, concerning it, Handel's biographers have missed three important facts, viz.:—The attendance of the Gentlemen of

[1] *Life of G. F. Handel*, p. 364.

COVENT-GARDEN.
By SUBSCRIPTION.
The Ninth Night.

AT the Theatre-Royal in Covent-Garden, Wednesday next, will be perform'd

A NEW SACRED ORATORIO.

A CONCERTO on the ORGAN,

And a Solo on the Violin by Mr. DUBOURG.

Tickets will be deliver'd to Subscribers on Tuesday next, at Mr. Handel's House in Brook-street.

Pit and Boxes to be put together, and no Person to be admitted without Tickets, which will be deliver'd that Day, at the Office in Covent-Garden Theatre, at Half a Guinea each. First Gallery 5 s. Upper Gallery 3 s. 6 d.

The Galleries will be open'd at Four o'Clock. Pit and Boxes at Five.

THE ANNOUNCEMENT IN THE DAILY PRESS OF THE FIRST PERFORMANCE OF *MESSIAH*—THEN CALLED THE SACRED ORATORIO—IN LONDON.

Tuesday last the Rev. Mr Sherlock Willis Rector of St. Christopher's Church in Threadneedle-street, was married to Miss Seller, Daughter of Mrs. Seller, of Cheshunt in Hertfordshire.

Yesterday was married at St. James's Church, Clerkenwell, Mr. Joseph Letch, youngest Son of Mr. Letch, of the Temple, to Miss Beazley, Niece of Walsingham Beazley, Esq; of St. John Street, and immediately after set out for their Father's House in Essex.

This Evening the Remains of Mr. Handel will be buried in Westminster Abbey. The Gentlemen of his Majesty's Chapels Royal, as well as the Choirs of St. Paul's and St. Peter's, will attend the Solemnity, and sing Dr. Croft's Funeral Anthem

Tuesday Night died, much lamented, Mrs. Turner, Wife of Mr. James Turner of Vine street in the Minories.

Wednesday Night died —— Riccards, Esq; at his House in the Minories; in the Commission of the Peace for the Tower Hamlets.

THE ANNOUNCEMENT OF HANDEL'S BURIAL IN THE *PUBLIC ADVERTISER* 20 APRIL 1759
The only known reference to the music sung at his funeral.

the Chapels Royal; the combined Choirs of St Paul's and St Peter's; and, the most important point, that the music played was Croft's.

So passed Handel, midst all the pomp and circumstance of a nation's reverence. How different from the passing of some of the masters who came after him! Chopin—his bones rattled over the cobbles of Paris on his way to Père Lachaise. Schubert—and his brother pawning his coat to bury him. Bizet—dying of starvation just as the acclaiming crowd poured out of the theatre after the first performance of *Carmen*. But each of the great ones, as they came, yielded his tribute to the feet of Handel. Beethoven, dying, pointed to the Arnold edition of Handel's works, which were piled up in a corner of the room, and exclaimed: 'There lies the truth!' Haydn worshipped his memory. And a greater judge than all—the musical world of two hundred years, has acknowledged the genius of Handel. To many, he remains as the greatest dreamer in music the world has ever known. His whole life was a dream. And his every effort was a votive offering to his temple of dreams—that temple which he sought to make beautiful.

He went to the Abbey as he would have wished—the acknowledged Master. Those who had laughed and jeered now came to mourn. Three thousand people gave him the tears of the world.

HANDEL'S DIFFICULTIES WITH HIS SINGERS

and notes on his score corrections

REFERENCE has been made in this volume to the continual difficulty which Handel had with his singers. Fortunately there still exist certain copies of Christopher Smith's transcriptions, which reveal not only these difficulties that necessitated frequent alterations, but the constant change of mood which made Handel adapt a song he had composed for one singer, in order to suit the voice of another.

Only six of the transcriptions remain, and these only in part, which bear such alterations. They are now in the State and University Library at Hamburg, and were previously in the possession of Victor Schoelcher, the Handel biographer, who bought them for a trifle at Bristol. Of the other Smith transcriptions existing, none of those in the British Museum, the Fitzwilliam Museum at Cambridge, nor in my own collection, bear the same corrections, which goes to prove that he cast his companies for his revivals from those now at Hamburg.

The six works in question, and the number of volumes of Smith's transcriptions of them, which are at Hamburg, are as follows: *Alexander's Feast*, 1 vol.; *L'Allegro*, 1 vol.; *Arianna*, 1 vol.; *Athalia,* 1 vol.; *Belshazzar*, 3 vols.; *Song for St Cecilia's Day*, 1 vol.

They are interesting from several points of view as they give us the names of the singers for whom the songs were composed, as well as those who were chosen for subsequent performances, while, apparently, Handel sometimes changed his mind in the choice of a singer for some particular performance. Apart from this, they show the shortenings, corrections, alterations, and interpolations, or substitutes of various numbers, which Handel made very frequently, partly for artistic reasons, and partly to suit the taste of his audiences. As comparatively little is known about these alterations, the following notes on the Hamburg copies may not be without interest.

ALEXANDER'S FEAST

The name of Sigr Avolio is pencilled against that of Mr Beard, while Signa Avolio, as well as Mrs Weichsell, appear against the name of Signa Strada. The name of the latter is written in Christopher Smith's hand against the words 'With ravish'd ears', while the name of Mrs Weichsell and Miss Brent are entered as cast for the part. The names of Mrs Weichsell and Mr Callogh are written in pencil at the beginning of the air: 'Bacchus ever Fair'. Callogh was evidently a high baritone, as Handel has pencilled in higher notes for the passage:

is the soldiers pleasure

of which the original setting was evidently for a lower voice.

If Handel had an artist whom he thought particularly suited to the effective rendering of the music, he would turn over a soprano song to a contralto, or even to a tenor, and transpose it accordingly, provided the text would permit of such a change.

'The mighty master smiled' was apparently composed for Beard in the first instance, for his name was placed at the beginning in Christopher Smith's handwriting. But it was later struck out in pencil, and next to it we find the name of Miss Brent. Callogh is written underneath Beard and crossed out again. Under Callogh we find Mrs Cibber's name, and Sigr Guardacci underneath that again, while next to the latter, under the first line, appears 'Mrs Weichsell'.

The original recitative, in the key of 'A minor', is in the tenor clef, while the arioso, 'Softly sweet', in 'D major', is in the soprano clef. Afterwards he transposed it a third higher, indicating the notes he wanted by placing their respective letters in pencil over the original notes, using the German form 'h' for the 'b natural'. The arioso, Largo No. 9, originally written for Signa Strada, was afterwards given to Miss B . . . (Brent, illegible in pencil). Next to it, likewise in pencil, is written 'Guardacci', a note higher, covered by a patch of paper. All is struck out again, and the arioso begins and gives the names of Signa Strada, Sigr Tend. (Tenducci), 'Mrs Cibber in contralto ex g♯', 'Mrs Weichsell ex A'. The whole of the recitative (in tenor clef) and the arioso are then struck out, and another version, in which the violin replaces the violoncello, is inserted.

'Let old Timotheus', originally given to Beard, appears to have been at one time intended for Mrs Cibber, whose name is written over the words by Handel in pencil, but struck out again and 'Williams' written by the side of it.

The entire score of *Alexander's Feast* is altered in this fashion, which is suggestive of Handel's difficulty in casting.

L'ALLEGRO

On this score, Handel has written an Italian translation in pencil over the words: 'There let Hymen', etc., while the original English words are retained of 'Me, when the Sun begins . . .', which is given to Frasi instead of Francesina, whose name was originally connected with it. 'And let their Sweetness through mine Ear', shows an alteration. Written in pencil is the name of Sigra Avolio, and underneath, very faintly, appears that of Signa Monza, while Frasi's name is very clearly written under the latter.

ARIADNE

There is little worth mentioning concerning the subject in this score. Here and there we find cuts of short passages, or perhaps a few bars, especially in the first act. The most interesting note is that which occurs in 'Ove son quall'orrore', which, in a rapid pencil scrawl, in parts almost illegible, gives the following directions: 'Tr a un mezzo tono più basso tutta questa scena'. (From a (?) a semitone lower the whole scene.)

ATHALIA

There are several cuts of varying length in the score of *Athalia*. The singers mentioned are Lowe, against whose name appears that of Beard in pencil, while the ladies were Signa Frasi and Miss Edwards. Some of the names are shortened and almost illegible.

Over the *Larghetto* (Joad): 'Will God whose mercies ever

flow', is written in pencil 'Boy'. This requires a short explanation.

Handel had rightly conceived the part of Joad, the High Priest, as a bass, as well as that of Abner, and these twain were the mainsprings of action in the oratorio, which would have given it the interesting feature of being a true bass oratorio. But, unfortunately, Montagnana, for whose powerful voice and artistic nature Handel had conceived the part, deserted him at the moment when the oratorio was completed.

It was thus a case of most regrettable emergency which caused Handel to rewrite the part for an alto voice, and to choose for its representative a 'boy' of the Chapel Royal. But in spite of the fact that the 'boy' was entrusted with this important solo part, he was not considered worthy of appearing under his own name.

Later on, the alterations in the score became more extensive.

In the chorus 'Around let acclamation ring', the words *Andante Allegro* were struck out, and *a tempo ordinario* substituted in pencil, as well as other words, which unfortunately have become illegible. In the following pages, underneath the words 'Royal Youth' (as well as other words, which unfortunately have become illegible), 'Hail Royal Youth, long live the King' is written in pencil, 'the Church and save the King' as alternative words.

The following recitative: 'Reviving Judah' had been altered in pencil to 'With firm united Hearts we all (shall?) conquer'; but all has been crossed out and 'Anthem; The King shall rejoice' written over it. Then follows the cembalo part (with obbligato trumpet indicated for the first, third, and fourth bars) of a chorus in D major '*Allegro* non *Presto*', fifty-four bars in all, which was intended as final chorus, as the words following it: 'End of the Oratorio', clearly prove. Of this chorus there is no full score. The recitative 'Reviving Judah' is continued with pencil notes of alternative words, but all is crossed out again.

Then comes a chorus: 'Bless the true Church and save the King', another recitative for Athalia, also crossed out, and in pencil: Chorus/around let acc-/mation/anthem the King shall rejoice/Fine/. Then comes a *Tutti unisono*: 'Oppression no longer I dread thee', Athalia, Recit.; Nathan, Recit. and Aria; Joad, Recit.; Athalia, Aria; 'To darkness eternal'; Joad, Recit., with a pencil note at the end; 'Aria' and two words which are undecipherable; Aria, duet for Joad and Josabeth; a Recitative for Ab(ner), and at the end of this: 'Concerto ex f (?)'. A chorus, 'Give Glory', is the final number.

BELSHAZZAR

In many places small alternative notes are added, especially in recitatives, in some cases merely to suit the compass of the singers' voices, in others, however, to ensure greater emphasis, or better declamation. In many places some bars are crossed out with ink or pencil, words are sometimes altered in Handel's writing, and some recitatives are crossed out entirely.

In Act I, MS. p. 21, an aria: 'Opprest with never ceasing grief' for Gobias, has been added, and, on p. 75, an aria for Nitocris: 'The leafy honours of the field.' Another aria which stood in its place has been cut out, as is evident from the five last bars of it

which appear on p. 80 of the manuscript.

The following recitative of Belshazzar is shortened by the omission of Nitocris's rejoinder, and the words are altered by Handel to connect the words of Belshazzar's recitative.

Throughout the score we find here and there a few bars eliminated by being pasted over with white paper. In the second act, p. 63*b* is altered and entirely rewritten in a different hand on p. 64*b* (p. 64*a* is left blank), and another and shorter *Finale* than the original one ending on p. 76, is added. Of the original *Finale*, which has a different text, the very florid ending, from p. 77*a* to p. 82*b* is preserved, and marked, like its shorter substitute: 'End of the 2nd Act.'

In Act III there is an aria for soprano (Nitocris?), *Larghetto* in D major, which is so bound that it follows the beginning (eighth bar) of Daniel's recitative 'Can the black Aethiop', while Nitocris's recitative 'Fain would I hope', is crossed out. As the aria opens with the words 'Fain would I know', it seems that it was intended to take the place of that recitative.

On p. 22*b*, after the 'Martial Symphony', a short recitative for Gobias is added, in Handel's own handwriting, but this is crossed out again with pencil. It is followed by an aria in D minor for Gobias, which replaces another setting of the same words in G minor, as is shown by the four closing bars of the latter, on p. 25.

A similar process has taken place with a duet in A minor between Nitocris and Cyrus, which replaces a previous one, in B minor, finishing on p. 37. At the end of this, is written in Handel's writing, 'Segue Cyrus to Daniel'. Another similar alteration has been made from p. 42*b* to p. 47*b*, as shown by the original bars of Cyrus's air on p. 48. Pages 49*b* and 50*a* are entirely crossed out in pencil.

THE SONG FOR ST CECILIA'S DAY

An interesting feature of this copy is the indication of Handel's troubles with the singers. The name of Mr Beard appears in Christopher Smith's hand for the part of the first tenor. At the top we find in Handel's writing the name of 'Savage' written in pencil, which has become very faint. Then we find Sigra Francesina as soprano. This is struck out with pencil, and next to it in Handel's writing the name of 'Avolio'.

At the top of the page is the name, 'Miss Brent', and, a little lower, Handel started another name and then rubbed the pencil writing out with his finger. All that is recognizable now, is 'E', which may point to the name of Miss Edwards.

At the beginning of 'The trumpets loud clangor', we find Mr Beard again, but at the top of the page, in pencil, appears Mr Corf, likewise struck out again. 'The soft complaining Flute' had Mrs Cibber as original interpreter, but in pencil we find the name of Guadagni.

At the bottom of this page (p. 35) there is a different ending, the bass alone finishing with 'late to retreat', followed by four final bars for the orchestra. Then comes another setting of 'The soft complaining Flute', with Traverse (flute) and Liuto (lute) solo, for 'Sigra Francesina'. Over this appear in Handel's pencil writing the names of Mrs Cibber, Sra Monza, and in a very neat (female?) hand 'Frasi'.

'Sharp violins', originally given to Mr Beard, was afterwards allotted, in pencil, to others. Two names appear faintly under 'Mrs Clive', one was 'Andreoni', the other has become indecipherable. Over the English words of this aria Handel wrote an Italian version in pencil. This was no doubt a concession to Francesina, whose name appears also at the beginning of the next aria, but 'Frasi' is written in pencil next to it, and where the voice enters, we find 'Miss Edwards' written over the words 'But oh!'

'Orpheus could lead'—apparently to trouble! 'Sigra Francesina' appears, in Christopher Smith's writing, as the singer for whom the part was originally intended. Underneath her name we find in pencil 'Miss Edwards', next to her 'Passerini', over the opening bars 'Mrs Scott', and above her name another which seems to begin with an H, and to end with A, but the restless composer has rendered it illegible by rubbing it out with his fingers. Miss Edwards's name appears again above the first words of the aria. Over the words 'But bright Cecilia' we find the name of 'Sr Avollo' (Avolio), at the top of the page 'Miss Brent', and both these names occur again over the opening words of the aria. Eleven bars are cut out, between 'and musick shall untune the skies' and 'the dead shall live' on pp. 58b and 59a.

These constant corrections and alterations indicate the changing moods of Handel, his restlessness, his ability to switch a song from one singer to another and sacrifice nothing of his Art. When one singer failed him he simply adapted his music to the requirements of another. He was never at a loss. Never did his genius fail to extricate him from the difficulties which beset his performing.

BIBLIOGRAPHY

COMPILED BY WILLIAM C. SMITH

Formerly Assistant Keeper, Department of Printed Books
in the British Museum

THE following bibliography, which is arranged in chronological order, includes all the separate works on Handel which have been traced, as well as a considerable number of miscellaneous publications containing matter of interest in connection with Handel and his times.

In addition to the works mentioned, numerous articles and references exist elsewhere, in newspapers, periodicals, programmes, histories, and dictionaries of music and musicians. It has been impossible to enumerate or examine in detail many of these probable sources of information. *Grove's Dictionary of Music and Musicians* gives a very full list of musical periodicals.

A few of the most important magazines and periodicals are mentioned and also some selected magazine articles. The catalogues of 'Periodical Publications' and 'Newspapers' at the British Museum, and the article 'Periodicals, musical' in *Grove's Dictionary of Music* give particulars of most of the British and much of the foreign periodical literature. For purposes of further reference various indexes should be consulted, such as Poole's *Index to Periodical Literature*, London, 1802, etc.; Guthrie's *Readers' Guide to Periodical Literature*, Minneapolis, 1905, etc.; *The Library Association Subject Index to Periodicals*; Palmer's *Index to the Times*.

Titles of some of the principal dictionaries, histories, and bibliographies of music are included in the bibliography, but it has not been considered necessary to indicate more than a very few out of the enormous number of general musical works which deal incidentally with Handel. The *Subject Catalogue of Printed Works in the British Museum*, 1881, etc., includes most of the publications from that date, and other useful bibliographies are *The English Catalogue of Books*; *The London Catalogue of Books*; Whistling's (Hofmeister's) *Handbuch der musikalischen Literatur*, Leipzig, 1817, etc.; *Jahrbuch der Musikbibliothek Peters*, Leipzig, 1895, etc.; Abcr's *Handbuch der Musikliteratur*, Leipzig, 1922.

Other miscellaneous sources, not mentioned in the main bibliography, are the collections of playbills, programmes, and libretti at the British Museum and elsewhere; the Mattheson manuscripts and opera text-books at the Hamburg Library; the sale catalogues of various London sale-rooms and second-hand music dealers, and *Book Prices Current*, although a few special catalogues are listed. The footnotes in the work include references to some sources not included in the bibliography.

Although the present volume does not deal with Handel and his work on the technical side, it may be of interest to indicate the whereabouts of some of the larger collections of his manuscripts and printed editions. A very good summary and index is to be found in Rockstro's *Life of Handel*, but since the publication of that work several of the collections have changed hands and other information has become available. A detailed catalogue of all the Handel manuscripts is needed; only the larger collections are mentioned here.

MANUSCRIPTS (AUTOGRAPHS AND COPIES)

1. *The British Museum* contains the Royal Collection from Buckingham Palace (given to the nation by H.M. Queen Elizabeth II), the Granville Collection (purchased in 1915), and miscellaneous items acquired at various times by purchase or gift.

Catalogues of the Royal Collection and of most of the manuscripts are available. Other catalogues are in preparation.

2. *The Fitzwilliam Museum, Cambridge*, contains the manuscripts mentioned in the catalogue by Fuller-Maitland and Mann, issued in 1893, and also the collection of manuscripts formerly in the possession of F. B. Lennard and acquired by the Fitzwilliam Museum in 1902.

3. *The Hamburg Library* collection of copies, formerly in the possession of Kerslake of Bristol and Victor Schoelcher.

4. *The Newman Flower Collection*, which includes most of the Aylesford manuscripts.

Catalogue issued 1921. A new catalogue is in preparation containing full details of the many additions to the collection made in recent years.

5. *The Foundling Hospital*. A small collection.

COLLECTIONS OF PRINTED EDITIONS AND HANDEL LITERATURE

1. *The British Museum*. The national collection of printed music includes an enormous number of Handel items, which has been considerably increased by editions in the Royal Collection, and by the acquisition of the Paul Hirsch Music Library completed in four volumes. The British Museum issues a one-volume catalogue of the Collection.

The works are catalogued as received, and catalogues of all works up to the end of 1800, and of the Royal Collection, are on sale. A special catalogue of the Paul Hirsch Library is being completed in four volumes which can be purchased.

2. *La Conservatoire de Musique, Paris*, contains Schoelcher's collection of many printed editions, and a vast array of Handel literature.

3. *The Newman Flower Collection*, besides the manuscripts already mentioned, includes some autograph MSS. and many first and other printed editions, pictures, contemporary portraits, and a considerable amount of Handel literature.

4. *The Library of the Royal College of Music* contains, amongst other collections, the works formerly in possession of the Sacred Harmonic Society.

Catalogue by W. Barclay Squire, issued in 1909.

5. *King's College, Cambridge*, including the Mann and Rowe collections.

6. *The Gerald Coke Collection*.

7. *The William C. Smith Collection*.

8. *The J. S. Hall Collection*.

9. *The National Library of Scotland*, Edinburgh, contains the collection of early editions formerly owned by Julian Marshall, the Earl of Balfour, and Viscount Traprain.

There are also various private collections, such as that of the Earl of Malmesbury, and other public collections, of which it is unnecessary to give the details here.

COLLECTED EDITIONS OF HANDEL'S WORKS

1. The works of Handel, edited in score by Samuel Arnold. London [1787–97].

Modifications in some of the volumes were made from time to time, and a revised and corrected edition of the series was advertised in 1802.

2. The works of Handel. Printed for members of the Handel Society. London, 1843–58.

3. George Friedrich Händel's Werke. Ausgabe der Deutschen Händelgesellschaft. Herausgegeben von F. Chrysander. Leipzig [1859–1902]. Preface to Vol. I dated 1858.

4. Harrison & Co., of Paternoster Row, London, published a cheap popular edition of a number of Handel's works, in serial form, from 1783 onwards. Copies of these works are extremely rare and are a valuable contribution to the subject.

Most of Handel's works were published during his lifetime by Cluer, Meares, or Walsh (father and son), but Walsh issues are very confusing and were subject to much modification. After the death of the younger Walsh (1766), Randall and Abell, followed by Randall alone, afterwards by Elizabeth Randall, Wright and Wilkinson, Wright & Co., and H. Wright, published a number of works, mostly full scores of oratorios, which had not been issued previously.

No adequate printed list of all the early editions is available, but a comprehensive catalogue is now in preparation by William C. Smith. Manuscript catalogues partly in French, formerly in the possession of Julian Marshall and now in the Royal Collection, British Museum, are attempts towards a bibliography of Handel's works. The Mann Library, King's College, Cambridge, contains the Victor Schoelcher manuscript, which appears to be largely an English version of the Marshall material in the Royal Collection.

Walsh and his successors issued several catalogues of their publications, including Handel's works, but they are not very detailed and are of little help in the identification of editions.

The titles as given in the following bibliography have been taken from copies of the works whenever possible, but in some cases the information has been obtained from other sources.

Brackets [] have been used to indicate matter which does not occur in the works referred to.

BIBLIOGRAPHY

The London Magazine. London, 1710–70.

GAY, JOHN: *Trivia; or The Art of Walking the Streets of London*. London [1716].

HAYM, N. F.: *Il Radamisto*, opera. [Libretto, with dedicatory epistle by Handel.] London, 1720.

MALCOLM, ALEX.: *A Treatise of Musick, Speculative, Practical, and Historical*. Edinburgh, 1721. Second edition. London, 1779.

SACHSEN, H.: *Einfältige Critique der Oper Julius Caesar in Aegypten*. Hamburg, 1725.
    An answer to this criticism is said to have been published at Altona.

CAREY, H.: *Poems on Several Occasions*. Third edition. London 1729.

Register of performances at London Theatres. 1710–29. (Egerton MSS., British Museum, 2321, 2322.)

WRIGHT, EDWARD: *Some Observations Made in Travelling through France, Italy, etc., in the years 1720, 1721, and 1722*. 2 vols. London, 1730.

The Gentleman's Magazine. London, 1731–1868.

Letters from the Academy of Ancient Music at London to Signor Antonio Lotti of Venise, with Answers and Testimonies. [A pamphlet.] London, 1732.

WALTHER, J. G.: *Musicalisches Lexicon*. Leipzig, 1732.

The Oxford Act: a New Ballad Opera. [A pamphlet]. London, 1733.

COLMAN, FRANCIS: Opera-Registers from 1712–34, etc. A brief account of operas performed at the Haymarket. (Add. MSS., British Museum, 11258.)

HUGHES, JOHN: *Poems on Several Occasions, with some Select Essays*. 2 vols. London, 1735.

CIBBER, COLLEY: *An Apology for the Life of Colley Cibber*. London, 1740.

GRASSINEAU, J.: *A Musical Dictionary*. London, 1740.

LOCKMAN, J.: *Rosalinda, a Musical Drama. . . . To which is prefixed an inquiry into the rise and progress of operas and oratorios*. London, 1740.

MATTHESON, J.: *Grundlage einer Ehren-Pforte*, etc. Hamburg, 1740. Neudruck herausgegeben von Max Schneider. Berlin, 1910.

The Public Register: or Weekly Magazine. London, 1741.

RICCOBONI, L.: *An Historical and Critical Account of the Theatres in Europe*. London, 1741.

An Ode to Mr Handel. London, 1745.

SCHEIBE, J. A.: *Johann Adolph Scheibens. . . . Critischer Musikus*. Leipzig, 1745.

WARD, EDW.: *A Complete and Humorous Account of all the*

Remarkable Clubs and Societies in the Cities of London and Westminster. London, 1745.

The Universal Magazine. London, 1747–1803.

ARBUTHNOT, J.: *The Miscellaneous Works of the late Dr Arbuthnot.* Second edition. 2 vols. Glasgow, 1751. Another edition. 2 vols. London, 1770.

WILLIAM HAYES: *The Art of Composing Music by a Method Entirely New, suited to the Meanest Capacity.* [A pamphlet.] London, 1751.

HILL, AARON: *The Works of the late Aaron Hill.* 4 vols. London, 1753.

DREYHAUPT, J. C. VON: *Pagus Neletici et Nudzici,* etc. 2 vols. Halle, 1755.

Reflections upon Theatrical Expression in Tragedy. London, 1755.

DE BLAINVILLE: *Travels through Holland, Germany, Switzerland, but especially Italy.* 3 vols. London, 1757.

The London Chronicle. London, 1757–1823.

Remarks upon Musick; to which are added Several Observations upon some of Mr Handel's Oratorios, and other parts of his Works. By a lover of harmony. [W. Hughes?] Worcester, 1758.

HUGHES, WILLIAM: *Remarks upon Church Music.* . . . Second edition. Worcester, 1763.

HILL, AARON: *The Dramatic Works of Aaron Hill.* 2 vols. London, 1760.

LANGHORNE, J.: *The Tears of Music: a Poem to the Memory of Mr Handel.* London, 1760.

MAINWARING, J.: *Memoirs of the Life of the late G. F. Handel. To which is added a Catalogue of his Works and Observations upon them.* London, 1760.

    Reviews of this work and extracts: *The Critical Review,* vol. 9, 1760; *The Gentleman's Magazine,* April 1760; *The London Chronicle,* June 1760; *The Universal Magazine,* vol. 26, 1760.

MATTHESON, J.: *Georg Friedrich Händel's Lebensbeschreibung.* [By John Mainwaring,] *nebst einem Verzeichnisse seiner Ausübungswerke und deren Beurtheilung übersetzet, auch mit einigen Anmerkungen. . . . versehen vom Legations-Rath Mattheson.* Hamburg, 1761.

An Examination of the Oratorios which have been performed this season at Covent Garden Theatre. London, 1763.

BAKER, D. E.: *The Companion to the Playhouse*. 2 vols. London, 1764. Another edition. *Biographia Dramatica*, etc. 2 vols. London, 1782. Another edition. 3 vols. London, 1812.

Wöchentliche Nachrichten und Anmerkungen die Musik betreffend, etc. Leipzig, 1766–70. Articles by J. A. Hiller.

ROUSSEAU, J. J.: *Dictionnaire de Musique*. Paris, 1768.

BARETTI, G. M. A.: *An Account of the Manners and Customs of Italy*. London, 1769.

GROSLEY, P. J.: *Observations sur l'Italie et sur les Italiens*. 4 vols. London, 1770.

HAWKINS, SIR JOHN: *An Account of the Institution and Progress of the Academy of Ancient Music. . . . By a Member*. [Sir John Hawkins.] London, 1770.

HOYLE, J.: *Dictionarium Musica*. London, 1770. Another edition. *A Complete Dictionary of Music*. London, 1791.

BURNEY, CHARLES: *The Present State of Music in France and Italy; or a Journal of a Tour through Those Countries*. London, 1771.

Letters by Several Eminent Persons Deceased, including the Correspondence of John Hughes, etc. 2 vols. London, 1772.

The literary part of the *Musical Magazine*. London, 1774–5.

LUXBOROUGH, LADY: *Letters written by the late Right Honourable Lady Luxborough to William Shenstone*. London, 1775.

BEATTIE, J.: *Essays on Poetry and Music*. Edinburgh, 1776.

BURNEY, CHARLES: *A General History of Music*. 4 vols. London, 1776–89.

HAWKINS, SIR JOHN: *A General History of the Science and Practice of Music*. 5 vols. London, 1776. Another edition. 2 vols. London, 1853. Another edition. 3 vols. London, 1875.

List of 'Dramas of Italian opera, acted in England' between 1705 and 1776. (Add.MSS.,Burn. 521B., British Museum.)

CIBBER, COLLEY: *The Dramatic Works of Colley Cibber*. 5 vols. London, 1777.

The Westminster Magazine, or the Pantheon of Taste. London, 1777.

A. B. C. Dario Musico. Bath, 1780. Another edition. London, 1780.

The European Magazine. London, 1782–1825.

CRAMER, C. F.: *Magazin der Musik*. Herausgegeben von C. F. Cramer. Hamburg, 1783–6.

'An Account of the Life of G. F. Handel', *The European Magazine*, March 1784. London.

Commemoration of Handel. Third performance, the Messiah . . . May 29th., 1784. [A programme.] London.

DIXWELL: *Life of Handel*. [London, 1784.] Referred to in *Critical Review*, 1784.

HILLER, J. A.: *Lebensbeschreibungen berühmter Musikgelehrten und Tonkünstler neuerer Zeit*. Leipzig, 1784.

ROBINSON, POLLINGROVE: *Handel's Ghost: An Ode*. [London, 1784.] Referred to in *Critical Review*, 1784.

BURNEY, CHARLES: *An Account of the Musical Performances in Westminster Abbey and the Pantheon, May 26th, 27th, 29th; and June the 3rd and 5th, 1784, in Commemoration of Handel*. London, 1785.

REICHARDT, J. F.: *G. F. Händels Jugend*. Berlin, 1785.

HILLER, J. A.: *Nachricht von der Aufführung des Händelschen Messias, in der Domkirche zu Berlin, den 19 May 1786*. Berlin [1786].

NEWTON, JOHN: *The Messiah. Fifty Expository Discourses on the Subject of the Celebrated Oratorio of Handel*. London, 1786.

The (London) Play Pocket Companion; or Theatrical Vade Mecum. London, 1789.

The Theatrical Dictionary. London, 1792.

Allgemeine musikalische Zeitung. Leipzig, 1798–1849; 1863–82.

COXE, W.: *Anecdotes of G. F. Handel and J. C. Smith*, etc. London, 1799.

HEPTINSTALL, T.: *The Sacred Oratorios as Set to Music by G. F. Handel. (The miscellaneous pieces . . . with the life of G. F. Handel.)* [Selected by T. Heptinstall.] 2 pts. London, 1799.

BUSBY, T.: *A Complete Dictionary of Music*. London [1800?]. Fourth edition. London, 1817.

DIBDIN, C.: *A Complete History of the English Stage*. 5 vols. London [1800].

HERDER, J. G. VON: *Händel: Seine Lebensumstände*. (Adrastea, vol. iii.) Leipzig, 1802.

MALCOLM, J. P.: *Anecdotes of the Manners and Customs of London during the Eighteenth Century*. London, 1808. Another edition. 2 vols. London, 1810.

CARTER, ELIZ., and TALBOT, CATH.: *A Series of Letters between Mrs Elizabeth Carter and Miss Catherine Talbot from the year 1741 to 1770*. 4 vols. London, 1809.

For the benefit of the Vulpicide and Anticubbite Societies. On Saturday, April 1st, 1809, will be performed by permission of the Shepherd of Arcadia, at the Temple of Pan, the grandest of all selections from the works of Handel. [A parody on airs in the works of Handel. 1809.]

WEISSEBECK, J. M.: *Der grosse Musikus Händel im Universalruhme*. Nuremberg, 1809.

CHORON, A. E., and FAYOLLE, F. J. M.: *Dictionnaire historique des Musiciens*. 2 vols. Paris, 1810–11.

LYSONS, D.: *History of the Origin and Progress of the Meeting of the Three Choirs of Gloucester, Worcester, and Hereford*, etc. Gloucester, 1812, and later editions.

A Series of Reflections on the Sacred Oratorio of the Messiah. By a Lady. London, 1812. Seventh edition. London, 1836.

BINGLEY, W.: *Musical Biography*. 2 vols. London, 1814. Second edition. 2 vols. London, 1834.

BURGH, A.: *Anecdotes of Music, Historical and Biographical*. 3 vols. London, 1814.

The Quarterly Musical Magazine and Review. London, 1818–28.

BUSBY, T.: *A General History of Music*. 2 vols. London, 1819.

REES, ABRAHAM: *The Cyclopaedia or Universal Dictionary of Arts, Sciences, and Literature*. 39 vols. London, 1819.

RING, J.: *The Commemoration of Handel; the second edition, and other poems*. London, 1819.

The Letters of J. Beattie . . . from Sir W. Forbes' Collection. 2 vols. London, 1820.

BLAZE (CASTIL-BLAZE), F. H. J.: *De l'Opéra en France*. 2 vols. Paris, 1820.

COLMAN, GEORGE: *Posthumous Letters from Various Celebrated Men; Addressed to Francis Colman and George Colman the Elder, with Annotations and Occasional Remarks by G. Colman, the Younger*. London, 1820.

CLARK, R.: *An Account of the National Anthem*, etc. London, 1822.

HAWKINS, L. M.: *Anecdotes, Biographical Sketches, and Memoirs*. London, 1822.

SPENCE, ELIZ. I.: *How to be Rid of a Wife*, etc. 2 vols. London, 1823.

A Dictionary of Musicians. 2 vols. London, 1824. Second edition. 2 vols. London, 1827.

HARDCASTLE, EPHRAIM [William H. Pyne]: *Somerset House Gazette and Literary Museum.* 2 vols. London, 1824.

BUSBY, T.: *Concert Room and Orchestra Anecdotes of Music and Musicians.* 3 vols. London, 1825.

CROSSE, J.: *An Account of the Grand Musical Festival held in September 1823 in the Cathedral Church of York.* York, 1825.

DANNELEY, J. F.: *An Encyclopaedia or Dictionary of Music.* London, 1825.

LICHTENTHAL, P.: *Dizionario e Bibliografia della Musica.* 4 vols. Milan, 1826. French edition. 2 vols. Paris, 1839.

A Catalogue of the Musical Library belonging to His Majesty's Concerts of Ancient Music. London, 1827

KRAUSE, C. C. F.: *Darstellungen aus der Geschichte der Musik* Göttingen, 1827. Second edition. Leipzig, 1911.

Revue Musicale. (Revue et Gazette musicale.) Paris, 1827–80.

CRADOCK, J.: *Literary and Miscellaneous Memoirs.* 4 vols. London, 1828.

MARX, A. B. *Ueber die Geltung Händel'scher Sologesänge für unsere Zeit.* Berlin [1828].

MILNES, K.: *Memoir Relating to the Portrait of Handel by Francis Kyte.* London, 1829.

ROCHLITZ, F.: *Für Freunde der Tonkunst.* Second edition. Vols. i. and iv. Leipzig, 1830–32.

GENEST, J.: *Some Account of the English Stage from . . . 1660 to 1830.* 10 vols. Bath, 1832.

MILDE, T.: *Über das Leben und die Werke der beliebtesten deutschen Dichter und Tonsetzer.* 2 vols. Meissen, 1834.

PARRY, JOHN: *An Account of the Royal Musical Festival held in Westminster Abbey, 1834.* London, 1834.

WALPOLE, HORACE: *Letters of Horace Walpole to Sir Horace Mann.* Third edition. 3 vols. London, 1834.

CLARK, RICH.: *Reminiscences of Handel, His Grace the Duke of Chandos, Powells, the Harpers, the Harmonious Blacksmith,* etc. London, 1836.

The Musical World. London, 1836–91.

'Biographie von Georg Friedrich Händel', *Fünfundzwanzigstes*

Neujahrsstück der allgemeinen Musik-Gesellschaft in Zürich, 1837.

FÉTIS, F. J.: *Biographie Universelle des Musiciens*, etc. 8 vols. Paris, 1837–44. Second edition, with supplement. 10 vols. Paris, 1860–80.

FOERSTEMANN, K. E.: *Gg. Fr. Händel's Stammbaum, nach Original-Quellen und authentischen Nachrichten aufgestellt und erläutert von K. E. Förstemann*. Leipzig, 1844.

The Musical Times. London, 1844, etc.

NORTH, HON. ROGER: *Memoirs of Musick*. Edited by Dr Rimbault. London, 1846.

BROWNLOW, J.: *Memoranda, or Chronicles of the Foundling Hospital*. London, 1847.

HERVEY, LORD JOHN: *Memoirs of the Reign of George the Second. Edited by J. W. Croker*. 2 vols. London, 1848. Another edition. 3 vols. London, 1884.

MACFARREN, SIR GEORGE A.: 'Handel and his Messiah', *Musical World*, vol. xxiv. London, 1849.

WINTERFELD, C. VON: *Alceste, 1674, 1726, 1769, 1776, von Lulli, Händel und Gluck*. Berlin, 1851.

CLARK, RICH.: *On the Sacred Oratorio of 'The Messiah', previous to the death of G. F. Handel, 1759*. London, 1852.

TOWNSEND, H.: *An Account of the Visit of Handel to Dublin: with Incidental Notices of his Life and Character*. Dublin, 1852.

MACFARREN, SIR GEORGE A.: *Messiah . . .* [Word Book], *with an Analysis of the Oratorio* [and a Preface] *. . . by G. A. Macfarren*. London [1853].

KUESTER, H.: *Ueber Händels 'Israel ins Aegypten'*. Berlin, 1854.

MOORE, JOHN W.: *Complete Encyclopaedia of Music*. Boston, 1854.

G. F. Händel: Eine Biographie mit Portrait. Cassel, 1855.

PUTTICK, J. F.: *Remarks on Roubiliac's Statue of Handel in the possession of the Sacred Harmonic Society*. [London ?, 1855.]

BISHOP, JOHN: *Brief Memoir of G. F. Handel*. London, 1856. Also included in Bishop's edition of Messiah, 1856.

BOWLEY, R. K.: *Grand Handel Musical Festival at the Crystal Palace in 1857. A Letter Addressed to the Members . . . of the Sacred Harmonic Society*. London, 1856.

GRINFIELD, T.: *Poetic Rehearsal of Handel's Sacred Oratoria*

'*The Messiah*'. London, 1856. Another edition. *Critical and Poetical Rehearsals of . . . The Messiah, with notes,* etc. London [1893].

BRAY, A. E.: *Handel: his Life, Personal and Professional.* London, 1857.

HEARNE, THOS.: *Reliquiae Hearnianae.* 2 vols. Oxford, 1857.

HUSK, W. H.: *An Account of the Musical Celebrations on St Cecilia's Day in the Sixteenth, Seventeenth, and Eighteenth Centuries.* London, 1857.

MACFARREN, SIR GEORGE A.: *Israel in Egypt; an Oratorio . . .* [libretto], *with an Analysis . . . by G. A. Macfarren.* London [1857].

MEYER, G. M.: *G. F. Händel: Eine biographische Charakteristik.* Berlin, 1857.

MORELL, T.: *Judas Maccabaeus. . . . Written by T. Morell. . . . With analytical remarks by W. Pole.* London, 1857.

Programmes of the Handel Festivals, Crystal Palace, 1857, etc.

SCHOELCHER, V.: *The Life of Handel.* [Translated from the French by J. Lowe.] London, 1857.

BROWNLOW, J.: *The History and Design of the Foundling Hospital.* London, 1858.

CHRYSANDER, FR.: *G. F. Händel.* Vols. 1; 2; 3, pt. i. Leipzig, 1858–67. Reprint. Leipzig, 1919.

CALLCOTT, W. H.: *A Few Facts in the Life of Handel . . . extracted from 'The Handel Album'.* London, 1859.

CHORLEY, H. F.: *Handel Studies.* 2 pts. London, 1859.

CHRYSANDER, FR.: *Handel Receiving the Laurel from Apollo. A poem by an unknown author, originally printed in the year 1724. Edited by F. Chrysander.* Leipzig, 1859.

MACFARREN, SIR GEORGE A.: *A Sketch of the Life of Handel: with Particular Notices of the Works selected for . . . performance at the Centenary Festival in the Crystal Palace.* London [1859].

Melbourne Philharmonic Society. Handel Centenary Celebration. First Concert, etc. [Programme, with *Some account of Handel and his times*]. Melbourne, 1859.

ELSASSER, C.: *The Life of Handel: a Sketch.* Melbourne [1860 ?].

DELANY, MARY: *Autobiography and Correspondence of Mary Granville, Mrs Delany.* 6 vols. London, 1861–2. Contains an account of Handel's death.

The Musical Standard. London, 1862, etc.

RAMSAY, EDW. B.: *Two Lectures on the Genius of Handel and the Distinctive Character of his Sacred Compositions.* Edinburgh, 1862.

BALL, T. H.: *Sketch of Handel and Beethoven.* London, 1864.

POHL, C. F.: *Mozart und Haydn in London.* 2 vols. Vienna, 1867.

GERVINUS, G. G.: *Händel und Shakespeare. Zur Ästhetik der Tonkunst.* Leipzig, 1868.

KEMPEN, F. J. VAN: *G. F. Händel: Een Leven.* Leyden, 1868.

LA MARA [i.e. MARIE LIPSIUS]: *Musikalische Studienköpfe von La Mara.* 5 vols. Leipzig, 1868–82. Ninth edition. Leipzig [1910, etc.]. 'Georg Friedrich Händel . . . Fünfte Auflage'. Leipzig, 1912. Reprinted from *Musikalische Studienköpfe.*

WRIGHT, THOS.: *Caricature History of the Georges.* London [1868].

BITTER, C. H.: *Ueber Gervinus' Händel und Shakespeare.* Berlin, 1869.

MENDEL, HERMANN: *Musikalisches Conversations Lexicon.* 11 vols. and supplement. Berlin, 1869–83. Second edition. Berlin, 1881, etc.

Catalogue of the Prints and Drawings in the British Museum . . . Political and Personal Satires. 4 vols. London, 1870–83.

FOWLE, T. L.: *Life of Handel for the Million.* London [1871]. With addenda. London [1874].

FRANZ, R.: *Offener Brief an E. Hanslick. Über Bearbeitungen älterer Tonwerke, namentlich Bach'scher und Händel'scher Vocalmusik.* Leipzig, 1871.

HAWEIS, H. R.: *Music and Morals.* London, 1871, and later editions.

POPE, ALEX.: *The Works of Alexander Pope.* 10 vols. London, 1871–89.

PROUT, E.: *The Monthly Musical Record.* London, 1871, etc. Various articles.

FROMMEL, E.: *Händel und Bach. (Erzählung für das Volk.)* Berlin, 1873. Other editions in *Gesammelte Schriften.* Berlin, 1878, etc.

Haendel's Oratorientexte. Uebersetzt von G. G. Gervinus. Berlin, 1873.

CUSINS, SIR WILLIAM G.: *Handel's Messiah. An Examination*

of the Original and of Some Contemporary MSS. London, 1874.

CROWDY, J.: *A Short Commentary for the Use of Audiences on Handel's Oratorio 'The Messiah'.* London [1875].

ENGEL, CARL: *Musical Myths and Facts.* 2 vols. London, 1876.

SCHÄFFER, H.: *F. Chrysander in seinen Klavierauszügen zur deutschen Händel-Ausgabe beleuchtet von J. Schäffer.* Leipzig, 1876.

Musical Opinion. London, 1877 etc.

Sammlung von Gesängen aus Händels Opern und Oratorien mit Clavierbegleitung versehen und herausgegeben von Victorie Gervinus. 7 vols. Leipzig [1877]. With preface, introduction and stories of the operas.

GROVE, SIR GEORGE: *A Dictionary of Music and Musicians.* 4 vols. London, 1879–89. Reprint with appendix. 4 vols. London, 1900. *Grove's Dictionary of Music and Musicians.* Edited by J. A. Fuller-Maitland. 5 vols. London, 1904–10. Edited by H. C. Colles. 5 vols. London, 1927–8. Supplement volume, 1940. Fifth edition, edited by Eric Blom. 9 vols. London, 1954. Vol. IV contains Handel article by Scott Goddard and Catalogue of works by William C. Smith.

MARSHALL, JULIAN: 'Handel' [Life], *Grove's Dictionary of Music and Musicians,* London, 1879, etc.

Händel. (Meister der Tonkunst in Biographien geschildert. No. 24.) Leipzig, 1880.

NIGGLI, A.: *Faustina Bordoni-Hasse.* Leipzig, 1880.

POLKO, E.: *Unsere Musikklassiker. Sechs biographische Lebensbilder.* (*G. F. Händel,* etc.) Leipzig, 1880.

SCHÄFFER, J.: *Neue Bearbeitungen Händel'scher Vocalcompositionen von R. Franz,* etc. Leipzig, 1880.

BUCHNER, WILHELM: *Georg Friedrich Händel: Ein Lebensbild.* Lahr [1881].

WEBSTER, CLARINDA A.: *Handel: an Outline of his Life.* Aberdeen, 1881.

REISSMANN, AUGUST: *Georg Friedrich Händel: Sein Leben und seine Werke.* Berlin, 1882.

WHITTINGHAM, A.: *The Life and Works of Handel.* London, 1882.

ADEMOLLO, A.: *Il carnevale di Roma nei secoli xvii e xviii.* Rome, 1883.

KRETZSCHMAR, A. F. H.: *Georg Friedrich Händel*. Leipzig, 1883.

MARSHALL, MRS JULIAN: *Handel*. London, 1883.

ROCKSTRO, W. S.: *The Life of G. F. Handel*. London, 1883.

WENTWORTH, THOMAS, EARL OF STRAFFORD: *The Wentworth Papers, 1705–39*. London, 1883.

DAVID, ERNEST: *G. F. Händel: sa Vie, ses Travaux et son Temps*. Paris, 1884.

HEINRICH, E.: *Georg Friedrich Händel, ein deutscher Tonmeister*. Leipzig, 1884.

MACFARREN, SIR GEORGE A.: 'Handel and Bach', *Proceedings of the Musical Association*. London, 1884–5.

CLARKE, ELIZA: *Handel*. London, 1885.

OPEL, J. O.: *Der Kammerdiener Georg Händel und sein Sohn Georg Friedrich*. (Zeitschrift für allgemeine Geschichte, etc.) Stuttgart, 1885.

OPEL, J. O. *Mitteilungen zur Geschichte der Familie des Tonkünstlers Händel, nebst einigen sich auf den letzteren beziehenden Briefen*. [Halle, 1885.]

SPITTA, FRIEDR.: *Haendel und Bach. Zwei Festreden*. Bonn, 1885.

STEVENSON, R. A. M.: 'Handel and His Portraits', *Magazine of Art*, Vol. 8. London, 1885.

Vierteljahrsschrift für Musikwissenschaft. Herausgegeben von F. Chrysander und P. Spitta. Leipzig, 1885–95.

VOIGT, W.: *Haendels Samson und Bach's Matthaeus-Passion*. Göttingen, 1885.

BALFOUR, ARTHUR JAMES, EARL OF BALFOUR: 'Handel', *Edinburgh Review*, January 1887. Edinburgh.

CHRYSANDER, FR.: 'Handels Instrumentalkompositionen für grosses Orchester', *Vierteljahrsschrift für Musikwissenschaft, 1887*. Leipzig.

FERRIS, G. T.: *Great Musical Composers*. London, 1887. Another edition. London [1893].

BENNETT, JOSEPH: 'Handel' [Life], *Musical Times*, November 1888–December 1889. London.

BOUCHOR, M.: *Israël en Egypte: Étude sur un Oratorio de G. F. Händel*. Paris, 1888.

HADDEN, J. C.: *George Frederick Handel*. London, 1888. Reprinted 1904.

ADEMOLLO, A.: *G. F. Haendel in Italia*. Milan, 1889.

BURNEY, FRANCES: *The Early Diary of F. Burney, 1768–1778.* 2 vols. London, 1889.

FULLER-MAITLAND, J. A., and SQUIRE, W. BARCLAY: 'Handel', *Dictionary of National Biography*, vol. xxiv. London, 1890.

RICCI, CORRADO: *Burney, Casanova e Farinelli in Bologna*, Milan [1890].

B[RITTON], C. E.: *Reminiscences of G. F. Handel.* London, 1891.

CULWICK, J. C.: *Handel's Messiah: Discovery of the Original Word-Book used at the First Performance in Dublin, April 13, 1742; with Some Notes.* Dublin, 1891.

CHRYSANDER, FR.: 'Der Bestand der Königlichen Privatmusik und Kirchenkapelle in London von 1710 bis 1755', *Vierteljahrsschrift für Musikwissenschaft, 1892.* Leipzig.

DOBSON, AUSTIN: *Eighteenth Century Vignettes.* 3 vols. London, 1892–6.

SPITTA, P.: 'Handel', *Famous Composers and Their Works. Edited by J. K. Paine, etc.* Boston [1892].

FULLER-MAITLAND, J. A. and MANN, A. H.: *Catalogue of the Music in the Fitzwilliam Museum, Cambridge.* London, 1893.

The Musical Times. Special Handel number. 14 December 1893. London.

ROBINSON, JOHN R.: *The Princely Chandos. A Memoir of James Brydges . . . afterwards the First Duke of Chandos.* London, 1893.

HERVEY, JOHN, FIRST EARL OF BRISTOL: *Letter-Books of John Hervey.* 3 vols. Wells, 1894.

The Story of 'The Messiah'. (Being an account of Handel's grand oratorio, with the complete words.) London [1894].

ARMSTRONG, B. J.: *Some Account of the Parish of Little Stanmore, alias Whitchurch, Middlesex . . . with a Supplement by E. Cutler* [on the relations of Handel with Whitchurch]. Edgware, 1895. Another edition. Edgware, 1908.

DAVEY, HENRY: *History of English Music.* London [1895]. Second edition. London, 1921.

Jahrbuch der Musikbibliothek Peters. Leipzig, 1895, etc.

SITTARD, J.: 'Händel, Der Messias. Erläutert von J. Sittard', *Musikführer*, etc., Nos. 42, 43. Frankfort on the Main, 1895.

WIDMANN, B.: 'Händel, Samson mit Textbuch. (Händel,

Frohsinn, Schwermut und Mässigung.) (Händel, Cäcilien-Ode.)' Erläutert von B. Widmann, *Musikführer*, etc., Nos. 21, 22, 26, 27, 31. Frankfort on the Main, 1895.

CROWEST, F. J.: 'Handel and English Music', Traill's *Social England*, vol. v. London, 1896.

SCHRADER, B.: *G. F. Händel. Biographie*. Leipzig, 1896.

WROTH, W.: *The London Pleasure Gardens of the Eighteenth Century*. London, 1896.

CHRYSANDER, FR.: *Händels biblische Oratorien in geschichtlicher Betrachtung*. Hamburg, 1897.

STREATFEILD, R. A.: *The Case of the Handel Festival*. London [1897].

VOLBACH, F.: *Georg Friedrich Händel. Ein Lebens- und Charakterbild*. Berlin, 1897. Second, enlarged edition, Berlin, 1907.

SHARP, ROBT. F.: *Makers of Music*. London [1898]. Fourth edition. London, 1913.

WEBER, WILHELM: *Händel's Oratorien überetzt und bearbeitet von F. Chrysander. Erläutert von Weber*. Augsburg, 1898, etc. 1. *Israel in Egypten*. 2. *Der Messias*.

Sammelbände der Internationalen Musikgesellschaft. Leipzig, 1899, etc.

VOLBACH, F.: *Die Praxis der Händel-Aufführung*. Bonn, 1899.

Zeitschrift der Internationalen Musikgesellschaft. Leipzig, 1899–1914.

ZUSCHNEID, K.: 'Händel G. F., Judas Makkabäus.' Erläutert von K. Zuschneid, *Musikführer*, etc., No. 151. Stuttgart, 1899.

EITNER, ROBT.: *Biographisch-bibliographisches Quellen-Lexikon der Musiker und Musikgelehrten*, etc. 10 vols. Leipzig, 1900–4.

KIDSON, F.: *British Music Publishers, Printers, and Engravers*. London [1900].

VERNIER, G.: *L'oratorio Biblique de Händel*. Cahors, 1901.

WILLIAMS, C. F. ABDY: *Handel, his Life and Works*. (Master Musicians, edited by F. J. Crowest.) London, 1901. Revised edition, edited by Eric Blom. London, 1935.

EDWARDS, F. G.: 'The Foundling Hospital and its Music', *Musical Times*, May, June, 1902. London.

EDWARDS, F. G.: 'Handel's Messiah. Some Notes on its History and First Performance', *Musical Times*, November 1902. London.

EGEL, H. W.: 'Händel, Josua.' Erläutert von H. W. Egel, *Musikführer*, etc. No. 286. Leipzig [1902].

FULLER-MAITLAND, J. A.: 'The Age of Bach and Handel', *Oxford History of Music*, vol. iv. Oxford, 1902.

MALMESBURY, THE EARL OF: 'Some Anecdotes of the Harris Family', *Ancestor*, No. 1. April 1902. London.

PATTERSON, A. W.: *The Story of Oratorio*. (Music Story Series.) London, 1902.

PROUT, E.: *The Messiah*. . . *Edited* [with Preface] . . *by E. Prout. Full Score*. London, 1902.

VETTER, THEO.: 'Johann Jakob Heidegger, ein Mitarbeiter G. F. Händels', *Neujahrsblatt herausgegeben von der Stadtbibliothek Zurich*, No. 258. [1902.]

BAKER, H. B.: *History of the London Stage . . . 1576–1903*. London, 1904.

BURNEY, FRANCES: *Diary and Letters of Madame D'Arblay, 1778–1840*. 6 vols. London, 1904–5.

CUMMINGS, W. H.: *Handel*. London, 1904.

BERNOULLI, E.: *Oratorientexte Händels. Streifzüge im Gebiete der Chrysander'schen Händelforschung*. Zurich [1905].

GARAT, J.: *La Sonate de Händel*. Paris, 1905.

SPENGEL, J.: *Belsazar. Oratorium: Textbuch und thematischer Führer bearbeitet von J. Spengel*. Leipzig [1905].

SEIFFERT, MAX: 'Die Verzierung der Sologesänge in Händels "Messias" ', *Sammelbände der Internationalen Musik-Gesellshaft*. Leipzig, 1906-7.

TAYLOR, SEDLEY: *The Indebtedness of Handel to Works by other Composers*. Cambridge, 1906.

VOLBACH, F.: 'Georg. Friedr. Händel und die Eigenart seines Schaffens', *Die Musik*, 6 Jahr, Heft 2. Berlin, 1906.

HEUSS, A.: *Saul. Kleiner Konzertführer*. Leipzig [1907].

LEE, VERNON: *Studies of the Eighteenth Century in Italy*. Second edition. London, 1907.

SEIFFERT, MAX: 'Händels Verhältnis zu Tonwerken älterer deutscher Meister', *Jahrbuch der Musikbibliothek Peters*. Leipzig, 1907.

WALKER, ERNEST: *A History of Music in England*. Oxford, 1907.

Catalogue of engraved British Portraits preserved in the Department of Prints and Drawings in the British Museum. London, 1908, etc.

LATHAM, M.: *The Messiah. Handel, 1685–1759. An explana-*

tory introduction [by Morton Latham] *and words. Written with special reference to the performance to be given at Farnham on 27th May 1908.* Farnham [1908].

ROBINSON, PERCY: *Handel and His Orbit.* London, 1908.

An illustrated Catalogue of the Music Loan Exhibition held . . . by the Worshipful Company of Musicians at Fishmongers' Hall, June and July 1904. London, 1909.

The Musical Antiquary. London, 1909–13.

SQUIRE, W. BARCLAY: 'Handel in 1745', *Riemann-Festschrift,* Leipzig, 1909.

STREATFEILD, R. A.: *Handel.* London, 1909.

STREATFEILD, R. A.: 'Handel in Italy, 1706–10', *Musical Antiquary,* October 1909. London.

CHOP, MAX: *G. F. Händel, Der Messias. Oratorium. Geschichtlich und musikalisch analysiert,* etc. Leipzig, 1910.

FRANZ, R.: *Gesammelte Schriften über die Wiederbelebung Bach'scher und Händel'scher Werke,* etc. Leipzig, 1910.

KRETZSCHMAR, H.: *G. F. Handel:* '*The Messiah*'. *Book of words and analytical notes by H. Kretzschmar.* London [1910].

LIGHTWOOD, E.: *The Choir. A Magazine,* etc. [Handel articles, 1918, 1920.] London, 1910, etc.

ROBINSON, P.: 'Handel's Journeys', *Musical Antiquary,* July 1910. London.

ROLLAND, ROMAIN: *Haendel.* (Les Maîtres de la Musique.) Paris, 1910. Translation by A . Eaglefield Hull. (Library of Music and Musicians.) London, 1916.

ROLLAND, ROMAIN: *Haendel. . . . Extrait de la Revue de Paris,* xvii, 8. Paris, 1910.

ROLLAND, ROMAIN: *Audition du Messie de Haendel par la Société Haendel de Paris,* etc. [A programme of the performance given at the Trocadéro, 23 April 1910, with the words of the oratorio translated into French, and an essay by Rolland entitled *Haendel et le Messie.*] Paris [1910].

SEIFFERT, MAX: 'Händels deutsche Gesänge. Nach Materialien in Fr. Chrysanders Nachlass', *Festschrift . . . Liliencron.* Leipzig, 1910.

MEE, J. H.: *The Oldest Music-Room in Europe. A record of Eighteenth-Century Enterprise at Oxford.* London, 1911.

SCHERING, A.: *Geschichte des Oratoriums.* Leipzig, 1911.

STREATFEILD, R. A.: 'The Granville Collection of Handel

Manuscripts', *Musical Antiquary*, July 1911. London.

BRENET, M.: *Hændel . . . Biographie critique*. Paris, 1912.

LAWRENCE, W. J.: 'Handeliana. Some Memorials of the Dublin Charitable Musical Society', *Musical Antiquary*, January 1912. London.

ROLLAND, ROMAIN, etc.: *Le Messie de G.-F. Haendel. 1741. Haendel et le Messie.*—Romain Rolland. *Textes du Messie.—Plan de l'oratorio.*—Félix Raugel. Paris, 1912.

SOTHEBY, WILKINSON and HODGE Sale Catalogues, especially: March 28th, 29th, 1912, Granville MSS.; December 21st, 22nd, 1915, Granville MSS.; May 17th–24th, 1917, Cummings' Library; May 13th, 1918, Aylesford MSS.; June 27th, 1932; December 18th, 1936; February 13th, 1939, Arkwright Collection.

STREATFEILD, R. A.: *Handel Autographs at the British Museum.* London, 1912.

DALE, WILLIAM: *Tschudi, the Harpsichord Maker.* London, 1913.

DAVEY, H.: *Handel and His Music.* (Masterpieces of Music.) London, 1913. *Handel.* (Mayfair Biographies.) London [1922]. A reissue of the text of the earlier work.

SQUIRE, W. BARCLAY: 'Handel in Contemporary Song-Books', *Musical Antiquary*, January 1913. London.

THORMALIUS, G.: *Georg Friedrich Händel.* Bielefeld, [1913].

CUMMINGS, W. H.: 'The Lord Chamberlain and Opera in London, 1700–40', *Proceedings of the Musical Association, 1913–14.* London.

CUMMINGS, W. H.: *Handel, the Duke of Chandos, and the Harmonious Blacksmith.* London, 1915.

The Musical Quarterly. New York, 1915, etc.

STREATFEILD, R. A.: *Handel, Cannons and the Duke of Chandos.* London, 1916.

CUMMINGS, W. H.: Sotheby, Wilkinson, and Hodge Sale Catalogue of the Library of Dr Cummings, 17–24 May 1917. London. A valuable record of Handeliana.

STREATFEILD, R. A.: 'Handel, Rolli, and Italian Opera in London in the Eighteenth Century', *Musical Quarterly*, July 1917. New York.

SIBLEY, J. C.: *Handel at Cannons: with a Description of the Church of St. Lawrence, Whitchurch.* London [1918].

TAYLOR, HARRY J.: *The Life of Handel.* (Musical booklets, No. 26). London, 1918.

SQUIRE, W. BARCLAY: 'Handel's Clock Music', *Musical Quarterly*, October 1919. New York.

ROLLAND, ROMAIN: *Voyage musical aux pays du passé*. Paris, 1919. Another edition. Paris, 1920. Review of the work in *La Revue Musicale*, No. 1. English edition. *A Musical Tour through The Land of the Past. Translated by B. Miall*. London, 1922.

EGMONT, EARL OF: *Manuscripts of the Earl of Egmont. Diary of Viscount Percival*, etc. (Historical Manuscripts Commission.) London, 1920, etc.

KIDSON, F.: 'Handel's publisher, John Walsh, his successors and contemporaries', *Musical Quarterly*, July 1920. New York.

FLOWER, SIR NEWMAN: *Catalogue of a Handel Collection formed by Newman Flower*. Sevenoaks [1921].

LAWRENCE, J. A.: 'The Early Years of the First English Opera House', *Musical Quarterly*, January 1921. New York.

MICHAEL, WOLFGANG: 'Die Entstehung der Wassermusik von Händel', *Zeitschrift für Musikwissenschaft*, August-September 1922. Leipzig.

LEICHTENTRITT, H.: *Händel*. Stuttgart, 1924.

SMITH, WILLIAM C.: 'George III, Handel, and Mainwaring', *Musical Times*, September 1924. London.

ROBINSON, P.: 'Handel's Early Life and Mainwaring', *Musical Times*, September 1925. London.

SMITH, WILLIAM C.: 'The Earliest Editions of Handel's Messiah', *Musical Times*, November 1925; December 1941. London.

BAIRSTOW, SIR EDWARD C.: *Handel's Oratorio 'The Messiah'*. London, 1928.

Händel-Jahrbuch im Auftrage der Händel Gesellschaft herausgegeben von Rudolf Steglich. Leipzig, 1928–33. 1933 consists of a bibliography: *Verzeichnis des Schrifttums über Georg Friedrich Händel von Kurt Taut*.

MANSFIELD, O. A.: *George Frederick Handel, 1685–1759*. London, 1928.

COOPERSMITH, J. M.: 'A List of Portraits, Sculptures, etc., of Georg Friedrich Händel', *Music and Letters*, April 1932, London.

JAMES, R. R.: 'Handel's Blindness', *Music and Letters*, April 1932. London.

MULLER-BLATTAU, J.: *Georg Friedrich Händel*. (Die grossen

Meister der Musik.) Potsdam, 1933.

DENT, E. J.: *Handel*. (Great Lives.) London, 1934.

COOPERSMITH, J. M.: 'Handelian Lacunae: a Project', *Musical Quarterly*, April 1935. New York.

Georg Friedrich Händel. Abstammung und Jugendwelt. Festschrift zur 250. Wiederkehr des Geburtstages Georg Friedrich Händels, etc. Halle, 1935.

'Handel Exhibits at the British Museum', *Musical Opinion*, April 1935. London.

The Letters and Writings of Georg Frideric Handel. Edited by E. H. Müller. London, 1935.

MULLER-BLATTAU, J.: 'Georg Friedrich Handels Leben und Werk', *Illustrierte Zeitung*, 14 February 1935. Leipzig.

Music and Letters, July, October, 1935. [Mainly articles on Handel and Bach.] London.

Musical Quarterly, April 1935. [Mainly articles on Handel and Bach.] New York.

NICHOLS, R. H. and WRAY, F. A.: *The History of the Foundling Hospital*. London, 1935.

Programme and Book of Words of the Handel Festival, June 9th to 14th 1935, organized by the Cambridge University Musical Society. Cambridge, 1935.

SMITH, WILLIAM C.: 'Handel's First Song on the London Stage', *Music and Letters*, October, 1935. London.

WRIGHT, R. W. M.: 'George Frederick Handel: his Bath Associations', *Musical Opinion*, July, August, 1935. London.

DENT, E. J.: *Händel in England. Gedächtnis-Rede anlässlich der 250. Geburtstagsfeier in Halle am 24. February 1935*. Halle, 1936.

FLOWER, DESMOND: 'Handel's Publishers', *English Review*, January, 1936. London.

SMITH, WILLIAM C.: 'Handel's Failure in 1745. New Letters of the Composer', *Musical Times*, July, 1936. London.

SMITH, WILLIAM C.: Recently discovered Handel Manuscripts, *Musical Times*, April, 1937. London.

SMITH, WILLIAM C.: Samson: the Earliest Editions, *Musical Times*, August 1938. London.

WEISSENBORN, B.: *Das Händelhaus in Halle. Die Geburtsstätte Georg Friedrich Händels*. Wolfenbüttel, 1938.

WESTRUP, J. A.: *Handel*. (Novello's Biographies of Great Musicians.) London [1938].

ROBINSON, P.: 'Handel up to 1720: a New Chronology', *Music and Letters*, January, 1939. London.

SMITH, WILLIAM C.: 'The Earliest Editions of Handel's "Water Music"', *Musical Quarterly*, January 1939. New York.

EISENSCHMIDT, JOACHIM: *Die szenische Darstellung der Opern Georg Friedrich Händels auf der Londoner Bühne seiner Zeit*. 2 vols. Wolfenbüttel and Berlin, 1940–41.

LOEWENBERG, A.: *Annals of Opera, 1597–1940*, Cambridge, 1943.

BLOM, ERIC: *Some Great Composers*. London, 1944.

MAINWARING, JOHN: *G. F. Händel. Nach Johann Matthesons deutscher Ausgabe von 1761 mit andern Dokumenten herausgegeben von Bernhard Paumgartner*. Zürich, 1947.

YOUNG, PERCY, M.: *Handel* (The Master Musicians New Series, edited by Eric Blom.) London, 1947.

HERBAGE, JULIAN: *Messiah* (The World of Music.) London, 1948.

SMITH, WILLIAM C.: *Concerning Handel: his life and works*. Essays. London, 1948.

CHERBULIEZ, ANTOINE E.: *Georg Friedrich Händel: Leben und Werk*. Olten, 1949.

MAINWARING, JOHN: *Georg Friedrich Händel. Biographie von John Mainwaring. Briefe und Schriften, Herausgegeben . . . von Hedwig und E. H. Mueller von Asow*. Lindau im Bodensee, 1949.

SERAUKY, WALTER: *Das Händelhaus in Halle an der Saale*. Halle, 1949.

YOUNG, PERCY M.: *The Oratorios of Handel*. London, 1949.

SMITH, WILLIAM C.: 'Handeliana,' *Music and Letters*, April, 1950. London.

Händelfest 1952 [etc.] *Halle. Festschrift*. Halle, Leipzig, 1952, etc.

FELLERER, KARL G.: *Georg Friedrich Händel: Leben und Werk*. Hamburg, 1953.

Wege zu Händel: eine Sammlung von Aufsätzen. Halle, 1953.

SMITH, WILLIAM C.: 'More Handeliana,' *Music and Letters*, January 1953. London.

ABRAHAM, GERALD: *Handel*. A Symposium edited by Gerald Abraham. London, 1954.

SIEGMUND-SCHULTZE, WALTHER: *Georg Friedrich Händel: Leben und Werk*. Leipzig, 1954.

DEUTSCH, OTTO E.: *Handel. A Documentary Biography*. London, 1955.

Händel-Jahrbuch im Auftrage der Georg-Friedrich-Händel-Gesellschaft Herausgegeben von Max Schneider und Rudolf Steglich. Leipzig, 1955, etc. 1955 includes a supplement to the Bibliography issued with the earlier series, 1928–1933.

PETZOLDT, RICHARD: *Georg Friedrich Händel: sein Leben in Bildern*. Leipzig, 1955.

HALL, JAMES S.: 'John Christopher Smith, Handel's Friend and Secretary,' *Musical Times*, March 1955. London.

HERIOT, ANGUS: *The Castrati in Opera*. London, 195´.

SERAUKY, WALTER: *Georg Friedrich Händel: sein Leben—sein Werk*. III Band. *Von Händels innerer Neuorientierung bis zum Abschluss des 'Samson'*. [1738–1743.] Leipzig, 1956.

Fünf Jahre Händel-Festspiele in Halle. Halle, 1957.

LARSEN, JENS P.: *Handel's Messiah: origins, composition, sources*. London, 1957.

INDEX